Mathematics
GRADE SIX

purposeful design®
p u b l i c a t i o n s
A Division of ACSI

Colorado Springs, Colorado

Purposeful Design Publications is the publishing division of the Association of Christian Schools International (ACSI) and is committed to the ministry of Christian school education, to enable Christian educators and schools worldwide to effectively prepare students for life. As the publisher of textbooks, trade books, and other educational resources within ACSI, Purposeful Design Publications strives to produce biblically sound materials that reflect Christian scholarship and stewardship and that address the identified needs of Christian schools around the world.

References to books, computer software, and other ancillary resources in this series are not endorsements by ACSI. These materials were selected to provide teachers with additional resources appropriate to the concepts being taught and to promote student understanding and enjoyment.

Unless otherwise identified, all Scripture quotations are taken from the Holy Bible, New King James Version (NKJV), © 1982 by Thomas Nelson, Inc. Used by permission. All rights reserved.

Printed in the United States of America
16 15 14 13 12 11 10 09 08 07   2 3 4 5 6 7

Mathematics, grade six
Purposeful Design Mathematics series
ISBN 978-1-58331-190-5   Student edition   Catalog #7220

Purposeful Design Publications
A Division of ACSI
PO Box 65130 • Colorado Springs, CO 80962-5130
Customer Service: 800/367-0798 • Website: www.acsi.org

ENABLING EDUCATORS SERIES

Grade Six
MATHEMATICS

Student Textbook

Author
Mae Branda

Grade Level Editor
Dr. Gary Kimball

Managing Editor
Paula Redfield

Senior Content Editor
Dr. James Schwartz

Assistant Managing Editor
JoAnn Keenan

Editing Team
Suzanne Clark
Anita Gordon
Christy Krenek

Design Team
Susanna Garmany
Phil Lear
Kristopher Orr
Dan Schultz

In His Image

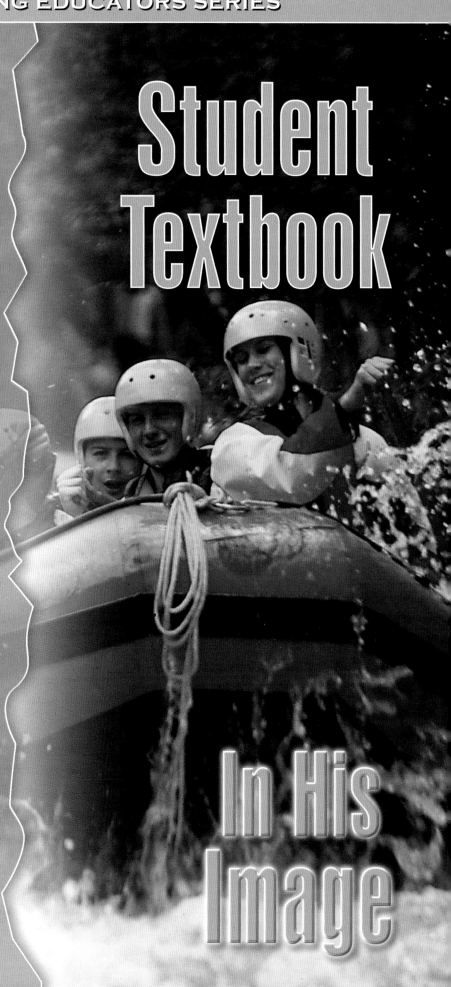

Grade 6

Table of Contents

Grade 6

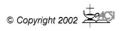

Chapter Theme

The theme of your sixth grade mathematics book is In His Image. Each chapter will focus on one aspect of the wonder of God's creation of mankind. The chapter 1 theme, Creativity, highlights God's gift of creativity to mankind. Man's creativity is far more limited than God's, yet He has given us the ability to appreciate and produce beautiful things, such as art and music. May you be encouraged to discover your own inventiveness as you learn about others who glorified God with their talents and abilities.

1 Chapter

Addition and Subtraction of Whole Numbers and Decimals

Lessons 1-15

So God created man in His own image; in the image of God He created him; male and female He created them.

Genesis 1:27

The Creation by Michelangelo

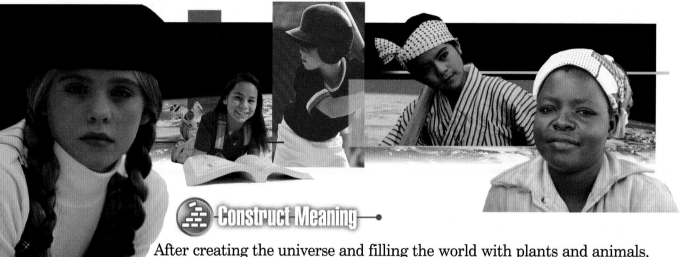

Construct Meaning

After creating the universe and filling the world with plants and animals, God saw that it was good. Then God made man and woman in His own image and blessed them. Even though every child is a unique individual, he or she is a descendant of that first family. It is God who gave man the ability to think creatively. He also has enabled man to study the complexities of the human body.

Periods →	trillions,			billions,			millions,			thousands,			ones		
Place Value →	hundred trillions	ten trillions	trillions	hundred billions	ten billions	billions	hundred millions	ten millions	millions	hundred thousands	ten thousands	thousands	hundreds	tens	ones
															4
										1	0	0,	0	0	0
									5,	0	0	0,	0	0	0
				1	0	0,	0	0	0,	0	0	0,	0	0	0
	6	3,	0	0	0,	0	0	0,	0	0	0,	0	0	0

Did You Know?

There are about . . .

quarts of blood in your body.
hairs on your head.
smelling receptors in your nose.
nerve cells in your brain.
red blood cells produced by your body yearly.

To express the **word form**, read the number followed by the period name, "sixty-three trillion."

Whole numbers can be expressed in **standard notation** using the digits 0, 1, 2, 3, 4, 5, 6, 7, 8, and 9. Commas separate the digits into groups of three digits called **periods**.

Check Understanding

Read each number. Use place value to tell what the underlined digit represents.

a. 5,<u>6</u>19

b. <u>3</u>5,816,700,952,608

c. 7<u>2</u>7,952

d. 9<u>6</u>4,718,500

e. 5,872,<u>6</u>93,247,104

f. 1,500,<u>0</u>00,080

Name the highlighted period.

1. 674,383,294,102,516

2. 356,139,863,103

3. 4,965,582,136,003

4. 27,732,518

Use place value to write what the 5 represents in each number.

5. 153,617,824

6. 580,736,912

7. 580,216,479,813,642

8. 154,637,132,616

Write the number in standard notation.

9. Six hundred five trillion, twenty-nine

10. Forty-nine million, two hundred six thousand, four

11. Three billion, seven thousand

12. Five hundred thirty-six thousand, one hundred thirteen

Write the letter of the most reasonable answer to each question.

13. How many bones are in the human body?

14. About how many times do you breathe each day?

15. About how many cows are in the country of India?

16. How many days would it take to drive from Portland, Oregon, to Portland, Maine?

a. 6
b. 30,000
c. 206
d. 200,000,000

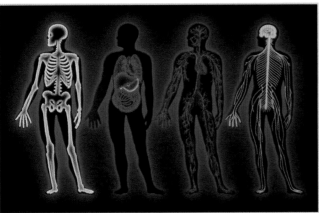

17. The human body consists of over seventy-five trillion cells. Write that number in standard notation.

18. There are about sixty-two thousand miles of blood vessels in the human body. Write that number in standard notation.

Construct Meaning

In the painting by the Dutch artist Rembrandt, notice the hand that appears to be writing on the wall. King Belshazzar held a lavish feast, praising gods of gold and silver instead of "the God who holds your breath in His hand and owns all your ways" (Daniel 5:23). He had not humbled his heart before God. The message on the wall was sent from God and interpreted by the prophet Daniel. Belshazzar had not measured up to God's standard, and that very night he lost his life.

Jackie visited a famous art museum that housed two million, three hundred seventy-five thousand, six hundred nine works of art. She calculated that even if she spent eight hours every day looking at the museum collection, it would take years to see it all!

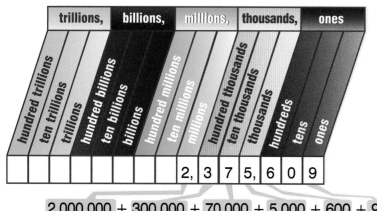

There are different forms or notations for writing the same number. The number of works of art could also be written in standard notation using digits with each period separated by commas.

Expanded notation shows the number as the sum of the nonzero digits with appropriate place value for each.

Check Understanding

Write each number in standard notation.

a. 300,000 + 50,000 + 2,000 + 500 + 60 + 2

b. 600,000,000 + 30,000,000 + 7,000,000

c. 90,000,000,000,000 + 1,000,000,000,000

d. sixty-seven million, five hundred thousand, fifty-seven

Write each number in expanded notation.

e. 9,452,762

f. 888,000,000,000,000

g. 18,743,301,021

h. three hundred million, five hundred

"Old Man Praying," by Rembrandt

Write the number in standard notation.

1. 6,000,000 + 500,000 + 2,000 + 300 + 30 + 7
2. 800 + 90 + 3
3. 20,000 + 5,000 + 300 + 8
4. 70,000,000,000,000 + 200,000,000,000 + 500,000,000

Write the number in expanded notation.

5. 528
6. 651,659,080
7. 3,006,147
8. 14,959,000,000,000
9. Four hundred fifty-two million
10. Ninety-seven thousand, six hundred forty-four

Write each number in expanded notation.

11. The museums of Los Angeles spent more than one million, six hundred thousand dollars on construction in a ten-year period.

12. In one of the museums, Gwen saw a replica of the *Titanic* made of seventy-five thousand toothpicks.

13. There were 952 antique duck decoys displayed at a local art museum.

14. The Metropolitan Museum of Art contains more than two million pieces of art from all parts of the world.

Consider the number 93,572,885,367,021. Write the digit that appears in the given place.

1. hundred millions
2. billions
3. ten millions
4. thousands
5. hundred thousands
6. millions

Lesson 3

Construct Meaning

People who have a special ability to communicate well often become authors. A Christian author named John Bunyan lived from 1628 to 1688. He is well-known for the book called *The Pilgrim's Progress*. The Bible, however, may be the most well-known book ever published.

The Old Testament alone has 2,728,100 of the total letters of the alphabet that make up the words in the Bible. In English, the Bible has 3,566,480 letters contained in its text.

Compare the two numbers by comparing the digits in each place value position.

3,566,480 Total number of letters in the Bible

2,728,100 Total number of letters in the Old Testament

By lining up the digits in place value position, you can easily start comparing the numbers at the left. 3 > 2, and it would make sense that the total number of letters in the Bible is greater than the total number in the Old Testament.

> Use what you just learned to estimate how many letters would be found in the New Testament.

Order the numbers in the place value chart from greatest to least.

	hundred trillions	ten trillions	trillions	hundred billions	ten billions	billions	hundred millions	ten millions	millions	hundred thousands	ten thousands	thousands	hundreds	tens	ones
a.			2	6	4	8	0	0	7	1	1	1	5	5	3
b.		3	2	7	2	4	9	0	0	8	2	2	0	0	0
c.		3	2	7	1	0	9	5	3	1	9	7	0	0	0
d.			2	9	1	5	5	3	6	0	0	0	4	6	7

Step 1 The two greatest numbers are b and c since they are the only ones with digits in the ten trillions. Both have a 3.

Step 2 Both b and c have a 2 in the trillions place and a 7 in the hundred billions place.

Step 3 No difference is found between the two greatest numbers until the ten billions place. 2 > 1, so b > c.

Step 4 Compare the remaining numbers. Since 9 > 6 in the hundred billions place, d > a.

> From greatest to least, the order is: b, c, d, a.

6

Compare and Order Whole Numbers

 Check Understanding

a. Order the numbers in the place value chart from least to greatest.

b. Why do you start at the left to compare numbers?

c. Order from least to greatest:
6,421,000,000,211   6,421,001,000,112   6,421,010,533,000

 Practice

Write >, < or = .

1. 4,361,208 ⬚ 4,352,462

2. 6,001,246,893 ⬚ 6,002,913,205

3. 730,121,302 ⬚ 730,121,203

4. 2,465,200,011,467 ⬚ 2,465,200,011,467

Use the sets of numbers below to answer questions 5 through 10.

875 , 462 , 003 , 500 , 921

5. Write the number above in word form.

6. Write the largest possible number in standard notation by rearranging the sets.

7. Write the smallest possible number in standard notation by rearranging the sets.

8. Using all the sets, write two different numbers and compare using >, < or =.

9. Write a number with 9 in the hundred millions place.

10. Write a number with 2 in the trillions place.

Population Statistics	
Russia	147,950,000
Indonesia	219,267,000
China	1,253,438,000
USA	276,621,000
India	1,012,909,000

Use the numbers in the chart to answer the following questions.

11. Which numbers are greater than 1 billion?

12. Which numbers are less than 280,000,000?

13. Which number is between 500,000,000 and 1,200,000,000?

14. Write the names of the countries in order from greatest to least population.

 Review

Use commas to separate the periods in the number.

1. 20046713942   2. 931400008235   3. 100993040   4. 213983

Use place value to tell what the orange digit represents.

5. 623,759,000   6. 30,517,922,588,000   7. 501,368,745,000   8. 94,225,650,000

Lesson 4

 **Construct Meaning**

Fanny J. Crosby (1820–1915) was a very talented person. She had a fine soprano voice; played the guitar, harp, piano, and organ; and wrote between 8,000 and 9,000 hymns. Even though she became blind at the age of six weeks, she regarded her childhood as happy. "I could climb a tree like a squirrel and ride a horse bareback." Check your church hymnal for some of her hymns titled: "Blessed Assurance," "Pass Me Not, O Gentle Savior," and "Praise Him, Praise Him."

Rounding is used when an exact quantity is unknown.
If she had written 8,364 hymns, to what thousand would you round that number?
If she had written 8,821 hymns, to what thousand would you round that number?

- Use a number line.

8,364 is less than halfway, so round it to 8,000.
8,821 is greater than halfway, so round it to 9,000.

- Follow these steps to round to any place value position.

    Step 1 Locate the target digit in the place to which you are rounding.　　　12,603,974

    Step 2 Find the digit to the right of the target digit.　　　12,603,974

    Step 3 If the digit to the right is 5 or greater, round up. If it is less than 5, round down, leaving the target digit the same.　　　13,000,000

    Step 4 Replace the digits to the right of the target place with zeros.

    Rounded to the nearest million, 12,603,974 is 13,000,000.

Explain why you might round a number.

 **Check Understanding**

- a. Write the number that is halfway between 60,000 and 70,000.
- b. Write the number that is halfway between 200,000 and 300,000.
- c. Write the thousands that the number 4,381 is between.
- d. Write the millions that the number 5,207,618 is between.
- e. Round 1,834,752,369 to the nearest billion.
- f. Round 72,097 to the nearest hundred.

Write the letter of the rounded number.

1. Round 39,542 to the nearest ten thousand.
   a. 39,000   **b.** 35,000   **c.** 40,000   **d.** none of these

2. Round 704,236,085,119 to the nearest hundred billion.
   a. 600,000,000,000   **b.** 700,000,000,000   **c.** 700,000,000   **d.** none of these

3. Round 85,135,906 to the greatest place value.
   a. 85,000,000   **b.** 86,000,000   **c.** 90,000   **d.** none of these

Round to the nearest hundred.

4. 981   5. 13,609

Round to the nearest thousand.

6. 250,918   7. 8,916

Round to the nearest million.

8. 710,240,687   9. 78,565,342

Round to the nearest hundred billion.

10. 516,304,826,794

Write each missing number.

Round to → 264,159,786,403	ten billions	hundred millions	thousands	hundreds
	11.	12.	13.	14.

15. Among the many Scriptures that Fanny Crosby memorized were the entire Pentateuch, the four Gospels, all of the Proverbs, the Book of Ruth, and the Song of Solomon. There are 6,969 verses in these books of the Bible. Round the number to the nearest ten.

16. Write two different numbers that round to 6,000.

Use place value to write what the 4 represents in each number.
1. 254,617,329   2. 423,180,953,286   3. 48,750

Write the number in expanded notation.
4. 937   5. eighty-six million, fourteen   6. 73,854

Write >, < or =.
7. 536,972,108 ▨ 537,972,108   8. 87,043,256 ▨ 78,403,526

Lesson 5

Construct Meaning

Woven clothes, rugs, blankets, and wall hangings are all types of textile art. Each is uniquely covered with designs and patterns. Many types of patterns are designed using numbers. These patterns help us make sense of numbers and predict the outcomes of the patterns.

Triangular Numbers

A number pattern can be made into a shape like a triangle. Using counters, we can build **triangular numbers**, which are numbers of a sequence that can be shown by dots arranged in the shape of a triangle.

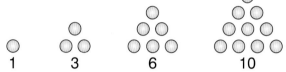

Can you find a relationship or pattern among the numbers?

Using counters, find the next triangular number. You can add a row of counters to the bottom of the triangle, then count the number of counters, and you will discover that the next triangular number is 15.

Here is the pattern: 1 + 2 = 3, 3 + 3 = 6, 6 + 4 = 10, 10 + 5 = 15. What will the next two equations be?

Patterns of Nine

0 + 9 = 9

1 + 8 = 9

2 + 7 = 9

3 + 6 = 9

4 + 5 = 9

Observe each column of addends. What is the pattern? Would this pattern occur if you began with zero and used the same method to find all of the addends for 15?

5 +   = 9

6 +   = 9

7 +   = 9

8 +   = 9

9 +   = 9

Check Understanding

a. Complete the multiplication facts for 9. What pattern do you see in the products?

$9 \times 1 = 9$ $9 \times 6 = $

$9 \times 2 = 18$ $9 \times 7 = $

$9 \times 3 = 27$ $9 \times 8 = $

$9 \times 4 = 36$ $9 \times 9 = $

$9 \times 5 = 45$ $9 \times 10 = $

b. In this pattern, nine is multiplied and the product is added to a sequence of numbers.

$(9 \times 0) + 1 = 1$
$(9 \times 1) + 2 = 11$
$(9 \times 12) + 3 = 111$
$(9 \times 123) + 4 = 1{,}111$

Predict the next equation.

 **Practice**

Copy and complete the pattern of equations. Use a calculator.

1. $(9 \times 1{,}234) + 5 = $ ▨
   $(9 \times 12{,}345) + 6 = $ ▨
   $(9 \times 123{,}456) + 7 = $ ▨
   $(9 \times 1{,}234{,}567) + 8 = $ ▨
   $(9 \times 12{,}345{,}678) + 9 = $ ▨
   $(9 \times 123{,}456{,}789) + 10 = $ ▨

2. $(9 \times 9) + 7 = $ ▨
   $(9 \times 98) + 6 = $ ▨
   $(9 \times 987) + 5 = $ ▨
   $(9 \times 9{,}876) + 4 = $ ▨
   $(9 \times $ ▨ $) + $ ▨ $ = $ ▨
   $(9 \times $ ▨ $) + $ ▨ $ = $ ▨
   $(9 \times $ ▨ $) + $ ▨ $ = $ ▨

Solve.

3. Extend the pattern of triangular numbers to find the largest triangular number less than or equal to 62.

4. How many triangular numbers are between 15 and 55?

5. How many rows of counters does the triangular number 91 have?

 Apply

6. An artist is making a design with triangular numbers and wants to use the number 120. How many rows would he need for the design?

7. A weaver is making a blanket with a triangular number design that is 15 feet long and each row is one foot. What is the largest triangular number that will fit on the blanket?

8. The cost of the tickets to the museum is $15 for three adults, $21 for four adults, and $27 for five adults. What is the cost for seven adults? What is the pattern?

 Construct Meaning

Traditional, unglazed pottery is used in Ghana, Africa, for preparing, cooking, and storing food. Each piece is skillfully made by a potter as an individual product of his or her artistic talent.

We are referred to as clay in the hands of God. Isaiah reminds us that the potter is to be held in higher esteem than the object formed. We should be careful to give God the credit for the abilities He has given to us and not to question His wisdom.

Commutative (Order) Property of Addition

Changing the order of addends does not change the sum.

Joseph counted 102 grinding bowls and 94 mixing bowls in his father's shop. How many bowls were there?

$$102 + 94 = 94 + 102$$
$$196 = 196$$

 196 bowls

But now, O LORD,
You are our Father;
We are the clay, and
You our potter;
And all we are the
work of Your hand.
Isaiah 64:8

Associative (Grouping) Property of Addition

Grouping addends differently does not change the sum.

Joseph's mother sold 72 bowls on Monday, 33 bowls on Tuesday, and 67 bowls on Wednesday. What was the total number of bowls sold?

$$(72 + 33) + 67 = 72 + (33 + 67)$$
$$105 + 67 = 72 + 100$$
$$172 = 172$$

 172 bowls

Compatible numbers are numbers that can be paired together in order to make mental computing easier. The Associative Property allows us to group addends into pairs that can be added mentally. How did grouping the addends differently make it easier to solve the above problem?

Zero Property of Addition

The sum of a number and zero is that number. The zero always identifies the other addend. It is also called the Identity Property of Zero.

$$172 + 0 = 172$$

 **Check Understanding**

Write the addition property shown by each equation. Write *Commutative Property,*
Associative Property, or *Zero Property.*

a. $(7 + 15) + 5 = 7 + (15 + 5)$ b. $49 + 61 = 61 + 49$
c. $27 + 0 = 27$ d. $22 + 23 + 24 = 24 + 22 + 23$
e. $152 + 0 = 152$ f. $(9 + 1) + 65 = 9 + (1 + 65)$

 **Practice**

Write the missing addend.

1. $(76 + 42) + 39 = 76 + (\boxed{} + 39)$ 2. $852 + \boxed{} = a + 852$
3. $\boxed{} + 0 = 759$ 4. $(\boxed{} + 2) + 4 = 19 + (2 + 4)$
5. $365 + \boxed{} = 365$ 6. $x + 6 + 5 + 4 = \boxed{} + x + 4 + 5$

Rewrite using the Associative Property of Addition. Solve.

7. $(2 + 15) + 15$ 8. $(62 + 95) + 5$ 9. $12 + (12 + 6)$
10. $(3 + 10) + 20$ 11. $1 + (49 + 23)$ 12. $(37 + 250) + 250$

13. How did using the Associative Property make it easier for you to solve problems
7 through 12?

14. Which pairs of addends would you group together to find the sum mentally?
State the sum.

15. Does the Commutative Property apply to subtraction? Give an example to
illustrate your answer.

 Review

Round each number to the nearest hundred.

1. 1,256 2. 952
3. 3,501 4. 76

Round each number to the greatest place value.

5. 809,532 6. 8,255
7. 15,753,211 8. 339

Norwegian
pottery

Construct Meaning

Albrecht Dürer is the artist who made this brush drawing entitled *Praying Hands*. He was one of eighteen children born to a poor family in Germany. In his diary, he wrote a prayer, "Deliver us at the right time, preserve in us the right, true Christian faith, gather your widely scattered sheep by your voice, which is called the Word of God in Scripture."

Dürer painted portraits and religious subjects, made copper engravings, and carved woodcuts. In his lifetime, he produced over a thousand works of art.

```
      1
  62,451
+ 24,329
  86,780
```

Use regrouping to add two addends.
Add the ones. (1 + 9 = 10)
Regroup 10 as 1 ten and 0 ones.
Add each remaining place value.

```
  62,000
+ 24,000
  86,000
```

Check your answer by estimating. Round the numbers to the nearest thousand and add.

Think: "86,780 is a reasonable answer compared to my estimate of 86,000."

```
    5 11
  87,6̸1̸5
- 52,383
  35,232
```

Use regrouping to subtract.
Subtract the ones.
Subtract the tens. Since 8 > 1, regroup 6 hundreds as 5 hundreds and 11 tens.
Subtract each remaining place value.

```
  88,000
- 52,000
  36,000
```

Check your answer by estimating. Round the numbers to the nearest thousand and subtract.
Is your answer reasonable?

Check Understanding

Solve. Check with estimating.

a.
```
  9,698
+ 3,813
```

b.
```
  91,867
- 63,749
```

c.
```
  282,413
-  73,521
```

d. 6,219 + 8,943 + 21,956

Add and Subtract Whole Numbers

Solve. Check 1 and 2 by estimating to the nearest thousand.

1.
$$96,421$$
$$+\ 36,584$$

2.
$$84,631$$
$$-\ 33,720$$

3.
$$746,540$$
$$-\ \ 80,955$$

4.
$$121,863$$
$$+\ 214,742$$

5.
$$8,941$$
$$-\ 3,151$$

6. $43,000 + 32,000 + 51,643$

7. $32,591 - 6,941$

Find the missing numbers.

8.
$$\ \ \ ,3\ \ \ $$
$$+\ 6,\ \ \ 51$$
$$\overline{11,176}$$

9.
$$2,\ \ \ \ \ $$
$$+\ 40,500$$
$$\overline{7\ \ \ ,364}$$

10.
$$439,\ \ 26$$
$$-\ 25\ \ ,2\ \ \ $$
$$\overline{\ \ \ 0,111}$$

11.
$$\ \ \ ,882$$
$$-\ \ \ \ \ 9\ \ \ $$
$$\overline{6,\ \ 52}$$

12. Mr. and Mrs. Gregory bought three paintings at an auction for a total cost of $46,445. Two of the paintings together cost $26,123. How much did the third painting cost?

13. The Lincoln Road Neighborhood Association is passing a petition to have a traffic light installed at a busy intersection. They need a total of 250,000 signatures. They have four lists with signatures: 32,435; 8,399; 56,488; and 900. How many signatures has the association collected?

"Armed Horseman"

14. Miss McMahon has a cattle stockyard in Stockton, California. She has three separate herds of different sizes: 1,246; 3,500; and 1,423. What is the total number of cattle in Miss McMahon's stockyard?

15. The city commissioner election was held last Thursday. One candidate received 2,320 votes from District 1 and 1,468 votes from District 2. 83 of the votes had to be thrown out because of ballot problems. How many total votes did the candidate receive?

Complete the pattern.

1. 8   24   72 ▨

2. 27   36 ▨   54 ▨

3. 7   12   17 ▨   27

Write the addition property shown by each equation. Write *Commutative Property*, *Associative Property*, or *Zero Property*.

4. $(12 + 57) + 23 = 12 + (57 + 23)$

5. $186 + 0 = 186$

6. $57 + 81 + 23 = 81 + 23 + 57$

Lesson 8

 Construct Meaning

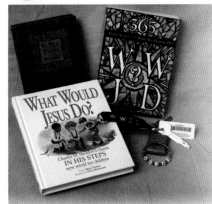

Charles Monroe Sheldon (1857–1946) was an American preacher who wrote stories and then read them to his congregation. Sheldon's popular book *In His Steps* asked the question, What would Jesus do? It was published in 1896 by Judson Press. For a sixty-year period this book was the largest-selling religious book in the United States after the Bible.

In 1993 Sheldon's great-grandson updated the book, leading to the fad of having WWJD printed on items.

At the beginning of the summer youth camp, one leader was given 425 WWJD wristbands to present to contest winners during the summer; another leader was given 180 T-shirts; and another leader was given 315 necklaces. At the final awards program, 35 awards were presented. After the program, 45 items remained in the summer inventory. How many awards had been presented prior to the final awards program?

Use the Problem-Solving Guide to answer the question.

Understand the question. How many awards were presented during the summer youth camp prior to the final program?

Analyze the data. At the beginning of camp, there were 425 WWJD wristbands, 180 T-shirts, and 315 necklaces. At the final program, 35 awards were presented and 45 items remained in inventory.

Plan the strategy. Total the quantity of WWJD items available at the beginning of camp. Add the quantity of items presented at the final program to the quantity remaining in inventory. Finding the difference between the two quantities is a subtraction problem.
Use rounding to estimate the answer.

$$920 \rightarrow 900 \text{ awards to begin camp}$$
$$- 80 \rightarrow 100 \text{ awards on final night and in inventory}$$
$$\overline{840} \rightarrow 800 \text{ awards presented prior to the final program}$$

Solve the problem.

$$\begin{array}{r} \overset{1\,1}{425} \\ 180 \\ +\,315 \\ \hline 920 \end{array} \qquad \begin{array}{r} \overset{1}{35} \\ +\,45 \\ \hline 80 \end{array} \qquad \begin{array}{r} \overset{8\,12}{\cancel{920}} \\ -\,80 \\ \hline 840 \end{array}$$

Evaluate the result.

Check your answer.
Compare it to the estimate.

$$\begin{array}{r} \overset{1}{840} \\ +\,80 \\ \hline 920 \end{array}$$

Compare the answer of 840 to the estimate of 800. Is the answer reasonable?

16

 **Practice**

1. How many years passed between the publication of *In His Steps* and when the updated version was published?

2. A Christian bookstore received a shipment of 3,000 WWJD items on September 1. It sold 587 of those items during that month and 1,106 items during October. How many items remained to be sold on November 1?

3. For family devotions, Cheryl's family has read 189 pages of *In His Steps*, which has 420 pages. Carolyn's family has read 188 pages of *What Would Jesus Do?* which has 416 pages. Whose family has the fewer number of pages to read to finish the book?

4. Four golfers were enjoying a round of golf. On the fourth tee, the first player drove the ball 302 yards, the second player drove the ball 294 yards, the third player drove the ball 358 years, and the last one drove the ball 275 yards. How many yards less than 1,230 yards is the combined total number of yards that all four players drove the golf ball?

5. The gymnasium has 2,650 seats. 1,872 of them have backs. Round to the greatest place value to tell about how many seats do not have backs.

6. On the first Monday in the month of March, Josh drove his truck 452 miles; on Tuesday he drove 367 miles; on Thursday he drove 397 miles; and on Friday he drove 436 miles. What is the difference in miles between the Monday–Tuesday route and the Thursday–Friday route?

7. There are 104 students in the four sixth grade classes at Stanton Christian School. During an extremely rainy day, there were 49 students absent. How many students were present?

8. Mrs. Gordon's class has 17 boys and 12 girls. Mrs. Krenek's class has 15 boys and 13 girls. Mrs. Boucher's class has 11 boys and 16 girls. Are there more boys or girls in the three classes? how many more?

9. One department store wrapped 2,481 presents during the holiday season. Another store wrapped 2,814 presents. Rounding to the greatest place value, about how many presents did the two stores wrap?

10. Dan's company owns three rental trucks. The odometers read 142,468; 138,027; and 151,476. When the mileage of his trucks totals 500,000 miles, he investigates the purchase of a new truck. How many more miles does he have before the investigation begins?

Construct Meaning

God has enabled men to write music and to invent musical instruments. The most complex instrument is man's voice. God wants us to use our voices to praise and worship Him. George Frideric Handel's most famous work, *Messiah*, is an example of music that glorifies God.

George Frideric Handel
(1685–1759)

For the annual performance of the *Messiah* at Trinity Christian College, all of the tickets were sold for the 2,000 available seats. Pat sold some tickets, but forgot to write down the number he sold. Shelley sold all the rest of the tickets, which was a total of 1,852 tickets. How many did Pat sell?

$$x + 1,852 = 2,000$$

number of tickets   number of tickets   total number
Pat sold   Shelley sold   of tickets

An **equation** is a mathematical sentence that has an equal sign.

In order to solve this equation, decide what operation is being performed on the unknown term, x. In this case, 1,852 is being added to x. To solve the equation, perform the inverse operation, subtraction. Remember that in order to keep both sides of the equation equal, the same operation must be done to both sides.

$$x + 1,852 - 1,852 = 2,000 - 1,852$$
$$x + 0 = 148$$
$$x = 148 \text{ tickets}$$

Check. Use 148 in place of x.
$$x + 1,852 = 2,000$$
$$148 + 1,852 = 2,000$$
$$2,000 = 2,000 \quad ✔$$

Solve this equation for the unknown term, y.

$$y - 16,443 = 92,555$$
$$y - 16,443 + 16,443 = 92,555 + 16,443$$
$$y = 108,998$$

The inverse operation would be addition.

Check.
$$y - 16,443 = 92,555$$
$$108,998 - 16,443 = 92,555$$
$$92,555 = 92,555 \quad ✔$$

Explore Algebra: Inverse Operations

Solve for the unknown. Check.

a. $x + 17,652 = 18,999$

b. $322 + y = 795$

c. $r - 80,000 = 50,000$

d. $s - 1,590 = 74$

e. $w - 3,200 = 9,560,000$

f. $\$205 + p = \$438$

Solve and check.

1. $p + 16 = 39$

2. $q - 52 = 14$

3. $105 + r = 216$

4. $10,500 + x = 20,000$

5. $y + 597 = 3,352$

6. $z - 1,000 = 974$

7. $592 + m = 6,744$

8. $n - \$152 = \$44$

9. $k + 200,000 = 250,000$

10. Mrs. Baker has a total of 83 sixth graders in band. There are 49 boys. Let g represent the number of girls in band. Write an addition equation and solve for g to determine how many girls are in Mrs. Baker's class.

11. Let n represent the number of band lockers in the music room. Thirty-five lockers contain instruments. Seventy-two lockers do not contain instruments. Write a subtraction equation and solve for n.

12. Samuel practiced the trumpet for 90 minutes this week. The requirement for band class is two hours per week. Choose a letter to represent the number of minutes he still needs to practice. Write an addition equation and solve.

I will sing a new song to You, O God; On a harp of ten strings I will sing praises to You. Psalm 144:9

© Copyright 2002

19

 Construct Meaning

Louis Pasteur is called the father of bacteriology. One of his goals as a scientist was to discover the mysteries and truths that God created.

Most bacteria can divide 4.125 times in just over two hours. However, some can divide up to 12 times in just over two hours. Compare rates of 4.125 and 4.250 on the number line.

The number 4.250 is to the right of 4.125 on the number line. Therefore, 4.250 > 4.125.

The rate of 4.250 times in over two hours is faster.

A visual model using squares can show the relationship between decimals.

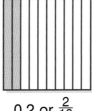 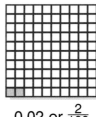 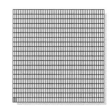

0.2 or $\frac{2}{10}$ 0.02 or $\frac{2}{100}$ 0.002 or $\frac{2}{1,000}$

Comparing and ordering decimals can be done by comparing the digits in each place value position.

- First, line up the numbers by place value.
- Next, compare the numbers two at a time. Because the 4 in the ones place is greater than 0, 0.6452 is the smallest number.

ones	tenths	hundredths	thousandths	ten-thousandths
4	4	2	5	1
4	4	2	5	7
0	6	4	5	2
4	4	2	6	5

- Because the 6 in the thousandths place is greater than 5, 4.4265 is greater than both 4.251 and 4.4257.

- Because the 7 in the ten-thousandths place is greater than 1, 4.4257 > 4.4251.

- Finally, list the numbers from greatest to least: 4.4265   4.4257   4.4251   0.6452.

 Check Understanding

Write >, < or =.

a. 5.67 ▒ 5.68   b. 0.642 ▒ 0.63   c. 1.030 ▒ 1.03   d. 0.0135 ▒ 0.0145

Order from least to greatest.

e. 2.136   2.146   2.016   f. 1.1895   1.1875   1.1892

Compare and Order Decimals

 **ractice**

Order from least to greatest.

1. 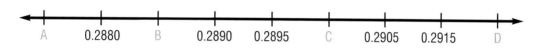 1.3250 1.3221 1.3255

2. 0.9751 0.9730 0.9752 0.98

Write >, < or =.

3. 2.564 ⬚ 2.563

4. 0.015 ⬚ 0.051

5. 0.0525 ⬚ 0.0552

6. 12.4301 ⬚ 12.43010

7. 1.450 ⬚ 1.04

8. 0.9905 ⬚ 0.99

Use the number line to write the letter that corresponds to each decimal location.

A 0.2880 B 0.2890 0.2895 C 0.2905 0.2915 D

9. 0.292

10. 0.2885

11. 0.290

12. 0.2875

 pply

Use the graph to answer problems 13 through 16.

13. Put the petri dishes in order of greatest to least weight.

14. Which petri dishes have a weight between 8.447 and 8.457 grams?

15. Which petri dishes have a weight between 9.0 and 8.459 grams?

Write >, < or =.

16. 8.452 ⬚ 8.456

17. 8.47 ⬚ 8.446

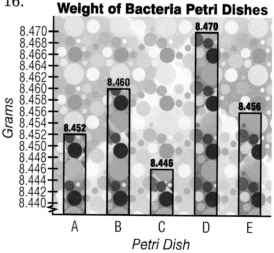

Weight of Bacteria Petri Dishes

18. Mr. Lowell has recorded five weights of petri dishes: 6.431 grams, 6.439 grams, 6.429 grams, 6.44 grams, and 6.433 grams. Which weight is the second greatest?

 **eview**

1. $d + 21 = 54$

2. $r - 300 = 4{,}252$

3. $33 + m = 649$

4. $10 + x = 47$

5. $319 + q = 8{,}421$

6. $s - 66 = 192$

Lesson 11

 **Construct Meaning**

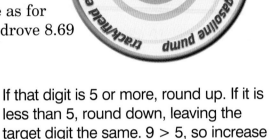

Decimal Usage

speedometer · electric meter · gasoline pump · track/field events · money

The beginning of a new school year usually means a shopping spree for new clothes! Wise planning is made possible because of the skill of rounding that provides an estimated amount.

○ The steps for rounding decimals are the same as for rounding whole numbers. The Barnes family drove 8.69 miles to their favorite mall.

Round 8.69 to the nearest tenth of a mile.

Find the digit in the place to which you will round.	Look at the digit to its right.	If that digit is 5 or more, round up. If it is less than 5, round down, leaving the target digit the same. 9 > 5, so increase the tenths digit by one.
8.6**9**	8.6**9**	**8.69 rounds to 8.7**

➤ **The Barnes family drove 8.7 miles to the mall.**

○ The decimal place value chart will help you.

ones	tenths	hundredths	thousandths	ten-thousandths	hundred-thousandths
2	5	1	6	3	
4	7	5	2	6	6

Round 2.5163 to the nearest hundredth.
Round 4.75266 to the nearest ten-thousandth.

○ Estimate how much the Barnes family spent if they spent $129.50 at one store and $179.25 at another. Use a number line to locate and round each amount before adding.

129.50   179.25

100.00   150.00   200.00

Which amount is closer to one hundred dollars?
Which amount is closer to two hundred dollars?
What is the halfway number between $100 and $200?

The Barnes family spent about $300.00 at both stores.

 **Check Understanding**

Round each number to the place of the underlined digit.

a. 247.3   b. 7.18<u>5</u>6   c. 90.<u>7</u>13   d. 0.824<u>7</u>1   e. 1<u>8</u>.824

Write the whole dollar amounts between which the money amount falls. Then write the nearest dollar to which it rounds.

f. $16.59   g. $200.85   h. $113.77   i. $84.00   j. $1.50

 **Practice**

1. Draw a number line with endpoints of $140 and $150. Locate and label the halfway number and the money amounts in the box.
   a. Which money amounts round to $140.00?
   b. Which money amounts round to $150.00?

   > $142.68
   > $147.15
   > $144.80 $146.33

Round to the nearest whole number.

2. 4.793	3. 283.4	4. 1,790.8	5. 0.961	6. 53.06

Round to the nearest dollar.

7. $4.35	8. $88.83	9. $44.17	10. $126.95	11. $299.51

Round to the nearest hundredth.

12. 7.814	13. 0.225	14. 31.492	15. 9.517	16. 513.163

Round to the nearest thousandth.

17. 4.3165	18. 17.3982	19. 45.6718	20. 0.2894	21. 119.3876

Round to the nearest ten-thousandth.

22. 0.72651	23. 1.98743	24. 37.96124	25. 2.38972	26. 0.57643

 Apply

27. A company estimated its utility costs for a four-month period to be between $19,000 and $20,000. After four months, their bill totaled $19,634.75.
    Visualize a number line having $19,000 and $20,000 for its endpoints.
    a. What is the halfway amount on the number line?
    b. To which endpoint is the bill closer?

28. Susie purchased a new outfit for $34.95. An additional $2.10 is added to the purchase as sales tax. She paid for the outfit with two twenty-dollar bills. How much change should she receive?

 **Review**

Use place value to tell what the underlined digit represents.

1. 4<u>5</u>,079	2. <u>9</u>,175,643	3. 76<u>4</u>,972,583,018	4. 8<u>5</u>6,799,452

Solve.

5.	6.	7.	8.	9.
80,000 − 59,321	2,796 + 8,354	417,528 − 14,978	574 + 89	1,001 − 872

Lesson 12

Construct Meaning

David Livingstone (1813–1873) left Scotland as a young doctor to find a path to the heart of Africa in order to take the gospel of Jesus Christ to an entire continent. He was the first white man to view the beautiful spectacle that he named Victoria Falls. Although he became known as a great explorer, teacher, and healer, his primary goal was to bring honor to God. "I am a missionary, heart and soul," he said. "In this service I hope to live and in it I wish to die." He endured hardship and loneliness to serve his Creator.

Victoria Falls is on the Zambezi River between the two southern African countries of Zambia and Zimbabwe. What is the difference in elevation between the highest and lowest points in Zimbabwe?

ELEVATIONS		
COUNTRY	ZAMBIA	ZIMBABWE
HIGHEST	2.301 km	2.592 km
LOWEST	0.329 km	0.162 km

```
  2.592
- 0.162
  2.430  km
```

What is the difference in elevation between the highest point in Zimbabwe and the highest point in Zambia?

```
  2.592
- 2.301
  0.291  km
```

When adding or subtracting decimals:
• Line up each place value and the decimal points.
• Add zeros after the decimal, if necessary, to make an equivalent decimal.
• Begin with the least place value, regrouping if necessary.
• Write the decimal point between the ones and the tenths.

```
      1
  12.1605
+ 15.7700
  27.9305
```

```
     610
   9.770
 - 1.043
   8.727
```

```
   11 1
   5.0500
  44.6000
+  9.9704
  59.6204
```

Decimal sums and differences can be estimated by rounding to the nearest whole number.

```
44.62 − 5.07
  ↓      ↓
 45  − 5  =  40
```

Check Understanding

Solve.

a. 9.732
  − 8.511

b. 59.7541
  + 60.8222

c. 19.3
  − 4.632

d. 24.5962
  + 30.33

e. 40 − 6.2999

f. 5.46 + 14.667 + 30.981

 **Practice**

Solve.

1. 283.006
   115.4
   + 703.4

2. 24.068
   − 13.521

3. 3.0079
   − 1.042

4. 3.1237
   + 0.024

5. 800
   + 4.24

6. 19.625 + 8.21 + 27.403

7. 6 − 4.218

8. 19.47 − 7.3211

9. 63 + 0.62 + 0.7

10. 46.7 − 2.503

11. 19.5605 + 8.043

Estimate by rounding to the nearest whole number before adding or subtracting.

12. 8.567 + 4.44

13. 105.17 − 4.62

14. 69.525 − 30.231

 Apply

15. What is the difference in elevation between the highest and lowest points in Zambia? Use the table on the previous page.

16. The country of Zimbabwe borders Botswana for 813 km, Mozambique for 1,231 km, South Africa for 225 km, and Zambia for 797 km. What is the total boundary length of Zimbabwe?

17. Julia has a collection of African tiles. She measured the thickness of three different tiles as 1.5 cm, 2 cm, and 1.85 cm. If those three tiles are stacked, what will be the total thickness?

18. Joel spent $12.52 on a book about monkeys and $3.79 for flowers for his mother. If he paid for these items with a twenty-dollar bill, how much change did he receive?

 **Review**

Round to the nearest tenth.

1. 44.6205

2. 5.777

3. 9.12

Write in order from least to greatest.

4. 10.4   10.392   10.39   10.04

Lesson 13

 Construct Meaning

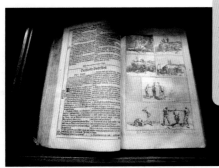

The idea of a movable-type printing press was perfected in Europe by Johannes Gutenberg in the 1450s. The first book printed was the Bible known as the *Gutenberg Bible*, in 1456. Forty-seven copies of this Bible remain in existence today.

Early Luther Bible

Gwendolyn purchased supplies for her small printing company and needs to balance her checkbook. Use your problem-solving guide techniques to solve the following problems.

CHECK REGISTER								
Number	**Date**	**Description**	**Payment** (–)			**Deposit** (+)		**Balance** $725.50
902	9/7	Ink	14.95		$			710.55
903	9/9	8½" x 11" Paper	123.95					586.60
904	9/9	Binders	5.01					
905	9/11	Blue pens	38.62					
—	9/11	Customer Receipt				243.05		

After making a payment or deposit, Gwendolyn records the amount in her check register. Then she calculates the balance.

$$\begin{array}{r} {}^{4\ 14\ 10} \\ \text{Balance} \quad \$72\cancel{5}.\cancel{5}\cancel{0} \longleftarrow \text{Regroup.} \\ -\,\text{Payment} \quad -\quad 14.95 \\ \hline \$710.55 \longleftarrow \text{Record in the Balance column.} \end{array}$$

$$\begin{array}{r} {}^{6\ 10\ 9\ 15} \\ \text{Balance} \quad \$7\cancel{1}\cancel{0}.\cancel{5}5 \longleftarrow \text{Regroup.} \\ -\,\text{Payment} \quad -\quad 123.95 \\ \hline \$586.60 \longleftarrow \text{Record in the Balance column.} \end{array}$$

 Check Understanding

a. After purchasing binders on September 9 for $5.01, what was Gwendolyn's balance?

b. What was the balance after check number 905 was written for $38.62?

c. If Gwendolyn deposited $243.05 from a customer, what was her balance?

1. Mrs. Loewen has $184.37 left from her paycheck. She paid an electric bill of $23.01, a phone bill, and spent $58.74 on food. If her paycheck was $310.35, how much was her phone bill?

2. Suzanne sold four of her grandmother's old books for $15.95, $4.30, $0.79, and $9.55. How much money did she make selling the books?

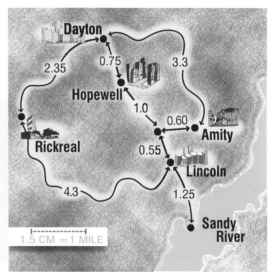

3. Colleen lives in the town of Dayton. She will be traveling to the Sandy River. Use the map to determine the route with the least number of miles.

4. Estimate how many miles it is from Dayton through Rickreal and Lincoln to the river.

5. In the newspaper advertisements, Elizabeth discovered that three stores were selling the same product for different prices—$132.50 minus a ten-dollar rebate, $121.95, and $126.85. What is the least expensive price?

6. Mr. Kropf is the president of a large automobile factory based in several countries. He currently is in charge of 35,628 employees. Because 500 workers are being transferred to another company, he will be hiring 762 more employees. How many total employees will be working for Mr. Kropf?

7. The sixth grade class at Williamette Christian School returned 480 recyclable cans to the store. They had discarded 21 cans that were not acceptable for recycle. What is the total number of cans the class collected?

8. The world population was approximately 3,000,000,000 in 1960; 4,500,000,000 in 1980; 6,000,000,000 in 2000; and will be 7,500,000,000 in 2020. What will be the approximate world population in 2040?

USING A CALCULATOR

9. Wolcott used a digital measurement tool to find the thickness of thin strips of metal. Five strips are measured and have thicknesses of 0.435 in., 0.325 in., 0.524 in., 0.095 in., and 0.269 in. What will be the total thickness of the strips?

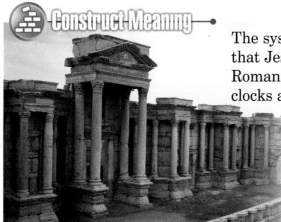

Construct Meaning

The system for writing numbers used during the time that Jesus lived on Earth was developed by the Romans. Roman numerals are still used today on clocks and monuments, for numbering the Olympic games, and in writing an outline. Where else have you seen Roman numerals? Because they do not use place value, multiplying and dividing Roman numerals could be a challenge. The Arabic system that we use makes these calculations much easier.

I	V	X	L	C	D	M
1	5	10	50	100	500	1,000

When the value of a symbol is greater than or equal to the value of the symbol to the right, add the values.

$$DCXII = 500 + 100 + 10 + 1 + 1 = 612$$

When the value of a symbol is less than the value of the symbol on the right, subtract that value. Then proceed with adding. Only I, X, and C can be placed before a symbol of larger value.

$$CDXCIV = (500 - 100) + (100 - 10) + (5 - 1) = 400 + 90 + 4 = 494$$

If a bar is placed over a Roman numeral, the value is multiplied by a thousand.

$$\overline{L} = 50,000 \qquad \overline{CX} = 110,000$$

When changing a number from standard notation to Roman numerals, consider one digit with its place value at a time.

$$649 = 600 + 40 + 9 = DC\ XL\ IX = DCXLIX$$

Check Understanding

Write the number using standard notation.

a. CCCXXI   b. CMV   c. $\overline{XI}$

d. DLIX   e. MMV

Write the Roman numeral.

f. 52

g. 3,524

h. 99

i. 408

j. The year you were born

Chapter One Study Guide

1. Write what each underlined digit represents in 7<u>3</u>9,55<u>5</u>,431. *Lesson 1*

2. Write 5,630,500 in expanded notation. *Lesson 2*

3. Write the numbers in order from least to greatest. *Lesson 3*
   439,562   440,508   439,495

4. *Lesson 4*

Round to the nearest	billion	hundred million	thousand
5,632,580,092			

5. Identify the pattern and determine the next number. *Lesson 5*
   4   20   100   500

6. a. 6 + ⬚ = 6   b. 7 + 2 = 2 + ⬚   c. 6 + (3 + 9) = (⬚ + 3) + 9   *Lesson 6*

7. a. 75,097 + 630,544   b. 59,000 − 6,322 *Lesson 7*

8. Martha and Louise each cataloged 525 books for the library at Trinity Christian School. If there are 2,672 books, how many are left to catalog? *Lesson 8*

9. Solve for x. Check.   a. $x − 352 = 1{,}976$ b. $451 + x = 35{,}491$ *Lesson 9*

10. Write the numbers in order from greatest to least.
    82.7321   82.743   83.00   *Lesson 10*

11. *Lesson 11*

Round to the nearest	tenth	hundredth	ten-thousandth
8.43533			

12. a. 29.5492 + 31.07   b. 600.982 − 5.49   *Lesson 12*

13. Kristen made $9.29 by recycling aluminum cans and $35.00 by mowing yards. Mrs. Stewart gave her a ten-dollar bill for washing windows. Did she earn enough to buy a pair of athletic shoes for $55.99?   *Lesson 13*

14. Write CDLIII using standard notation.   *Lesson 14*

Roman arena in France

Count the Amount

Write the letter of the explanation that matches each term.

1. Final step of the Problem-Solving Guide
2. Compatible numbers
3. Standard notation
4. Periods
5. Equation
6. Word form
7. Expanded notation

a. Groups of three digits
b. 4,681,534,702
c. Four trillion, one hundred nine
d. Mathematical sentence that has an equal sign
e. Evaluate the result
f. 10,000 + 6,000 + 300 + 90 + 9
g. Make mental math easier

Equiangular
Spiral Curve

Complete the missing periods in the place value chart.

hundred trillions	ten trillions	8.	hundred billions	9.	billions	hundred millions	ten millions	10.	11.	ten thousands	thousands	hundreds	12.	ones

Write >, < or =.

13. 634 ⬚ 436
14. 1.08 ⬚ 1.3
15. 534,877 ⬚ 538,477
16. 835.237 ⬚ 835.2370
17. 5,261,354 ⬚ 5,262,354

Copy and complete the chart.

Round to →	billions	ten millions	hundred thousands
5,613,259,784	18.	19.	20.

Estimate by rounding to the greatest place value.

21. $\begin{array}{r} 7,463 \\ + 1,854 \\ \hline \end{array}$

22. $\begin{array}{r} 86.634 \\ + 12.986 \\ \hline \end{array}$

23. $\begin{array}{r} 4,776 \\ - 2,187 \\ \hline \end{array}$

24. $\begin{array}{r} 28.104 \\ - 6.953 \\ \hline \end{array}$

25. $\begin{array}{r} 95,532 \\ 33,705 \\ + 61,071 \\ \hline \end{array}$

Trifolium Curve

26. Identify the pattern and determine the next number.

   8   20   32   44   ⬚

Write the letter of the addition property illustrated by each number sentence.

27. 42.6 + (6.32 + 8.43) = (42.6 + 6.32) + 8.43
28. 28 + 29 = 29 + 28
29. 9 + 6 + 7 = 6 + 9 + 7
30. 49 + 0 = 49

a. Commutative (Order) Property
b. Associative (Grouping) Property
c. Zero Property

Solve.

31. If 128 + x = 128, then x = :::::.

32. a + b = b + :::::

33. (r + s) + t = r + (s + :::::)

34. n + 25 + 49 + 11 = ::::: + n + 11 + 49

35.
```
   863
   784
   212
 + 131
```

36.
```
   461
 - 325
```

37.
```
   239,554
 +   9,844
```

38.
```
   4,900
 -   758
```

39. 890 − 742

40.
```
   663.8721
 + 873.25
```

41.
```
   82.094
 - 38.6
```

42.
```
   117.38
 +  53.002
```

43.
```
   0.6
 - 0.0043
```

44. 35 + 49 + 18

Solve for n. Check.

45. n − 124 = 376

46. 241 + n = 17,651

Write the number in standard notation.

47. DCII

48. XLVII

49. MCMXCIII

50. Covenant Christian School sold $3,195.25 in books on the first day of the book fair and $4,273.95 on the second day. The total two-day sales amount last year was $7,354.75. What is the difference in sales between this year and last year?

Maria Agnesi's Curve

Cayley's Sextic Curve

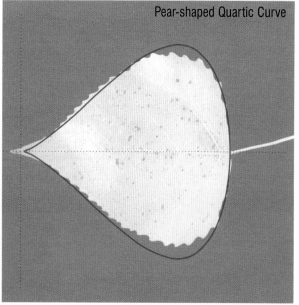
Pear-shaped Quartic Curve

Chapter Theme

God gave mankind the desire and ability to communicate with Him and with each other. The chapter 2 theme of Communication will focus on both the spoken and written forms. We know that God gave us the gift of speech, for in the second chapter of Genesis we read of God bringing the beasts to Adam "to see what he would call them." God gave us the example of writing, as recorded in Exodus 31:18, "And when He had made an end of speaking with him on Mount Sinai, He gave Moses two tablets of the Testimony, tablets of stone, written with the finger of God." Listening is also a form of communication that God wants us to value and practice. He gave us Christ as an excellent model who listened to others and responded with wisdom, power, and loving actions.

2

Chapter

Multiplication of Whole Numbers and Decimals

Lessons 16-30

"For then I will restore to the peoples a pure language,
That they all may call on the name of the Lord,
To serve Him with one accord."

Zephaniah 3:9

Lesson 16

 **Construct Meaning**

Language is an important aspect that shows how man is made in God's image. The ability to communicate through a complex language sets us apart from the animals. There are 6,809 known languages in the world.

If six countries each have about 23 different languages, how many languages are found in those six countries?

$$23 + 23 + 23 + 23 + 23 + 23 = 138$$

or

$$23 \times 6 = 138$$

Multiplication is repeated addition. Multiplying the factors results in the product.

$$\begin{array}{r} 23 \leftarrow \text{factor} \\ \times\ 6 \leftarrow \text{factor} \\ \hline 138 \leftarrow \text{product} \end{array}$$

Properties of Multiplication

(1) Zero Property of Multiplication
Multiplying any factor by 0 results in a product of zero.
$$36 \times 0 = 0$$
$$0 \times 700 = 0$$

(2) Multiplication Identity Property of One
If one factor is 1, the product will be the other factor.
$$1 \times 55 = 55$$
$$3,000 \times 1 = 3,000$$

(3) Commutative (Order) Property of Multiplication
The order of the factors may change without changing the product.
$$11 \times 6 = 66$$
$$6 \times 11 = 66$$

(4) Associative (Grouping) Property of Multiplication
The grouping of factors may change without changing the product.
$$10 \times (8 \times 4) = 320$$
$$(10 \times 8) \times 4 = 320$$

(5) Distributive Property
The product remains the same whether the factor is multiplied by the sum of the addends or by each addend.
$$3 \times (5 + 8) = 39$$
$$(3 \times 5) + (3 \times 8) = 39$$

 **Check Understanding**

Name the multiplication property demonstrated by each number sentence.

a. $42 \times 1 = 42$

b. $75 \times 0 = 0$

c. $35 \times (2 \times 10) = (35 \times 2) \times 10$

d. $50 \times 5 = 5 \times 50$

e. $6 \times (5 + 8) = (6 \times 5) + (6 \times 8)$

f. $r \times (3 \times 4) = (r \times 3) \times 4$

g. $5 \times a = 5$

h. $6 \times (s + 1) = (6 \times s) + (6 \times 1)$

34

Properties of Multiplication

 Practice

Write the missing factor and identify the property of multiplication.

1. $24 \times \boxed{} = 24$

2. $(70 \times 4) \times 5 = \boxed{} \times (4 \times 5)$

3. $32 \times \boxed{} = 0$

4. $\boxed{} \times 9 = 9 \times 4$

5. $12 \times 1 = \boxed{}$

6. $6 \times (2 + 3) = (\boxed{} \times 2) + (\boxed{} \times 3)$

Write the value of the unknown.

7. $a \times (10 + 4) = (9 \times 10) + (a \times 4)$

8. $n \times 12 = 12 \times 3$

9. $(53 \times 2) \times 7 = s \times (2 \times 7)$

10. $8 \times (p + 3) = (8 \times 2) + (8 \times 3)$

Use the Distributive Property to rewrite each expression. Solve.

11. $6 \times (3 + 5)$

12. $(8 \times 4) + (8 \times 6)$

13. $(11 \times 2) + (11 \times 3)$

14. $5 \times (16 + 9)$

Write a number sentence to illustrate each property.

15. Distributive Property

16. Commutative Property of Multiplication

17. Zero Property of Multiplication

18. Associative Property of Multiplication

19. Multiplication Identity Property of One

Mentally evaluate each number sentence. Write *true* or *false*.

20. $23 \times (1 \times 17) < (23 \times 16) \times 1$

21. $5 \times 33 > 32 \times 5$

22. $41 \times 8 = 8 \times 1 \times 41$

23. $5 \times 5 \times 4 = 100$

24. $(15 \times 45) \times 29 > 15 \times (45 \times 29)$

Apply

25. Let r represent the total number of languages in a particular country. If the country is divided into five regions, each with about six different languages, approximately how many different languages are spoken in that country? Write an equation to show this relationship and solve for r.

Construct Meaning

Language is mainly a job of the left side of the brain and develops in stages as a small child matures. At seven days old, an infant can distinguish its mother's voice from another woman's voice, and the father's voice can be distinguished when the infant is two weeks old.

AGE	LANGUAGE SKILLS
10 Months	First true words Babbling
20 Months	Understands about 300 words Words are 65% intelligible
30 Months	Understands about 900 words Has trouble with consonants

When you count by tens, as in 10, 20, 30, you are counting in multiples of 10. A **multiple** is the product of a select number and another whole number. Mental math is done easily with multiples of 10, 100, and 1,000.

$18 \times 10 = 18$ tens $= 180$

$18 \times 100 = 18$ hundreds $= 1,800$

$18 \times 1,000 = 18$ thousands $= 18,000$

$15 \times 20 =$ twice 15 tens $=$ ▦

$15 \times 200 =$ twice 15 hundreds $=$ ▦

$15 \times 2,000 =$ twice 15 thousands $=$ ▦

Using the Distributive Property and multiples of 10 will help you multiply mentally.

Find 8 × 46 mentally.

$8 \times 46 = 8 \times (40 + 6)$ Think of 46 as 40 + 6.

$= (8 \times 40) + (8 \times 6)$ Multiply each addend by 8.

$= 320 + 48$ Add the products.

$= 368$

Find 7 × 830 mentally.

$7 \times 830 = 7 \times (800 + 30)$ Think of 830 as 800 + 30.

$= (7 \times 800) + (7 \times 30)$ Multiply each addend by 7.

$= 5,600 + 210$ Add the products.

$= 5,810$

Check Understanding

a. 30×40 b. 40×600 c. $63 \times 1,000$

Solve using the Distributive Property.

d. $3 \times 26 = 3 \times ($ ▦ $+$ ▦ $)$

$= (3 \times$ ▦ $) + (3 \times$ ▦ $)$

$=$ ▦ $+$ ▦

$=$ ▦

e. 5×120

Use mental math.

1. 20 × 40
2. 20 × 100
3. 60 × 20
4. 50 × 70

5. 500 × 30
6. 1,000 × 9
7. 400 × 8
8. 1,000 × 40

9. 10,000 × 8
10. 4,000 × 50
11. 50,000 × 2
12. 30,000 × 3

Write the missing factor. Use the Distributive Property.

13. 9 × 21 = 9 × (▓ + ▓)
    = (9 × ▓) + (9 × ▓)
    = ▓ + ▓
    = ▓

14. 4 × 410 = 4 × (▓ + ▓)
    = (4 × ▓) + (4 × ▓)
    = ▓ + ▓
    = ▓

Use the Distributive Property to multiply mentally.

15. 7 × 32
16. 5 × 44
17. 3 × 96

18. 3 × 81
19. 3 × 150
20. 8 × 42

21. 50 × 74
22. 20 × 32
23. 9 × 85

Use mental math.

24. Gulnara bought a rug for her house that was 100 feet by 35 feet. Will the rug fit into a room with an area of 350 square feet? Explain.

25. Zachery rode the train in Europe 200 miles a month. If he maintained this mileage for one year, how many total miles would he travel?

26. Leisa bought 12 yards of fabric at $6 per yard. She paid for it using only ten-dollar bills. How many bills did she give to the clerk? What change did she receive?

27. In Kazakhstan it costs $5,000 to build a new house. How much would it cost to build five houses?

 **Construct Meaning**

Speech is produced with the help of the lips, palate, tongue, and vocal cords. When you speak, air from the lungs passes over the vocal cords. This rapid pulsation of air produces sound. The sound of the human voice can be measured in hertz.

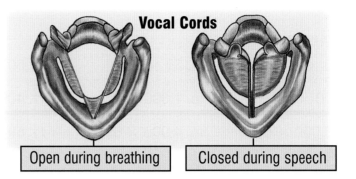

Vocal Cords

Open during breathing | Closed during speech

If Barry made a sound with his voice that measured 4,351 hertz and Jessica made a sound three times that, how many hertz did Jessica's sound produce?

Multiply the ones and tens. Regroup 15 tens as 1 hundred and 5 tens.	Multiply the hundreds. 3 × 3 hundreds = 9 hundreds. Add the regrouped hundred.	Multiply the thousands. 3 × 4 thousands = 12 thousands. Add the regrouped thousand.
$\begin{array}{r} \overset{1}{4{,}35\!\!1} \\ \times\quad 3 \\ \hline 53 \end{array}$	$\begin{array}{r} \overset{1\ \ 1}{4{,}351} \\ \times\quad 3 \\ \hline 053 \end{array}$	$\begin{array}{r} \overset{1\ \ 1}{4{,}351} \\ \times\quad 3 \\ \hline 13{,}053 \end{array}$

When multiplying large numbers, pay close attention to place values. You can also use the Distributive Property. Find the product of 531,642 × 4.

| 5 hundred thousands
3 ten thousands
1 thousand
6 hundreds
4 tens
2 ones | $500{,}000 \times 4 = 2{,}000{,}000$
$30{,}000 \times 4 = 120{,}000$
$1{,}000 \times 4 = 4{,}000$
$600 \times 4 = 2{,}400$
$40 \times 4 = 160$
$2 \times 4 = +\ \ \ \ 8$
$\overline{2{,}126{,}568}$ | Multiply the number in each place by 4.

Add the products. |

 **Check Understanding**

Multiply to find the product.

a. $\begin{array}{r} 1{,}530 \\ \times\quad 8 \\ \hline \end{array}$

b. $\begin{array}{r} 3{,}369 \\ \times\quad 4 \\ \hline \end{array}$

c. $\begin{array}{r} 21{,}064 \\ \times\quad 6 \\ \hline \end{array}$

d. $\begin{array}{r} 6{,}431 \\ \times\quad 8 \\ \hline \end{array}$

e. If a Bible conference center had 2,825 visitors in 1998, and that figure tripled in 2000, how many people visited in 2000?

Solve.

1. 265 × 6	2. 324 × 2	3. 61,340 × 5	4. 5,471 × 4	5. 52,142 × 5

6. 942 × 7	7. 73,366 × 8	8. 4,685 × 9	9. 331,454 × 3	10. 257,122 × 6

11. 5,382 × 8   12. 21,520 × 3   13. 12,326 × 4   14. 105,649 × 5

Find the missing factor.

15. 452 × ▦ 1,356	16. 618 × ▦ 2,472	17. 329 × ▦ 2,303	18. 6,054 × ▦ 30,270

19. A music store ordered 125 music books during its first year of business. The number of books ordered has doubled each year since then. If the store is in its sixth year of business, how many books were ordered this year?

20. If your vocal cords open and close about 7,640 times while reading a paragraph, approximately how many times would they open and close while reading eight paragraphs?

21. Mrs. Glendale drives 115 miles per week to give nine voice lessons. She deducts the cost of eight gallons of gasoline at two dollars per gallon from her profit. If she charges $35 for each voice lesson, what is her profit for one week?

22. Libby is a hearing-aid sales representative. She sells a pair of hearing aids for $1,342. On average, she sells four pairs a month. What is her average sales total for one month?

1. Of the 100 stalls in the market bazaar, twenty sell clothes, ten sell hardware items, thirty sell kitchenwares, and the rest sell food. How many stalls sell food?

Solve using the Distributive Property and mental math.

2. 3 × 46   3. 6 × 52   4. 8 × 99   5. 2 × 49

Lesson 19

Construct Meaning

Sandy Bay, Cape Town, South Africa

Bible translation is an important worldwide ministry. There are 31 languages in South Africa, and the republic of Nambia has 28 languages. Thirty-one is a prime number, and twenty-eight is composite.

A **prime number** is a whole number that has exactly two factors, 1 and the number itself.

Example:

31 17 13 2 3 5

Example:

28 114 12 9 6 25 8 42

A **composite number** is a whole number that has more than two factors.

48 is a composite number since it has more than two factors. You can use a factor tree to factor the number until all the numbers are prime. This is called **prime factorization**.

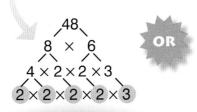

48
8 × 6
4 × 2 × 2 × 3
2 × 2 × 2 × 2 × 3

The prime factors of 48 are 2 × 2 × 2 × 2 × 3.

OR

Repeatedly divide by prime numbers.
Start with 2 since it is the smallest prime number.
Other primes are 3, 5, 7, 11, 13 . . .

3
2)6
2)12
2)24
2)48

You are finished when the final quotient is prime.

Continue to divide the quotient by 2 because it divides evenly.

Start by dividing by 2 since it is the smallest prime number.

Find the prime factors of the number 210.

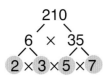

210
6 × 35
2 × 3 × 5 × 7

OR

7 ← Seven is prime.
5)35 ← 3 does not divide evenly. Try 5.
3)105 ← 2 does not divide evenly. Try 3.
2)210 ← **Start** with 2.

The prime factors of 210 are 2 × 3 × 5 × 7.

Check Understanding

Copy and complete.

a.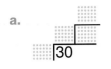
)30

b.
2)12

c.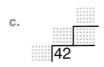
)42

d.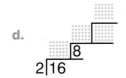
8
2)16

Write *prime* or *composite*.

1. 56   2. 41   3. 30   4. 92   5. 19   6. 47

Copy and complete.

7. 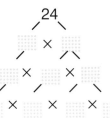   8. 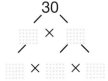   9.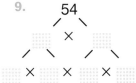

List the prime factors.

10. 6   11. 10   12. 36

13. 54   14. 42   15. 35

Copy and complete.

16.   17. 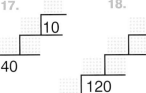   18.   19.

Repeatedly divide by prime numbers to find the prime factors.

20. 18   21. 92   22. 63   23. 340   24. 58

1. 36,041
    ×   4

2. 4,006
    ×   7

3. 1,436,935
    +   558,436

4. 2,361,410
    −   895,163

5. 63.42 − 4.05   6. 0.031 + 1.045   7. 1.1437 − 0.5610

Solve for the missing factor.

8. $r + 6 = 32$ 9. $q - 62 = 218$ 10. $a + 99 = 166$

There are 6,809 languages in the world, and Bible translators estimate that about 3,000 of those language groups do not have any part of the Bible in their language. In Asia, there are about 1,200 language groups without the Bible. All of these people have the need of Jesus as their greatest common factor.

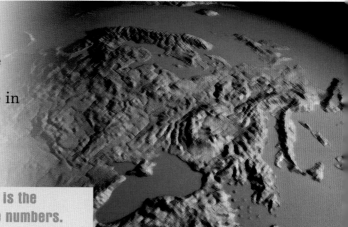

> The greatest common factor (GCF) is the largest common factor of two or more numbers.

You can find the greatest common factor of two numbers by listing the factors or by prime factorization. The Strategies for Factoring below will help you find the GCF.

List the factors of 12 and 36.

12 → 1, 2, 3, 4, 6, 12
36 → 1, 2, 3, 4, 6, 9, 12, 18, 36

Circle the common factors.
The greatest common number among the factors is the GCF, 12.

OR

Find all the common prime factors and multiply.

$$2 \times 2 \times 3 = 12$$

Circle the common prime factors. Because there are two 2's and one 3 as prime factors for both numbers, multiply $2 \times 2 \times 3$ to find the GCF, 12.

Strategies for Factoring

If a number is divisible by:

2 The digit in the ones place will be an even number. (0, 2, 4, 6, 8)

3 The sum of the digits will be divisible by 3. (15, 30, 45, 57)

5 The digit in the ones place will be 5 or 0. (15, 20, 25, 30)

6 It will be divisible by 2 and 3. (12, 18, 24, 36)

9 The sum of the digits will be divisible by 9. (18, 27, 45, 72)

10 The digit in the ones place will be 0. (20, 30, 40, 50)

Find the GCF of 20, 30, and 40.

20 → 1, 2, 4, 5, 10, 20
30 → 1, 2, 3, 5, 6, 10, 15, 30
40 → 1, 2, 4, 5, 8, 10, 20, 40

OR

$$2 \times 5 = 10$$

The greatest common factor is 10.

Greatest Common Factor

Use both methods to find the greatest common factor.

a. 9 and 21   b. 25 and 45   c. 24, 8, and 12

List the factors to find the GCF.

1. 35 and 21   2. 12 and 30   3. 26 and 6   4. 55 and 33

5. 15 and 45   6. 35 and 55   7. 13 and 26   8. 20 and 28

Use prime factorization to find the GCF.

9. 54 and 12   10. 30 and 18

11. 36 and 42   12. 50 and 10

13. 14, 28, and 42   14. 49 and 63

15. 81 and 72   16. 12, 30, and 66

Write *true* or *false*.

17. The GCF of 48 and 80 is 16.

18. The GCF is the largest common factor of one number.

19. To find the GCF using prime factorization, you need to subtract.

20. Prime numbers help you find the GCF.

21. Hannah is making a mosaic tile art piece that is 112 inches by 98 inches. What is the largest size square tile she could evenly fit into the piece?

22. Home Warehouse received a shipment of 36 matching plywood boards and 76 bags of nails. The plywood and nails must be placed in identical stacks with the largest possible number of boards and nails in each stack. How many stacks should be made? How many boards and bags of nails will be in each stack?

23. The science teacher, Miss Perry, is setting up a laboratory. She has to divide 12 microscopes, 42 slides, and 18 tubs of pond water evenly among classroom stations. How many stations should she make? How many microscopes, slides, and tubs will be at each station?

MANGER SQUARE

Lesson 21

Construct Meaning

Members of the Hazebute tribe, who live in a remote area of the hot, dry country of Tanzania, East Africa, use brush to build their homes and to fence in their animals. Their language sounds like clicking noises made with the tongue. If for the past 13 years this area had an average of 326 dry days a year, how many days without rain have they had?

$$\begin{array}{r} \overset{1}{3}26 \\ \times\ \ 13 \\ \hline 978 \end{array}$$ Multiply the ones.

$$\begin{array}{r} 326 \\ \times\ \ 13 \\ \hline 978 \\ +\ 3260 \\ \hline 4{,}238 \end{array}$$ Multiply the tens.

Add the partial products.

4,238 days without rain

Method 1

Check your answer by multiplying the factors, rounded to the greatest place value, to see if the product is reasonable. The answer 4,238 is reasonable because $300 \times 10 = 3{,}000$.

> Make sure you have the correct number of digits.

Solve $4{,}261 \times 247$.

$$\begin{array}{r} \overset{1\ 4}{4{,}}261 \\ \times\ \ \ 247 \\ \hline 29827 \end{array}$$ Multiply the ones.

$$\begin{array}{r} \overset{1\ 2}{4{,}}261 \\ \times\ \ \ 247 \\ \hline 29827 \\ 170440 \end{array}$$ Multiply the tens.

$$\begin{array}{r} \overset{1}{4{,}}261 \\ \times\ \ \ 247 \\ \hline 29827 \\ 170440 \\ +\ 852200 \\ \hline 1{,}052{,}467 \end{array}$$ Multiply the hundreds.

Add the partial products.

Method 2

Check your answer by rounding each factor to the nearest hundred and multiplying.

$$4{,}300 \times 200 = 860{,}000$$

Method 3

Check your answer by rounding the first factor to the greatest place value and using the Distributive Property to obtain a closer estimate.

$$(4{,}000 \times 200) + (4{,}000 \times 40) + (4{,}000 \times 7) =$$
$$800{,}000\ \ +\ \ 160{,}000\ \ +\ \ 28{,}000\ = 988{,}000$$

> Compare your estimates.

Check Understanding

Multiply. Check your answer by estimating.

a. $$\begin{array}{r} 356 \\ \times\ 24 \end{array}$$

b. $$\begin{array}{r} 327 \\ \times 254 \end{array}$$

c. $$\begin{array}{r} 5{,}382 \\ \times\ \ 216 \end{array}$$

Two- and Three-Digit Multipliers

Find the product. Check your answer.

1.	35 × 15	2.	46 × 34	3.	113 × 23	4.	245 × 19

5.	536 × 47	6.	747 × 335	7.	1,826 × 468	8.	2,641 × 265

9.	3,112 × 65	10.	5,371 × 55	11.	6,513 × 119	12.	3,645 × 621

Choose the best estimate.

13. 537 × 35
20,000 or 15,000

14. 639 × 57
360,000 or 36,000

15. 5,382 × 68
200,000 or 371,000

16. A round-trip airplane ticket to Dar es Salaam, Tanzania, from Portland, Oregon, costs $2,609. A team of 23 people are flying from Portland on January 3 to Tanzania. What is the total price of all their tickets?

17. A missionary team is going to distribute bags of corn to the 120 bush tribes of Tanzania. Each tribe averages about 70 people. Use the Distributive Property and mental math to determine the number of people in 120 tribes.

18. Each 15-pound bag of corn costs two U.S. dollars. If each U.S. dollar is worth 896 Tanzanian shillings, how many shillings will the team spend on 750 bags of corn?

19. If 4,699 people passed through a checkpoint between Uganda and Rwanda in one month, about how many people pass through the checkpoint in two years?

Lesson 22

 Construct Meaning

George Mueller and his wife Mary started an orphanage in Bristol, Germany, in the 1830s without an income. They diligently prayed and asked God to supply every need. When without food for breakfast, they would bring the need to God and He would provide money or groceries through other people. After one year, the orphanage was caring for 100 children, and by 1870 there were 2,000 children being cared for in several orphanages.

Multiply 1,026 × 70. Notice the zeros in each factor.

```
  1,026   Multiply the ones.
×    70   Since there are no ones,
   0000   write zero for each place value.
```

```
  1,026     Multiply the tens.
×    70     Write a zero as a placeholder
   0000     to show multiplication by ten.
+ 71,820    Add.
  71,820
```

Multiply 482 × 306.

```
  41
  482        2           2
×306        482         482
────       ×306        ×306
2892       ────        ────
           2892        2892
           0000        0000
                    +144600
                     147,492
```

Estimate to check your answer by rounding to the nearest hundred.

```
    500
  × 300      147,492 is a
  150,000    reasonable answer.
```

USING A CALCULATOR

Use a calculator to multiply factors with zeros.
(4,091 × 700) + (4,091 × 2)

```
4,091 × 700 = ⬭
4,091 × 2   = + ⬭
              ⬭
```

Follow the calculator steps to find the answer.

4 0 9 1 × 7 0 0 M+ 4 0 9 1 × 2 M+ MRC   2871882.

OR Use the Distributive Property to rewrite the problem before multiplying on the calculator.

(4,091 × 700) + (4,091 × 2) = 4,091 × (700 + 2) = 4,091 × 702

4 0 9 1 × 7 0 2 =   2871882.

 **Check Understanding**

Solve.

a. 699 × 209   b. 2,609 × 40   c. 307 × 42

 **Practice**

Multiply. Check by estimating.

1. 407	2. 960	3. 370	4. 1,008	5. 9,051
× 605	× 360	× 501	× 470	× 802

Round to the nearest hundred to estimate the product.

6. 1,463	7. 2,390	8. 6,421	9. 2,009	10. 4,009
× 150	× 605	× 960	× 308	× 560

 **USING A CALCULATOR**

Solve using a calculator and the Distributive Property when needed.

11. 6,301 × (400 + 60)   12. (431 × 200) + (431 × 90)   13. 9,036 × 673

 Apply

14. An orphanage in Romania made 262,800 meals in one year, then doubled that amount the next year. How many additional meals were made the second year?

15. A monthly gift of $1,096 was given anonymously to a missions foundation for a period of 360 months. What was the total amount of money given? Over how many years was the money given?

16. If the World Prayer Center sent out a prayer alert to 203 different people each day for 104 days, how many people were notified?

17. The printing and mailing costs for the first 50 days were $90 per day and increased to $109 per day for the next 54 days. Did the World Prayer Center stay within their budget of $11,000? Explain.

 Review

Write *prime* or *composite*.

1. 21   2. 41   3. 97   4. 144   5. 73

 **Construct Meaning**

In the 1870s, a simple stone church and cloistered walkway were erected on the Mount of Olives to commemorate the passage of Scripture known as the Lord's Prayer. On decorative tile panels the prayer is presented in 111 different languages, including Arabic, Hebrew, and even Ojibway Indian. The Church of the Lord's Prayer is open for visitors to view the beautiful tiles and to pause for a moment of quiet prayer.

Vater unser im Himmel, geheiligt werde Dein Name. Dein Reich komme. Dein Wille geschehe wie im Himmel so auf Erden. Unser tägliches Brot gib uns heute. Und vergib uns unsere Schuld, wie auch wir

Our Father in heaven,
Hallowed be Your name.
Your kingdom come.
Your will be done
On earth as it is in heaven.
Give us this day our daily bread.
And forgive us our debts,
As we forgive our debtors.
And do not lead us into temptation,
But deliver us from the evil one.
For Yours is the kingdom and the
power and the glory forever. Amen.
Matthew 6:9–13

What number is represented by the tiles in this array?

- standard notation   64
- product of factors 8×8
- using exponents 8^2

Write: 8^2 ← exponent
            ← base

Read: eight to the second power, or eight squared.

═══ The **exponent** tells the number of times the **base number** is used as a factor. ═══

The prime factorization of a number can be written using exponents.

$$\begin{array}{r} 2 \\ 2\overline{)4} \\ 2\overline{)8} \\ 2\overline{)16} \\ 2\overline{)32} \\ 2\overline{)64} \end{array}$$

$2 \times 2 \times 2 \times 2 \times 2 \times 2$

Write: 2^6
Read: two to the sixth power

Squared means to the second power. **Cubed** means to the third power.

Powers of ten can be expressed using exponents.

$10 = 10 \times 1 = 10^1$
$100 = 10 \times 10 = 10^2$
$1{,}000 = 10 \times 10 \times 10 = 10^3$

The base number is 10.

Scientific notation is a way of expressing a number as a decimal between one and ten multiplied by a power of ten.

Write: 3.4×10^2 **Read:** three and four-tenths times ten to the second power.
   decimal   power of ten $3.4 \times 10 \times 10 = 340$

Write 260 in scientific notation.

Move the decimal to the left until it is a number between one and ten.	**260.**
The number of places the decimal was moved determines the power of 10.	$260 = 2.6 \times 10^2$

 **Check Understanding**

Write the prime factorization using exponents.

a. 32   b. 72   c. 81

Write in scientific notation.

d. 390   e. 4,800   f. 62,000

 **Practice**

Write using exponents.

1. $3 \times 3 \times 3 \times 3 \times 3$ 2. $2 \times 2 \times 2 \times 8 \times 8 \times 8$ 3. $3 \times 3 \times 7 \times 7$

4. 9 squared   5. Six to the eighth power   6. Three to the eleventh power

 **USING A CALCULATOR**

Write the following in standard notation.

7. 6^4 8. 8^3 9. 5^5 10. 3^2 11. 88^2

Write the prime factorization using exponents.

12. 24   13. 49   14. 50   15. 12   16. 75

Write the following in scientific notation.

17. 3,200   18. 46,000   19. 64   20. 5,000   21. 160,000

22. 160   23. 2,000   24. 9,900   25. 79,000

 Apply

Write the answer in scientific notation.

26. If each design in the Church of the Lord's Prayer has 60 tiles and there are 111 designs, what is the total number of tiles?

27. It is about 7,000 miles one way from Seattle, Washington, to Jerusalem, Israel. How many miles is the round trip?

28. Miss Behrens traveled from Quito, Equador, east along the equator around the world, returning to Quito. She traveled a quarter of her trip in 6,250 miles. How many total miles was her trip?

Lesson 24

 **Construct Meaning**

"Blessed are those who hear the word of God and keep it." Luke 11:28b

At the age of 24, George Whitefield (1714–1770) preached in England. His first open-air sermon was to miners, and the crowd grew to 10,000 within a few days. Adoniram Judson (1788–1850), America's first foreign missionary, served the Lord in India six years before he baptized the first believer. Jonathan Goforth (1859–1936) went to China as an evangelist. Hearing the Word of God motivates His children to do His will.

ENGLAND   CHINA   INDIA

Brian worked with the neighbor on a computer job and was challenged to give $12.50 each month to support the missions work in his church. How much would he give in 10 months?

The number of zeros in 10, 100, and 1,000 tells you how many places to move the decimal to the right when multiplying a decimal by a multiple of 10.

1 × $12.50 = $12.50	10 × $12.50 = $125.00	100 × $12.50 = $1,250.00	1,000 × $12.50 = $12,500.00
	one zero Move the decimal **one** place to the right.	**two** zeros Move the decimal **two** places to the right.	**three** zeros Move the decimal **three** places to the right after writing a zero.

After 10 months, Brian had given $125.00 to the missions ministry.

Brian's family drove 24.5 miles to church, using approximately 1.609 gallons of gasoline. Use the number of miles and gallons of gasoline to notice how each number becomes greater as the decimal point moves to the right.

Observe the pattern by using mental math.

1 × 24.5 = 24.5 miles	1 × 1.609 = 1.609 gallons of gasoline
10 × 24.5 = 245	10 × 1.609 = 16.09
100 × 24.5 = 2,450 ◄— Write one or more	100 × 1.609 = 160.9
1,000 × 24.5 = 24,500 zeros as needed to	1,000 × 1.609 = 1,609

move the decimal.

 **Check Understanding**

Multiply. Observe the pattern.

a. 1 × 8.2
10 × 8.2
100 × 8.2
1,000 × 8.2

b. 1 × $24.99
10 × $24.99
100 × $24.99
1,000 × $24.99

c. 1 × 6.135
10 × 6.135
100 × 6.135
1,000 × 6.135

d. 1 × $3.40
10 × $3.40
100 × $3.40
1,000 × $3.40

Multiples of Ten and Decimals

Multiply. Write the letter of the correct answer.

Christ the King School, Côte D'Ivoire

1. 100 × 4.062
2. 10 × 0.42
3. 1,000 × 0.0064
4. 100 × 64.2
5. The product of 0.4 and 1,000
6. The product of 100 and 6.24

a. 400
b. 6,420
c. 624
d. 6.4
e. 4.2
f. 406.2

Multiply. Use mental math.

7. 10 × 0.48
8. 100 × 92.4
9. 21.8 × 100
10. 7.62 × 1,000
11. 1.1 × 10
12. 245.326 × 100
13. 0.0017 × 1,000
14. 10 × 131.74
15. 1,000 × 357.06
16. 100 × 0.3333

Copy and complete each table.

r	2.5	7.64	16.9846	0.4	0.097
100 × r	17.	18.	19.	20.	21.

Reverend Cheiwlu M. Bargeboe II

n	22.	139.4	1.3	25.	0.0063	27.
10 × n	16.42	23.	24.	20.40	26.	1.035

28. 1.097 × n = 109.7
29. 0.00814 × n = 8.14
30. 15.81063 × n = 15,810.63

Complete.

31. To solve 1,000,000,000 × 381.6 mentally, move the decimal ▒ places to the right. How many zeros will you need to add to the product?

32. A computer monitor uses $0.12 of electricity per kilowatt hour. How much does it cost to have the monitor turned on for 10 hours? 100 hours?

33. Twenty-four dollars per month will cover the support (tuition, a uniform, hot lunch) of a child in Côte D'Ivoire. The children are orphans from Liberia who fled because of their Christian faith. How much will it cost to support 1,000 orphans for one month?

1. 63	2. 1,085	3. 827	4. 132,006	5. 37,211
× 8	× 247	× 16	× 9	× 75

 Construct Meaning

God created us with ears to be able to enjoy the sounds of nature, the beautiful music of an orchestra, and the sweet voice of a friend. The outer and middle sections of the ear allow us to hear. The inner ear helps to provide balance to the body.

Kay's dad worked in a machine shop environment, leaving him with a hearing problem that necessitates a hearing aid. For each of the previous 12 check-ups, the doctor's report showed a 0.06 hearing loss. How much of his hearing has he lost?

The graph paper is divided into hundredths to find $12 \times 0.06 = x$.

$$\begin{array}{r} 0.06 \\ \times\ 12 \end{array}$$

Seventy-two hundredths is the amount of hearing loss that Kay's dad has experienced.

Multiply as if you were multiplying whole numbers.

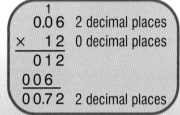

$$\begin{array}{r} 1 \\ 0.0\,6 \quad \text{2 decimal places} \\ \times\quad 1\,2 \quad \text{0 decimal places} \\ \hline 0\,1\,2 \\ 0\,0\,6 \\ \hline 0\,0.7\,2 \quad \text{2 decimal places} \end{array}$$

Place the decimal point in the product by counting the total number of decimal places to the right of the decimal point in both factors.

How many decimal places would be counted in the product of 87×1.98764?

Estimating can help you determine where to place the decimal. The cost for Kay to heat her lunch in the microwave is about 4.8¢ daily. You can also write this cost as $0.048. About how much does it cost to heat her lunch for a fifteen-day period?

4.8¢ $\xrightarrow{\text{round}}$ 5.0¢ Is it easier to work in cents or dollars?

$$\begin{array}{r} 4.8\text{¢} \\ \times\ 15 \end{array} \qquad \begin{array}{r} \$0.048 \\ \times\ 15 \end{array}$$

Actual amount in cents	Actual amount in dollars
$\begin{array}{r} 4.8\text{¢} \\ \times\,1\,5 \\ \hline 2\,4\,0 \\ 4\,8 \\ \hline 7\,2.0\text{¢} \end{array}$	$\begin{array}{r} \$\,0.0\,4\,8 \\ \times\qquad 1\,5 \\ \hline 0\,2\,4\,0 \\ 0\,0\,4\,8 \\ \hline \$\,0\,0.7\,2\,0 \end{array}$

Is 75¢ a reasonable amount to heat Kay's lunch for a fifteen-day period?

 Check Understanding

Copy the equation that matches the model.

a. 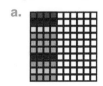 b. 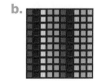 c.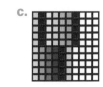

$13 \times 0.05 = 0.65$

$10 \times 0.04 = 0.4$

$10 \times 0.10 = 1$

Write the number of decimal places counted for each product.

1. 14 × 0.61 = r   2. 8 × 7.6438 = r   3. 9,542 × 1.3 = r   4. 101 × 1.101 = r

Find the product.

| 5. 6.4 × 27 | 6. 7.348 × 49 | 7. 4.23 × 25 | 8. 3.25 × 216 | 9. 7.9542 × 13 |

| 10. 25 × 0.3 | 11. 416 × 0.04 | 12. 5.13 × 28 | 13. 4.52 × 638 | 14. 32 × 0.9 |

15. 47 × 0.1   16. 240 × 0.02   17. 8,006 × 9.27   18. 6.4 × 4,601   19. 9 × 9.9

Copy and complete the chart.

×	Estimate	Actual amount in cents	Actual amount in dollars
45	2.8¢	2.8¢	$0.028
	20.	21.	22.

23. Is your estimated answer reasonable?

Complete.

24. Is the product of a number multiplied by 0.5 greater or less than the number?

25. If a number is multiplied by 1.2, is the product greater or less than the number?

26. A vitamin contains 0.5 milligrams of vitamin C. How many milligrams of vitamin C do 360 tablets have?

27. John uses 0.75 gallons of gasoline every time he drives to and from work. How much gasoline does he use in five days to commute to and from work?

28. Tasha saved 8.9¢ on every dollar she made baby-sitting. After making $20, how much had she saved?

29. Van rides his bicycle 3.25 kilometers each day. About how many kilometers does he ride in 15 days? (Round the decimal number only.)

| 1. 68.14 − 19.53 | 2. 489 + 762 | 3. 7.594 + 3.165 | 4. 50,018 − 19,127 | 5. 705 × 614 |

Lesson 26

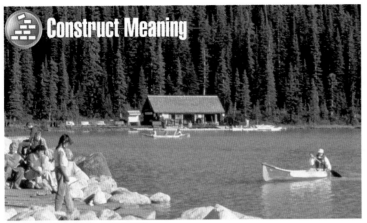

Construct Meaning

It was time for the sixth grade retreat to Camp Gilead. Instructions on policies and procedures took 0.8 of the first hour. 0.2 of that time was spent praying for safety and behavior. Mr. Kruger read and discussed Isaiah 50:4.

Name the part of the first hour that was spent in prayer. Solve $0.8 \times 0.2 = x$.

DECIMAL MODEL

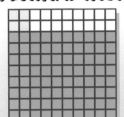

Eight-tenths are shaded horizontally. Two-tenths are shaded vertically. The part where the colors overlap is the product.
0.16

$$\begin{array}{r} 0.8 \\ \times\ 0.2 \\ \hline 0.1\,6 \end{array}$$

0.8 Multiply as you do with whole numbers.
× 0.2 Count the decimal places in both factors. (2)
0.1 6 Show the product with that number of decimal places. (2)

When both factors are less than one, the product is less than one.

Discuss each multiplication example below.

$$\begin{array}{r} 0.0\,9 \\ \times\ \ 0.7 \\ \hline 0.0\,6\,3 \end{array} \qquad \begin{array}{r} 0.0\,0\,9 \\ \times\ \ \ \ \ \ 7 \\ \hline 0.0\,6\,3 \end{array}$$

Why do both products have three decimal places?

MORE EXAMPLES

Count the decimal places.

$$\begin{array}{r} 0.5\,1 \\ \times\ \ 0.7 \\ \hline 0.3\,5\,7 \end{array}$$

2 decimal places
+ 1 decimal place
▓ decimal places

$$\begin{array}{r} 7\,4.5\,2\,1 \\ \times\ \ \ \ \ 0.3\,2 \\ \hline 1\,4\,9\,0\,4\,2 \\ +\ 2\,2\,3\,5\,6\,3\,0 \\ \hline 2\,3.8\,4\,6\,7\,2 \end{array}$$

▓ decimal places

Find 9.59×0.30.

$$\begin{array}{r} \$9.5\,9 \\ \times\ \ \ \ 0.3\,0 \\ \hline \$2.8\,7\,7\,0 \end{array}$$

rounded to the nearest cent is ▓.

Compute mentally, then place the decimal.
Write extra zeros in the product if needed.
Look for a pattern.

$0.4 \times 0.6 = 0.24$
$0.4 \times 0.06 = 0.024$
$0.4 \times 0.006 = $ ▓

Check Understanding

Write the equation that matches the model.

a. 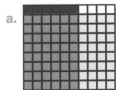 b. 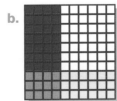 c.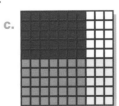

$0.3 \times 0.4 = 0.12$

$0.5 \times 0.7 = 0.35$

$0.9 \times 0.6 = 0.54$

Rewrite the product with the decimal in the correct place.

1. 8.4	2. 36.7	3. 2.36	4. 23.5	5. 0.008
× 6.7	× 0.09	× 6.408	× 0.98	× 0.9
5628	3303	1512288	2303	72

Multiply.

6. 0.17	7. 0.003	8. 7.57	9. 86.52	10. 16.4376
× 0.04	× 23	× 0.524	× 0.037	× 0.8

Compute mentally, then place the decimal.

11. 0.6 × 0.7
0.6 × 0.07
0.6 × 0.007

12. 0.3 × 0.8
0.3 × 0.08
0.3 × 0.008

13. 0.5 × 0.04
0.5 × 0.004
0.5 × 0.0004

14. 0.9 × 0.2
0.09 × 0.2
0.009 × 0.2

15. Carl works 5.5 hours each day. He earns $7.50 per hour. How much money does he earn in one day?

16. Suzan baby-sits for $2.75 an hour. How much money does she make in 3.5 hours? Round to the nearest cent.

17. Becky saved $19.25. She needs 2.4 times that amount to purchase a pair of sandals. What is the price of the sandals?

18. Chad used a fifty- and a twenty-dollar bill to pay for a yearly pass to an amusement park. The pass cost $54.75. How much change did he receive?

19. Half of the day at Camp Gilead was free time. Ben spent 0.3 of his free time swimming. What portion of the day did Ben spend swimming?

Review

1. 43.819
51.367
+ 16.021

2. 8,003
− 4,739

3. Factor 36 by using a factor tree and the repeated division method.

**Construct Meaning**

Christian organizations have strategic plans to evangelize the world. When God's people speak His written word, and those words fall on ears ready to receive them, then a person is ready to believe in Christ. God gave His Son so believers could have eternal life—the ultimate expression of God's love to mankind.

Two different churches sent youth to participate in a Vacation Bible School for Vietnamese immigrants in Tennessee. 17 youth went from the first church. 21 youth from the second church traveled on the same bus. 17 + 21 is an expression that represents the number of youth on the bus.

A **numerical expression** such as 17 + 21 uses numbers and at least one operation symbol to name a known quantity.

Another example

| **Expression:** 41 + 18 | **Phrase:** the sum of 41 and 18 |

An **algebraic expression** contains at least one variable and one operation symbol. A **variable** is a letter or symbol that stands for an unknown quantity. The letter or symbol can represent one number or a set of numbers.

What if the youth from a third church traveled on the same bus?

Evaluate the expression if the variable b is equal to 23.
Write the expression. $(17 + 21) + b$
Substitute 23 for b. $38 + 23$
Solve.   61
What if the variable b is equal to 20?

> Calculate inside the ( ) first.

Multiplication in algebraic expressions can be written four different ways. The phrase "8 times a number" can be written: $8 \times n$ $8 \cdot n$ $8(n)$ $8n$

**Check Understanding**

Evaluate each algebraic equation by rewriting the expression substituting the given value for the variable.

a. $a + 72$ for $a = 9$ b. $(18 - b) + 14$ for $b = 4$
c. $t \div 8$ for $t = 64$ d. $(5m) - 29$ for $m = 9$

Write as a numerical expression.
- e. 8 greater than 2
- f. 9 less than 15
- g. 6 times 8
- h. 15 divided by 5

Write as an algebraic expression.
- i. A number greater than 8
- j. 9 less than a number
- k. 6 times a number
- l. A number divided by 5

Evaluate each algebraic expression.

1. $h + 29$ for $h = 17$
2. $x \div 3$ for $x = 396$
3. $32 + (f - 4)$ for $f = 8$
4. $(j + k) \times 2$ for $j = 9$ and $k = 6$
5. $(b \times 5) \div c$ for $b = 4$ and $c = 2$

Substitute 6 for x, 9 for y, and 12 for z to evaluate each algebraic expression.

6. $(z - y) + x$
7. $(x \cdot y) \div 3$
8. $z + (y - x)$
9. $(3 \cdot x) - z$

Write as a numerical expression.
10. The product of 9 and 12
11. The difference of 15 and 7
12. 10 greater than 10
13. 4 less than 4 times 4

Write as an algebraic expression.
14. 25 less than a number
15. A number decreased by 8
16. A number divided by 210
17. 12 more than twice a number

18. Write a numerical expression to show that Sue bought seven colored pencils on Monday and four more on Tuesday.

19. Write a phrase for the algebraic expression $3 \times n$.

20. Is the expression 7 less than 9 the same as 9 less than 7? Why or why not?

21. Should h have the same value or a different value each time it is used in the expression $h + 6 + h$? Explain.

22. Jill's parents bought a car priced at $14,775.00. They made a down payment of $8,895. How much was left to pay? Write an equation and solve.

23. Mrs. Reagan put this challenge on the board. The students were to identify the whole number each letter represents. (Hint: v, w, x, y, and z have the same value for all the equations.) $v + w = 4$ $v \div z = v$ $x \cdot y = 35$ $z + x = 13$ $v \cdot w = v$

Solve and check.

1. $r + 18 = 37$
2. $b - 49 = 19$
3. $643 + r = 4,907$
4. $n - \$2.16 = \$30$

Lesson 28

Man's ability to communicate has been revolutionized by technology. Samuel Morse's telegraph of 1844 and Alexander Bell's telephone of 1876 opened new avenues of communication. A computer called ENIAC, completed in 1945, was to have a profound impact on the field of communication technology. ENIAC stands for the Electrical Numerical Integrator and Computer.

Solve.

1. Within a five-minute period, the huge ENIAC could complete approximately ten million addition or subtraction problems of ten-digit numbers. At that rate, about how many problems would be calculated in half an hour?

2. The period of time the ENIAC required to complete a problem with a ten-digit multiplier was a little less than 0.003 of a second. What period of time would be needed to multiply 100 similar problems?

3. The ENIAC contained almost 18,000 vacuum tubes, occupied a 30- by 50-foot room, and weighed 30 tons. Would this enormous computer fit into a room with an area of 1,600 square feet?

4. Today, a large corporation might purchase laptop computers for its employees. If a company had budgeted $75,000 for the computers, what is the maximum number that can be purchased at a cost of $2,099.87 each? (Use a calculator.)

5. Eight years ago, fifty students in a college dormitory had cellular phones. If seven times as many students in the dorm now have cell phones, how many students have them today?

6. Twenty-five sets of headphones will be purchased for a "listening tour" in a museum. If a total of $1,800 may be spent for the headphones, will the museum purchase sets that cost $79.95 each or buy the less expensive models at $69.95 each? Round each amount and use the Distributive Property to solve mentally.

Alexander Graham Bell Museum, Nova Scotia

58

7. There are ten digits on a push-button phone. The first three digits of a seven-digit phone number are called the "exchange." When you are assigned your phone number, there are 8 possible choices for the first digit, 10 for the second digit, and 10 for the third digit. Because 8 × 10 × 10 = 800, there are 800 possible exchanges. How many possible combinations are there for the last four digits of a phone number if any digit may be used in any position? Express your answer using an exponent.

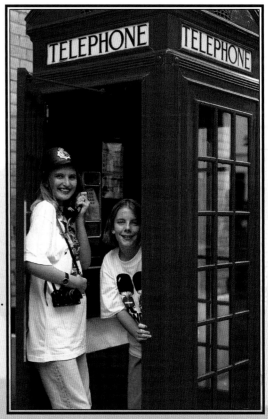

8. Miss Ortega's class of 24 students and Mr. Winston's class of 32 students will attend a program about the history of communication. The chairs will be set up so each class is seated on either side of a center aisle. What is the greatest number of chairs that can be placed in a row if the rows on each side of the aisle have an equal number of chairs?

Use the chart to answer the following.

9. Which phone plan will be less expensive for Mrs. Bell, who makes about 100 minutes worth of long-distance calls each month?

LONG-DISTANCE CALLING PLANS		
Plan	**Monthly Fee**	**Cost Per Minute**
Phone Giant 1	$3.95	$0.07
Phone Giant 2	$3.50	$0.08

10. How much will Mrs. Bell save in one month by using the plan you selected?

11. Suppose the Save More Phone Company, which has no monthly fee, offered Mrs. Bell a $0.06 per minute long-distance rate but required a $25 fee to begin the service. After six months, would she have spent more or less money than she would have using the Phone Giant plan you selected? State the difference.

JUST FOR FUN

12. If five students can drink five milk shakes in twelve minutes, how many milk shakes can the same five students drink in two hours?

 **Construct Meaning**

Multiplying a number by itself gives the **square** of that number.

| seven squared | $7^2 = 7 \times 7 = 49$ |

"Undoing" the multiplication gives the **square root** of a number, the number which, when multiplied by itself, yields the given number. The symbol $\sqrt{}$ means "the square root of."

| the square root of forty-nine | $\sqrt{49} = \sqrt{7 \times 7} = 7$ |

Mrs. Pierce cut 144 squares of fabric from old jeans to make a quilt for her son. If she uses all 144 pieces and arranges them into a square, how many pieces will be on each edge of the pattern?

$$\sqrt{144} = \sqrt{12 \times 12} = 12 \text{ pieces on each side.}$$

The blocks will be in a 12 by 12 array.

If she had 164 pieces, could she arrange them all in a square array?

$\sqrt{164} = ?$

$12 \times 12 = 144$ too small   There is no whole number times itself that equals 164.
$13 \times 13 = 169$ too large   The square root of 164 is a decimal between 12 and 13.
She cannot arrange 164 pieces into a square array.

 **USING A CALCULATOR**

Find the square root of 3,844.

Find 5.2 squared. $5 . 2 \; x^2$ 27.04

 **Check Understanding**

Solve.

a. 5^2 b. 100^2 c. 6^2 d. $\sqrt{16}$ e. $\sqrt{400}$ f. $\sqrt{25}$

Solve using a calculator.

g. 56^2 h. $\sqrt{625}$ i. $\sqrt{2.25}$ j. 1.6^2 k. $\sqrt{3{,}025}$ l. 19^2

Chapter Two Study Guide

1. What property is illustrated by $4 \times 8 = 8 \times 4$? *Lesson 16*

2. Use the Distributive Property to mentally multiply 5×23. *Lesson 17*

3. Solve $4,969 \times 8$. *Lesson 18*

4. Write the prime factors of 54. *Lesson 19*

5. Find the greatest common factor of 30 and 75. *Lesson 20*

6. Solve 987×124. *Lesson 21*

7. Solve $7,057 \times 622$. *Lesson 22*

8. Write 193,000 in scientific notation. *Lesson 23*

9. Solve $245.37 \times 10,000$. *Lesson 24*

10. Solve 3.233×71. *Lesson 25*

11. Solve 16.42×8.67. *Lesson 26*

12. Use n to write an algebraic expression for six times a number. *Lesson 27*

13. Mr. Schneider needs to purchase twenty-four phones for his employees. He can buy them individually for $26.95 each with free delivery or in cases of 12 for $288.50 per case plus a $24 delivery fee for the entire order. Which is less expensive? *Lesson 28*

14. Find $\sqrt{121}$. *Lesson 29*

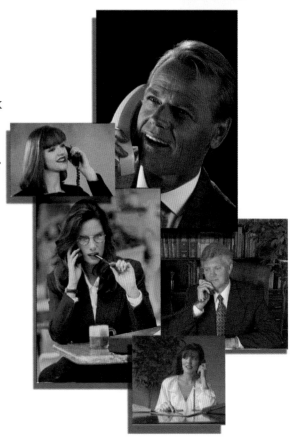

Magnified Messages

Write the letter to match the property with the equation.

1. $4 \times 7 = 7 \times 4$

2. $6 \times (3 + 5) = (6 \times 3) + (6 \times 5)$

3. $19 \times 0 = 0$

4. $8 \times (5 \times 2) = (8 \times 5) \times 2$

5. $1 \times 49 = 49$

a. Zero Property of Multiplication
b. Multiplication Identity Property of One
c. Commutative Property of Multiplication
d. Associative Property of Multiplication
e. Distributive Property

Mentally use the Distributive Property to solve.

6. Gracie gave 52 blankets to each of five separate groups of homeless people. What is the total number of blankets she gave away?

7. 89×6

8. 602×3

9. 250×7

10. 15×8

11. 52×9

Solve.

12. $\begin{array}{r} 45{,}602 \\ \times\qquad 8 \\ \hline \end{array}$

13. $\begin{array}{r} 3{,}894 \\ \times\qquad 23 \\ \hline \end{array}$

14. $\begin{array}{r} 6{,}431 \\ \times\qquad 355 \\ \hline \end{array}$

15. $\begin{array}{r} 607 \\ \times\quad 20 \\ \hline \end{array}$

16. $\begin{array}{r} 90{,}430 \\ \times\qquad 4 \\ \hline \end{array}$

17. $\begin{array}{r} 489 \\ \times\, 601 \\ \hline \end{array}$

18. $\begin{array}{r} 50{,}406 \\ \times\qquad 306 \\ \hline \end{array}$

19. $\begin{array}{r} 406 \\ \times\, 208 \\ \hline \end{array}$

20. $\begin{array}{r} 905 \\ \times\, 300 \\ \hline \end{array}$

21. $\begin{array}{r} 3{,}690 \\ \times\qquad 44 \\ \hline \end{array}$

22. A chapel has four rooms with mosaic tile floors. If each floor has 56 tiles per square foot and each floor is 32 square feet, how many tiles are on the chapel floor?

Write as exponents.

23. $8 \times 8 \times 8 \times 2 \times 2 \times 2$

24. $6 \times 6 \times 6 \times 6 \times 6 \times 6$

25. 5 squared

26. Nine to the seventh power

27. $2 \times 2 \times 2 \times 2 \times 2 \times 3$

28. Eleven to the fourth power

Write the prime factors using exponents.

29. 32

30. 16

31. 52

32. 72

33. 49

Find the greatest common factor.

34. 32 and 16   35. 14 and 49   36. 21 and 81   37. 24 and 62

Write as an algebraic expression using r.

38. A number times 6   39. 23 more than twice a number

40. 144 divided by a number   41. A number increased by 16

42. The sum of two buckets of apples if one bucket has nine fewer than the other

Solve.

43. Collette lives in the Netherlands and needs to purchase 26 loaves of bread and 13 rounds of cheese. If each loaf costs $2.15 and each round costs $4.56, how much will she spend for the items?

44. To be a member of the Salem Home Builders Association, Arnie is required to pay $335 for the first year and $310 for each following year. If Arnie is a member for five and a half years, how much money will he pay to the association?

45.   0.9
   × 0.3

46.   2.75
   × 3.5

47.   4.89
   × 0.05

48.   16.34
   ×   4.6

Use the table to answer the following questions.

49. Mr. Murphy made a list of several items and their prices that he needed to purchase for an inner-city outreach. While figuring the cost of the items, he made a mistake. Which items on the list have the cost figured incorrectly?

50. What is the correct total cost of all the items?

PRICE LIST			
Items	Quantity	Price	Cost
blankets	5	$8.95	$44.75
Bibles	8	$23.04	$18.43
balloon packages	4	$1.99	$7.66
toothbrushes	50	$2.06	$1.03
		Total	

Chapter Theme

What a blessing to know that because we belong to God, our bodies are indwelt by His Holy Spirit. As we mature both spiritually and physically, it becomes evident that our heavenly father expects us to take care of our bodies. The chapter 3 theme of Healthy Choices explores some of the ways we can make wise decisions in the area of health. Your lessons will include examples of men and women of God who were pioneers in the field of medicine. Their contributions made a profound difference in the health care we receive today. However, God the Father is the ultimate source of all healing. His Son demonstrated His power and love in the healing miracles described in the Bible.

3

Chapter

Division of Whole Numbers and Decimals

Lessons 31-45

Or do you not know that your body is the temple of the Holy Spirit who is in you, whom you have from God, and you are not your own?

1 Corinthians 6:19

For You formed my inward parts;
You covered me in my mother's womb.
My frame was not hidden from You,
When I was made in secret,
And skillfully wrought in the lowest parts of the earth.
Your eyes saw my substance, being yet unformed.
And in Your book they all were written,
The days fashioned for me,
When as yet there were none of them. Psalm 139:13, 15–16

When a baby is 154 days old, how many weeks old is she?

Since there are seven days in a week, divide 154 by 7.

The baby is 22 weeks old.

$$\text{divisor} \longrightarrow 7 \overline{)154} \longleftarrow \text{dividend}$$

quotient = 22

$$\begin{array}{r} 22 \\ 7\overline{)154} \\ \underline{14} \\ 14 \\ \underline{14} \\ 0 \end{array}$$

Division can be shown in three ways: $7\overline{)154}$, $154 \div 7$,   or $\frac{154}{7}$.

Division can be understood in three ways.

• **Division involves finding sets.**
Copy and complete the chart by first counting the number of desks in your classroom.

Total Number of Desks in Class	Arranged in Groups of:	How many sets?	Any remaining desks?
Example: 25	2	12	1
	3		
	4		
	5		
	6		
	7		
	8		
	9		

• **Division is the inverse of multiplication.**

$$\begin{array}{r} 3 \\ 7\overline{)21} \\ \underline{21} \\ 0 \end{array}$$ $7 \times \boxed{} = \boxed{}$

• **Division may be shown as repeated subtraction.**

$$\begin{array}{r} 4 \\ 8\overline{)32} \\ \underline{32} \\ 0 \end{array}$$ $32 - 8 = \boxed{}$, $\boxed{} - 8 = \boxed{}$, $\boxed{} - 8 = \boxed{}$, $\boxed{} - 8 = \boxed{}$

4 groups of 8 may be taken from 32.

Division Rules

1. When any number except 0 is divided by itself, the quotient is 1.
2. Any number divided by 1 will be that number.
3. Zero divided by any number will be 0.
4. It is impossible to divide by zero.

 **Check Understanding**

a. $9\overline{)36}$ $\quad$ $36 - 9 = $ ⬚ , $\quad$ ⬚ $- 9 = $ ⬚ , $\quad$ ⬚ $- 9 = $ ⬚ , $\quad$ ⬚ $- 9 = $ ⬚

b. $4\overline{)48}$ $\quad$ $4 \times$ ⬚ $= $ ⬚

c. If there are 72 people, how many teams of nine can be made?

 Practice

Solve.

1. $7\overline{)63}$ $\qquad$ 2. $8\overline{)56}$ $\qquad$ 3. $4\overline{)36}$ $\qquad$ 4. $8\overline{)72}$ $\qquad$ 5. $4\overline{)44}$

6. $124 \div 2$ $\qquad$ 7. $175 \div 5$ $\qquad$ 8. $162 \div 3$ $\qquad$ 9. $146 \div 2$ $\qquad$ 10. $152 \div 8$

Solve for the unknown.

11. $25 \div 5 = a$ $\qquad$ $5 \times a = 25$

13. $150 \div 5 = m$ $\qquad$ $5 \times m = 150$

12. $8 \times r = 40$ $\qquad$ $40 \div 8 = r$

14. $7 \times c = 21$ $\qquad$ $21 \div 7 = c$

15. $35 \div 5 = s$ $\qquad$ $5 \times s = 35$

16. $4 \times t = 36$ $\qquad$ $36 \div 4 = t$

Match the correct division rule from page 66 with the equation.

17. $8 \div 1 = 8$ $\qquad$ 18. $5 \div 5 = 1$

19. $t \div 0 = $ no solution

20. $0 \div 9 = 0$

 **Apply**

21. Kari has 24 oranges that she is grouping in sets. List the ways she could group the oranges.

22. Johan is cutting wood for his fireplace. Each piece must be 3 feet long. The log he is cutting is 63 feet long. How many pieces can he cut?

Challenge

23. If one human egg cell divides in half once every 24 hours, how many cells will there be after 192 hours?

Construct Meaning

Because we are the temple of the Holy Spirit, it is important to maintain our health. Bread, macaroni, potatoes, rice, cereal, beans, and milk are foods rich in carbohydrates. A healthy person should eat 6–11 servings of carbohydrates a day.

Geoff eats three meals a day, each having two servings of carbohydrates. How many days will it take Geoff to eat 138 servings of carbohydrates?

First, multiply mentally to determine the number of servings of carbohydrates he eats each day.

Think 3 meals × 2 servings of carbohydrates per meal = 6 servings a day

Divide 138 by 6.

6)138   6 >1   The first digit of the quotient will not be in the hundreds place.

```
    2
6)138      Divide the tens.
  12       Multiply.
   1       Subtract.
           Compare, 6 > 1
```

```
   23
6)138      Divide the ones.
  12↓      Multiply.
   18      Subtract.
   18
    0
```

It will take Geoff 23 days to eat 138 servings of carbohydrates.

Find 3,250 ÷ 4.

Find the greatest number of fours in 32.

4 × 8 = 32

```
     8
4)3,250
  32
   0
```

```
    81
4)3,250
  32↓
   05
    4
    1
```

quotient
```
        8 1 2  R2
divisor 4)3,250
        32
         05
          4↓
          10
           8
    remainder  2
```

Check by multiplying.
```
      8 1 2  ← quotient
   ×      4  ← divisor
    3 2 4 8
   +      2  ← remainder
    3,2 5 0
```

 **Check Understanding**

Solve and check.

a. 5)320   b. 3)617   c. 2)4,052   d. 6)2,153

Solve and check.

1. 2)240

2. 4)56,044

3. 8)942

4. 6)12,468

5. 3)1,095

6. 4)325

7. 6)498

8. 7)968

9. 11,570 ÷ 5

10. 822 ÷ 6

11. 3,171 ÷ 7

12. 1,710 ÷ 5

13. $\frac{3,744}{9}$

14. $\frac{1,102}{5}$

15. $\frac{45,555}{5}$

16. $\frac{729}{6}$

17. Mrs. Nayamatsu spent a total of $75 at the grocery store. She purchased $30 worth of canned goods, and the remainder was spent on the strawberries she needed to make jam. If the strawberries cost $3 per pint, how many pints did she purchase?

18. Annette's age is three times that of Tim, who is twice as old as his five-year-old brother Evan. How old is Annette's sister, who is half of Annette's age?

19. Three groups of three students are contacting people for a school survey about eating habits. There are a total of 117 students remaining to be surveyed. If the students conducting the survey divide the remaining students equally, how many people must each one contact?

20. Organizers of a school health fair have a total of 4,800 square feet of floor space to use. If one-half of the space is designated for student exhibits, how much space will each of the eight medical exhibitors be able to use?

R eview

1. 3,640
   × 20

2. 369
   × 400

3. 780
   × 504

4. 25.24
   × 6.09

5. 25.75
   × 72.99

6. $465.86
   − 328.62

7. 963.95
   + 745.22

8. 0.963
   − 0.872

Lesson 33

 **Construct Meaning**

A teenage girl should eat about 2,200 calories a day and a teenage boy should eat about 2,800 calories a day. Greg, Joan, and Thomas counted the number of calories they ate in one day. They compared their records with the table showing the amount of each food group they should consume in one day.

FOOD GROUP	SERVING SIZE	NUMBER OF SERVINGS (girls)	NUMBER OF SERVINGS (boys)
Bread	1 slice or $\frac{1}{2}$ cup cereal	9	11
Vegetables	$\frac{1}{3}$ cup raw	4	5
Fruit	1 medium size	3	4
Milk	1 cup	2 or 3	2 or 3
Meat	2–3 ounces	6 ounces	7 ounces
		2,200 calories	2,800 calories

As she counted her calories, Joan realized that most of the items she ate on Tuesday had about 110 calories each. How many 110-calorie items can Joan eat in a day and stay within a 2,200-calorie limit?

$$2,200 \div 110 = $$

Division patterns can help you divide by multiples of 10.

$22 \div 11 = 2$
$220 \div 110 = 2$
$2,200 \div 110 = 20$
$22,000 \div 110 = 200$

$28 \div 7 = 4$
$280 \div 70 = 4$
$2,800 \div 70 = 40$
$28,000 \div 70 = 400$

Think of the division problem $2,200 \div 110$ as a fraction where the dividend is the numerator.

$$\frac{2,200 \div 10}{110 \div 10} = \frac{220}{11}$$

We can divide the numerator and denominator by any common factor to simplify before dividing. Choose a multiple of 10.

Find $420,000 \div 20,000$.

$$\frac{420,000 \div 10,000}{20,000 \div 10,000} = $$

Divide by a multiple of 10 with as many zeros as are common to the dividend and divisor.

 **Check Understanding**

Divide.

a. $3,300 \div 300$
d. $1,800 \div 600$

b. $100,000 \div 10,000$
e. $39,000 \div 3,000$

c. $924,000 \div 6,000$
f. $860,000 \div 5,000$

Divide.

1. 580 ÷ 10

2. 6,300 ÷ 100

3. 75,000 ÷ 100

4. 21,000 ÷ 70

5. 28,000 ÷ 40

6. 16,000 ÷ 50

Solve mentally.

7. 360 ÷ 60

8. 3,600 ÷ 60

9. 3,600 ÷ 600

10. 270 ÷ 9

11. 2,700 ÷ 900

12. 27,000 ÷ 90

Find the missing number.

13. 350 ÷ 50 = a

14. 2,400 ÷ 30 = r

15. 48,000 ÷ 80 = t

16. 720 ÷ 9 = s

17. 4,900 ÷ 70 = m

18. 32,000 ÷ 400 = y

19. The Listella family consumed 14,000 calories of carbohydrates in one day. If each member ate about 2,800 calories, how many members are in the Listella family?

20. A food bank has received 63,000 cans of food packed as thirty cans per box. If each needy family gets two boxes, how many families will receive food?

21. Antonio has a 600-gram carbohydrate limit for candy bars in one week. Look on the Nutrition Facts label and determine the number of grams of carbohydrates one of his candy bars contains. How many candy bars can Antonio eat and remain within his carbohydrate limit?

Nutrition Facts	CANDY BAR	
	Total Fat 11g	Total Carb. 44g
	Sat Fat 6g	Fiber 1g
Serv. Size 1 bar	Cholest. 0 mg	Sugars 30 g
Calories 270	Sodium 120 mg	Protein 3 g
	Vitamin A 0% • Vitamin C 0% • Calcium 0% • Iron 0%	

Divide.

1. 6)146

2. 8)9,132

3. 4)840

4. 5)615

Lesson 34

Construct Meaning

As a 17-year-old, Jim Ryun became the first high school student to run a mile in under four minutes. It takes great self-discipline and training to be a good runner. Your body depends on exercise to be healthy, and running is one way to become fit.

If you want to run 360 miles in a 12-month period, how far will you have to run each month?

```
      3            30         Check by         30
12)360        12)360         multiplying.    × 12
   36            36                            60
    0            00                         + 300
                  0                           360
                  0
```

You will have to run 30 miles a month.

Find 720 ÷ 120. Check.

```
      6           120
120)720          ×   6
   720            720
     0
```
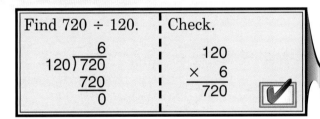

Find 880 ÷ 125. Check. 125

```
    7 R5               ×   7
125)880               875
   875                +   5
     5                  880
```

Find 3,596 ÷ 62.

```
      5              58
62)3,596        62)3,596
   310              310
    49              496
                    496
                      0
```

You may use estimation to check that the quotient is reasonable.
Estimate with numbers compatible with mental math.

```
3,600 ÷ 60 = 60
```

USING A CALCULATOR

Find 18,772 ÷ 104.

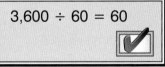

Check Understanding

Estimate using numbers compatible with mental math.

  a. 22)442   b. 39)396   c. 51)3,162   d. 103)1,272

72

Two- and Three-Digit Divisors

Solve and check with multiplication.

1. 12)960
2. 15)375
3. 40)600
4. 33)363

5. 25)1,575
6. 82)3,362
7. 130)1,560
8. 125)3,875

9. 105)2,310
10. 214)13,482
11. 45)1,664
12. 24)745

13. 32)2,724
14. 230)10,352
15. 320)2,563
16. 115)17,200

Estimate the quotient using numbers compatible with mental math.

17. 24)744
18. 12)1,812
19. 40)1,621
20. 39)11,640

21. 179)3,561
22. 162)4,798
23. 26)1,522
24. 18)2,400

USING A CALCULATOR

Solve. If needed, round the quotient to the nearest hundredth.

25. $3,680 \div 110$
26. $18,439 \div 223$
27. $46,802 \div 46$

28. $17,712 \div 144$
29. $73,872 \div 162$
30. $9,546 \div 516$

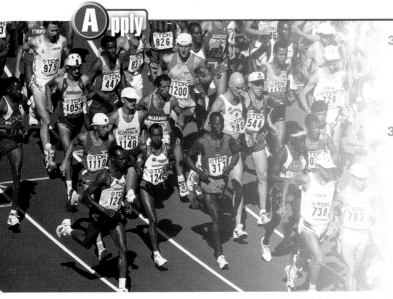

Apply

31. At the Prefontaine Classic track meet $332,208 was made selling tickets. If each ticket cost $18, how many tickets were sold?

32. The Heart Marathon had 15,600 total entries for the past thirteen years, and each entry fee was $11. If they had the same number of entries each year, what was the total income for one year?

. . . forgetting those things which are behind and reaching forward to those things which are ahead, I press toward the goal for the prize of the upward call of God in Christ Jesus. Philippians 3:13–14

Construct Meaning

Alex displays his collection of model cars on four shelves in his room. There are five cars on each shelf. If he received two additional cars for his birthday, how many cars will be in his collection?

The expression that represents the number of cars is $(5 \times 4) + 2$. The parentheses indicate which operation is done first. If n equals the number of cars that will be in the collection, then:

$$(5 \times 4) + 2 = n$$
$$20 + 2 = n$$
$$22 = n$$

Do the operation in parentheses first.

There will be 22 cars in Alex's collection.

Will the answer be the same if you do <u>not</u> multiply first?

$$5 \times 4 + 2 = n$$
$$5 \times 6 = n$$
$$30 = n$$

The answer is not the same.
The rules for **order of operations** in mathematics must be followed.

Order of Operations
1. Do the operation(s) in parentheses first.
2. Multiply and divide from left to right.
3. Add and subtract from left to right.

Solve the equation for x. $50 + 9 \times 4 = x$
If you follow the rules for order of operations, $x = 86$.

$50 + 9 \times 4 = 86$

$$10 - 6 \div 2 + 9 \times 5 = y$$
$$10 - 3 + 45 = y$$
$$7 + 45 = y$$
$$52 = y$$

Explain why the problem shown was computed in this order.

Check Understanding

Solve.

a. $8 \times (7 + 4.5)$ b. $15 + 9 \div 3$ c. $(25 + 15) - 12$ d. $40 - 8 \times 4$

Solve for the unknown.

1. $16 + 40 \div 5 = n$ 2. $7 + (4 \div 4) \times 8 = r$ 3. $36 \div (12 \div 2) - 2 = s$
4. $(10 + 19) \times (13 - 3) = y$ 5. $7 \times 7 + 3 + 15 = x$ 6. $5 \times (43 - 13) \div 10 = t$
7. $33 - 81 \div 9 + 3 \times 3 = a$ 8. $2 \times (16 \div 4 + 4) = b$ 9. $(11 + 8) \times (5 - 1) = c$

Write the order of operations for each problem.

Example:

$2 + 7 \times (6 \div 2)$

parentheses, multiply, add

10. $20 \div (8 - 3) + 4$ 11. $16 + 18 \div 6$ 12. $88 - 9 \times 5$

13. $35 + 14 \div 7 - 2 \times 1$ 14. $60 \div (7 + 15) \times 8$

A pply

15. Brett and Matt used calculators to solve $15 + 40 \times 5$. Matt's calculator display read 275, but Brett's displayed 215. Who had the calculator that performed order of operations?

16. Mr. Dunn challenged his students to write the symbols $+$, $-$, $\times$, or $\div$ to make the equations true. Write each equation with the correct symbols.

   a. $10 \quad 6 \quad 4 = 34$ b. $7 \quad 8 \quad 2 = 28$ c. $8 \quad 5 \quad 4 = 28$

17. How should the problem $240 \div 80 \times 30 - 10$ be written if the operation of subtraction is to be done first?

18. Jenny rode her bicycle five miles on Thursday and six miles on Friday. On Saturday, the number of miles she rode was three times the sum of the previous two days. Write the equation for the length of Saturday's ride and solve. (Hint: Use parentheses.)

19. If a problem consists of only addition, does the order in which the digits are added matter? What about the order of digits for subtraction, multiplication, or division? Consider the examples. Write a statement to summarize your findings.

   $6 + 4 + 2 \quad 9 - 5 - 3 \quad 2 \times 5 \times 4 \quad 8 \div 4 \div 2$

Lesson 36

Construct Meaning

The history of dental hygiene began many years ago. In 1500 B.C., one documented recipe for toothpaste called for oysters, eggshells, cattle hooves, and horns. Are you glad that the recipe for toothpaste has changed?

Your permanent teeth, when taken care of, should last your entire life. Mrs. Hudsen is 32,850 days old and brushes her teeth twice daily.

How many years old is Mrs. Hudsen?

Since there are 365 days in a year, 32,850 ÷ 365 will show us the age of Mrs. Hudsen.

Decide where to place the first digit. Divide the tens. Multiply. 9 × 365 = 3,285 Subtract.

$$
\begin{array}{r}
9 \\
365\overline{)32850} \\
3285 \\
\hline
0
\end{array}
$$

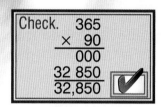

Check.
$$
\begin{array}{r}
365 \\
\times\ 90 \\
\hline
000 \\
32\ 850 \\
\hline
32,850
\end{array}
$$ ✔

Bring down. Zero divided by any number is zero. Multiply. 0 × 365 = 0 Subtract.

$$
\begin{array}{r}
90 \\
365\overline{)32850} \\
3285\!\downarrow \\
00 \\
\underline{0} \\
0
\end{array}
$$

Mrs. Hudsen is 90 years old.

Find 12,072 ÷ 12.

$$
\begin{array}{r}
1 \\
12\overline{)12,072} \\
12 \\
\hline
0
\end{array}
$$

Decide where to place the first digit in the quotient.

$$
\begin{array}{r}
1,0 \\
12\overline{)12,072} \\
12\!\downarrow \\
\hline
00 \\
\underline{0} \\
0
\end{array}
$$

Zero divided by any number is zero.

$$
\begin{array}{r}
1,00 \\
12\overline{)12,072} \\
12 \\
\hline
00 \\
\underline{0}\!\downarrow \\
07 \\
\underline{0} \\
7
\end{array}
$$

There are not enough tens, so a zero is put in the tens place of the quotient.

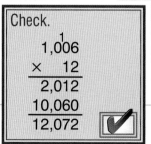

Check.
$$
\begin{array}{r}
1 \\
1,006 \\
\times\ \ 12 \\
\hline
2,012 \\
10,060 \\
\hline
12,072
\end{array}
$$ ✔

$$
\begin{array}{r}
1,006 \\
12\overline{)12,072} \\
12 \\
\hline
00 \\
\underline{0} \\
07 \\
\underline{0}\!\downarrow \\
72 \\
\underline{72} \\
0
\end{array}
$$

Bring down. Divide the ones.

Check Understanding

Write the quotient. Check by multiplying.

a. $4\overline{)1,232}$ b. $62\overline{)6,386}$ c. $13\overline{)13,104}$

Write the quotient. Check by multiplying.

1. 23)4,623
2. 44)4,534
3. 55)16,610
4. 32)6,595

5. 113)$23,165
6. 219)22,119
7. 411)41,923
8. 323)65,246

9. 13)13,105
10. 21)$42,084
11. 18)18,720
12. 12)12,096

Write the quotient.

13. 97,875 ÷ 75
14. 124,226 ÷ 31
15. 56,169 ÷ 28

16. 34,544 ÷ 114
17. 63,129 ÷ 126
18. 16,926 ÷ 42

19. 73)657,365
20. 526)4,255,340
21. 321)327,099

22. 32,064 ÷ 16
23. 31,500 ÷ 45
24. 23)9,315

25. Dr. Duval purchased dental equipment on two different occasions for $18,450 and $11,502. Altogether he purchased 144 items. If each item had the same price, how much did each item cost?

26. The population of Shoreline, Washington, is about 55,200 people, and about 200 dentists work there. If $\frac{1}{2}$ of the population are equally distributed among the dentists, how many patients would each dentist have?

Solve for the unknown.

1. $y + 12 = 47$
2. $8 + a = 63$
3. $42 - t = 16$

4. $8 \times r = 96$
5. $q \times 15 = 945$
6. $18 - x = 7$

 **Construct Meaning**

Antony van Leeuwenhoek was a Dutch biologist. He made over 400 microscopes and was the first person to observe a protozoa (single-celled animal) with a microscope. Protozoans can cause diseases such as malaria, giardiasis, and African sleeping sickness.

Simon is ill from malaria. His doctor has ordered a medication, called quinine, to treat him and other malaria patients. The doctor ordered 623 bottles of quinine, and the bottles are packaged in special boxes that hold twelve bottles.

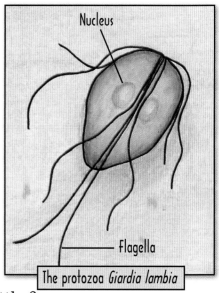

Nucleus

Flagella

The protozoa *Giardia lambia*

How many boxes will be needed to hold all of the bottles?

Interpreting the Remainder

* Round the quotient to the next higher number.
* Drop the remainder.
* Use the remainder as the answer.

$$\begin{array}{r} 51 \text{ R11} \\ 12\overline{)623} \\ 60 \\ \hline 23 \\ 12 \\ \hline 11 \end{array}$$

R11 What about the remainder?

First consider the question, How many boxes will hold **all** of the bottles?

In this case, round the quotient to the next higher number.

All the bottles will fit in 52 boxes.

How many boxes will be completely filled?

$$\begin{array}{r} 51 \text{ R11} \\ 12\overline{)623} \\ 60 \\ \hline 23 \\ 12 \\ \hline 11 \end{array}$$

Consider the question.

In this case, drop the remainder.

51 boxes will be completely filled.

How many bottles will there be in the partially filled box?

$$\begin{array}{r} 51 \text{ R11} \\ 12\overline{)623} \\ 60 \\ \hline 23 \\ 12 \\ \hline 11 \end{array}$$

Consider the question.

In this case, use the remainder as the answer.

11 bottles will be in the partially filled box.

 **Check Understanding**

Kalee had 803 soda cans to recycle. The store gave her 15 bags, which she filled equally with cans.

a. How many cans were in each of the 15 bags?
b. How many cans remained after the 15 bags were filled?
c. Could Kalee have filled another half of a bag with the remaining cans?

 ractice

1. The Red Cross clinic has 114 people waiting to be given a free malaria test. There is only enough time for eight equal groups of people to be administered the test in one day. How many people will have to come back the next day to be given the test?

2. The Asante Primary School has 266 volunteers who want to play in a soccer tournament during recess. Each team will be made of 13 participants. How many volunteers will not be placed on a team?

3. 320 patients affected by an outbreak of giardia are to be divided equally among six hospitals. The rest of the patients will be taken to an emergency clinic. How many patients should the clinic expect?

4. Andrew and Zachery packaged medication in order to send it overseas. They packaged 235 bottles into boxes that each held 50 bottles. How many boxes were needed to hold all of the bottles?

5. One of Mrs. Gordon's chocolate cakes serves eight people. How many cakes will she need to bake to serve 115 people at the picnic?

6. At the picnic, there were 362 slices of watermelon. Each person ate three slices, and fewer than three slices remained uneaten. How many people were at the picnic?

7. How many watermelons at $3 each will Jacob have to sell to earn at least $350?

Practice

Edward Jenner was a revolutionary thinker and problem solver. He studied how the diseases cowpox and smallpox were related, and hypothesized that being exposed to cowpox may make the body immune to smallpox. In 1796, he developed the first vaccine. Today, immunization is widespread, helping to eradicate this harmful disease.

Solve

1. The pharmacy will be receiving 50 boxes of smallpox vaccine with each box containing 45 bottles. On Wednesday, the store received 16 boxes. How many more bottles will be arriving?

2. The protozoa *Neospora* causes cows to give birth to their calves prematurely. 400,000 doses of vaccine preventing this have been sold between January 1999 and May 2001. Each cow needs two doses to ensure a full-term pregnancy. If each dose costs about $3, how much money has been spent purchasing the vaccine?

3. Mr. Stevens estimates that he will need 2,965 pounds of insecticide to kill off a certain population of malaria-carrying mosquitos. His plane will carry 225 pounds at a time. How many times will Mr. Stevens need to reload his plane in order to kill all of the mosquitos?

4. Tickets to the Oregon Museum of Science and Industry cost $14 each. One sixth grade class purchased $448 worth of tickets and another class purchased $420 worth of tickets. How many students went to the museum?

5. Tujong earns $3.25 an hour working in the rice paddies with ten other workers. If he has worked for six hours, with a 30-minute lunch break without pay, how much money has Tujong earned?

6. Roma has been waiting to see the doctor for 1 hour and 23 minutes. There are three people in front of her in line and it takes about 35 minutes per patient. How many total minutes will she have waited for the doctor?

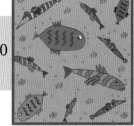

7. By the end of the day, the dock crew had distributed 6,450 pounds of fish to holding bins in the factory. If each bin held 250 pounds of fish, how many bins were filled to capacity?

8. Mrs. LeLaCheur has a shop that delivers flowers. Today she received four orders for three bouquets, three orders for two bouquets, and twelve orders for one bouquet. If her car holds nine bouquets at a time, how many trips will she have to make to deliver all the flowers?

9. Greg has $942 in his savings account. He just purchased a new bike and will have equal payments of $27 a month for nine months. How much money will Greg have left in his savings account after he has paid for the bike?

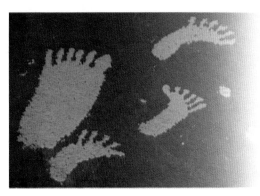

10. Each team for the walk-a-thon needed to complete 1,115 miles. Team Red consisted of Allen's group and Otis's group. Allen's group walked a total of 565 miles, but Otis's group lost count. Let m represent the number of miles Otis's group walked. Solve for m.

11. Jodi used two pieces of wood to make a picture frame of four equal sides. One piece was 26 inches long and the other piece was 29 inches. What is the largest size of frame she can make?

12. Mr. Hagen determined that one oak log weighed about 995 pounds and he needs to transport 16 logs on his truck. If the carrying capacity of his truck is 13,000 pounds, how many trips will he need to make?

13. Nurse Lorane administers immunizations to children each day. Using the average number of shots given in one day, find the average number of shots she will give in one year.

Day	Number of Shots
Monday	22
Tuesday	14
Wednesday	19
Thursday	16
Friday	20
Saturday	14
Sunday	14

Lesson 39

Construct Meaning

In the late 1800s a Quaker doctor named Joseph Lister became known for his work with carbolic acid to kill germs during surgical procedures and to keep wounds free from infection.

During a soccer game, Vince received a foot injury. His medical treatment required five visits to the doctor. Vince's mother drove a total of 159.5 miles to the doctor for those visits. How many miles was each round-trip visit to the doctor?

When solving 159.5 divided by 5, you are dividing a decimal by a whole number.

```
5)159.5
```

```
   31.9
5)159.5
   15
    09
     5
    45
    45
     0
```

- Place the decimal in the quotient by lining it up with the decimal in the dividend.

- Perform the division as with whole numbers.
  Divide the tens. 15 ÷ 5
  Divide the ones. 9 ÷ 5
  Divide the tenths. 45 ÷ 5

Each visit to the doctor was 31.9 miles.

MORE EXAMPLES

zero in the dividend	zero in the quotient	zero in the divisor and the dividend

```
zero in the dividend

    2.24
17)38.08
   34
    40
    34
    68
    68
     0
```

```
zero in the quotient

     1.064
43)45.752
   43
    27
     0
    275
    258
     172
     172
       0
```

```
zero in the divisor
and the dividend

      57.3
50)2,865.0
   250
    365
    350
    150
    150
      0
```

Check Understanding

Divide.

a. 0.84 ÷ 7   b. 2.16 ÷ 24   c. $6.30 ÷ 9   d. 192.2 ÷ 31   e. $21.84 ÷ 14

f. 21)3.234   g. 17)20.4   h. 42)214.62   i. 63)80.01   j. 79)0.0553

82

Chapter 3 • *Mathematics* Grade 6

Dividing Decimals by Whole Numbers

Divide. Remember to place the decimal first. Use multiplication to check your answers on problems 1–5.

1. 8)12.8   2. 5)0.0485   3. 12)$7.56   4. 3)2.58   5. 6)3.654

6. 22.66 ÷ 11   7. 0.3195 ÷ 9   8. 157.5 ÷ 25   9. $179.52 ÷ 44   10. $681.92 ÷ 16

11. 4)0.8272   12. 39)3.2175   13. 46)17.802   14. 52)$20.28   15. 12)1.5648

16. The Chargers soccer team stays fit by running an equal number of miles before each practice session. Last week, they had soccer practice five times. If their total distance was 12.5 miles, how far did they run each time?

17. Jake, Monica, and Amy wanted to surprise their mom with a cordless phone for her birthday. The phone cost $44.49. How much would each child pay if they shared the cost of the phone equally?

18. Al bought four new tires for his truck. The total bill before tax was $299.96. What was the cost per tire?

19. Hans can buy each monthly issue of *The Sport of Soccer* at the newsstand for $1.75 or he can buy a yearly subscription for $18. Which is the better buy?

20. A six-pack of soda cost $1.45. Estimate the price per can by using compatible numbers. About how much would Jill pay for two cans?

21. Bruce and Will's families share the traveling cost of the season's soccer tournaments by renting a van. This season's total bill was $480.98. How much should each family contribute to the expense?

1. 14,592 ÷ 24   2. 39,824 ÷ 524

3. Is 7,536 evenly divisible by 4?

4. Round to the highest place value to estimate 4,792 ÷ 79.

5. 52.6 × 2.55   6. 2.07 × 0.034

7. 2,700 ÷ 3
8. 2,700 ÷ 30
9. 2,700 ÷ 300

Lesson 40

Construct Meaning

What a blessing! People from every country have benefitted from his discovery. In 1842, Crawford Long used ether as an anesthetic to perform the first painless surgery. There is a museum in Jefferson, Georgia, to honor him. He was a Christian.

Gary had anesthesia during surgery after breaking his arm by falling at the fourth event on an obstacle course. The course was 3 miles long and the events were spaced 0.25 of a mile apart. How many events were there?

Find 3 ÷ 0.25.

$$0.25\overline{)3}$$

Division cannot be performed with a decimal in the divisor. Follow these steps to turn the divisor into a whole number.

- Multiply the dividend and divisor by the same power of 10 (10, 100, 1,000, etc.).

$$0.25\overline{)3.00}$$
$$\times 100 \quad \times 100$$

- When multiplying by a power of 10, place the decimal point to the right as many times as there are zeros in the power of 10. In this problem, multiply both the divisor and dividend by 100. This is the same as moving the decimal point of both numbers two places to the right since there are two zeros in 100.

$$\begin{array}{r} 12. \\ 25\overline{)300.} \end{array}$$

- The divisor is now a whole number. You are ready to divide.

There were 12 events in the 3-mile obstacle course.

Another Example:

$$0.6\overline{)192} \longrightarrow 0.6\overline{)192.0} \longrightarrow 6\overline{)1920.}$$

Division cannot be performed since there is a decimal in the divisor.

Multiply both numbers by 10. Write the needed 0. Write the decimal in the quotient.

Divide as usual.

Check Understanding

Tell what power of 10 each number should be multiplied by to make it a whole number. Then multiply and move the decimal point accordingly.

a. 0.125   b. 0.1   c. 0.12   d. 0.649   e. 0.0374

Solve.

f. How many nickels are there in three dollars?

g. $0.4\overline{)22}$ h. $0.07\overline{)56}$ i. 6 ÷ 0.375   j. Divide 36 by 0.016.

Practice

Write the power of 10 each number should be multiplied by to make it a whole number.

1. 0.5
2. 0.008
3. 0.32
4. 0.0725
5. 0.316

Multiply each number by a power of 10 to make it a whole number. Move the decimal and rewrite the number.

6. 0.619
7. 0.1
8. 0.74
9. 0.004
10. 0.93

Divide.

11. $0.8\overline{)28}$
12. $0.04\overline{)5}$
13. $0.025\overline{)3}$
14. $0.12\overline{)4,824}$
15. $0.26\overline{)8,034}$

16. $0.36\overline{)27}$
17. $0.875\overline{)21}$
18. $1,272 \div 0.16$
19. Divide 255 by 0.3.

Solve mentally. Use multiplication to verify that the answer is correct.

20. $0.5\overline{)30}$
21. $0.5\overline{)3}$
22. $0.03\overline{)24}$
23. $0.003\overline{)24}$
24. Divide 5 by 0.25.

For problems 25 through 27, note that dividend ÷ divisor = quotient.

25. Write a division problem where the quotient is smaller than the dividend.
26. Write a division problem where the quotient is larger than the dividend.
27. State in your own words when the quotient will be larger than the dividend.

Apply

28. Mrs. Young bought a calling card for her daughter to use at college. From a multiple selection of cards, she chose one that offered 675 minutes priced at $27. What was the rate per minute of the card she selected?

29. The parents' organization raised $2,275 for the purchase of T-shirts to be worn on orientation day at Providence Christian Academy. The school logo and verse for the year were printed on each T-shirt that cost $6.25. How many shirts can be purchased with the money they raised?

Review

1. Write these decimals from least to greatest.
    0.009   0.09   0.05   0.5   0.005   5.9

Round to the nearest whole number.

2. 4.986
3. 254.482
4. 54.76
5. 1,039.8

6. Fred and Philip competed in the 800-meter freestyle swim. Fred finished in 7 minutes 29.31 seconds. Philip finished in 7 minutes 29.309 seconds. Who was faster?

Moments with Careers

My dad works as an anesthesiologist. In his work he uses math to work with equipment and to do his job well.

Timothy
Corvallis, OR

Lesson 41

 **Construct Meaning**

In 1945 Sir Alexander Fleming from Scotland won the Nobel Prize in medicine for his discovery of penicillin. Penicillin, with its curing effect on a number of infections, became known as the miracle drug. Various drugs are used therapeutically to treat diseases, disorders, allergies, and injuries.

Miss Patty bought a wrapped package of several bottles of pain reliever. Each bottle weighed 4.75 oz. The total weight of the package was 28.5 oz. How many bottles were in the wrapped package?

Find $28.5 \div 4.75$. Follow the steps to divide a decimal by a decimal.

STEP 1   Decide by what power of 10 to multiply the divisor.   *Multiply by 100* $4.75\overline{)28.5}$

STEP 2   Multiply both the divisor and the dividend by the same power of 10 to move the decimals. $4.75\overline{)28.50}$
           $\times\, 100$ $\times\, 100$

You may need to add zero(s) to place the decimal correctly.

STEP 3   Write a decimal in the quotient. $475.\overline{)2850.}$

STEP 4   Divide.
$$475.\overline{)2850.} \quad \begin{array}{c} 6. \\ \underline{2850} \\ 0 \end{array}$$

> Six bottles were in the wrapped package.

Multiply to check.
$$\begin{array}{r} 4.75 \\ \times\ \ \ 6 \\ \hline 28.50 \end{array}$$

MORE EXAMPLES

Multiply by 10
$$3.6\overline{)9.684} \quad \begin{array}{c} 2.69 \\ \underline{72} \\ 248 \\ \underline{216} \\ 324 \\ \underline{324} \\ 0 \end{array}$$

Multiply by 100
$$0.52\overline{)31.20} \quad \begin{array}{c} 60. \\ \underline{312} \\ 00 \end{array}$$

Multiply by 1,000
$$0.003\overline{)2700} \quad \begin{array}{c} 900. \\ \underline{27} \\ 000 \end{array}$$

$$0.8\overline{)0.00376} \quad \begin{array}{c} 00047 \\ \underline{32} \\ 56 \\ \underline{56} \\ 0 \end{array}$$

 **Check Understanding**

Multiply each number by a power of 10 to make it a whole number. Rewrite the number.

a. 4.6   b. 907.89   c. 0.1764   d. 218.36   e. 6.525

f. Set up the problem $1.64 \div 0.0002$. Draw the arrows to decide by what power of 10 to multiply. Divide.

Divide.

g. $1.41 \div 0.003$ h. $0.7\overline{)\$2.03}$ i. $0.09\overline{)0.00648}$ j. $8.5 \div 0.5$ k. $0.12\overline{)0.264}$

Dividing a Decimal by a Decimal

 **Practice**

Rewrite each number after multiplying it by a power of 10 to make it a whole number.

1. 6.3
2. 85.317
3. 0.92
4. 8.6981
5. 1,069.222

Divide.

6. $0.25\overline{)1.8}$
7. $0.155\overline{)7.75}$
8. $0.33\overline{)3.135}$
9. $9.6 \div 1.2$
10. $\$2.19\overline{)\$8.76}$

For problems 11–13, check your answers by multiplying.

11. $0.04\overline{)0.6}$
12. $1.8\overline{)0.558}$
13. Divide 49.6 by 6.2.

Eileen computed the following division problems. If the problem is correct, write *C*. If it is incorrect, write the correct answer.

14. $0.13\overline{)0.26}$ (answer 2)
15. $0.06\overline{)4.8}$ (answer 8)
16. $0.8\overline{)0.64}$ (answer 0.08)
17. $2.3\overline{)103.5}$ (answer 45)
18. $0.145\overline{)1.740}$ (answer 1.2)

 Apply

19. Mrs. Jenkins saw gasoline priced at $1.61 per gallon. She stopped at the station and bought $14.49 worth of gasoline to fill her tank. How many gallons of gasoline did she put into her car?

20. The area of a large mural is 8.2075 square meters. The height of the mural is 2.45 meters. What is the width?

21. Nicholas has an older brother who goes to college. This year's tuition with room and board totaled $16,400. He received a $1,500 scholarship which is deducted from his total bill. He also has to pay a $50 enrollment fee. What monthly amount will Nicholas' parents pay if the amount is spread over ten months?

 **Review**

Compute mentally.

1. $79 \times 65 \times 0$
2. $374 + 187 = \_\_\_ + 374$
3. $5 \times 89 \times 2$
4. $(19 + 23) + 48 = 19 + (\_\_\_ + 48)$
5. $10 \times 100 \times 1,000$

Identify the properties used in these equations.

6. 86×1
7. $427 + 66 = 66 + 427$
8. $95 \times 0 = 0$
9. $5 + (1 + 6) = (5 + 1) + 6$
10. $1.3 + 25.8 + 4.16 = 4.16 + 25.8 + 1.3$

 Construct Meaning

Dr. Tom Dooley, a medical missionary, founded MEDICO, which is an organization that provides free medical, dental, and eye care to poor areas of the world. Much of his work was done in Asia.

The medical outreach team needed $83.50 to provide care for a child in Vietnam. Len purposed to save $6.25 per week. How many weeks will it take Len to reach the needed amount?

It will take Len about 14 weeks to reach the needed amount.

First, estimate by rounding to the nearest dollar.

$83.50 ⟶ $84.00 $84 ÷ $6 = 14
$6.25 ⟶ $6.00

Next, divide to find a more precise number of weeks.

```
        1 3.3 6
6.25)835.0000
       625
      2100
      1875
      2250
      1875
       3750
       3750
          0
```

The estimate (14 weeks) shows the answer (13.36 weeks) is reasonable.

Sometimes a quotient gets carried out to more places than you need. A calculator may do this.

24.87912064

Round the quotient by dividing one place beyond the place to which you are rounding.

Round to the nearest cent.	Round to the nearest thousandth.	Round to the nearest dollar.
$ 2.1 4 2 ⟶ $2.14 1.4)$3.0000	0.7 8 2 6 ⟶ 0.783 3.6)2.81736	$ 2.7 8 ⟶ $3 2.51)$7.0000

 Check Understanding

Estimate first by rounding both numbers to the nearest whole number. Find the quotient.

a. 3.1)17.98   b. 6.2)47.74   c. 8.6)54.18   d. 1.4)8.4   e. 5.73)138.2076

Round the quotient to the nearest hundredth.

f. 4.25)13.28

g. 2.37)0.77

Round to the nearest dollar.

h. 3.5)$15.05

i. 2.75)$30.25

 **Practice**

Estimate by rounding to the nearest whole number. Find the quotient.

1. 4.2)27.72
2. 1.35)38.34
3. 7.4)42.402
4. 2.06)4.2848
5. 0.89)60.52

Divide. Round the quotient to the nearest tenth.

6. 0.06)4.6524
7. 3.2)0.256
8. 5.18)2.7454
9. 0.162)1.01250
10. 3.3)1.947

Use the quotient 8.7293 to round to the nearest place value.

tenths	hundredths	thousandths	ones
11.	12.	13.	14.

Complete.

15. Write the power of 10 you multiply by when dividing 6.348 by 24.17.
16. If the divisor has a decimal in it, change the decimal to a ▓▓▓ to make it easier to divide.
17. Evaluate $y \div z$ if $y = 3.76$ and $z = 0.8$.
18. Find $8.7694 \div 2.4$. Round the quotient to the ten-thousandths place. (Continue dividing to one place beyond the ten-thousandths place by writing zeros in the dividend.)

 Apply

19. A bundled package of 12 paper towel rolls costs $11.76. Another store has 10 rolls for $9.90. Which is a cheaper price per roll, 12 rolls for $11.76, or 10 rolls for $9.90?

20. A box of medical supplies such as bandages is advertised at a price of $9.92. Each bandage is at the low price of $0.04. How many bandages are in each box?

 Review

1. 220 ÷ 110
2. 1,800 ÷ 600
3. 882,000 ÷ 6,000
4. 16,000 ÷ 50
5. 13,065 ÷ 13
6. $27)$11,016
7. 436)3,488
8. $x + 18 = 61$
9. $762 - a = 603$
10. $25 \times t = 2,500$
11. 20,178 ÷ 342
12. 1,278 ÷ 9

Practice

Florence Nightingale (1820–1910) is known as the founder of modern nursing. She supervised the nurses in the army hospitals during the Crimean War (1853–1856) and received the British Royal Red Cross.

Solve.

1. In February, 1855, the mortality rate at the military hospital where Miss Nightingale worked was 42.7%. After implementing her ideas for change, the mortality rate declined to 2.2%. If 43 people died at the hospital every month, but after the reform two people died every month, how many lives would be saved in a year as a result of the changes?

2. Seven Oaks Hospital is recognized for its outstanding healthcare to the community. The Nursing Service received 27 awards, Radiology received 35, Physical Therapy received 18, the Emergency Room received 48, and Surgery received 39 awards. How many times has the hospital been recognized for its performance in these areas?

3. Polk region records the average rainfall on a bi-monthly basis. Use the information on the graph to determine the average bi-monthly rainfall.

4. Principal Garrett purchased raincoats for outdoor education at $7 each. On his first trip to the store, he purchased 28 coats, and on his second trip he purchased 14 coats. How much money did Principal Garrett spend on the raincoats?

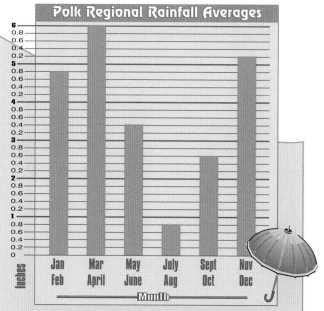

Store	Cost
Joe's Mart	$3.50
One Stop	$4.00
Meyer's	$3.69
Louie's Market	$4.25
Lincoln Store	$3.45

5. Darlene compared the price of her favorite hand cream at five different stores. What is the average price of the hand cream? (Round to the nearest cent.) Which store sold the hand cream priced nearest the average?

6. Use a calculator to help Mrs. Barker find her current checkbook balance. On June 12, Mrs. Barker had $937.58 in her checking account. On June 13, she paid the house payment of $436.15. She deposited $15.95 into her account on June 14. On June 15, a trip to the grocery store cost $134.29. On June 16, she bought a pair of sunglasses priced at $12.99. Mrs. Barker received a statement from the bank indicating her balance is $370.10. Does her checking account balance agree with the bank's statement?

7. At the balloon festival there were six balloons floating over a ranch with three people in each basket. One other balloon was floating over a pond with four people in the basket. Write and solve an equation that shows how many people were riding in hot air balloons.

8. Use the picture to write a numerical expression that represents the number of men on horses and the number of men walking.

9. Write an algebraic expression that shows there are 12 more pelicans than two times the number of hippos.

10. Mrs. Eubanks planned a sixth grade graduation party. She bought several trays of food. Each tray serves 15 people.

meat tray	$19.99
cheese tray	$16.99
sandwich tray	$12.99
fruit tray	$18.99
veggie tray	$14.99

a. What is the cost per serving of each tray? (Round to the nearest cent.)

b. What is the cost per serving of the fruit and veggie trays combined?

c. What is the cost per serving of the cheese and sandwich trays combined?

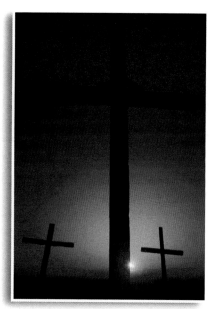

Construct Meaning

When he heard that Jesus had come out of Judea into Galilee, he went to Him and implored Him to come down and heal his son . . . Jesus said to him, "Go your way; your son lives . . ." John 4:47, 50.
God is the true source of healing, both spiritually and physically.

During the winter season, many people contract the flu virus. Usually your body will recover from the virus within 24 hours to five days. The average number of flu virus cases in Oregon between 1918–1981 was 15,589 cases per year.

What was the average number of cases per year between 1996 and 2000?

OREGON FLU

Year	Number of Cases
1996	100
1997	82
1998	77
1999	75
2000	132

HOW SHALL I FIND THE AVERAGE?

Find the sum.　　**D**ivide by the number of items.

```
  100
   82
   77
   75
+ 132
─────
  466
```

```
        93.2  ← average
   5)466.0
     45       ← sum
     ──
     16
     15
     ──
     10
     10
     ──
      0
```

number of years

Round the average to the nearest whole number.

Check Understanding

There was an average of 93 flu cases.

Find the average of the following sets of numbers. Round to the nearest whole number.
a. 16 12 14 25 62 37
b. 100 510 98 162 103

Apply

Find the average.
1. The patients in Dr. Marks' waiting room were aged 68, 29, 50, 43, 36, and 62. What was the average age of the patients?

2. Teresa recorded the scores of her math tests throughout the term as: 89, 78, 95, 92, 85, 90, and 88. What was Teresa's average test score? Round to the nearest whole number.

3. Ronald bought groceries twice a month. His bills were: $102 and $64; $59 and $108; $92 and $85; $89 and $76. What was Ronald's average monthly grocery bill?

Chapter Three Study Guide

1. Write 35 ÷ 7 as a repeated subtraction problem. *Lesson 31*

2. 5,624 ÷ 8 *Lesson 32*

3. 36,000 ÷ 1,000 *Lesson 33*

4. 14,670 ÷ 52 *Lesson 34*

5. 10,032 ÷ 114 *Lesson 34*

6. 16 – 2 × 6 *Lesson 35*

7. 24 ÷ 3 + 3 *Lesson 35*

8. 65,246 ÷ 323 *Lesson 36*

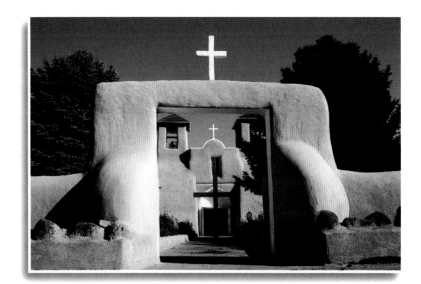

9. The physical education teacher divided the students into softball teams. If there were 328 students with twelve members per team, how many students were not able to play? *Lesson 37*

10. Josey deposited $240 into her savings account every month for two years. If she continues doing this for five more years, how much money will she have in her savings account? *Lesson 38*

11. 6.235 ÷ 5 *Lesson 39*   12. 2,305 ÷ 1.25 *Lesson 40*   13. 12.65 ÷ 6.25 *Lesson 41 and 42*

14. Angelica sold 1,124 tickets one day and 741 tickets the next day for the cancer benefit concert. Ricardo also sold tickets but misplaced the record sheet. There were 2,160 tickets available to sell. Write an addition equation and solve for Ricardo's tickets. *Lesson 43*

15. Mrs. Miller just completed a 363-mile trip in her antique MG Tourer. She used 25.5 gallons of gasoline. How many miles per gallon did her car average on her trip? Round to the nearest whole number. *Lesson 44*

Lesson 45

Fitness Training in Division

Use the Word Bank to complete the sentence.

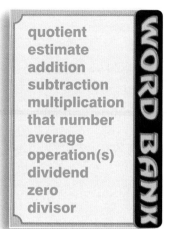

WORD BANK
quotient
estimate
addition
subtraction
multiplication
that number
average
operation(s)
dividend
zero
divisor

1. Division is the inverse of ░░ .
2. Any number divided by one equals ░░ .
3. In an equation, do the ░░ in parentheses first.
4. Division cannot be performed with a decimal in the ░░ .
5. To find an ░░ , you add then divide.
6. The answer in a division problem is the ░░ .
7. Division may be shown as repeated ░░ .

Write *yes* or *no* if the number is evenly divisible by 2, 3, 4, 5, 6, 9, and 10.

	2	3	4	5	6	9	10
1,017	8.	9.	no	10.	11.	12.	13.
4,640	14.	15.	16.	yes	17.	18.	19.

Complete the pattern.

20.   33 ÷ 11

21.   330 ÷ 110

22. 3,300 ÷ 110

23. 33,000 ÷ 110

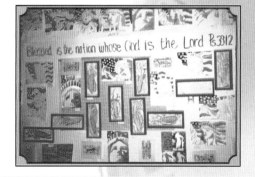

Divide.

24. 6,300 ÷ 90

25. 420 ÷ 70

26. 918,000 ÷ 6,000

27. 7)91

28. 30)2,460

29. 4)$7.36

30. 66)7,128

31. 8)40,784

32. 43)215

33. 0.09)0.612

34. 112)5,824

35. 0.36)54

36. 0.5)32

37. 27)0.8586

38. 6.25)0.3125

Find the average.

39. 86   100   96   82

Estimate with numbers compatible with mental math.

40. $89\overline{)651}$ 16,104 ÷ 317

Apply the order of operations to solve the equations.

42. $(8 \times 9) + 2 = x$ 43. $30 + 6 \times 5 = y$ 44. $12 - 8 \div 2 + 7 \times 4 = z$

45. Round the quotient to the nearest cent. $1.7\overline{)\$4}$

46. Round the quotient to the nearest dollar. $3.74\overline{)\$9.23}$

47. Round the quotient to the nearest thousandth. $0.5\overline{)0.84629}$

---

48. Mr. Anza purchased supplies for his art class.

   a. If he spent $21.48 on scissors that cost $1.79 each, how many pairs of scissors did he purchase?

   b. Seven boxes of markers cost $24.43. How much does one box of markers cost?

49. SmartArt charges $3.50 for a package of modeling clay. DeluxeArt charges $4.00 per package, and the Creative Store charges $3.69. What is the average price for a package of modeling clay in these three stores?

50. A roll of craft paper measures 19.5 yards. For each project in Mr. Anza's class, 2.3 yards of craft paper will be used. Approximately how many projects can be made from one roll of craft paper?

"Oh Blessed health . . . thou art above all gold and treasure . . . He that has thee, has little more to wish for."

Laurence Sterne
(1713–1768)

Chapter Theme

God desires for His people to worship Him. If you reside in America, you live in a country founded by people seeking the freedom to worship God. The chapter 4 theme of Worship reminds us that it is part of God's plan for mankind to worship Him. The beautiful chapel of the United States Air Force Academy is seen on the opposite page, but people express their true worship of God in a variety of places. In some parts of the world, believers may gather to worship God at the risk of their own lives. Thank God if you live in a location where you can worship openly and with great joy. Each of us may also show our daily worship to our Father by simply living in obedience to Him.

4

Chapter

Geometric Properties

Lessons 46-61

"God is Spirit, and those who worship Him must worship in spirit and truth."

John 4:24

Lesson 46

 **Construct Meaning**

It would be impossible to describe the chapel pictured on the previous page without using geometric terms. Try using some of the terms below.

Geometric Terms

point	An exact location in space. It is identified by a capital letter.	A •	Point A
line	A straight path of points that extends without end in both directions. It is named by any two points.		Line AB or Line BA $\overleftrightarrow{AB}$ or $\overleftrightarrow{BA}$ Line n
line segment	A part of a line between two endpoints. **Congruent** line segments have the same length.	A B C D	Segment AB or Segment BA $\overline{AB}$ or $\overline{BA}$ $\overline{AB} \cong \overline{CD}$
ray	A part of a line that begins at one point and extends without end in one direction.	A B	Ray AB $\overrightarrow{AB}$
plane	A two-dimensional flat surface that extends without end in all directions. It is named by a script letter and represented by a four-sided figure although it extends past the edges.	$\mathcal{R}$	Plane $\mathcal{R}$

 **Construct Congruent Line Segments**

Congruent line segments can be drawn using a ruler. Using only a straightedge and a compass, a line segment congruent to any given line segment can be constructed.

Construct a segment congruent to $\overline{PR}$.
- Draw a segment that is longer than $\overline{PR}$.
- Adjust the compass opening to the length of $\overline{PR}$. Label it $\overline{XY}$.
- Place the compass point on X without adjusting the setting and draw an arc on $\overline{XY}$. Label the point of intersection Z.

$\overline{PR}$ is congruent to $\overline{XZ}$
$\overline{PR} \cong \overline{XZ}$

 **Check Understanding**

Draw and label.
a. $\overleftrightarrow{CD}$ b. Ray JK c. $\overline{OP}$ d. Line XY e. Plane $\mathcal{B}$ f. Point X

g. Draw a 3-inch line segment using a ruler. Construct a congruent line segment using a compass and straightedge.

98

Chapter 4 • *Mathematics* Grade 6

Identify the geometric term for each figure. Name each figure using the appropriate symbol.

1.

2. •K

3. M N

4.

5.

6.

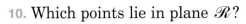

7. Trace the figure from problem 3. Construct and label a congruent figure, $\overline{OP}$, using a compass and straightedge.

Consider the drawing at the right for problems 8 through 14.

8. Name as many line segments as possible.

9. Give three different names for the vertical line.

10. Which points lie in plane $\mathscr{R}$?

11. Are $\overline{AB}$ and $\overline{BC}$ congruent line segments?

12. Do $\overrightarrow{FB}$ and $\overrightarrow{BF}$ represent the same figure?

13. Could a line contain points A, E, and C?

14. Do $\overline{AB}$ and $\overline{BA}$ represent the same figure?

15. The wise men who came to worship the young child Jesus were guided by a star. What geometric term is suggested by the light coming from a star?

16. Arlene entered her kiwi pie in the county fair. After the judges removed one slice for tasting, how many plane surfaces were on her entry?

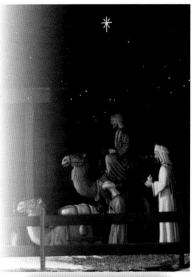

"We have seen His star in the East and have come to worship Him."
Matthew 2:2b

17. Consider three rays: $\overrightarrow{AB}$, $\overrightarrow{AC}$, and $\overrightarrow{AD}$. What do these rays have in common? Draw all three rays where points A, B, C, and D are on the same line.

1. 1.98 + 0.045

2. 3.4 + 8

3. 7.31 − 5.08

4. 3.5 − 0.19

5. 0.22 × 5

6. 0.902 × 0.6

7. 0.64 ÷ 8

8. 270 ÷ 7.5

Construct Meaning

The freedom to worship God as they pleased was the reason many Europeans came to America. This freedom was so precious to the Pilgrims that they were willing to endure a long sea journey and the hardships of living in a new land. Today visitors can view a living-history museum of the 17th-century Pilgrims' colony at Plimoth Plantation and see a replica of the original *Mayflower*.

Mayflower II

Use the map of Plymouth, Massachusetts, to find examples of intersecting, parallel, and perpendicular lines.

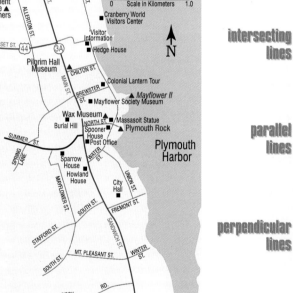

Geometric Terms

intersecting lines	Lines that meet at a point. The point at which they meet is the point of **intersection**.	$\overrightarrow{AB}$ and $\overrightarrow{CD}$ intersect at point X.
parallel lines	Lines in a plane that never intersect.	$\overrightarrow{EF} \parallel \overrightarrow{GH}$
perpendicular lines	Lines that intersect to form right (90°) angles.	$\overrightarrow{IJ} \perp \overrightarrow{KL}$
skew lines	Lines that are not in the same plane and do not intersect.	

Check Understanding

Find an example of the following types of line segments in your classroom.

a. intersecting   b. parallel   c. perpendicular   d. skew

e. The mast of the *Mayflower II* and Brewster Street would be an example of what kind of line segments listed above?

Practice

Draw and label.

1. $\overleftrightarrow{AB} \perp \overleftrightarrow{CD}$

2. $\overleftrightarrow{WX}$ intersects $\overleftrightarrow{YZ}$ at point P.

3. $\overline{QR} \parallel \overline{ST}$

4. $\overleftrightarrow{CH}$ and $\overleftrightarrow{BR}$ are skew.

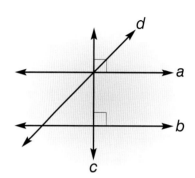

Use the figure on the right for problems 5 through 8. Give one answer for each description.

5. A pair of parallel lines.

6. A pair of $\perp$ intersecting lines.

7. A pair of intersecting lines that are not perpendicular.

8. Why are none of the lines skew?

Apply

9. Draw the following figure. $\overleftrightarrow{AT} \parallel \overleftrightarrow{BY}$ and $\overleftrightarrow{BY} \parallel \overleftrightarrow{NO}$.

10. What is the relationship between $\overleftrightarrow{AT}$ and $\overleftrightarrow{NO}$ in the figure you drew for problem 9?

11. On the map of Plymouth, is Water Street parallel to Main Street? Why or why not?

12. Find two streets that represent parallel line segments.

13. Draw three lines in the same plane that have the following number of points of intersection.

   a. zero   b. one   c. two   d. three

Review

Write the letter for the most reasonable answer.

1. There are about ▦ pages in a Bible with both the Old and New Testaments.

   a. 100   **b.** 1,000   **c.** 10,000

2. A child with a low fever has a temperature of ▦ degrees Fahrenheit.

   a. 50   **b.** 70   **c.** 100

3. A normal width for a stop sign would be ▦ inches.

   a. 10   **b.** 30   **c.** 50

4. A bag of dried cranberries costs $2.25 at the Plimoth Plantation gift shop. What is the greatest number of bags you can purchase with $10.00? How much change should you receive?

Construct Meaning

Many people worship God in churches around the world. The age, size, and style of these buildings vary greatly. Notice the different angles in the architecture of these churches. An **angle** is formed by two rays with a common endpoint called the **vertex**. The two rays are called the **sides** of the angle.

Swiss church   Croatian church   Danish church

An angle can be named by one point from each ray on either side of the vertex or simply by the vertex. **Congruent** angles have the same measure.

acute angle	measures less than 90°		∠ABC ∠B
right angle	measures 90°		∠DEF ∠E
obtuse angle	measures greater than 90° but less than 180°		∠GHI ∠H
straight angle	measures 180°		∠JKL ∠K
reflex angle	measures greater than 180°		∠XYZ ∠Y
complementary angles	sum of the measures of two angles is 90°		∠NMO and ∠OMP are complementary
supplementary angles	sum of the measures of two angles is 180°		∠RQS and ∠SQT are supplementary

Types of Angles

Measuring Angles

A **degree** (°) is the standard unit of measurement for angles. A **protractor** is used for measuring angles. Imagine a circle divided into 360 wedges. Each angle would be 1°. One-sixth of the entire circle would be 60°.

- Place the center point of the protractor on the vertex of the angle.
- Place the zero line on one side of the angle.
- Read the measure of the angle using that scale.

a. Draw an acute angle. Use a protractor to measure your angle.

b. Draw an obtuse angle. Use a protractor to measure your angle.

c. What is the measure of a right angle? straight angle?

d. An angle measuring 145° and one measuring 35° are ▦▦▦ angles.

Classify each angle as *acute*, *right*, *obtuse*, *straight*, or *reflex*. Find the exact measure of each angle using a protractor.

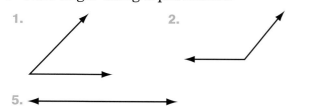

1.   2.   3.   4.

5.   6.

Use a protractor and a straightedge to construct an angle with the given measure. Begin by drawing a ray with a dot representing the vertex, then mark a point to draw the second ray.

7. 75°   8. 160°   9. 5°

10. Can two obtuse angles be supplementary? Explain.

11. Without using a protractor, find the measure of the other three angles formed by two intersecting lines.

Use this figure for problems 12 through 15.

12. Name three different angles.

13. Name the rays that form the sides of ∠CAD. What is the vertex?

14. Use a protractor to measure ∠CAD.

15. If ∠BAC and ∠CAD are complementary angles, what is the measurement of ∠BAD?

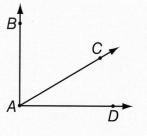

Write in Roman numerals.

1. 37   2. 299   3. 1,450

Write in standard form.

4. XXIII   5. LIV   6. CMX

It is good to give thanks to the LORD,
And to sing praises to Your name, O Most High;
To declare Your lovingkindness in the morning,
And Your faithfulness every night. Psalm 92:1–2

French church

Lesson 49

Construct Meaning

In the picture, the double yellow line **bisects**, or divides in half, the road as it appears to converge and form an angle. Bisection produces two congruent parts. A **compass**, a tool used for constructing circles and arcs, can be used with a straightedge to construct congruent line segments and angles. The compass may also be used to bisect lines and angles.

Construct a Congruent Angle

Construct an angle congruent to ∠B.

- Draw a ray $\overrightarrow{YZ}$.
- Place the compass point on B and draw an arc that intersects both sides. Label the points of intersection A and C.
- Leave the compass adjusted to the length of $\overline{BC}$.
- Place the compass point on Y and draw an arc intersecting $\overrightarrow{YZ}$. Label the point of intersection T.
- Adjust the compass to the length of $\overline{AC}$. Place the point on T and draw an arc that intersects the first arc. Label the point of intersection X.
- Draw $\overrightarrow{YX}$ using a straightedge.

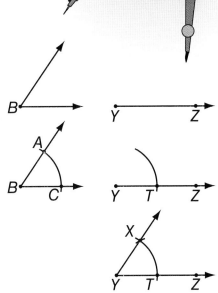

∠ABC is congruent to ∠XYZ
∠ABC ≅ ∠XYZ

Bisect a Line Segment

Bisect $\overline{AB}$.

- Adjust the compass to more than half of the length of $\overline{AB}$.
- Place the compass on A. Draw an arc extending above and below the line.
- Place the compass on B and repeat.
- Label the intersection points X and Y.
- Draw a line connecting X and Y.
- Label the point at which it intersects $\overline{AB}$ as C.

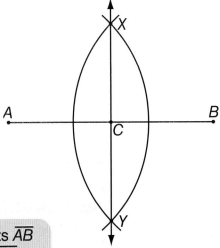

$\overleftrightarrow{XY}$ bisects $\overline{AB}$
$\overline{AC} \cong \overline{CB}$

Bisect an Angle

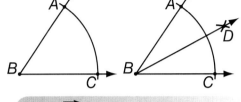

Bisect ∠*ABC*.

- With the compass point on *B*, draw an arc that intersects both sides. Label the points *A* and *C*.
- With the compass point on *A*, draw an arc between the two sides.
- Place the compass point on *C* and repeat. Label the intersection of the two arcs *D*.
- Draw $\overrightarrow{BD}$ using a straightedge.

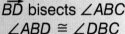

$\overrightarrow{BD}$ bisects ∠*ABC*
∠*ABD* ≅ ∠*DBC*

Check Understanding

a. When you construct a bisector of a line segment, what is true about the angles formed?

b. Would the bisector of an obtuse angle form two acute, right, or obtuse angles? Explain.

c. Josh found a starfish that had grown an extra arm halfway between two of the five evenly-spaced arms. This additional arm is a ▨▨▨ of the angle formed by the original arms.

Practice

Trace each angle. Construct and label a congruent angle using a compass and straightedge.

1.
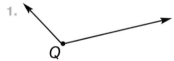
Q

2. *F*

Trace and bisect each figure using a compass and straightedge.

3. *X* ———— *Y* 4. *T* ———— *V* 5. *R* ←————→ 6. 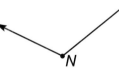 *N*

Apply

7. Jacque planned to plant a row of marigolds down the center of a triangular corner of a garden plot. How can she find the bisector of the angle using a piece of rope?

8. Can an angle formed by two short rays be congruent to an angle formed by two long rays? Explain.

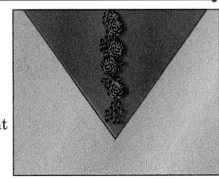

 **Construct Meaning**

Examine the triangles suggested in this photograph of a Romanian church. How would you describe them? A **triangle** is a polygon with three sides. It also has three angles and three vertices.

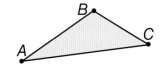

The sum of the measures of the angles of a triangle is 180°.

measure of ∠A + measure of ∠B + measure of ∠C = 180°

CLASSIFICATION BY SIDE LENGTH

	equilateral triangle	three congruent sides
	isosceles triangle	at least two congruent sides
	scalene triangle	no congruent sides

What can be said about the measures of the angles of an equilateral triangle?

What is true about the angles opposite the congruent sides of an isosceles triangle?

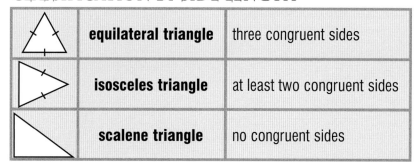

Similar triangles have angles of equal measures.

Congruent triangles have sides of equal lengths.

CLASSIFICATION BY ANGLE MEASUREMENT

	acute triangle	three acute (less than 90°) angles
	right triangle	one right (90°) angle
	obtuse triangle	one obtuse (greater than 90°) angle

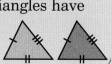 **Check Understanding**

Use the drawing for problems a through c.

a. Name the three triangles formed.

b. Classify each triangle by side length and by angle measurement.

c. What is the sum of the two acute angles in any right triangle?

d. A regular polygon has all congruent sides and all congruent angles. Which type of triangle is a regular polygon?

e. How can you prove that the sum of the measures of the angles in a triangle is 180°?

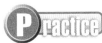

Practice

$\triangle QRT$ is an equilateral triangle. $\triangle QRS$ is a right triangle. Find the measure of each angle without using a protractor.

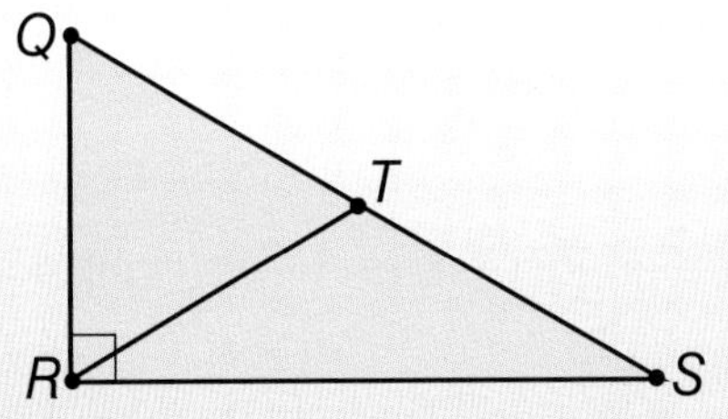

1. $\angle QRT$
2. $\angle QTR$
3. $\angle RQT$
4. $\angle TRS$
5. $\angle RTS$
6. $\angle TSR$
7. If the length of $\overline{QT}$ is 1.5 ft, what is the length of $\overline{TS}$?

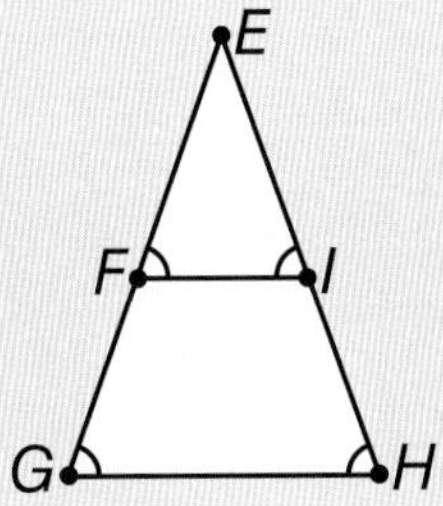

8. Classify $\triangle EFI$ and $\triangle EGH$ by their side lengths.
9. Are the two triangles similar? congruent?
10. The measure of $\angle GHI$ is 70°. What is the measure of $\angle FEI$? $\angle EFI$?
11. Is it possible to draw an obtuse equilateral triangle? Explain.
12. Can a triangle have more than one obtuse angle? Explain.
13. Draw an obtuse scalene triangle.

Apply

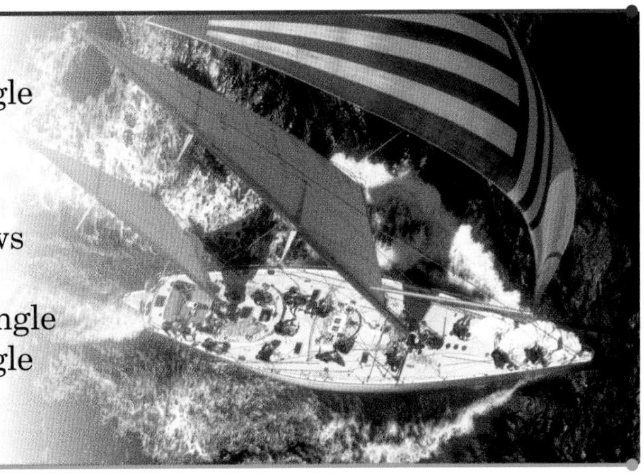

14. The sail for Gary's boat is a right triangle with one angle of 30°. What angle is formed by the other corner of the sail?
15. Johanna planted lettuce in diagonal rows across one corner of her rectangular garden. If one of the rows made a 45° angle with the side of the garden, at what angle did it intersect the other side?

Review

1. 13×9
2. 862×8
3. 208×16
4. $6{,}045 \times 44$
5. 717×39
6. 100×505
7. 621×517
8. 900×80

Lesson 51

![icon] **Construct Meaning**

A **quadrilateral** is a polygon with four sides. Quadrilaterals are classified by the length of their sides and whether or not the sides are parallel.

Classifying Quadrilaterals

parallelogram ------ a quadrilateral having opposite sides parallel and congruent

rectangle --------- a parallelogram with opposite sides congruent and four right angles

square ------------ a rectangle having all sides congruent

rhombus --------- a parallelogram with all sides congruent

trapezoid --------- a quadrilateral having only one pair of parallel sides, called **bases**

For any quadrilateral, the sum of the measures of the angles will be 360°.

This is obvious for a square or rectangle since four right angles add up to 360°. Examine these other quadrilaterals. Remember that the sum of the measures of the angles in a triangle is 180°.

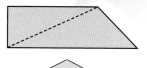

Think: 180° + 180° = 360°

For any parallelogram, opposite sides have the same length and opposite angles have the same measure.

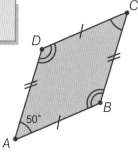

$$\overline{DC} \cong \overline{AB} \qquad \angle D \cong \angle B$$
$$\overline{AD} \cong \overline{BC} \qquad \angle A \cong \angle C$$

The measure of $\angle A$ is 50°. Find the measure of each other angle.
Since $\angle A \cong \angle C$, what is the measure of $\angle C$?

$\angle C = 50°$

measure of $\angle A$ + measure of $\angle B$ + measure of $\angle C$ + measure of $\angle D$ = 360°
50° + ? + 50° + ? = 360°

What is the sum of 50° and 50°?
What is the sum of the two missing numbers?

Remember that $\angle B \cong \angle D$, so both the missing numbers are the same.

If the sum of the measures of $\angle B$ and $\angle D$ is 260°, what is the measure of each angle?

$\angle B$ is 130° $\angle D$ is 130°

 **Check Understanding**

Use grid paper to draw the following.

- a. Draw a parallelogram that is not a rhombus or a rectangle.
- b. Draw a quadrilateral that is not a parallelogram or a trapezoid.
- c. Draw a square. Draw a similar square that is not congruent to the first.
- d. Draw a quadrilateral that has four congruent sides and four congruent angles.
- e. Draw a quadrilateral that has four congruent sides, but the angles are not all congruent.
- f. Draw a trapezoid with a pair of congruent sides.

 **Practice**

Use the figure at the right for problems 1 through 4.

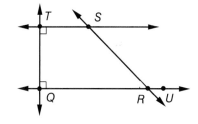

1. Figure *QRST* is what kind of quadrilateral?
2. The measure of ∠*QRS* is 45°.
   What is the measure of ∠*RST* if *TS* ∥ *QR*?
3. What is the measure of ∠*SRU*?
4. Is figure *QRST* a parallelogram? Explain.

 Apply

5. A trapezoid having a pair of congruent sides forms the base of a steel arch. If the two lower angles are both 86°, what is the measure of each of the top two angles?

6. Scott noticed that his kite contained four triangles. Since the sum of the measures of the angles of a triangle is 180°, is the sum of the measures of the angles in the kite shape four times 180°? Why or why not?

7. Name each class of quadrilaterals shown in the drawing.

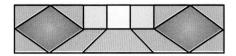

Lesson 52

The mission team prepared colored paper shapes for a craft project for the Russian orphans. The children were very artistic and designed beautiful illustrations resembling stained glass windows for each Bible lesson taught by the team.

Each shape was a **polygon**, a closed plane figure formed by line segments. If all the sides of a polygon are congruent and all angles are congruent, the figure is a **regular polygon**. Name each of the above figures and tell if it is a regular polygon.

A **diagonal** is a line segment connecting two vertices, but is not a side.

Regular Polygon	Number of Sides	Number of Diagonals
triangle	3	0
square	4	2
pentagon	5	5
hexagon	6	9
heptagon	7	14
octagon	8	20
nonagon	9	
decagon	10	
hendecagon	11	
dodecagon	12	

+2 +3 +4 +5

What pattern do you see in the number of diagonals as the number of sides increases? Complete the chart.

All regular polygons are **convex**, since for any two points inside the polygon, a line segment between them is completely within the polygon.

For a **concave** polygon, it is possible to draw a line segment between two points inside the polygon and have part of the line segment lie outside the polygon.

 **Check Understanding**

a. What is the specific name for a regular polygon with three sides?
b. Construct an equilateral triangle using only a compass and a straightedge.

 **Construct an Equilateral Triangle**

- Draw line segment $\overline{AB}$.
- Place the compass point on A and adjust it to the length of $\overline{AB}$.
- Keeping the compass on A, draw an arc above $\overline{AB}$.
- Repeat at point B and label the intersection as C.
- Draw line segments to form sides $\overline{AC}$ and $\overline{BC}$.

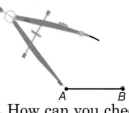

c. How can you check your triangle to make sure it is an equilateral triangle?

110

Chapter 4 • *Mathematics* Grade 6

Identify each polygon. Write whether it is *convex* or *concave*.

1.
2.
3.
4.

5. Why is a rhombus not necessarily a regular polygon?
6. Construct a square using only a compass and a straightedge.

Construct a Square

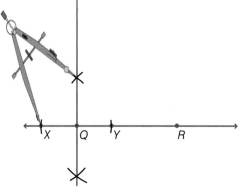

- Draw a line and label a segment as one side of the square, $\overline{QR}$.
- At Q, construct a perpendicular line by marking an arc on the line on each side of Q. Label X and Y.
- Adjust the compass to a larger opening and make an arc above and below Q from point X.
- Repeat at point Y.
- Using the points of intersection above and below Q, draw a line ⊥ to $\overline{QR}$ at Q.
- Adjust the compass to the exact length of $\overline{QR}$. Mark this same length above Q on the perpendicular line. Label this point T.
- Without changing the compass, make an arc above R with the compass on T and an arc above R with the compass on R. Label the point of intersection S.
- Draw $\overline{TS}$ and $\overline{RS}$. Your square should be figure $QRST$.

7. Check your drawing using a protractor. What is the measure of each angle?
8. Check your drawing with a ruler. What is the length of each side?
9. Copy and complete the chart.

Regualar Polygon	Number of Sides	Number of Lines of Symmetry
triangle	3	3
square	4	
pentagon		
hexagon		
heptagon		
octagon		

10. Write an equation to express the relationship between the number of sides, s, and the number of lines of symmetry, l, in a regular polygon.

Pure and undefiled religion before God and the Father is this: to visit orphans and widows in their trouble, and to keep oneself unspotted from the world. James 1:27

Lesson 53

Construct Meaning

Archaeologists do not know exactly how the Egyptian pyramids were built, but their construction was an amazing feat of engineering. They served as tombs for royalty, as well as places for religious activities. Rulers were mummified and placed in pyramids for passage into the afterlife. The Egyptians did not worship God, but worshiped many false gods. How sad that they put their faith in something which could not help them. When God delivered the Israelites from Egypt, He reminded them that they were to worship Him alone.

"You shall have no other gods before Me." Exodus 20:3

A **polyhedron** is a three-dimensional figure made of flat surfaces that are polygons. A **pyramid** is a polyhedron named for its base. All other faces are triangles that meet at a common vertex.

triangular pyramid

square pyramid

rectangular pyramid

Count the faces, vertices, and edges for each pyramid.

How many faces would an octagonal pyramid have? Must the base of a pyramid be a regular polygon? What can you predict about the shape of a slice through a pyramid that is parallel to its base?

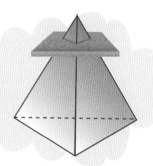

A **prism** is a polyhedron named for its two congruent and parallel bases. All other faces are parallelograms.

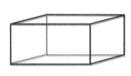

triangular prism   **cube**   **rectangular prism**

Could you have a square prism that is not a cube?

Check Understanding

Write *prism*, *pyramid*, or *neither* for each figure.

a.

b.

c.

d.

Pyramids and Prisms

e. Write the number of faces, vertices, and edges for the figure shown in problem b.

Copy and complete the chart.

Polyhedron	**F** Number of Faces	**V** Number of Vertices	**E** Number of Edges
1. Triangular pyramid			
2. Triangular prism			
3. Square pyramid			
4. Cube			
5. Rectangular pyramid			
6. Rectangular prism			
7. Pentagonal prism			

8. Write an equation that shows the relationship between the number of faces, F, of a prism and the number of sides, S, of its base.

9. Write an equation that shows the relationship between the number of faces, F, of a pyramid and the number of sides, S, of its base.

10. Does Euler's formula, which relates the number of edges, faces, and vertices, work for all pyramids and prisms? Use this formula to check each polyhedron in problems 1 through 7.

Euler's Formula
$$E = F + V - 2$$

11. Suzie bought a Christmas ornament that looked like two square pyramids with a common base. How many faces does it have?

12. Todd's house is a rectangular prism with a rectangular pyramid as its roof. How many roof faces would need to be covered with shingles?

13. What regular polygons are used to make a soccer ball? The colors might remind you of the flags of some countries where soccer is a popular sport. Is this soccer ball a polyhedron? Explain.

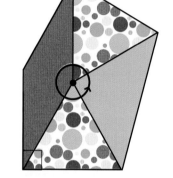

Practice

1. Draw a large scalene triangle. Using a compass and a straightedge, construct the bisector for each of the angles. What do you notice about the three bisectors?

2. Martha is designing a quilt pattern. The square corner is formed by a rhombus and an equilateral triangle. What are the measures of the angles of the rhombus? Do not use a protractor. What are the measures of the angles of the isosceles triangle that is between the two equilateral triangles? (Hint: There are 360° in a circle.)

3. Gabriella has a box that is a hexagonal prism. All of the sides are equal in length. What is the measure of the angle formed by two sides?

4. In a class of 24 students at Blue Ridge Christian Academy, 12 students have a brother and ten students have a sister. Seven students have both a sister and a brother. How many students have only brothers? How many have no sisters or brothers?

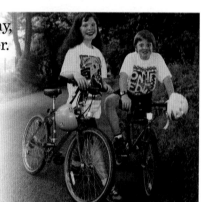

5. Draw the next figure in the given pattern. Name each polygon.

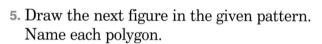
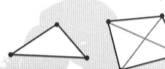

6. Six students from different schools attended summer camp together. They have agreed that each one will talk on the phone with each of the other campers sometime during the month after returning home. The call can be made by either person. No person can repeat a call. How many phone calls will be made? (Hint: Think of each person as a point on a circle. A line segment drawn between them can represent the call.)

7. Mitchell is thinking of a number that when divided by 3 has a remainder of 2, when divided by 5 has a remainder of 1, and when it is divided by 7 the remainder is 4. Continue the chart to determine Mitchell's number.

n	remainder n ÷ 3	remainder n ÷ 5	remainder n ÷ 7
1	1	1	1
2	2	2	2
3	0	3	3
4	1	4	4
5	2		

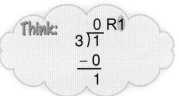

Think:
$$3\overline{)1}\;\;\begin{array}{r}0\ R1\\-0\\\hline1\end{array}$$

8. Corbin examined some copper sulfate crystals and noticed that they all had the same shape. Use a protractor to measure the four angles on one of the crystal surfaces. Name the shape of the crystal.

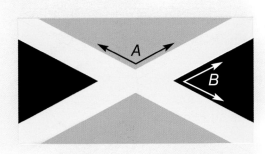

9. Examine the Jamaican flag. Measure ∠A of the green triangle using a protractor. Calculate the measure of the other two angles of the green triangle. Do not use a protractor. ∠A and ∠B are supplementary angles. Calculate the measure of ∠B. Calculate the measures of the other two angles of the black triangle.

10. Name the 15 triangles formed by these line segments.

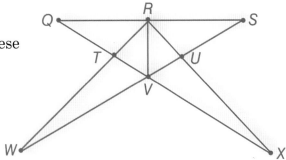

Lesson 55

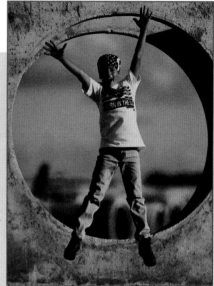

🧱 Construct Meaning

A **circle** is a set of points in a plane that are all an equal distance from a fixed point, the **center**. The **radius** (*r*), is the distance from the center to any point on the circle. The distance from one side of the circle to the other through the center is the **diameter** (*d*). What is the relationship between the radius and the diameter for any given circle?

Michael can reach up to six feet from the ground. Would this distance be an estimate for the diameter or the radius of the circular opening in the picture? Michael's foot is 34 inches from his waist. This would be an estimate of what distance? Would Michael be correct if he says that a pipe with a radius of two feet will fit through the opening?

Construct a Circle

- Use a compass and a ruler.
- Open the compass to the desired measure on the ruler.
- Place the point on the center and rotate the pencil the entire 360°.

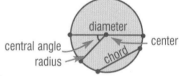

> An angle formed by two radii is a **central angle**. The sum of the measures of the central angles of a circle is 360°.

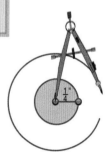

A line segment drawn between any two points on the circle is a **chord**. Is a diameter a chord? Circles that lie in the same plane and have the same center are **concentric** circles. Jessica drew six concentric circles, each time doubling the radius of the previous circle. If the first circle had a radius of $\frac{1}{4}$ inch, what was the radius of the sixth circle? How did the diameters change?

✔ Check Understanding

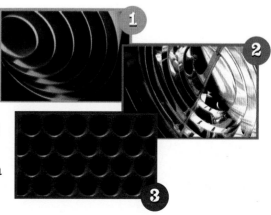

a. Which picture represents concentric circles? Explain.

b. If the diameter of one circle in picture 3 is 6 mm, what is the radius?

c. The line across the middle circle in picture 2 represents what dimension of the circle?

d. Can a chord of length 5 inches be drawn in a circle with a radius of 2 inches? Explain.

116

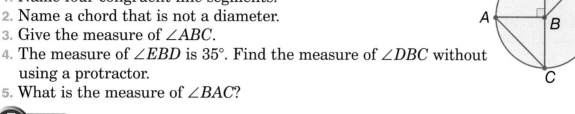

Use the drawing at the right for problems 1 through 5.

1. Name four congruent line segments.
2. Name a chord that is not a diameter.
3. Give the measure of ∠ABC.
4. The measure of ∠EBD is 35°. Find the measure of ∠DBC without using a protractor.
5. What is the measure of ∠BAC?

6. In the lamp glass shown in picture 2 on page 116, the diameter of the lens increases by four centimeters on each successive lens. How does the radius increase? If the third lens has a diameter of ten centimeters, what is the diameter of the fifth lens?

7. For the circles in picture 3 on page 116, Joshua measured 1.8 cm from the center of one to the center of the one beside it. If the distance between the edges of the circles at the closest point is 0.6 cm, what is the radius of each circle?

8. Ashley wants to divide her circular flower bed into fourths with decorative picket fencing. If the diameter is 9 feet, how many feet of fencing will she need to make the dividers? She can purchase 3-foot pieces for $3.79 each, or a 20-foot roll for $24.99. Which would be more economical for her project?

Low picket fence

rock border

9. Brittany gave Ashley a sundial to place in her garden. How many degrees are represented by the passage of the hour from 6:00 A.M. to 7 A.M. if it is one-twentieth of the entire circle?

10. Construct a regular octagon using only a compass and a straightedge. (Hint: Begin by drawing a circle. Draw a diameter. Bisect the angles formed until you have eight equal angles.)

1. Find the average score for the following set of scores:

      99   87   94   83   100   89

2. Solve. $6 + 5 (8 + 2) - 4 \times 10 =$

Lesson 56

Construct Meaning

In the late 1800s, a cylinder made of a brittle wax-like material was used to record sounds. It could be played on a home phonograph. Each cylinder typically played about two minutes of music. They were very fragile and repeated playing would damage them. How different from our modern digital compact discs which provide hours of uninterrupted music!

Thomas Edison, inventor of the phonograph

A **cylinder** is a three-dimensional figure with two circular bases that are congruent and parallel.

A **cone** is a three-dimensional figure with a circular base and a curved surface that forms the vertex opposite the base.

A **sphere** is a three-dimensional figure where every point is the same distance from the center.

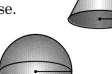

Check Understanding

Jasmine collects postcards sent to her from many different countries by her grandparents. Look closely for whole or parts of cones, cylinders, and spheres. Some may have more than one of these surfaces. For each picture, write *cylinder*, *cone*, or *sphere*, if you observe that figure.

a.
b.
c.
d.

e.
f.
g.
h.
i.

Cylinders, Cones, and Spheres

1. Drew wanted to make a cone with a circular base having a two-inch radius. He constructed a two-inch circle and cut it out. He was not sure how big to make the half circle he planned to use for the curved surface. He thought that if he doubled the radius of the base circle that the distance around the larger circle would be twice that of the base circle. Since he planned to use only half the larger circle, the distances should match.

Using a compass, construct the two pieces and cut them out. Assemble a cone using tape. Was Drew right?

2. Megan compared a cylindrical vase and one shaped like a cone. They were the same height and the openings at the top were the same size. Which vase would hold more water?

4"

2"

Use the figure below for problems 3 through 6.

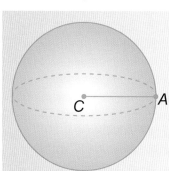

3. If the length of $\overline{AC}$ is 10 inches and the length of $\overline{BC}$ is 15 inches, is point B inside or outside of the sphere?

4. If the length of $\overline{CD}$ is 6 inches, is point D inside or outside of the sphere?

5. What can you determine about the maximum length of $\overline{AD}$?

6. What is the minimum length of $\overline{AD}$?

7. Traffic cones are used to mark road hazards and to divert traffic. Why is a cone a better shape to use than a cylinder of the same height and average diameter?

8. Scott wanted to store a spherical Christmas decoration in a box that would just fit on all sides. Which shape of box should he use?

9. The radius of Scott's ornament was 2.5 cm. The boxes he found were cubes with edges measuring 4.3 cm, 5.2 cm, and 6.1 cm. Which box should he use?

1. $4\overline{)6.44}$ 2. $0.6\overline{)48}$ 3. $0.7\overline{)0.371}$ 4. $3\overline{)3.204}$ 5. $6.3\overline{)1.701}$

Construct Meaning

Isaac was helping his brother, Samuel, measure and cut the wooden framework for his model airplane. They noticed several facts to be true about the sides and angles of triangles that were congruent. Knowing these facts made it possible to calculate the length to cut some of the pieces, even before they began to put the model together. **Congruent** means equal, or the same.

Congruent Triangles

Side
Side
Side   If three sides of a triangle are congruent with three sides of another triangle, the triangles are congruent.

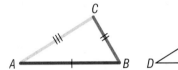
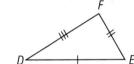
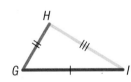

We can easily tell that △ABC and △DEF are congruent. What about △GIH? This may not be as obvious, but since $\overline{AB} \cong \overline{GI}$, $\overline{BC} \cong \overline{GH}$, and $\overline{CA} \cong \overline{HI}$, the two triangles are congruent. How is △ABC different from △GIH?

Side
Angle
Side   If two sides of a triangle are equal to two sides of another triangle and the angles between those two sides are congruent, the triangles are congruent.

Think about it. If you draw two sides with a given angle between them, there is only one possible length for the third side. Since $\overline{XZ} \cong \overline{QS}$, as well as the other corresponding sides being congruent, △XYZ ≅ △QRS.

Angle
Side
Angle   If two angles of a triangle are congruent to two angles of another triangle and the sides between those two angles are congruent, the triangles are congruent.

The rays forming the two angles will always meet at the same point, so $\overline{HJ} \cong \overline{LN}$ and $\overline{IJ} \cong \overline{MN}$. Therefore, △HIJ ≅ △LMN.

a. Which of the following show congruent triangles?

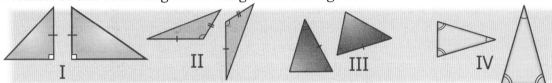

For each pair of congruent triangles, find the value of *x*.

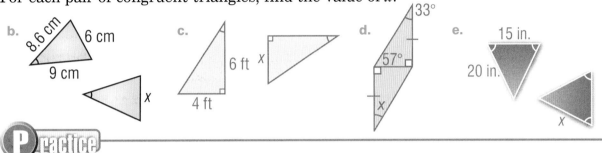

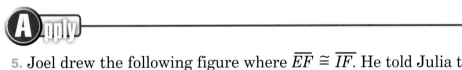

Use the drawing for problems 1 through 4.

1. If ∠CAB ≅ ∠DCA, what is true about △ABC and △ACD? Explain.

2. If the length of $\overline{DC}$ = 60 in., what is the length of $\overline{AB}$?

3. What side of △ABC is congruent to $\overline{AD}$?

4. If the measure of ∠B is 138°, what is the measure of ∠ACB? ∠DAC? ∠D?

5. Joel drew the following figure where $\overline{EF} ≅ \overline{IF}$. He told Julia that the length of $\overline{EJ}$ was the same as $\overline{IG}$. Julia said that $\overline{EJ}$ was longer than $\overline{IG}$. Who is right? Do not use a ruler. Explain your reasoning.

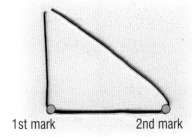

1st mark   2nd mark

6. Ben made triangles out of copper wire by measuring and marking two sides of the triangle and bending it into a right angle. He finished the triangle by bending another angle and cutting the wire where the two ends meet. Will his triangles all be congruent if he does not measure the third side? Explain.

Lesson 58

Construct Meaning

Glenn built a model of his grandparents' house. He took his measurements from a picture that was smaller than his model. He measured the roof, then cut his pieces twice the length of those in the picture.

23 mm   23 mm   46 mm   46 mm
32 mm   64 mm

The two triangles are similar since they have the same shape but not necessarily the same size. Corresponding sides are proportional to each other. Proportional, or similar, figures are used when constructing a model, drawing a map, or making an enlargement. Similar triangles have equal measures for all corresponding angles. The corresponding sides of similar triangles are in proportion and form equivalent fractions. Show that Glenn's model is similar to the picture.

$$\frac{picture\ roof\ side\ length}{model\ roof\ side\ length} = \frac{picture\ base\ length}{model\ base\ length}$$

$$\frac{23}{46} = \frac{32}{64}$$

Since both fractions can be reduced to $\frac{1}{2}$, they are equal.

Why is the model in proportion to the actual house as well as to the picture?

Study the following similar triangles and relationships between their sides. Use this information to find the length of $\overline{JH}$.

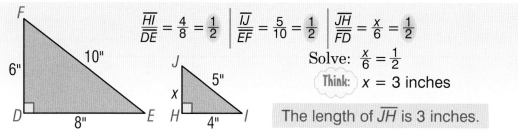

$$\frac{HI}{DE} = \frac{4}{8} = \frac{1}{2} \quad \frac{IJ}{EF} = \frac{5}{10} = \frac{1}{2} \quad \frac{JH}{FD} = \frac{x}{6} = \frac{1}{2}$$

Solve: $\frac{x}{6} = \frac{1}{2}$

Think: $x = 3$ inches

The length of $\overline{JH}$ is 3 inches.

If two sides of a triangle are proportional to two sides of another triangle, are the two triangles necessarily similar?

Check Understanding

Determine if the triangle pairs are similar. Write *yes* or *no*.

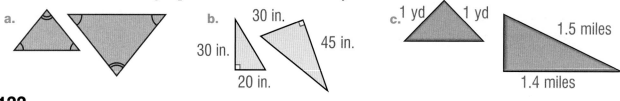

a.

b. 30 in.
30 in.   45 in.
20 in.

c. 1 yd   1 yd
                    1.5 miles
          1.4 miles

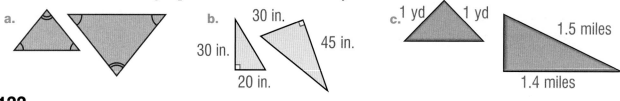

The following represent similar triangles. Find the value of *x*.

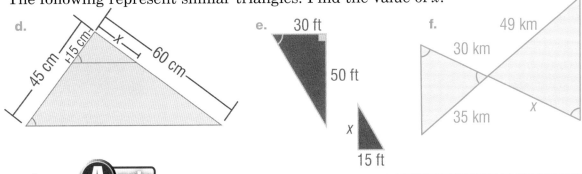

d. 45 cm 15 cm *x* 60 cm

e. 30 ft 50 ft *x* 15 ft

f. 49 km 30 km 35 km *x*

A**pply**

1. 40 ft 15 ft ground attachment point

A 50-foot line stretched from the top of a 40-foot pole is attached to the ground at a point 30 feet from its base. Another pole is placed 15 feet to the right of the first pole in line with the ground attachment point so that it just touches the line. How tall is the second pole?

2. Erica cut a rectangular piece of cloth into two congruent triangles by cutting it on the diagonal. Each piece was an isosceles triangle. If the length of the fabric before cutting was 45 inches, what was the width?

3. Kristen has a picture of her brother, Nory, standing beside their grandparents' cabin. Nory is 1 inch tall in the picture and the cabin is 7 inches tall. Kristen knows that her brother is 36 inches tall. Give the actual height of the cabin in feet.

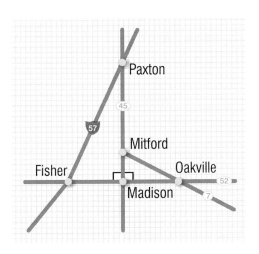

Paxton 45 57 Mitford Fisher Oakville 52 Madison 7

4. Determine the distance from Fisher to Paxton on Highway 57 if the distance from Fisher to Oakville is 60 miles and Madison is half-way between Fisher and Oakville. The distance between Madison and Mitford is 15 miles, Mitford to Oakville is 33.5 miles, and Paxton to Madison is 60 miles.

Lesson 59

Construct Meaning

Kimberly and Adam worked together to determine how many different ways they could arrange four cubes.

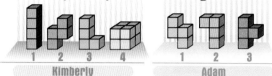

Kimberly   Adam

Kimberly noticed that her third arrangement and Adam's second arrangement were the same if one was **rotated** (turned) and **translated** (slid) until it matched the other.

> A **transformation** is a change in the location or position of a figure, but not its size or shape. Congruent figures can be transformed by a translation, rotation, and/or reflection.

Adam said his first arrangement and Kimberly's second arrangement were the same if you **reflected** (flipped) one of them. These two designs represent congruent figures.

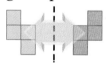

Together they made three more arrangements.

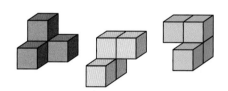

> Which two arrangements are mirror images of each other? Are they the same arrangement? Since no number of transformations can make them the same shape, they are not congruent, even though they are mirror images.

A **plane of symmetry** divides a figure into two parts that are mirror images of each other. Visualize the plane of symmetry for this figure.

Plane of symmetry

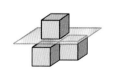
Not a plane of symmetry

Check Understanding

Determine the number of planes of symmetry that exist for the following.

a.

b.

c.

d. How many <u>different</u> arrangements did Kimberly and Adam make?

Write *rotation*, *translation*, or *reflection* for each of the following representations.

e.

f.

g.

Each of these arrangements contains five cubes. Use cubes to construct each one to help you determine congruency.

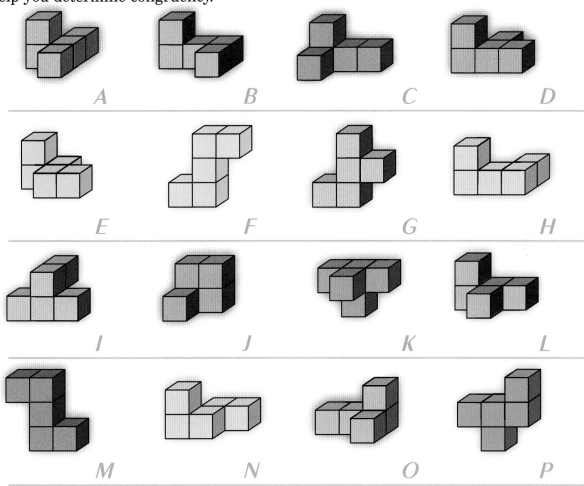

1. Match each pair of congruent figures. You may perform translations, rotations, and reflections.

2. Identify each pair of figures that can be mirror images but cannot be transformed into congruent figures.

3. Which figures have neither an identical match nor a mirror image?

4. Which figures possess a plane of symmetry?

5. For each pair of congruent figures you found in problem 1, identify the transformations necessary to go from one position to the other.

Construct Meaning

The Vogt family visited Petra, Jordan, and viewed the ruins and excavations of this ancient city, carved into red sandstone cliffs nearly 3,000 years ago. By the time of Christ, the once-magnificent city had fallen into ruins. Today Petra is the site of excavations and many preserved buildings and artifacts. Archeologists use grids to serve as a record of the location of each item. The grid can be marked on the ground and the coordinate grid is made on paper.

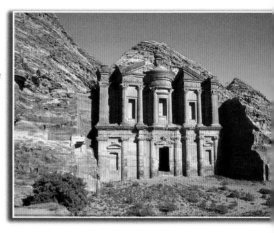

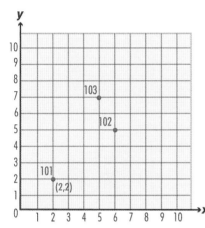

The horizontal axis is the **x-axis** and the vertical axis is the **y-axis**. The location of any given point is named by an **ordered pair**, (x, y). The **x-coordinate** of the point is always given first and tells how far to move from the origin in a horizontal direction. The **y-coordinate** follows the x-coordinate and tells how far to move in a vertical direction. The **origin** on a coordinate grid is the point (0,0). The plane on which points are described as ordered pairs is called a **coordinate plane**.

Josh found a storage jar, item 101, at point (2,2). From the origin, move two units to the right and then up two units. Read the coordinates for item 102. At what point was item 103 found?

1. Draw a coordinate grid similar to the one above. Using Josh's data, mark the location for each item he uncovered. Label each point with the item number and ordered pair.

ITEM	DESCRIPTION	LOCATION
201	oil lamp, small	(4,2)
202	coin, bronze	(7,5)
203	terra cotta figure	(0,3)
204	winged statuette	(3,8)
205	jar handle	(8,8)

2. A line segment is drawn between two points on a coordinate grid. If the value for x is the same for both points, is the line horizontal or vertical? What if the y value is the same for both points and the x values are different?

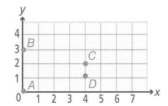

3. Write the coordinates as an ordered pair for points A, B, C, and D.

4. What geometric figure is formed by connecting points A, B, C, and D?

Chapter Four Study Guide

Use the figure at the right for problems 1 through 4.

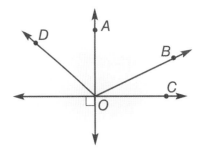

1. Name four line segments. *Lesson 46*

2. Name two perpendicular lines. *Lesson 47*

3. Name two complementary angles and find the measure of each using a protractor. *Lesson 48*

4. Trace ∠DOB on your paper. Using a compass and a straightedge, construct a congruent angle and label it ∠XYZ. Bisect ∠XYZ using a compass and a straightedge. *Lesson 49*

5. Classify △QRU by its side length. Determine the measure of each of its angles without using a protractor. *Lesson 50*

6. Give two names for figure QSTU if $\overline{UT} \parallel \overline{QS}$, and $\overline{QU} \parallel \overline{ST}$. Determine the measure of ∠UTS without using a protractor. *Lesson 51*

7. a. Draw a convex hexagon.
   b. Draw a concave octagon. *Lesson 52*

8. Identify each prism or pyramid specifically. *Lesson 53*

a.   b.   c.   d.   e.

9. Jill has 12 parallelograms, some of each of three different shapes. Four of them are not rectangles, six are rhombus shapes, and eight are rectangles. What is the other shape? *Lesson 54*

10. John says that all circles are similar figures. Explain why you think John is correct or incorrect. *Lesson 55*

11. Identify each geometric figure. *Lesson 56*

a.   b.   c.

12. a. Explain why △ABD is congruent to △CBD. *Lesson 57*
    b. If the measure of ∠DAB is 67°, what is the measure of ∠BDC?

13. △RHS is similar to △ABD in problem 12. The length of $\overline{AB}$ is 6 inches and the length of $\overline{BD}$ is 12 inches. Find the length of $\overline{RH}$ if $\overline{HS}$ is 32 inches. *Lesson 58*

14. Does the change between position 1 and position 2 represent a rotation, reflection, or translation of the figure? *Lesson 59*

15. Give the coordinates for the orange face of the figure on the left side of the grid. *Lesson 60*

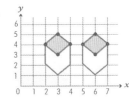

Lesson 61

Looking from a Different Angle

Write the letter of the correct word for each definition.

1. A part of a line that begins at one point and extends without end in one direction
2. A two-dimensional flat surface that extends without end in all directions
3. Lines in a plane that never intersect
4. Lines that meet at a point
5. An exact location in space
6. A straight path of points that extends without end in both directions
7. Lines that are not in the same plane and do not intersect
8. Lines that intersect to form right angles
9. A part of a line between two endpoints
10. Measures greater than 180°
11. Angles that have the same measure
12. Measures greater than 90° but less than 180°

a. point
b. line
c. ray
d. line segment
e. plane
f. intersecting
g. parallel
h. perpendicular
i. skew
j. obtuse angle
k. congruent
l. reflex angle

Use a protractor and a straightedge to construct each angle.

13. An angle having a measure of 90°
14. An angle having a measure of 120°
15. A straight angle
16. An acute angle

Write *true* or *false*.

17. An angle of 120° is an obtuse angle.
18. 80° and 100° are complementary angles.
19. A diameter is a chord.
20. The supplement of a 120° is a 60° angle.
21. A radius is a chord.
22. An isosceles triangle has no congruent sides.
23. Parallel lines can be perpendicular.
24. Congruent angles result if an obtuse angle is bisected.

25. The wings of this *blue and yellow triangle* butterfly represent a
    a. rotation
    b. reflection
    c. translation

Draw a circle. Draw and label each of the following.

26. A radius $\overline{AB}$
27. A diameter $\overline{CD}$
28. A chord $\overline{EF}$

128

Chapter Four Check-Up

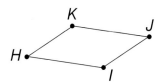
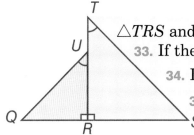

29. Name the figure at the left if $\overline{HI} \parallel \overline{KJ}$ and $\overline{KH} \parallel \overline{IJ}$.
30. If the measure of $\angle K$ is 100°, what is the measure of $\angle J$?
31. What is the sum of the measure of the angles for figure $HIJK$?
32. Is this figure a regular polygon?

$\triangle TRS$ and $\triangle URQ$ are similar triangles.
33. If the measure of $\angle T$ is 45°, what is the measure of $\angle Q$?
34. If $\overline{TR} \cong \overline{RS}$, then $\overline{UR} \cong$ ▦ .
35. Are $\triangle TRS$ and $\triangle URQ$ isosceles triangles?

Draw a coordinate grid.
36. Label each axis.　37. Plot point $A(3,2)$.　38. Plot point $B(0,1)$.
39. Plot point $C(1,5)$.　40. Plot point $D(5,5)$.
41. Connect the points and name the polygon formed.
42. Name the angle with the greatest measure.
43. $\overline{CD}$ is parallel to which axis?

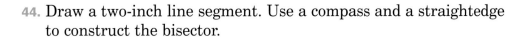
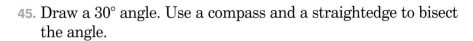

44. Draw a two-inch line segment. Use a compass and a straightedge to construct the bisector.

45. Draw a 30° angle. Use a compass and a straightedge to bisect the angle.

46. In Mrs. Hensen's class, 12 of the students have dogs. Nine students have cats, and 6 of the 24 students have neither a dog nor a cat. How many students have both a dog and a cat? (Hint: Use a diagram.)

Identify the shape of each lighthouse as a square pyramid, hexagonal pyramid, a cylinder, or a cone. (It may be only a portion of the figure, such as only the lower half of a cone.)

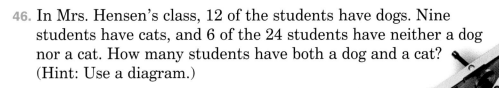

47. 　48. 　49. 　50.

129

Chapter Theme

The theme of chapter 5 is The Heart. God the Father designed mankind in such a manner that the heart and circulatory system are essential for physical life. It should not be a surprise, then, that Christianity is essentially a matter of the heart. God delights in the relationship with those of His children who have completely given their hearts to Him. He longs to share your joys and sorrows as you make Him your trusted confidant. His desire is that your heart is open to receive the unconditional love that comes only from Him. If our faith is only a matter of rules and traditions, we will miss the most loving, heart-warming relationship that will ever be available to us.

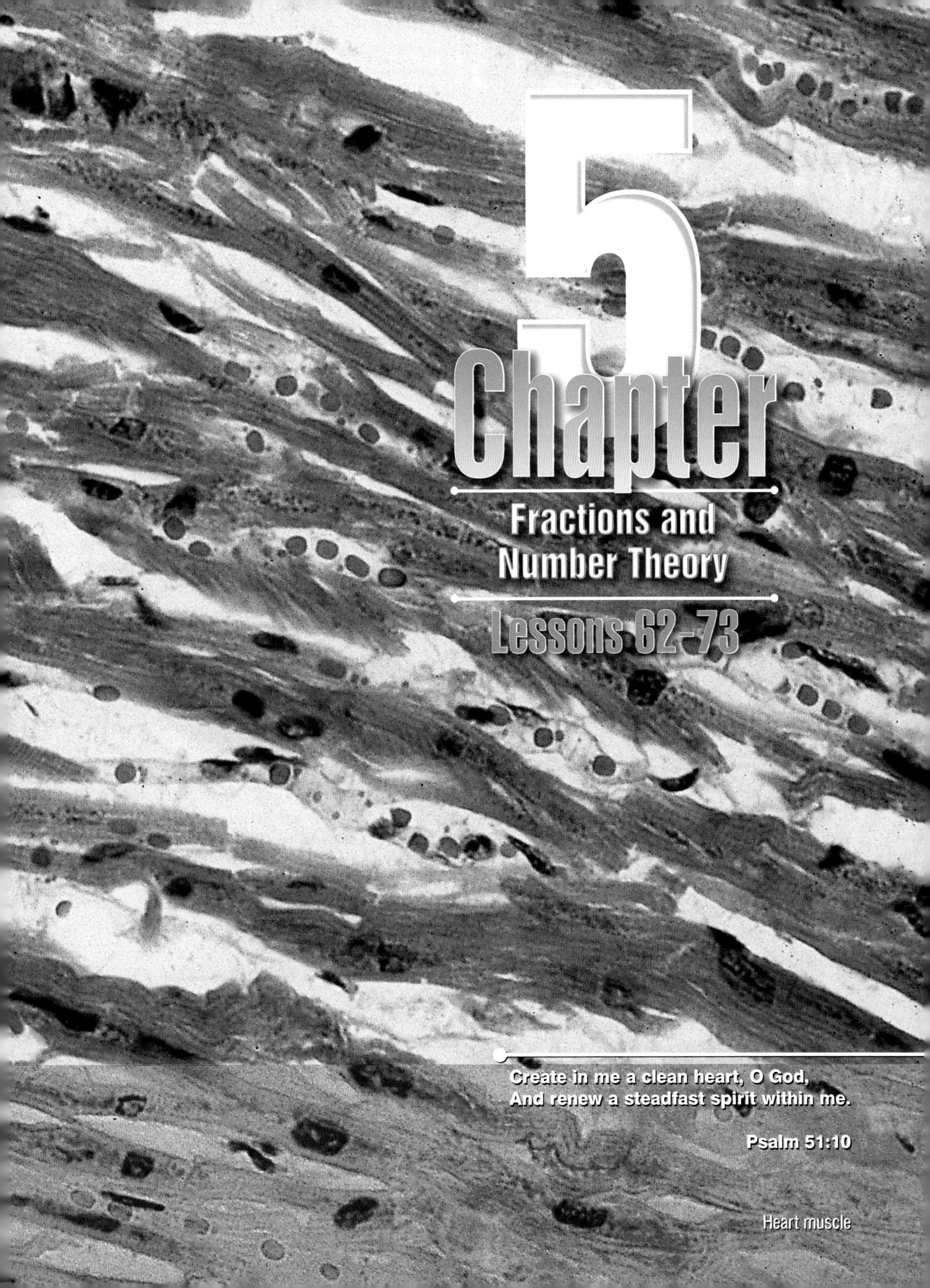

5

Chapter

Fractions and Number Theory

Lessons 62-73

Create in me a clean heart, O God,
And renew a steadfast spirit within me.

Psalm 51:10

Heart muscle

Construct Meaning

"And you shall love the LORD your God with all your heart, with all your soul, with all your mind, and with all your strength." Mark 12:30a

Jesus tells us to love God with everything we have and all of our being, not with just part of our heart or with a fraction of our heart, but with ALL of our heart.

The fraction one-half refers to a part of a whole.

A **fraction** describes part of a whole when the whole is divided into equal parts or part of a set.

The **denominator** tells the total number of equal parts in a whole.

The **numerator** tells the number of equal parts being considered.

numerator

$\frac{1}{2}$

denominator

About two out of five Americans die due to cardiovascular disease.

This fraction involves part of a set.

If two submarine sandwiches are to be divided equally among three students, how much will each student receive?

  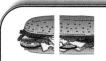

This FRACTION is THE RESULT of division.

Each student will receive $\frac{2}{3}$ of a sandwich.

Multiply or divide the numerator and denominator of a fraction by the same non-zero number to obtain an **equivalent fraction**, a fraction that names the same amount.

$\frac{6}{8}$ $\frac{6 \div 2}{8 \div 2} = \frac{3}{4}$

$\frac{3}{4}$ $\frac{3 \times 2}{4 \times 2} = \frac{6}{8}$ $\frac{3}{4}$ and $\frac{6}{8}$ are equivalent fractions.

 $\frac{2}{3} = \frac{}{9}$ 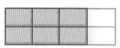 $\frac{2 \times 3}{3 \times 3} = \frac{6}{9}$ $\frac{2}{3}$ and $\frac{6}{9}$ are equivalent fractions.

 Check Understanding

a. $\frac{2 \times }{3 \times } = \frac{}{12}$ b. $\frac{15 \div }{25 \div } = \frac{}{5}$ c. What does the fraction $\frac{9}{10}$ represent?

d. The plane ride from Cape Long to John's Bay is 240 miles. If the plane has traveled two-thirds of the trip, how many miles has the plane flown?

$$\frac{2 \times \square}{3 \times \square} = \frac{\square}{240}$$

Write the fraction in simplest form.

1.

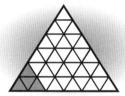

What fraction of the largest triangle is shaded?

2.

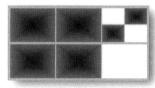

What fraction of the largest rectangle is shaded?

3.

What fraction of the largest square is shaded?

Write an equivalent fraction.

4. $\frac{3}{9}$ **5.** $\frac{6}{10}$ **6.** $\frac{1}{2}$ **7.** $\frac{8}{9}$ **8.** $\frac{11}{12}$ **9.** $\frac{5}{8}$ **10.** $\frac{7}{12}$

Use a diagram to solve.

11. Divide three pies among eight people.

12. Draw and color the four triangles to show how they could be divided into three equal groups.

Find the missing number.

13. $\frac{1}{3} = \frac{\square}{9}$ **14.** $\frac{\square}{4} = \frac{2}{8}$ **15.** $\frac{2}{3} = \frac{4}{\square}$ **16.** $\frac{\square}{45} = \frac{4}{9}$

17. Write two equivalent fractions for the shaded region below.

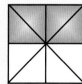

Apply

18. A scale drawing of a ping-pong table is 3 inches wide by 5 inches long. If the actual table is 5 feet 3 inches wide, how long is the table?

19. The trip from Wilmer to Jonestown is 800 miles. If Jerry has driven five-eighths of the trip, how many miles has he driven?

Lesson 63

Construct Meaning

Blood can be thought of as the transporter of life. It delivers necessary nutrients to all parts of the body. The Bible says in Leviticus 17:11a, "For the life of the flesh is in the blood." By taking blood samples, a doctor can tell whether a person is ill and what is causing the illness.

The hospital shuttle stops at the nursing home every 20 minutes, and the bus stops every 15 minutes. If they both begin their routes at the same time, when will they meet at the hospital?

List the multiples of 20 and 15.

Shuttle: 20, 40, 60, 80
Bus: 15, 30, 45, 60, 75

60 is the **least common multiple** of 20 and 15. The **LCM** is the smallest multiple that is common to two or more numbers.

The shuttle and bus meet at the hospital every 60 minutes.

When performing operations with fractions, it is often necessary to find the **least common denominator** (**LCD**), the least common multiple of two or more denominators.

3:	3	6	9	12	15	18
5:	5	10	15	20		

The LCM of 3 and 5 is 15.

$\frac{2}{3}$:	$\frac{2}{3}$	$\frac{4}{6}$	$\frac{6}{9}$	$\frac{8}{12}$	$\frac{10}{15}$
$\frac{4}{5}$:	$\frac{4}{5}$	$\frac{8}{10}$	$\frac{12}{15}$	$\frac{16}{20}$	

The LCD of $\frac{2}{3}$ and $\frac{4}{5}$ is 15.

4:	4	8	12	16	20	24
6:	6	12	18	24	30	36
8:	8	16	24	32	40	48

The LCM of 4, 6, and 8 is 24.

$\frac{3}{4}$:	$\frac{3}{4}$	$\frac{6}{8}$	$\frac{9}{12}$	$\frac{12}{16}$	$\frac{15}{20}$	$\frac{18}{24}$
$\frac{5}{6}$:	$\frac{5}{6}$	$\frac{10}{12}$	$\frac{15}{18}$	$\frac{20}{24}$		
$\frac{1}{8}$:	$\frac{1}{8}$	$\frac{2}{16}$	$\frac{3}{24}$			

The LCD of $\frac{3}{4}$, $\frac{5}{6}$, and $\frac{1}{8}$ is 24.

Check Understanding

Find the least common multiple.
a. 3 and 5   b. 4 and 10   c. 5 and 7

Find the least common denominator.
d. $\frac{3}{4}$ and $\frac{7}{16}$ e. $\frac{6}{9}$ and $\frac{21}{27}$ f. $\frac{2}{3}$ and $\frac{6}{8}$

134   Chapter 5 • *Mathematics Grade 6*

Find the least common multiple.

1. 3 and 7   2. 5, 6, and 10   3. 12, 4, and 8   4. 4, 5, and 8

Find the least common denominator. Use the LCD to rewrite the fractions.

5. $\frac{2}{8}$ and $\frac{1}{5}$ 6. $\frac{1}{2}$ and $\frac{1}{3}$ 7. $\frac{2}{3}$ and $\frac{7}{8}$ 8. $\frac{1}{2}$ and $\frac{3}{15}$

9. $\frac{5}{6}$ $\frac{2}{3}$ $\frac{4}{5}$ 10. $\frac{1}{2}$ $\frac{7}{8}$ $\frac{1}{6}$ 11. $\frac{11}{12}$ $\frac{1}{3}$ $\frac{3}{4}$ 12. $\frac{8}{9}$ $\frac{1}{15}$ $\frac{2}{5}$

13. Write a fraction for each picture and find the LCD of all three fractions.

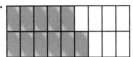
a.

b.

c.

14. The hospital ship makes regular trips between Simbala port and Hardcraft port. Each trip takes 15 days. By car, the trip takes 25 days. How many days will pass before the boat and car meet in port on the same day? How many more trips will the boat have taken than the car?

15. It took Blake $\frac{3}{8}$ of an hour to complete the spelling test and it took Haley $\frac{9}{24}$ of an hour to complete the same test. Did both Blake and Haley complete the test in the same amount of time? Explain.

Challenge

16. Jerry uses $\frac{1}{4}$ of a can of paint every 15 minutes and Patti uses $\frac{2}{5}$ of a can every 15 minutes. Who will be the first one to use up all the paint in their can?

Lesson 64

Construct Meaning

Lines of heritage and parental distinction can be
determined by blood group. The four main blood groups
are A, B, AB, and O. The O blood group, thought to be
from a Celtic line of heritage, is called the universal donor
because O blood can be given to anyone needing blood.
Approximately 44 out of 100 people have O type blood.

$\frac{44}{100}$ ○ ○ shows 44 out of 100 as a fraction.
Simplify the fraction using the greatest
common factor of the numerator and
denominator.

Use prime factorization to find
the GCF.

$$
\begin{array}{r}
5 \\
11 \qquad 5\overline{|25} \\
2\overline{|22} \qquad 2\overline{|50} \\
2\overline{|44} \qquad 2\overline{|100}
\end{array}
$$

$2 \times 2 = 4$
The GCF is 4.

OR

List the factors of each number in
numerical order to find the GCF.

44: 1 **2 4** 11 22 44
100: 1 **2 4** 5 10 20 25 50 100

The GCF is 4.

Next, simplify the fraction by dividing both the numerator and denominator
by the GCF.

$$\frac{44 \div 4}{100 \div 4} = \frac{11}{25}$$

A fraction is in **simplest form** or lowest terms, when
the GCF of the numerator and denominator is 1.

Simplify $\frac{6}{28}$.

$$
\begin{array}{r}
3 \\
2\overline{|6}
\end{array}
\qquad
\begin{array}{r}
7 \\
2\overline{|14} \\
2\overline{|28}
\end{array}
$$

The GCF is 2.

OR

6: 1 2 3 6
28: 1 2 4 7 14 28

The GCF is 2.

$$\frac{6 \div 2}{28 \div 2} = \frac{3}{14}$$

Dividing the numerator and denominator by any common factor until the GCF
is 1 will also simplify a fraction.

$\frac{16}{24}$ $\quad \frac{16 \div 4}{24 \div 4} = \frac{4}{6}$ $\quad \frac{4 \div 2}{6 \div 2} = \frac{2}{3}$

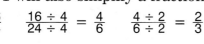

$\frac{16}{24}$ $\qquad \frac{4}{6}$ $\qquad \frac{2}{3}$

Check Understanding

Simplify each fraction.

a. $\frac{9}{12}$
b. $\frac{8}{36}$
c. $\frac{15}{45}$
d. $\frac{16}{48}$

136

Chapter 5 • *Mathematics* Grade 6

Is the fraction in simplest form? Write *yes* or *no*. Simplify all fractions not in simplest form.

1. $\frac{2}{8}$ 2. $\frac{3}{27}$ 3. $\frac{6}{28}$ 4. $\frac{3}{48}$ 5. $\frac{9}{48}$ 6. $\frac{22}{88}$

7. $\frac{6}{35}$ 8. $\frac{18}{26}$ 9. $\frac{9}{41}$ 10. $\frac{33}{39}$ 11. $\frac{15}{57}$ 12. $\frac{30}{65}$

Write the GCF for each pair of denominators.

13. $\frac{1}{6}$ and $\frac{2}{9}$ 14. $\frac{4}{30}$ and $\frac{1}{27}$ 15. $\frac{2}{25}$ and $\frac{1}{35}$

16. $\frac{7}{24}$ and $\frac{5}{32}$ 17. $\frac{4}{21}$ and $\frac{6}{49}$ 18. $\frac{5}{6}$ and $\frac{7}{18}$

Write a fraction represented by the portion of the model indicated by the black lines. Simplify.

19.    20. 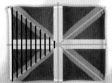   21.    22.

23. Mrs. Brooks is remodeling the guest bedroom in her house. If the bedroom has four windowless walls and one roll of wallpaper will cover $\frac{6}{18}$ of a wall, how many rolls of wallpaper will she need?

24. The chart shows the fraction of the population that has a certain blood group. Write the fractions in simplest form.

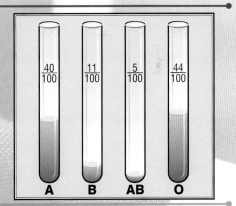

Review

Divide.

1. $0.269\overline{)3.228}$ 2. $0.25\overline{)2.5}$ 3. $12\overline{)28.50}$ 4. $0.8\overline{)20}$

Are the fractions equivalent? Write *yes* or *no*.

5. $\frac{3}{4}$ and $\frac{12}{24}$ 6. $\frac{14}{16}$ and $\frac{7}{8}$ 7. $\frac{2}{3}$ and $\frac{26}{39}$ 8. $\frac{9}{10}$ and $\frac{7}{15}$

 **Construct Meaning**

Blood pressure is a measurement of pressure exerted by heart contractions on blood vessels, arteries, and veins. Blood pressure enables the heart to pump about $4\frac{4}{5}$ quarts of blood in one minute.

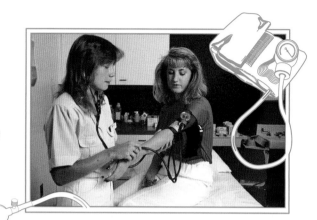

Improper fractions have a numerator equal to or greater than the denominator.

$$\frac{24}{5}$$

Mixed numbers have a whole number part and a fraction part.

$$4\frac{4}{5}$$

$\frac{24}{5}$ and $4\frac{4}{5}$ are equivalent fractions.

Rename the improper fraction $\frac{24}{5}$ as a mixed number.

$$\begin{array}{r} 4\frac{4}{5} \\ 5\overline{)24} \\ \underline{20} \\ 4 \end{array}$$

Divide the denominator into the numerator.

Write the remainder over the divisor as a fraction in the quotient.

Rename the mixed number $4\frac{4}{5}$ as an improper fraction.

$5 \times 4 = 20$ Multiply the denominator by the whole number.

$20 + 4$ Add the numerator.

$\frac{24}{5}$ Write the sum over the denominator.

An improper fraction may be renamed as a whole number: $\frac{45}{9} \longrightarrow 9\overline{)45}\,^{5}$

A whole number may be renamed as an improper fraction. $15 \longrightarrow \frac{15}{1}$

 **Check Understanding**

Write the improper fraction and the mixed number for each example.

a.

b.

Rename as an improper fraction or a mixed number.

c. $\frac{21}{15}$ d. $\frac{8}{5}$ e. $2\frac{6}{8}$ f. $5\frac{1}{4}$

Improper Fractions and Mixed Numbers

 ractice

Write the improper fraction and the mixed number for each example.

1. 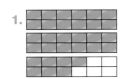　　2. 　　3.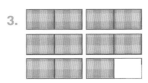

Rename the mixed number as an improper fraction.

4. $1\frac{2}{3}$　　5. $4\frac{1}{2}$　　6. $3\frac{3}{8}$　　7. $8\frac{1}{9}$　　8. $6\frac{5}{6}$

9. $19\frac{2}{5}$　　10. $9\frac{5}{8}$　　11. $6\frac{2}{5}$　　12. $10\frac{1}{3}$　　13. $14\frac{7}{8}$

Rename as a whole number or mixed number.

14. $\frac{7}{4}$　　15. $\frac{17}{8}$　　16. $\frac{36}{4}$　　17. $\frac{44}{5}$　　18. $\frac{91}{10}$

19. $\frac{82}{7}$　　20. $\frac{70}{14}$　　21. $\frac{59}{23}$　　22. $\frac{42}{6}$　　23. $\frac{81}{27}$

Draw a model to represent each number.

24. $2\frac{4}{5}$　　　　25. $3\frac{6}{10}$　　　　26. $\frac{13}{6}$

 pply

27. The recipe calls for $2\frac{1}{2}$ cups of sliced strawberries. David wants to make this recipe, but he can only find the $\frac{1}{2}$-cup measure. How many $\frac{1}{2}$ cups of strawberries should he use?

Milk Shake

$2\frac{1}{2}$ cups vanilla ice cream

$2\frac{1}{2}$ cups sliced strawberries

$\frac{1}{2}$ cup milk

$\frac{1}{4}$ cup honey

28. The East Library ordered four additional bookshelves for the new library books. The shelves are each divided into eight sections and each shelf holds 120 books. If the library ordered 390 books, how many sections (eighths) of the bookshelves are full?

29. The class ordered three large pizzas for their party, but several pieces were uneaten. What was the total amount of pizza that was eaten? Express your answer as a mixed number.

© Copyright 2002 ACSI

139

Construct Meaning

King David is one of many biblical heroes. When choosing David to be king, the Lord said that David was a man after His own heart. I Samuel 16:7b says, "For the LORD does not see as man sees; for man looks at the outward appearance, but the LORD looks at the heart."

It is good to remember that comparing and judging people by outward appearance is not important. Instead, consider who they are in their hearts.

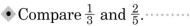

◆ Compare $\frac{1}{3}$ and $\frac{2}{5}$.

Use the least common multiple to find the LCD.

3: 3 6 9 12 15
5: 5 10 15

The LCD is 15.

Write equivalent fractions for $\frac{1}{3}$ and $\frac{2}{5}$ in order to compare.

$$\frac{1 \times 5}{3 \times 5} = \frac{5}{15}$$

$$\frac{1}{3} = \frac{5}{15}$$

$$\frac{2 \times 3}{5 \times 3} = \frac{6}{15}$$

$$\frac{2}{5} = \frac{6}{15}$$

Compare the numerators. $\frac{6}{15} > \frac{5}{15}$

Therefore, $\frac{2}{5} > \frac{1}{3}$

An **inequality** statement shows that two expressions are not equal.

◆ Compare mixed numbers $3\frac{3}{5}$ and $3\frac{2}{7}$.

Compare whole numbers first.
3 = 3

Compare the fractions.
Find the LCD of $\frac{3}{5}$ and $\frac{2}{7}$.

$$\frac{3}{5} = \frac{}{35} \qquad \frac{2}{7} = \frac{}{35}$$

$$\frac{3 \times 7}{5 \times 7} = \frac{21}{35} \qquad \frac{2 \times 5}{7 \times 5} = \frac{10}{35}$$

$$\frac{3}{5} > \frac{2}{7}$$

Compare the mixed numbers.

$$3\frac{3}{5} > 3\frac{2}{7}$$

◆ Order $\frac{2}{3}$, $\frac{5}{6}$, and $\frac{1}{2}$ from least to greatest.

Find the LCD of $\frac{2}{3}$, $\frac{5}{6}$, and $\frac{1}{2}$ by using the LCM of 3, 6, and 2.

Write equivalent fractions for $\frac{2}{3}$, $\frac{5}{6}$, and $\frac{1}{2}$ in order to compare them.

$$\frac{2}{3} = \frac{4}{6} \qquad \frac{5}{6} \text{ is not changed.} \qquad \frac{1}{2} = \frac{3}{6}$$

Therefore, $\frac{1}{2} < \frac{2}{3} < \frac{5}{6}$

◆ Order mixed numbers by comparing whole numbers, then fractions.

Use mental math to order $2\frac{1}{9}$, $2\frac{2}{3}$, and $2\frac{1}{6}$.
The whole numbers are equal.
Which fraction is greatest? least?

$$2\frac{2}{3} > \qquad >$$

140

Complete each inequality statement using > or <.

a. $\frac{5}{6}$ ⬚ $\frac{3}{5}$

b. $3\frac{1}{6}$ ⬚ $3\frac{2}{9}$

c. $1\frac{1}{7}$ ⬚ $\frac{9}{4}$

d. $9\frac{1}{16}$ ⬚ $8\frac{9}{16}$

Order from least to greatest.

e. $\frac{5}{6}$ $\frac{1}{2}$ $\frac{3}{4}$

f. $5\frac{3}{4}$ $5\frac{2}{3}$ $4\frac{9}{10}$ $5\frac{5}{6}$

g. $\frac{11}{4}$ 2 $\frac{9}{4}$

Write >, < or =.

1. $\frac{5}{6}$ ⬚ $\frac{4}{5}$

2. $\frac{8}{16}$ ⬚ $\frac{1}{2}$

3. $\frac{1}{2}$ ⬚ $\frac{2}{9}$

4. $\frac{3}{4}$ ⬚ $1\frac{11}{16}$

5. $\frac{4}{7}$ ⬚ $\frac{7}{12}$

6. $2\frac{14}{15}$ ⬚ $2\frac{12}{15}$

7. $6\frac{4}{9}$ ⬚ $7\frac{1}{7}$

8. $\frac{7}{8}$ ⬚ $\frac{5}{6}$

9. $3\frac{2}{10}$ ⬚ $\frac{13}{4}$

10. $\frac{12}{7}$ ⬚ $1\frac{10}{14}$

11. $\frac{26}{9}$ ⬚ $2\frac{11}{12}$

12. $9\frac{5}{10}$ ⬚ $9\frac{1}{2}$

Order from least to greatest.

13. $\frac{1}{4}$ $\frac{5}{12}$ $\frac{1}{6}$

14. $\frac{2}{9}$ $\frac{1}{3}$ $\frac{5}{6}$

15. $\frac{1}{2}$ $\frac{5}{6}$ $\frac{3}{4}$ $\frac{5}{8}$

16. $1\frac{2}{3}$ $1\frac{1}{2}$ $1\frac{3}{4}$

17. $2\frac{5}{8}$ $\frac{16}{3}$ $2\frac{1}{4}$

18. $\frac{9}{2}$ $4\frac{2}{3}$ $\frac{6}{7}$ $1\frac{9}{10}$

19. Abigail is cleaning out the kitchen drawer. She found the following measuring cups: 1 cup, $\frac{1}{3}$ cup, $\frac{1}{8}$ cup, $\frac{1}{2}$ cup, $\frac{2}{3}$ cup, and $\frac{1}{4}$ cup. To stack them within each other, she needs to put them in order with the biggest on the bottom. Order the cups from the one that holds the greatest amount to the one that holds the least amount.

20. Leslie and Jennie decided to meet each other at the park. Leslie rode her bike two-fifths of a mile and Jennie rode her bike three-tenths of a mile. Who rode her bike the greater distance?

21. At the ice-cream social the first day of school, the students ate $4\frac{7}{8}$ gallons of chocolate ice cream, $4\frac{3}{5}$ gallons of peppermint ice cream, and $\frac{29}{6}$ gallons of vanilla ice cream. Did the students eat more chocolate, vanilla, or peppermint ice cream?

Construct Meaning

The heart is one of the most important organs in the body. The size of your heart is about the size of your fist. Your average resting heart rate is about 72 beats per minute.

The goal of aerobic exercise is for your actual heart rate to approach your "target" heart rate. To determine the target heart rate on the chart below, multiply the Maximum Heart Rate (MHR) by 0.8.

MHR	
Age	Beats Per Minute
11	209
12	208
13	207

The target heart rate for an eleven-year-old:

$$\begin{array}{r} 209 \\ \times\ \ 0.8 \\ \hline 167.2 \end{array}\text{ beats per minute}$$

Practice

Write your answer in simplest form.

1. Chaz has a sister who is thirteen years old. What is her target heart rate? (Round to the nearest whole number.) If her pulse is 20 beats in ten seconds, is she meeting her goal?

2. A wrist heart rate monitor costs $95.50. Randy's mother will pay half of the cost and Randy will make two equal monthly payments. How much will Randy pay each month? Round your answer to the nearest cent.

3. Mr. Rocker spends $\frac{3}{5}$ of his day resting, $\frac{1}{8}$ of his day doing strenuous exercise, and $\frac{6}{24}$ of his day working at the office. What does Mr. Rocker spend the least amount of time doing?

4. Hans needed to cut a $\frac{3}{5}$-yard piece of wood from a piece that measured $\frac{5}{6}$ of a yard. Was his piece long enough to make the cut?

5. Mr. Stephens will cut five boards to make a flower box. The lengths of the boards are $\frac{1}{8}$ yard, $\frac{3}{6}$ yard, $\frac{3}{8}$ yard, $\frac{2}{3}$ yard, and $\frac{1}{4}$ yard. List the lengths of the boards from least to greatest.

6. During exercise, a fifteen-year-old's target heart rate is about 27 beats for every ten seconds. How many times would a fifteen-year-old's heart beat in 15 minutes if it remained at the target heart rate?

7. A basement room is being fitted with sound-proofing panels. If each panel covers $\frac{12}{15}$ of one wall and $\frac{12}{15}$ of the ceiling, how many panels will be needed to cover four walls and one ceiling?

8. Three spinners of different colors were made for the sixth grade statistics unit. Write four simplified fractions expressing the total fraction of colors.

   a. red   b. blue

   c. green   d. yellow

9. The mighty Pharaoh, Ketedut II, wrote in his will to divide his fortune among his four sons. Kabo received $\frac{2}{18}$, Ceiro received $\frac{6}{36}$, Petro received $\frac{2}{3}$, and Zelo received $\frac{1}{18}$ of the fortune. Who received the greatest part of the fortune?

10. The Pharaoh's younger brother Dutkamen worked as a chariot racer for $\frac{9}{12}$ of his life, a merchant for $\frac{6}{48}$ of his life, and a sculptor for $\frac{2}{16}$ of his life. For which occupations did he work an equal amount of time?

11. A set of measuring cups contains a $\frac{1}{4}$, $\frac{1}{3}$, $\frac{1}{2}$, and one-cup measure. Julee has to measure out $\frac{6}{8}$ cup of flour. How many of which measuring cup(s) should she use?

12. The hiking store has a variety of 32 pairs of socks. Eight are silk, six are wool, and 18 are cotton. What fraction of the pairs are cotton?

13. Victor takes three minutes to run one lap, Cindy takes five minutes to run one lap, and Kaleb runs one lap in six minutes. If each person started at the same time, how many minutes will elapse before they are all at the same point on the track?

14. Lance ran $\frac{4}{9}$ lap in two minutes, Jon ran $1\frac{2}{3}$ laps in two minutes, and Jeff ran $\frac{3}{2}$ laps in the same amount of time. Who ran at the fastest pace?

Lesson 68

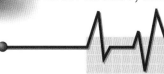

Long-lasting heart disease, such as coronary artery disease and multiple heart attacks, or viral infection may cause irreversible damage to the heart. People who cannot be treated through any other procedure may be candidates for heart transplants. The first heart transplant was performed in 1967. In 1999, there were 2,184 heart transplants.

Bleeding Heart Flower

If 0.7, or seven-tenths, of an individual's heart is damaged, that person may undergo a heart transplant.

The decimal 0.7 can be written as a fraction in simplest form.

$0.7 = \frac{7}{10}$ Since 0.7 is <u>seven-tenths</u>, use 10 as the denominator.

    $\frac{7}{10}$ is shaded.

The decimal 0.4 can also be written as a fraction in simplest form.

$0.4 = \frac{4}{10}$ The GCF of 4 and 10 is 2.

$$\frac{4 \div 2}{10 \div 2} = \frac{2}{5}$$

$$0.4 = \frac{2}{5}$$

 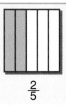

$\frac{4}{10}$ $\frac{2}{5}$

Rewrite 2.875 as a fraction.

- First write the decimal as a mixed number.

  $2\frac{875}{1,000}$ Since 0.875 goes to the thousandths place, use 1,000 as the denominator.

- Simplify the fraction.

  $\frac{875}{1,000}$ The GCF of 875 and 1,000 is 125.

  $$\frac{875 \div 125}{1,000 \div 125} = \frac{7}{8}$$

$$2.875 = 2\frac{875}{1,000} = 2\frac{7}{8}$$

Check Understanding

Write each decimal as a fraction in simplest form.

a. 0.3   b. 0.375   c. 2.6   d. 1.125   e. 0.2

f. 0.16   g. 0.1   h. 0.875   i. 0.6   j. 1.5

 **Practice**

1. $0.2 = \frac{2}{10} = \frac{1}{}$

2. $0.8 = \frac{8}{} = \frac{}{5}$

3. $0.625 = \frac{625}{} = \frac{}{8}$

Write each answer in simplest form.

4. 0.125 of a figure is shaded. What fraction of the figure is shaded?

5. 0.03 of a figure is shaded. What fraction of the figure is shaded?

6. 2.4 of a figure is shaded. What fraction of the figure is shaded?

Write as a fraction or mixed number in simplest form.

7. 0.6 8. 0.005 9. 0.9 10. 1.97 11. 0.16

12. 6.65 13. 6.001 14. 4.4 15. 4.875 16. 1.125

Write as a decimal and a fraction or mixed number in simplest form.

17. Two and twelve-hundredths 18. One and six-tenths

19. Three and six hundred twenty-five thousandths

 Apply

20. In one month, 0.375 of the letters received by the international office were from foreign sites. What fraction of the total letters does the number represent?

21. Mr. Gailey received eight letters while he was in the hospital. He had two heart attacks. One damaged 0.125 of his heart and the other damaged another 0.1875 of his heart. What fraction of his heart was damaged by both heart attacks?

22. Mrs. Nichols has a package of ground meat that weighs 1.27 pounds and another weighing 0.98 pounds. If she plans to use $1\frac{1}{2}$ pounds to make tacos, will she need to open both packages? State as a fraction the amount of meat she will have left after making the tacos.

 Review

1. Name two parallel lines.
2. If $\angle CAB$ measures 33°, what is the measurement of $\angle ACB$?
3. Name two perpendicular lines.
4. Classify $\triangle ABC$ by two names.

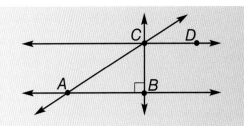

Construct Meaning

Your blood contains three types of cells: red blood cells, white blood cells, and platelets. The red blood cells carry oxygen throughout the body. About nine-tenths of your blood is made up of red blood cells.

Fractions with denominators that are powers of 10 are easily expressed as decimals.

Nine-tenths is the word form. $\frac{9}{10}$ is the fraction. 0.9 is the decimal. $\frac{9}{10} = 0.9$

Other Examples

75 hundredths $= \frac{75}{100} = 0.75$

309 thousandths $= \frac{309}{1,000} = 0.309$

Fractions with denominators that are factors of 10, 100, or 1,000 may be renamed and expressed as a decimal.

Multiply to find an equivalent fraction having 10, 100, or 1,000 as the denominator.

$\frac{2}{5} = \frac{}{10}$

$\frac{2 \times 2}{5 \times 2} = \frac{4}{10}$

$\frac{2}{5} = \frac{4}{10} = 0.4$

$\frac{11}{20} = \frac{}{100}$

$\frac{11 \times 5}{20 \times 5} = \frac{55}{100}$

$\frac{11}{20} = \frac{55}{100} = 0.55$

$\frac{25}{125} = \frac{}{1,000}$

$\frac{25 \times 8}{125 \times 8} = \frac{200}{1,000}$

$\frac{25}{125} = \frac{200}{1,000} = 0.200$

If the denominator is not a factor of 10, 100, or 1,000, divide the numerator by the denominator.

$\frac{7}{8}$ means $7 \div 8$.

$\frac{7}{8} = 0.875$

$$\begin{array}{r} 0.875 \\ 8\overline{)7.000} \\ \underline{64} \\ 60 \\ \underline{56} \\ 40 \\ \underline{40} \\ 0 \end{array}$$

You may also use a calculator.

Check Understanding

Write each fraction as a decimal.

a. $\frac{27}{1,000}$ b. $\frac{1}{2}$ c. $\frac{5}{16}$ d. $\frac{7}{100}$ e. $\frac{1}{5}$

 **Practice**

Write each fraction as a decimal.

1. $\frac{33}{100}$
2. $\frac{591}{1,000}$
3. $\frac{3}{8}$
4. $\frac{1}{10}$
5. $\frac{3}{5}$

 **USING A CALCULATOR**

6. $\frac{5}{8}$
7. $\frac{3}{4}$
8. $\frac{7}{10}$
9. $\frac{3}{1,000}$
10. $\frac{41}{100}$

Write each fraction as a decimal by using an equivalent fraction with a denominator of 10 or 100.

11. $\frac{31}{50}$
12. $\frac{9}{20}$
13. $\frac{13}{25}$
14. $\frac{1}{2}$
15. $\frac{4}{5}$

Choose the decimal in the box that matches the fraction.

16. $\frac{3}{16}$
17. $\frac{12}{15}$
18. $\frac{18}{48}$

19. $\frac{14}{100}$
20. $\frac{21}{24}$
21. $\frac{1}{1,000}$

Decimal Matches	
0.375	0.1875
0.8	0.875
0.001	0.14

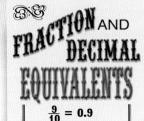 **FRACTION AND DECIMAL EQUIVALENTS**

$\frac{9}{10}$ = 0.9

$\frac{7}{8}$ = 0.875

$\frac{4}{5}$ = 0.8

$\frac{3}{4}$ = 0.75

$\frac{7}{10}$ = 0.7

$\frac{5}{8}$ = 0.625

$\frac{3}{5}$ = 0.6

$\frac{1}{2}$ = 0.5

$\frac{2}{5}$ = 0.4

$\frac{3}{8}$ = 0.375

$\frac{3}{10}$ = 0.3

$\frac{1}{4}$ = 0.25

$\frac{1}{5}$ = 0.2

$\frac{1}{8}$ = 0.125

$\frac{1}{10}$ = 0.1

$\frac{1}{20}$ = 0.05

$\frac{1}{25}$ = 0.04

 Apply

22. In one year, 78 of the 208 donations received by the Red Cross exceeded $25,600. Write the fraction of donations as a decimal.

23. Conrad, the receptionist at the Red Cross, spends $\frac{1}{5}$ of his day reading, $\frac{3}{10}$ of his day typing, $\frac{3}{8}$ of his day answering phones, and $\frac{1}{8}$ of his day eating. Use the table at the left to determine the decimal equivalency of each of Conrad's daily activities.

24. About $\frac{3}{50}$ of blood contains platelets and $\frac{3}{2,000}$ contains white blood cells. Write the total platelet and white blood cell content of blood as a decimal.

25. Esteban spent $\frac{5}{8}$ of his monthly paycheck on medical expenses, $\frac{1}{5}$ on food, $\frac{1}{10}$ on clothing, and $\frac{1}{20}$ on a new tire for his car. Use the table at the left to change the fractions to decimals. Write as a decimal the part of Esteban's paycheck that remained.

Lesson 70

 **Construct Meaning**

Let the words of my mouth and the meditation of my heart
Be acceptable in Your sight,
O LORD, my strength and my redeemer. Psalm 19:14

King David wrote this psalm when he opened himself to the Lord and allowed Him to perform "heart surgery" to purify him.

About 1.4 open heart surgery procedures begin every minute. 1.4 is an example of a **terminating decimal** where the digits end on the right.

$$1.4 = 1\frac{2}{5}$$

$$\frac{2}{5} \rightarrow 5\overline{)2.0} = 0.4$$
$$\underline{2.0}$$
$$0$$

A terminating decimal results when the numerator of a fraction is divided by the denominator leaving a zero remainder.

Use pencil and paper to divide 2 by 5. Check your work with a calculator.

All fractions can be expressed as decimals, but many will not be terminating decimals. What happens if you divide 1 by 3 using pencil and paper?

The decimal equivalent of $\frac{1}{3}$ is an example of a repeating decimal. The digits of a **repeating decimal** from some point on will repeat in a pattern. A repeating decimal results when the numerator of a fraction is divided by the denominator and a remainder of zero cannot be obtained.

$$3\overline{)1.000} = 0.333$$
$$\underline{9}$$
$$10$$
$$\underline{9}$$
$$10$$
$$\underline{9}$$
$$1$$

$$\frac{1}{3} = 0.\overline{3}$$

A bar is placed over the digit that repeats.

Use your calculator to find the decimal equivalent of $\frac{1}{12}$.

1 ÷ 1 2 = **0.083333**

The quotient is written $0.08\overline{3}$.

What pattern is seen in the digits of the decimal equivalent of $\frac{3}{13}$?

3 ÷ 1 3 = **0.23076923**

The calculator truncates, or shortens, the answer of 0.230769230769. . . .

$$\frac{3}{13} = 0.\overline{230769}$$

148

Terminating and Repeating Decimals

a. Is the bar placed over all the digits of a repeating decimal?

b. Explain the relationship of a zero remainder to a terminating decimal and to a repeating decimal.

c. If $\frac{1}{3} = 0.\overline{3}$, what is the decimal equivalent of $\frac{2}{3}$?

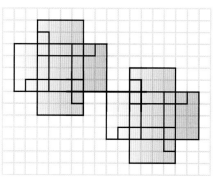

Repeating decimal pattern $0.\overline{71534}$

Practice

Write *terminating* or *repeating* for each decimal or decimal equivalent.

1. $\frac{1}{10}$ 2. $4\frac{1}{8}$ 3. 8.016 4. $\frac{5}{11}$ 5. $\frac{1}{2}$

6. $0.1\overline{6}$ 7. $1\frac{1}{3}$ 8. $4\frac{84}{125}$ 9. $\frac{9}{11}$ 10. 21.12516

Rewrite the decimal or decimal equivalent and use a bar to show a repeating decimal.

11. 0.376376 12. 0.623491348 13. 0.089999 14. $\frac{1}{9}$

15. $\frac{3}{125}$ 16. 0.44444 17. 6.62346234 18. 0.00151515

USING A CALCULATOR

Express each fraction or mixed number as a decimal.

19. $\frac{5}{7}$ 20. $2\frac{3}{16}$ 21. $\frac{8}{11}$ 22. $6\frac{1}{12}$

23. $\frac{5}{18}$ 24. $\frac{7}{12}$ 25. $\frac{10}{33}$ 26. $9\frac{2}{5}$

27. $7\frac{1}{18}$ 28. $\frac{3}{8}$ 29. $3\frac{24}{25}$ 30. $\frac{3}{10}$

31. $4\frac{1}{6}$ 32. $\frac{6}{7}$ 33. $\frac{9}{11}$ 34. $\frac{76}{37}$

Repeating decimal pattern $0.\overline{376}$

35. $4\frac{1}{8}$ 36. $\frac{47}{18}$ 37. $\frac{2}{3}$ 38. $\frac{4,766}{3,333}$

Review

1. Using a ruler, draw a line segment that is four inches long. Using a compass and straightedge, construct a perpendicular bisector of that line.

2. Using a protractor and a straightedge, construct an angle having a measure of 80°. Bisect the angle using a compass and straightedge.

Lesson 71

 Construct Meaning

But those who wait on the LORD
Shall renew their strength;
They shall mount up with wings like eagles,
They shall run and not be weary,
They shall walk and not faint. Isaiah 40:31

In order for a heart to be effective at pumping all
of the blood components, it needs to be exercised.

At the JayCee Relays track meet, T-shirts sold for $12 each. By the end of the day the
JayCees collected $2,400. How many T-shirts were sold? Write an equation to show
this relationship. Use a letter to represent the number of T-shirts sold.

$$y \quad \times \quad \$12 \quad = \quad \$2,400$$

| number of T-shirts sold | price per T-shirt | total money collected |

Notice that the unknown, y, is being <u>multiplied</u>.

To solve for y, perform the <u>inverse operation</u>, <u>division</u>.

To keep both sides of the equation equal, the same operation must be done
on both sides.

$y \times 12 = 2,400$ — Write the inverse operation
of division in fraction form.

$\dfrac{y \times 12}{12} = \dfrac{2,400}{12}$

$y \times \dfrac{12}{12} = \dfrac{2,400}{12}$ — The operation of division is
performed on both sides of
the equation.

$y \times 1 = \dfrac{2,400}{12}$

$y = \dfrac{2,400}{12}$

$y = 200$

Check the answer by substituting
200 in place of y.

$$y \times 12 = 2,400$$
$$200 \times 12 = 2,400$$
$$2,400 = 2,400 \quad ✓$$

Solve for t if $t \div 8 = 63$.

$\dfrac{t}{8} = 63$

$\dfrac{8 \times t}{8} = 63 \times 8$

$\dfrac{8}{8} \times t = 63 \times 8$

$1 \times t = 63 \times 8$

$t = 504$

Rewrite $t \div 8$ as a fraction.

Because t is being <u>divided</u> by 8, the
<u>inverse operation</u> of <u>multiplication</u>
is used.

The operation of multiplication is
performed on both sides of the equation.

Check the answer
by substituting
504 for t.

$\dfrac{t}{8} = 63$

$\dfrac{504}{8} = 63$

$63 = 63 \quad ✓$

150

Chapter 5 • *Mathematics* Grade 6

Explore Algebra: Inverse Operations

 **Check Understanding**

Solve for the unknown. Check your answer by substituting the correct value.

a. $b \times 14 = 350$ b. $20 \times a = 1{,}240$ c. $y \times 29 = 870$

d. $m \div 12 = 14$ e. $10 = \frac{n}{35}$ f. $\frac{t}{18} = 80$

 **Practice**

Solve and check.

1. $\$50 \times a = \$350$ 2. $30 \times c = 2{,}400$ 3. $80 \times b = 48{,}000$

4. $r \div 6 = 26$ 5. $\frac{s}{20} = 20$ 6. $y \div 3 = 27$

7. $\frac{t}{70} = 70$ 8. $22 \times f = 176$ 9. $n \times 9 = 144$

 Apply

10. At the state track meet there are 112 people in the 400-meter dash. They will be divided into 14 heats. Let r represent the number of runners in each heat. Copy the equation and solve for r.
$$\frac{112}{r} = 14$$

11. Let g represent the number of soccer games that Ellenore played. She played a total of 186 minutes and averaged 31 minutes a game. Copy the equation and solve for g.
$$31 \times g = 186$$

 Review

Write the letter of the correct word for each definition.

1. A parallelogram with four congruent sides
2. A polyhedron with two congruent bases and rectangular sides
3. Two angles forming a staight angle of 180°
4. A chord that passes through the center of a circle
5. An angle that measures less than 90°
6. Figures with the same shape

a. prism
b. acute
c. similar
d. supplementary
e. rhombus
f. diameter

 Construct Meaning

How precious is Your lovingkindness, O God!
Therefore the children of men put their trust under the
shadow of Your wings.
They are abundantly satisfied with the fullness of
Your house. Psalm 36:7–8a

A **prime number** has exactly two
factors, one and itself.
Five is a prime number.

1 × 5   *5 × 1*

A **composite number** has
more than two factors.
Six is a composite number.

1 × 6   *6 × 1*

2 × 3
3 × 2

The *proper factors* of a number include all of its
factors except the number itself. Composite
numbers are categorized by their proper factors.

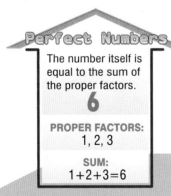

Perfect Numbers
The number itself is
equal to the sum of
the proper factors.
6
PROPER FACTORS:
1, 2, 3
SUM:
1+2+3=6

Abundant Numbers
The proper factor
sum is greater than
the number itself.
20
PROPER FACTORS:
1, 2, 4, 5, 10
SUM:
1+2+4+5+10=22
22 > 20

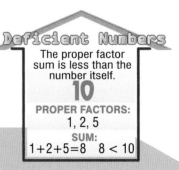

Deficient Numbers
The proper factor
sum is less than the
number itself.
10
PROPER FACTORS:
1, 2, 5
SUM:
1+2+5=8   8 < 10

 Check Understanding

Write the proper factors of each number using every number in the box one time.

a. 18   b. 32   c. 65   d. 76   e. 22

38	19	4	3	1
1	6	16	1	2
2	8	13	4	2
1	9	11	5	2	1

Write *perfect*, *abundant*, or *deficient* for each number.

f. 4   g. 15   h. 28   i. 40   j. 54

152

Chapter Five Study Guide

1. Write an equivalent fraction for $\frac{3}{8}$. *Lesson 62*

2. Write the least common multiple of 4, 5, and 10. *Lesson 63*

3. Rewrite the fractions $\frac{3}{7}$, $\frac{2}{3}$, and $\frac{4}{21}$ using the least common denominator. *Lesson 63*

4. Simplify $\frac{10}{24}$. *Lesson 64*

5. Write simplified fractions for the shaded portion of each model. *Lesson 64*

   a.   b.    c.    d.

6. Rename as a whole or mixed number. *Lesson 65*

   a. $\frac{16}{2}$ b. $\frac{82}{9}$ c. $\frac{18}{4}$ d. $\frac{115}{14}$

7. Order from greatest to least. $\frac{3}{8}$ $\frac{9}{10}$ $\frac{4}{5}$ $\frac{1}{2}$ *Lesson 66*

8. Write >, < or =. *Lesson 66*

   a. $\frac{2}{8}$ ⬚ $\frac{1}{4}$ b. $3\frac{2}{10}$ ⬚ $\frac{13}{4}$ c. $\frac{3}{10}$ ⬚ $\frac{1}{9}$ d. $\frac{25}{52}$ ⬚ $\frac{61}{104}$

9. During the All Sports Day at school, the students consumed $7\frac{7}{8}$ gallons of water, $7\frac{3}{5}$ gallons of sport drink, and $\frac{37}{5}$ gallons of juice. Did the students drink more water, sport drink, or juice? *Lesson 67*

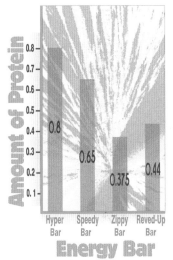

10. Using the table at the left, write each amount of protein per energy bar as a fraction. *Lesson 68*

11. Write each fraction as a decimal. *Lesson 69*

    a. $\frac{12}{25}$ b. $\frac{16}{20}$ c. $\frac{3}{5}$ d. $\frac{7}{8}$

12. Write each fraction as a repeating decimal. *Lesson 70*

    a. $\frac{6}{14}$ b. $\frac{8}{15}$ c. $\frac{15}{22}$ d. $\frac{2}{3}$

Lesson 73

Fraction Frontiers

Write the fraction represented by the shaded portion of each example.

1.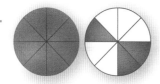
2.
3.

Find the missing number.

4. $\frac{2}{5} = \frac{8}{}$

5. $\frac{5}{9} = \frac{}{27}$

6. $\frac{6}{25} = \frac{24}{}$

7. $\frac{12}{31} = \frac{60}{}$

Find the LCM.

8. 5 and 35

9. 12 and 18

10. 9 and 27

11. 8 and 48

Find the GCF.

12. 9 and 30

13. 48 and 16

14. 36 and 24

15. 6 and 8

Day	Inches	Day	Inches
Monday	$\frac{1}{8}$	Thursday	$\frac{1}{3}$
Tuesday	$\frac{3}{4}$	Friday	$\frac{2}{3}$
Wednesday	$\frac{6}{8}$		

16. During a workweek in February, it snowed every day. Use the table to see if equal amounts of snow fell on any of the days. Explain.

Simplify.

17. $\frac{6}{9}$

18. $\frac{15}{36}$

19. $\frac{27}{90}$

20. $\frac{18}{24}$

21. $\frac{16}{32}$

Rename as an improper fraction.

22. $1\frac{3}{4}$

23. $4\frac{2}{7}$

24. $6\frac{8}{9}$

25. $2\frac{14}{15}$

26. $3\frac{3}{25}$

27. Marty walks to school every weekday. He chooses between the three paths shown on the diagram. Which path is the shortest route?

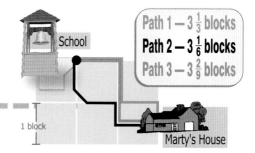

Path 1 — $3\frac{1}{3}$ blocks
Path 2 — $3\frac{1}{6}$ blocks
Path 3 — $3\frac{2}{9}$ blocks

School

1 block

Marty's House

Trust in the LORD with all your heart,
And lean not on your own understanding;
In all your ways acknowledge Him,
And He shall direct your paths. Proverbs 3:5–6

Rename as a mixed or whole number.

28. $\frac{28}{5}$ 29. $\frac{39}{13}$ 30. $\frac{52}{2}$ 31. $\frac{63}{4}$ 32. $\frac{37}{9}$

Write >, < or =.

33. $\frac{3}{8}$ ⬚ $\frac{2}{5}$ 34. $\frac{5}{6}$ ⬚ $\frac{7}{9}$ 35. $\frac{4}{7}$ ⬚ $\frac{48}{84}$ 36. $\frac{16}{23}$ ⬚ $\frac{8}{9}$

Write the fractions from least to greatest.

37. $\frac{3}{4}$ $\frac{5}{8}$ $\frac{2}{3}$ 38. $\frac{7}{9}$ $\frac{4}{5}$ $\frac{2}{3}$ 39. $\frac{7}{10}$ $\frac{1}{3}$ $\frac{1}{2}$

40. The hardware store has 36 bins of screws, 2 bins are filled with $\frac{3}{4}$-inch screws. 12 bins are filled with $\frac{1}{2}$-inch screws. 8 bins are filled with $\frac{1}{3}$-inch screws and 14 bins are filled with $\frac{1}{4}$-inch screws.

   a. What fraction of the bins are filled with $\frac{1}{2}$-inch screws?

   b. What fraction of the bins are filled with $\frac{1}{3}$-inch screws?

Write each decimal as a fraction in simplest form.

41. 0.9   42. 0.55   43. 0.625   44. $0.\overline{3}$

45. Jerry was making lemonade from frozen concentrate. The directions said to empty one can of the concentrate into a one-gallon container and add three cans of water. What fraction of the lemonade is water?

46. The tickets for the motocross competition were $16 each. The total value of the tickets sold was $56,000. Let p equal the number of people in attendance at the competition. Write a multiplication equation and solve for p.

Solve for the unknown factor.

47. $y \times 8 = 184$ 48. $\frac{s}{17} = 5$

Write each fraction as a decimal rounded to the nearest hundredth.

49. $\frac{9}{32}$ 50. $\frac{4}{7}$

Chapter Theme

In chapter 6, we consider the theme of Attitude and Friendship. We are to have an attitude that is pleasing to God, putting us in a position to be His friend as well as a friend to others. Jesus said that we are His friends if we obey Him. His life is the perfect model of a friend who serves, loves, supports, and forgives. In the twelfth chapter of Romans, Paul explains what it means to be "transformed by the renewing of your mind." We become more like Christ when we are able to love without hypocrisy, show brotherly love, and bless those who persecute us. The challenges of sharing the triumphs and defeats of others, and of having an attitude of humility are given in Romans 12:15–16. Read the entire chapter and ask God to give you the attitude that a friend of Jesus would have.

6 Chapter

Addition and Subtraction of Fractions

Lessons 74–82

Let this mind be in you which was also in Christ Jesus.

Philippians 2:5

Lesson 74

 Construct Meaning

Friends share with each other what is happening in their lives. They also share tangible items such as food, books, and toys. In Bible times Abraham believed in God and was called His friend.

The study of fractions can help you know how to share evenly. Your teacher will give you fraction circles with which to add and subtract.

Look at the circle that is labeled "Work Mat." What fraction of the circle is each of the sections?

Solve $\frac{1}{12} + \frac{5}{12}$. Take a $\frac{1}{12}$-piece and place it on the work mat. How can $\frac{5}{12}$ be represented? Place five $\frac{1}{12}$-pieces next to the $\frac{1}{12}$-piece. How many $\frac{1}{12}$-pieces are there? The sum is $\frac{6}{12}$, which can be simplified to $\frac{1}{2}$.

Solve $\frac{1}{4} + \frac{1}{12}$. Place a $\frac{1}{4}$-piece and a $\frac{1}{12}$-piece next to each other on the work mat. How many sections of the work mat does this cover? Since each of the sections represents $\frac{1}{12}$, the sum is $\frac{4}{12}$, which can be simplified to $\frac{1}{3}$.

Solve $\frac{2}{3} + \frac{1}{4}$. Place two $\frac{1}{3}$-pieces and a $\frac{1}{4}$-piece side by side. How many sections of the work mat are covered? Since each of the sections represents $\frac{1}{12}$, the sum is $\frac{11}{12}$.

Solve $\frac{1}{2} - \frac{1}{6}$. Place a $\frac{1}{2}$-piece on the work mat. As it is, $\frac{1}{6}$ cannot be removed from $\frac{1}{2}$. How many $\frac{1}{6}$-pieces does it take to make the $\frac{1}{2}$-piece? Replace the $\frac{1}{2}$-piece with three $\frac{1}{6}$-pieces. Now a $\frac{1}{6}$-piece can be removed. Two $\frac{1}{6}$-pieces are left. The answer is $\frac{2}{6}$, which can be simplified to $\frac{1}{3}$.

Solve $1 - \frac{1}{3}$. Think of the whole work mat as 1. How many $\frac{1}{3}$-pieces are needed to cover the whole work mat? Cover the work mat with three $\frac{1}{3}$-pieces. Subtracting $\frac{1}{3}$ means taking away a $\frac{1}{3}$-piece. How many $\frac{1}{3}$-pieces remain? The answer is $\frac{2}{3}$.

Use your fraction circles to solve. Write your answer in simplest form or lowest terms.

a. $\frac{7}{12} + \frac{1}{12}$ b. $\frac{1}{2} + \frac{1}{3}$ c. $\frac{2}{3} - \frac{1}{6}$ d. $\frac{1}{3} - \frac{1}{12}$

Use your fraction circles to solve. Write your answer in simplest form.

1. $\frac{1}{4} + \frac{1}{6}$ 2. $1 - \frac{3}{4}$ 3. $\frac{5}{12} + \frac{1}{4}$ 4. $\frac{5}{6} - \frac{2}{3}$

Use the fraction circles to write two solutions for each of the following.

5. Which three pieces add up to 1?
6. Which four pieces add up to 1?

Use your fraction circles if needed.

7. At Rob's twelfth birthday party, $\frac{2}{3}$ of the cake was eaten and $\frac{5}{6}$ of the ice cream was eaten. Did the guests eat a larger fraction of cake or of ice cream?

8. One-half of his presents were wrapped with red bows, one-third of his presents were in bags with bows, and the remaining ones were wrapped without bows. What fraction of all the presents were wrapped without bows?

9. $\frac{3}{4}$ of Rob's friends wore some type of jeans. Of that group, $\frac{3}{8}$ wore jean pants. The rest wore jean shorts. What fraction of his friends wore jean shorts?

10. $\frac{2}{6}$ of the group played soccer. $\frac{3}{6}$ played basketball. What fraction of Rob's friends were playing a sport?

1.	2.	3.	4.	5.
950 + 64	375 − 26	4,019 − 2,768	396 × 409	27)9,693

6.	7.	8.	9.	10.
9)0.378	0.25)375	2.7)16.2	587.4 − 390.57	1,796.38 + 54.7

 Construct Meaning

Heather volunteers in the church nursery. The nursery committee values her spirit of helpfulness. Can you think of something that is of value to God? 1 Peter 3:4 says that a gentle and quiet spirit is precious in God's sight.

$\frac{3}{8}$ of Heather's time is spent playing games and $\frac{2}{8}$ of her time is spent reading to the children.

What fraction of her time is spent playing games and reading to the children?

To add fractions with the same or common denominator,

$\frac{3}{8} + \frac{2}{8} = \frac{5}{8}$ ⟶ Add the numerators together and write the sum over the common denominator.

Write the answer in simplest form.
Read: three-eighths + two-eighths = five-eighths
$\frac{5}{8}$ of Heather's time is spent playing games and reading to the children.

The remainder of Heather's time in the nursery is spent supervising the rest and snack times. What fraction of her time is spent doing this supervision?

To subtract fractions with the same or common denominator,

$\frac{8}{8} - \frac{5}{8} = \frac{3}{8}$ ⟶ Subtract the numerators and write the difference over the common denominator.

Write the answer in simplest form.
Read: eight-eighths – five-eighths = three-eighths
$\frac{3}{8}$ of Heather's time is spent supervising the rest and snack times.

The sum of two or more fractions may be an improper fraction. In that case, rename the sum as a mixed number in simplest form or as a whole number.

$$\underset{\substack{\text{improper}\\\text{fraction}}}{\frac{6}{7} + \frac{3}{7} = \frac{9}{7}} = \underset{\substack{\text{mixed}\\\text{number}}}{1\frac{2}{7}} \qquad \underset{\substack{\text{whole}\\\text{number}}}{\frac{7}{12} + \frac{5}{12} = \frac{12}{12} = 1}$$

 Check Understanding

Write the sum or difference in simplest form.

a. $\frac{7}{25} + \frac{8}{25}$ b. $\frac{16}{17} - \frac{5}{17}$ c. $\frac{3}{9} + \frac{6}{9}$ d. $\frac{16}{21} - \frac{8}{21}$ e. $\frac{5}{7} + \frac{6}{7}$

f. $\frac{6}{8}$ g. $\frac{10}{12}$ h. $\frac{3}{6}$ i. $\frac{4}{5}$ j. $\frac{21}{24}$
$-\frac{4}{8}$ $+\frac{3}{12}$ $+\frac{3}{6}$ $-\frac{2}{5}$ $-\frac{18}{24}$

Add and Subtract with Like Denominators

Write the sum or difference in simplest form.

1. $\frac{3}{8}$
$+\frac{1}{8}$

2. $\frac{5}{7}$
$-\frac{2}{7}$

3. $\frac{9}{14}$
$+\frac{2}{14}$

4. $\frac{13}{16}$
$-\frac{9}{16}$

5. $\frac{9}{23}$
$-\frac{4}{23}$

6. $\frac{32}{45} + \frac{7}{45}$

7. $\frac{19}{36} - \frac{13}{36}$

8. $\frac{69}{74} - \frac{26}{74}$

9. $\frac{7}{11} + \frac{4}{11}$

10. $\frac{5}{8} + \frac{7}{8} + \frac{3}{8}$

Find the missing addend.

11. $\boxed{} + \frac{2}{6} = \frac{5}{6}$

12. $\frac{3}{4} + \boxed{} = 1\frac{1}{2}$

13. $\frac{7}{10} + \boxed{} = 1\frac{3}{10}$

14. $\boxed{} + \frac{5}{12} = \frac{11}{12}$

15. $\frac{10}{20} + \boxed{} = \frac{15}{20}$

Complete each equation.

16. $\frac{13}{15} - \boxed{} = \frac{7}{15}$

17. $\frac{16}{17} - \boxed{} = \frac{1}{17}$

18. $1 - \boxed{} = \frac{1}{11}$

19. $1\frac{3}{8} - \boxed{} = \frac{5}{8}$

20. $\frac{19}{26} - \boxed{} = \frac{9}{26}$

21. Mike and Tony ordered a large pizza. Mike ate $\frac{5}{16}$ of the pizza. Tony ate $\frac{3}{16}$ of the pizza. How much more of the pizza did Mike eat?

22. The morning worship service at Heritage Baptist Church begins with $\frac{3}{4}$-hour of announcements, offering, and music. The pastor concludes the service with a $\frac{3}{4}$-hour sermon. How long is the worship service?

23. Brooke is planning to grow a vegetable garden in her backyard. $\frac{3}{8}$ of the land area is used for tomatoes, $\frac{2}{8}$ of the land for cucumbers, and $\frac{1}{8}$ for carrots. What fraction of the land remains for growing other vegetables?

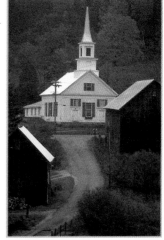

Find the least common multiple (LCM).

1. 4 and 5   2. 8 and 20   3. 16 and 12   4. 2, 4, and 6   5. 2, 5, and 8

Find the greatest common factor (GCF).

6. 6 and 4   7. 14 and 28   8. 36 and 24   9. 8, 12, and 15   10. 12 and 18

© Copyright 2002

161

Lesson 76

The circle graph shows the rescue calls responded to by the North Central Fire District. When rescue efforts are successful, there is an overwhelming response of thankfulness and gratitude on the part of those being rescued.

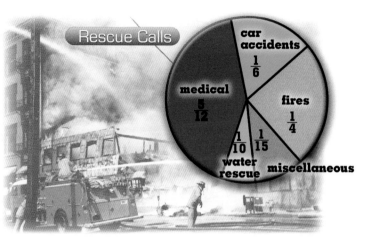

Rescue Calls

car accidents $\frac{1}{6}$

medical $\frac{5}{12}$

fires $\frac{1}{4}$

$\frac{1}{10}$ $\frac{1}{15}$

water rescue   miscellaneous

What fraction of the calls were related to fires and car accidents?
Fractions need a common denominator before they can be added or subtracted.

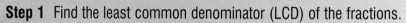

Steps to follow when adding or subtracting fractions with unlike denominators:

Step 1 Find the least common denominator (LCD) of the fractions.

Step 2 Write equivalent fractions with the LCD as the denominator.

Step 3 Add or subtract the numerators. Write the sum or difference over the LCD.

Step 4 Write the answer in simplest form.

Solve $\frac{1}{4} + \frac{1}{6}$.

Step 1: The LCD of $\frac{1}{4}$ and $\frac{1}{6}$ is 12.

Step 2:
$$\frac{1 \times 3}{4 \times 3} = \frac{3}{12}$$
$$+\frac{1 \times 2}{6 \times 2} = \frac{2}{12}$$

Step 3:
$$\frac{5}{12}$$

$\frac{5}{12}$ of the calls were related to fires and car accidents.

In fractional terms, how many more of the calls were related to fires than to water rescue?

Solve $\frac{1}{4} - \frac{1}{10}$.

The LCD is 20.

$$\frac{1 \times 5}{4 \times 5} = \frac{5}{20}$$
$$-\frac{1 \times 2}{10 \times 2} = \frac{2}{20}$$
$$\frac{3}{20}$$

There were $\frac{3}{20}$ more calls related to fires than to water rescue.

Solve.

a. $\frac{3}{7} + \frac{1}{14}$ b. $\frac{5}{6} - \frac{1}{10}$ c. $\frac{5}{7} + \frac{2}{3}$ d. $\frac{1}{4} - \frac{1}{8}$ e. $\frac{2}{3} + \frac{3}{4}$

Add and Subtract with Unlike Denominators

 ractice

Find the least common denominator.

1. $\frac{1}{2}$ $\frac{3}{8}$
2. $\frac{4}{7}$ $\frac{2}{5}$
3. $\frac{1}{6}$ $\frac{5}{8}$
4. $\frac{2}{3}$ $\frac{4}{9}$
5. $\frac{3}{10}$ $\frac{2}{15}$

Add or subtract. Write the answer in simplest form.

6. $\frac{1}{12} + \frac{2}{3}$
7. $\frac{5}{6} - \frac{3}{4}$
8. $\frac{1}{3} + \frac{4}{5}$
9. $\frac{1}{3} + \frac{2}{9}$
10. $\frac{2}{3} - \frac{1}{2}$

11. $\frac{1}{6}$ $+ \frac{3}{4}$
12. $\frac{13}{15}$ $- \frac{1}{5}$
13. $\frac{5}{6}$ $+ \frac{1}{3}$
14. $\frac{3}{4}$ $- \frac{5}{12}$
15. $\frac{5}{9}$ $+ \frac{7}{12}$

16. $\frac{8}{15}$ $+ \frac{1}{6}$
17. $\frac{7}{8}$ $- \frac{9}{20}$
18. $\frac{7}{12} + \frac{2}{3} + \frac{1}{4}$
19. $\frac{3}{10} + \frac{1}{4} + \frac{2}{5}$

 pply

Use the circle graph of rescue calls to answer the following.

20. Name two types of rescue calls having a sum that is an equivalent fraction for the number of medical calls.

21. Name three types of rescue calls having a sum that is an equivalent fraction for the number of medical calls.

22. What is the difference in the fraction of medical and miscellaneous calls responded to?

23. What is the difference in the fraction of fires and car accident calls responded to?

24. Write a fraction that represents the whole circle graph using the least common denominator of the fractions.

25. The North Central Fire District received 55 calls on Monday, 48 on Tuesday, 67 on Wednesday, 59 on Thursday, and 86 on Friday. What was the average number of calls received for the five-day period?

 eview

Identify the place value of 7.

1. 63,743
2. 78,856,109
3. 7.5106
4. 44.617
5. 626,716,834

 **Construct Meaning**

The Kim family is visiting Yosemite National Park. It took them $6\frac{1}{2}$ hours to hike to the top of Half Dome. The hike down took $4\frac{1}{4}$ hours. Mr. Kim commended the family for their cooperative spirit and for not grumbling and complaining. How long was the hike?

Solve $6\frac{1}{2} + 4\frac{1}{4}$.

Follow these steps to add or subtract mixed numbers with unlike denominators.

Step 1 **Rename the fractions with the LCD.**	**Step 2** **Add or subtract the fractions.**	**Step 3** **Add or subtract the whole numbers.**	**Step 4** **Write the answer in simplest form.**
$6\frac{1}{2} \longrightarrow 6\frac{2}{4}$ $+4\frac{1}{4} \longrightarrow +4\frac{1}{4}$	$6\frac{2}{4}$ $+4\frac{1}{4}$ $\overline{\quad\frac{3}{4}}$	$6\frac{2}{4}$ $+4\frac{1}{4}$ $\overline{10\frac{3}{4}}$	**The hike took** $10\frac{3}{4}$ **hours.**

Think — What is the LCD of $\frac{1}{2}$ and $\frac{1}{4}$? 4 is a multiple of 2. The LCD is 4. Only $\frac{1}{2}$ is renamed.
$\frac{1}{2} = \frac{}{4} \quad \frac{1 \times 2 = 2}{2 \times 2 = 4}$

How much longer was the hike up to Half Dome than the hike coming down?

$6\frac{1}{2} \longrightarrow 6\frac{2}{4}$ $6\frac{2}{4}$ $6\frac{2}{4}$
$-4\frac{1}{4} \longrightarrow -4\frac{1}{4}$ $-4\frac{1}{4}$ $-4\frac{1}{4}$
$\overline{\quad\quad}$ $\overline{\quad\frac{1}{4}}$ $\overline{2\frac{1}{4}}$

The hike up to Half Dome took $2\frac{1}{4}$ hours longer than the hike coming down.

MORE EXAMPLES

Rename with the LCD, then add.
$5\frac{1}{3} \longrightarrow 5\frac{2}{6}$
$+2\frac{1}{6} \longrightarrow +2\frac{1}{6}$
$\overline{7\frac{3}{6} = 7\frac{1}{2}}$

Rename with the LCD, then subtract.
$18\frac{3}{4} \longrightarrow 18\frac{9}{12}$
$-9\frac{5}{12} \longrightarrow -9\frac{5}{12}$
$\overline{9\frac{4}{12} = 9\frac{1}{3}}$

 **Check Understanding**

Solve. Write the answer in simplest form.

a. $3\frac{1}{4}$
$+2\frac{2}{5}$

b. $7\frac{5}{6} - 4\frac{2}{3}$

c. $24\frac{3}{6} + 5\frac{1}{2}$

d. $9\frac{7}{10} - 3\frac{1}{2}$

e. $37\frac{5}{7}$
$-14\frac{9}{14}$

Add and Subtract Mixed Numbers

Write the least common denominator needed to solve each problem.

1. $5\frac{3}{4}$
   $+ 1\frac{2}{8}$

2. $13\frac{5}{6}$
   $- 8\frac{4}{12}$

3. $9\frac{1}{2} - 4\frac{1}{3}$

4. $2\frac{9}{10} - 1\frac{4}{5}$

5. $14\frac{2}{8} + 6\frac{2}{3}$

Solve. Write the answer in simplest form.

6. $6\frac{3}{4}$
   $- 3\frac{1}{2}$

7. $5\frac{9}{10}$
   $- 1\frac{2}{5}$

8. $2\frac{1}{3}$
   $+ 8\frac{2}{9}$

9. $14\frac{1}{3}$
   $+10\frac{5}{12}$

10. $9\frac{3}{8}$
    $+ \frac{1}{6}$

11. $25\frac{1}{2} - \frac{2}{7}$

12. $26\frac{9}{40} + 4\frac{1}{8}$

13. $43\frac{5}{8} - 31\frac{7}{12}$

14. $1\frac{1}{2} + 4\frac{1}{4} + 2\frac{1}{6}$

15. $13\frac{2}{5} + 15\frac{1}{10} + 25\frac{1}{3}$

Complete.

16. Two numbers have a sum of $8\frac{7}{12}$. One of the numbers is $6\frac{1}{4}$. What is the other number?

17. Two numbers have a sum of $22\frac{4}{5}$. One of the numbers is $9\frac{1}{2}$. What is the other number?

18. Erick jogged $4\frac{1}{3}$ kilometers past the beautiful Sequoia trees on Monday. As a result of a shin splint, he only jogged $1\frac{1}{4}$ km on Tuesday. On those two days, how many kilometers did he jog?

19. The humidifier holds $3\frac{2}{3}$ gallons of water. In a six-hour period of time, it uses $1\frac{1}{2}$ gallons. How much water remains in the humidifier after six hours?

20. Farmer Dan has enough tomato plants to cover $5\frac{3}{4}$ acres of land. He has enough strawberry plants to cover $5\frac{4}{5}$ acres of land. Will the tomato or the strawberry plants cover more acreage?

21. The Endres family spent an afternoon at the zoo. Mr. Endres paid the entrance fee of $4.25 each for his wife and himself. He paid $3.50 for each of his two children. Grandpa and Grandma each took advantage of the $2.00 senior citizen rate. How much did the Endres family pay for admission to the zoo?

Now when the people complained, it displeased the LORD. Numbers 11:1a

Lesson 78

 **Construct Meaning**

Baking cookies for her classmates and a loaf of bread for her teacher are ways Kaneesha demonstrates love, kindness, and goodness—three of the nine fruits of the Spirit. The recipe for a batch of cookies calls for $1\frac{3}{4}$ cups of flour. The recipe for a loaf of bread calls for $3\frac{1}{2}$ cups of flour. How many cups of flour will she need for both recipes?

$$\begin{array}{r}1\frac{3}{4}\\+3\frac{1}{2}\end{array}$$ — Use the LCD → $$\begin{array}{r}1\frac{3}{4}\\+3\frac{2}{4}\\\hline 4\frac{5}{4}\end{array}$$

When the fractional part of the sum is improper, rename the improper fraction as a mixed number.

$$4\frac{5}{4} = 4 + 1\frac{1}{4} = 5\frac{1}{4}$$

The two recipes require $5\frac{1}{4}$ cups of flour.

How much more flour is needed to make the bread than the cookies?

$$\begin{array}{r}3\frac{1}{2}\\-1\frac{3}{4}\end{array}$$ — Use the LCD → $$\begin{array}{r}3\frac{2}{4}\\-1\frac{3}{4}\end{array}$$

The whole numbers can be subtracted, but the fractions cannot. Since $\frac{3}{4}$ cannot be subtracted from $\frac{2}{4}$, rename $3\frac{2}{4}$ to increase the numerator of its fraction.

Rename $3\frac{2}{4}$ in order to subtract $1\frac{3}{4}$.

$$\begin{aligned}3\frac{2}{4} &= 3 + \frac{2}{4}\\ &= 2 + 1 + \frac{2}{4}\\ &= 2 + \frac{4}{4} + \frac{2}{4}\\ &= 2 + \frac{6}{4}\\ &= 2\frac{6}{4}\end{aligned}$$

$3\frac{2}{4}$

$2\frac{6}{4}$

Use the renamed number to subtract.

$$\begin{array}{r}2\frac{6}{4}\\-1\frac{3}{4}\\\hline 1\frac{3}{4}\end{array}$$

The recipe for bread requires $1\frac{3}{4}$ more cups of flour than the recipe for cookies.

MORE RENAMING

$$\begin{array}{r}10\\-3\frac{5}{7}\end{array}$$ — Rename → $$\begin{array}{r}9\frac{7}{7}\\-3\frac{5}{7}\\\hline 6\frac{2}{7}\end{array}$$

Rename 10 as $9\frac{7}{7}$, since 7 is the denominator of the fraction. Subtract.

$$\begin{array}{r}5\frac{2}{15}\\-4\frac{5}{6}\end{array}$$ Use the LCD $$\begin{array}{r}5\frac{4}{30}\\-4\frac{25}{30}\end{array}$$ — Rename → $$\begin{array}{r}4\frac{34}{30}\\-4\frac{25}{30}\\\hline \frac{9}{30}=\frac{3}{10}\end{array}$$

$$\begin{array}{r}13\frac{7}{12}\\+8\frac{2}{3}\end{array}$$ Use the LCD $$\begin{array}{r}13\frac{7}{12}\\+8\frac{8}{12}\\\hline\end{array}$$

$$21\frac{15}{12} = 21 + 1\frac{3}{12} = 22\frac{3}{12} = 22\frac{1}{4}$$

Add and Subtract with Renaming

 **Check Understanding**

a. Is it in adding or subtracting fractions that you can find a numerator too small to perform the operation? Explain how you increase the numerator in order to solve the problem.

Rename each mixed number as a whole number with an improper fraction.

b. $4\frac{2}{3}$　　　c. $13\frac{1}{4}$　　　d. $8\frac{3}{8}$　　　e. $2\frac{3}{10}$　　　f. $6\frac{1}{2}$

Add or subtract, renaming when necessary. Write the answer in simplest form.

g. $3\frac{1}{8} - 2\frac{6}{8}$　　h. $7\frac{2}{3} - 4\frac{5}{6}$　　i. $9\frac{1}{4} + 6\frac{3}{4}$　　j. $12 - 5\frac{2}{9}$　　k. $2\frac{3}{5} + 4\frac{4}{5}$

 **Practice**

Add. Write the answer in simplest form.

1. $3\frac{2}{3}$ $+7\frac{1}{2}$
2. $1\frac{17}{30}$ $+6\frac{7}{10}$
3. $8\frac{2}{3}$ $+2\frac{3}{5}$
4. $2\frac{4}{7}$ $+1\frac{3}{7}$
5. $4\frac{11}{18}$ $+2\frac{1}{2}$

Subtract. Write the answer in simplest form.

6. 6 $-1\frac{2}{3}$
7. $8\frac{4}{9}$ $-3\frac{7}{9}$
8. $3\frac{1}{2}$ $-2\frac{4}{5}$
9. $7\frac{3}{10}$ $-5\frac{5}{6}$
10. 5 $-4\frac{2}{6}$

Add or subtract. Write the answer in simplest form.

11. $7\frac{4}{5}$ $+4\frac{1}{3}$
12. $16\frac{5}{12}$ $-4\frac{3}{4}$
13. $4\frac{3}{5}$ $+9\frac{13}{20}$
14. $16\frac{4}{7}$ $-10\frac{11}{14}$
15. $4\frac{8}{9}$ $+2\frac{1}{6}$

 Apply

16. Two numbers have a sum of 7. One number is $4\frac{1}{6}$. What is the other number?

17. The difference between two numbers is $7\frac{3}{4}$. If the greater number is $12\frac{1}{2}$, what is the other number?

18. Polly made $2\frac{1}{2}$ dozen chocolate chip cookies, $4\frac{1}{3}$ dozen peanut butter cookies, and $1\frac{3}{4}$ dozen oatmeal raisin cookies for a bake sale.

　a. How many dozen cookies did she contribute?

　b. How many more dozen peanut butter cookies were there than chocolate chip and oatmeal raisin combined?

Construct Meaning

Sandra listened to five songs on her favorite CD. The lengths of the songs were $3\frac{2}{15}$, $4\frac{7}{12}$, $2\frac{1}{10}$, $3\frac{4}{5}$, and $2\frac{17}{20}$ minutes. Approximately how long did it take her to listen to all five songs?

▶ To estimate mixed number sums and differences, round to the nearest whole number. Round the length of each song to the nearest minute and add the estimates.

$$3\frac{2}{15} + 4\frac{7}{12} + 2\frac{1}{10} + 3\frac{4}{5} + 2\frac{17}{20}$$

$$3 \;+\; 5 \;+\; 2 \;+\; 4 \;+\; 3 \;=\; 17 \text{ minutes}$$

A merry heart does good, like medicine,
But a broken spirit dries the bones.
Proverbs 17:22

It took Sandra approximately 17 minutes to hear the five songs.

- If the fraction part of a mixed number is less than $\frac{1}{2}$, use the whole number given. Round $3\frac{2}{15}$. Since $\frac{2}{15} < \frac{1}{2}$, round $3\frac{2}{15}$ to 3.

- If the fraction part of a mixed number is $\frac{1}{2}$ or greater, round to the next greater whole number. Round $4\frac{7}{12}$. Since $\frac{7}{12} > \frac{1}{2}$, round $4\frac{7}{12}$ to 5.

Try rounding these mixed numbers to the nearest whole number before adding or subtracting.

$$8\frac{2}{7} + 3\frac{7}{10} \qquad\qquad 6\frac{7}{8} - 5\frac{1}{6}$$

$$\boxed{} + \boxed{} = \boxed{} \qquad \boxed{} - \boxed{} = \boxed{}$$

▶ To estimate fraction sums and differences, round to the nearest half.

- If the numerator is small in comparison to the denominator, round the fraction to 0. Explain why $\frac{2}{25}$, $\frac{1}{8}$, and $\frac{9}{40}$ round to 0.

- If the numerator is about one-half of the denominator, round the fraction to $\frac{1}{2}$. Explain why $\frac{6}{11}$, $\frac{2}{5}$, and $\frac{20}{43}$ round to $\frac{1}{2}$.

- If the numerator and denominator are close in number, round the fraction to 1. Explain why $\frac{15}{17}$, $\frac{6}{7}$, and $\frac{29}{33}$ round to 1.

Try rounding these fractions to the nearest half before adding or subtracting.

$$\frac{4}{7} + \frac{3}{16} + \frac{5}{6} \qquad\qquad \frac{3}{5} + \frac{1}{7} \qquad\qquad \frac{17}{19} - \frac{7}{8}$$

$$\boxed{} + \boxed{} + \boxed{} = \boxed{} \qquad \boxed{} + \boxed{} = \boxed{} \qquad \boxed{} - \boxed{} = \boxed{}$$

 **Check Understanding**

Round each mixed number to the nearest whole number before adding or subtracting.

a. $2\frac{1}{5} + 3\frac{7}{9}$ b. $8\frac{5}{6} + 1\frac{7}{10}$ c. $5\frac{3}{14} - 2\frac{8}{11}$ d. $9\frac{1}{8} - 7\frac{2}{9}$ e. $4\frac{1}{2} + 8\frac{2}{3}$

Round each fraction to the nearest half.

f. $\frac{7}{8}$ g. $\frac{3}{7}$ h. $\frac{19}{21}$ i. $\frac{5}{23}$ j. $\frac{1}{10}$

Round each mixed number to the nearest half and estimate the sum or difference.

k. $7\frac{1}{6} - 5\frac{6}{13}$ l. $3\frac{5}{9} + 4\frac{4}{7}$ m. $4\frac{6}{7} + 3\frac{2}{15}$ n. $9\frac{3}{8} - 3\frac{4}{19}$ o. $5\frac{6}{7} - 1\frac{1}{8}$

 **Practice**

Estimate by rounding each mixed number to the nearest whole number.

1. $9\frac{1}{2} - 2\frac{1}{3}$ 2. $6\frac{1}{4} - 4\frac{5}{6}$ 3. $1\frac{2}{3} + 5\frac{3}{4}$ 4. $7\frac{2}{7} + 8\frac{3}{8}$ 5. $12\frac{7}{11} - 7\frac{2}{9}$

Estimate by rounding each fraction to the nearest half.

6. $\frac{13}{15} - \frac{5}{11}$ 7. $\frac{4}{9} + \frac{3}{8}$ 8. $\frac{7}{8} - \frac{1}{8}$ 9. $\frac{3}{4} - \frac{1}{3}$ 10. $\frac{5}{6} + \frac{3}{4}$

Use estimation. Write > or <.

11. $3\frac{9}{11} + 7\frac{4}{5}$ ▒ 13   12. $9\frac{1}{7} - 6\frac{4}{9}$ ▒ 1   13. $10\frac{1}{6} - 3\frac{5}{13}$ ▒ 6   14. $1\frac{7}{8} + 4\frac{3}{4}$ ▒ 8

 Apply

15. The media center sells CD player headsets with cords that vary from four feet to nine feet in length. Mr. Rice needs one that is $6\frac{7}{10}$ feet long. Should he buy one that is $6\frac{1}{2}$ feet long or one that is 7 feet long?

16. To the nearest foot, estimate the difference in the length of two cords that are $4\frac{7}{8}$ feet long and $8\frac{1}{4}$ feet long. What is the actual difference in the length of the two cords?

17. Dora's positive attitude is displayed in her enjoyment of music, God's Word, and her right relationship with others. She enjoys photography and arranges pictures of her friends creatively in an album. At four different sittings, she completed $3\frac{3}{8}$ pages, $4\frac{1}{2}$ pages, $3\frac{5}{8}$ pages, and $4\frac{3}{8}$ pages. She estimates that she has finished approximately 16 pages of the album. Is her estimate reasonable?

Lesson 80

Construct Meaning

Use the Problem-Solving Guide as a tool to help you solve the word problem.

At the zoo, $\frac{3}{5}$ of the animals are mammals, and $\frac{2}{15}$ of the animals are reptiles. What fraction of the zoo animals are neither mammals nor reptiles?

PROBLEM-SOLVING GUIDE

1. UNDERSTAND THE PROBLEM.
What fraction of the zoo animals are <u>not</u> mammals or reptiles?

2. ANALYZE THE DATA.
$\frac{3}{5}$ of the zoo animals are mammals and $\frac{2}{15}$ are reptiles.

3. PLAN THE STRATEGY.
Planning the strategies may mean deciding which operations to use. Sometimes it is a good strategy to make a reasonable guess and check to see if it is the solution.

Addition and subtraction are the operations that will provide the fraction of zoo animals that are neither mammals nor reptiles.

4. SOLVE THE PROBLEM.

$$\begin{array}{c} \frac{3}{5} = \frac{9}{15} \\ + \frac{2}{15} = \frac{2}{15} \\ \hline \frac{11}{15} \end{array} \qquad \begin{array}{c} \frac{15}{15} \\ - \frac{11}{15} \\ \hline \frac{4}{15} \end{array}$$

$\frac{15}{15}$ ← represents all of the animals at the zoo.

$\frac{4}{15}$ ← is the fraction of zoo animals that are neither mammals nor reptiles.

5. EVALUATE THE RESULT.
The fraction bars show $\frac{3}{5} + \frac{2}{15} = \frac{11}{15}$ and $\frac{4}{15}$ remain.

KEY
☐ mammals
☐ reptiles

America's First Zoo
1874 Philadelphia, PA

Solve. Write the answer in simplest form.

1. A paint store mixed $4\frac{3}{4}$ cans of blue paint and $7\frac{2}{3}$ cans of white paint to make the color the Guzmans wanted to paint their house. How many cans of paint did this mixture make?

2. A small watermelon weighs $11\frac{3}{8}$ pounds. A larger watermelon weighs $8\frac{1}{4}$ pounds more than the smaller one. How much do the watermelons weigh together?

3. Stacy is cropping photos for a photo album. The photo of her cat is trimmed to $3\frac{1}{4}$ inches wide. The photo of a teddy bear is $2\frac{5}{8}$ inches wide. Her photo of herself is $3\frac{1}{2}$ inches wide and a photo of the family dog is $2\frac{3}{8}$ inches wide. She used two of the photos to fit a space of $6\frac{1}{8}$ inches. Which two photos did she use?

4. A softball has a diameter of $3\frac{13}{16}$ inches. A baseball has a diameter of $2\frac{7}{8}$ inches. How much greater in diameter is a softball than a baseball?

5. On Saturday afternoon Trevor had $2\frac{1}{2}$ hours between hockey practice and dinner. He spent $1\frac{1}{3}$ hours doing his homework and $\frac{1}{6}$ hour cleaning his room. The rest of the time was free time. How much free time did he have?

6. Brian was given the responsibility of counting the coins in the collection plate. All the coins were either dimes or quarters. Brian counted $6.80 in change altogether. If $\frac{1}{4}$ of the coins were dimes, how many quarters were given?

Estimate. Explain why an answer is rounded up or down.

7. Estimate the amount of fencing material Mr. Swanson should buy for a rectangular garden that measures $12\frac{1}{4}$ feet by $29\frac{4}{5}$ feet.

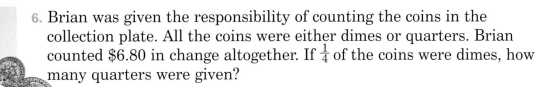

$\longleftarrow 29\frac{4}{5}' \longrightarrow$

$12\frac{1}{4}'$

8. Marty's music teacher requires that he practices the trumpet for at least $3\frac{1}{2}$ hours every week. On Monday, he practiced $\frac{5}{6}$ hour. Tuesday's practice was $\frac{7}{10}$ hour. He did not practice on Wednesday. Thursday's practice was $1\frac{1}{4}$ hours and Friday's practice was $\frac{2}{5}$ hour. Estimate to see if Marty needs to practice on the weekend.

 **Construct Meaning**

Use logical thinking to find similar relationships and make an analogy.

ANALOGY: Ice skates are to skater as skis are to skier.

Study the analogy to find a relationship.

RELATIONSHIP: Telling what is needed to perform

Use the relationship of the first part of the analogy to complete the second part.

ANALOGY: Addition is to subtraction as multiplication is to ▦ .

RELATIONSHIP: Addition and subtraction are inverse operations; multiplication and division are inverse operations.

FIND THE RELATIONSHIP AND THEN COMPLETE THE ANALOGY.

Dollar is to money as 12:30 A.M. is to ▦ .

2 is to prime number as 15 is to ▦ .

7 is to 8 as 70 is to ▦ .

Triangle is to polygon as triangular pyramid is to ▦ .

Use logical thinking to study a list of items for a sequence. Study the list of items to discover a pattern that will give a clue to the next one in the list.

SEQUENCE: 1,600   1,595   1,590   ▦   PATTERN: Counting back by 5

Examine each list to find the next item in the sequence.

1 4 2 5 3 ▦   8.4367 84.367 843.67 8,436.7 ▦ $\frac{1}{2}$ $\frac{2}{3}$ $\frac{5}{6}$ 1 ▦

 **Check Understanding**

Find a relationship. Write the word that completes the analogy.

a. Inch is to customary as centimeter is to ▦ .

LENGTH	METRIC	KILOMETER	MILLIMETER

b. Product is to multiplication as quotient is to ▦ .

DIVISOR	DIVIDEND	DIVISION	FACTOR

c. ▦ is to 1.00 as ▦ is to ▦ .

O.IO	O.OI	O.OOI	O.OOOI

Find a pattern. Write the number that completes the sequence.

d. $79.70 $79.80 $79.90 ▦

e. 1 2 4 7 11 16 ▦

f. $12\frac{1}{4}$ $12\frac{1}{2}$ $12\frac{3}{4}$ 13 ▦

Chapter Six Study Guide

Write each answer in simplest form.

1. Use the fraction bars to solve. *Lesson 74*

$\frac{2}{3} + \frac{1}{4} =$

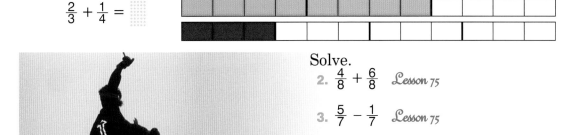

Solve.

2. $\frac{4}{8} + \frac{6}{8}$ *Lesson 75*

3. $\frac{5}{7} - \frac{1}{7}$ *Lesson 75*

4. $\frac{1}{3} + \frac{5}{6}$ *Lesson 76*

5. $\frac{2}{5} - \frac{3}{15}$ *Lesson 76*

6. $8\frac{1}{4} + 3\frac{3}{8}$ *Lesson 77*

7. $12\frac{3}{9} - 10\frac{1}{6}$ *Lesson 77*

8. $2\frac{4}{6} + 5\frac{1}{2}$ *Lesson 78*

9. $9\frac{1}{2} - 3\frac{2}{3}$ *Lesson 78*

10. Estimate by rounding to the nearest whole number. *Lesson 79*
    $5\frac{3}{4} + 2\frac{1}{4} + 8\frac{5}{6}$

11. Estimate by rounding to the nearest half. *Lesson 79*
    $4\frac{6}{10} - 1\frac{2}{5}$

12. Erin was working on an art project that required one
    whole piece of poster board. Her mother did not have time
    to make a trip to the store, so she taped two shorter pieces
    of poster board together. The pieces taped together were $\frac{2}{3}$
    of a whole and $\frac{3}{4}$ of another whole. After taping the pieces
    together, how much did she have to cut off since she only
    needed one whole? *Lesson 80*

13. Use logical thinking to complete the analogy. *Lesson 81*
    $\frac{2}{4}$ is to $\frac{1}{2}$ as $\frac{2}{6}$ is to ⬚ .

14. Complete the logical sequence. *Lesson 81*
    0.3   0.44   0.6   0.44   0.9   0.44   0.12   0.44

Lesson 82

Friends Forever — Not Just a Fraction of Time

Write the letter of the correct match.

1. LCD of $\frac{1}{3}$ and $\frac{1}{8}$
2. $4\frac{2}{15}$ rounded to the nearest whole number
3. $\frac{1}{6} = \frac{2}{12}$
4. $8\frac{3}{4} \longrightarrow 8\frac{9}{12}$
5. $\frac{7}{9}$ $\frac{1}{9}$
6. 100 is to 50 as 12 is to 6
7. $3\frac{7}{4}$
8. $\frac{8}{3} = 2\frac{2}{3}$
9. $\frac{1}{8}$ $\frac{1}{16}$ $\frac{1}{32}$ $\frac{1}{64}$ $\frac{1}{128}$
10. $8\frac{6}{11}$ rounded to the nearest half

a. Renamed with the LCD of 12
b. Fractions having common denominators
c. Logical sequence
d. Renamed as $4\frac{3}{4}$
e. 24
f. $8\frac{1}{2}$
g. Analogy
h. 4
i. Renamed as a mixed number
j. Equivalent fractions

Use each fraction model to write the equation.

11.

12.

Solve. Write the answer in simplest form.

13. $\frac{4}{7} + \frac{2}{7}$

14. $\frac{7}{8} - \frac{3}{8}$

15. $\frac{2}{6} + \frac{4}{6}$

16. $\frac{7}{11} - \frac{4}{11}$

17. $\frac{4}{10} + \frac{8}{10}$

18. $\frac{1}{2}$
    $+ \frac{1}{6}$

19. $\frac{3}{4}$
    $- \frac{5}{12}$

20. $\frac{7}{10}$
    $- \frac{1}{4}$

21. $\frac{5}{8}$
    $+ \frac{4}{5}$

22. $\frac{2}{3}$
    $- \frac{2}{9}$

23. $4\frac{3}{7}$
    $+ 6\frac{1}{2}$

24. $5\frac{1}{2}$
    $- 1\frac{1}{8}$

25. $9\frac{5}{6}$
    $- 5\frac{1}{12}$

26. $1\frac{6}{16}$
    $+ 3\frac{5}{8}$

27. $6\frac{7}{20}$
    $+ 3\frac{2}{5}$

28. $2\frac{3}{4} + 4\frac{1}{2}$

29. $5\frac{1}{2} - 3\frac{3}{4}$

30. $4\frac{7}{12} + 3\frac{2}{3}$

31. $3\frac{1}{4} + 1\frac{4}{5}$

32. $6 - 3\frac{2}{5}$

Estimate by rounding to the nearest whole number.

33. $4\frac{3}{15} + 1\frac{6}{10} + 2\frac{1}{9} + 5\frac{1}{2}$ **34.** $21\frac{7}{8} - 18\frac{1}{3}$ **35.** $1\frac{2}{13} - 1\frac{1}{20}$

Estimate by rounding to the nearest half.

36. $\frac{2}{21} + \frac{6}{7}$ **37.** $\frac{4}{9} - \frac{1}{7}$ **38.** $\frac{13}{14} - \frac{10}{19}$

Solve. Write the answer in simplest form.

39. To the back of the house, the Kroll family added a deck that measured $81\frac{1}{2}$ square feet and a spa that measured $64\frac{3}{4}$ square feet. How much area did the designer plan for these two additions?

 **40.** The Westwood city planning committee approved a new swimming pool for the northwest side of town. $\frac{1}{3}$ of the pool area is designated for laps, $\frac{1}{4}$ of the area is designated for the slide, and $\frac{1}{6}$ is designated for free swimming, and the rest is play area. How much area is designated as a play area?

41. Courtney enjoys making gifts using grapevines. She planned to design and decorate a wreath that would require $3\frac{1}{4}$ feet of grapevine. She cut that length from a piece of grapevine that measured $9\frac{3}{8}$ feet in length. How many feet of grapevine remained for other projects?

42. $\frac{1}{6}$ of Mrs. Tangretti's class has a birthday in June. $\frac{3}{8}$ of the class has a birthday in August. What fraction of the class does not have a birthday in June or August?

43. Two of the fractions have a sum of $1\frac{5}{12}$. What are the fractions? $\frac{3}{4}$ $\frac{2}{3}$ $\frac{11}{12}$

Write the word that completes the analogy.

44. Ounce is to pound as milligram is to ░░. | gram | cup | meter

45. 12:00 P.M. is to 12:00 A.M. as 2:00 P.M. is to ░░. | 12:00 A.M. | 4:00 A.M. | 2:00 A.M.

46. Pictograph is to symbol as bar graph is to ░░. | line | bar | circle

47. Pentagon is to five as octagon is to ░░. | 6 | 8 | 10

Write the number that completes the sequence.

48. 2,176 3,176 4,176 ░░

49. 4 4^1 4^2 4^3 ░░

50. 4 1 5 2 6 3 ░░

A man who has friends
must himself be friendly,
But there is a friend who sticks
closer than a brother.
Proverbs 18:24

Young friends in Singapore

Chapter Theme

The theme of chapter 7 is God's Wisdom and Man's Intelligence. In our years of formal education, we gain in academic knowledge and develop our intellectual abilities. How blessed we are that God gave us the ability to learn. Men and women with brilliant minds have made discoveries that have changed the way we live on a daily basis. However, when we think of the brightest person we have read about or known, we should remember how man's intellect fades when compared with the wisdom of God. Jeremiah 51:15 says, "He has made the earth by His power; He has established the world by His wisdom, and stretched out the heaven by His understanding." Mankind, made in the image of God, has the opportunity to pray, study, and seek God's wisdom. When the Christian walk brings us to a place of totally submitting to God and seeking His wisdom, we can begin to receive from Him a wise and understanding heart.

7

Chapter

Multiplication and Division of Fractions

Lessons 83-94

O Lord, how manifold are Your works!
In wisdom You have made them all.
The earth is full of Your possessions.

Psalm 104:24

Construct Meaning

Left Hemisphere

Your brain has two hemispheres or sides. The right hemisphere is the main center for musical ability, recognition of faces, visual patterns, and the expression of emotions. The left hemisphere largely controls the ability to use language, math, and logic.

Right Hemisphere

Mr. Turner spoke on mathematics and logic at three schools. Each presentation lasted $\frac{3}{4}$ of an hour. What was the total time he spoke?

Use a model to show the repeated addition.

$3 \times \frac{3}{4}$

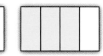

$$3 \times \frac{3}{4} = \frac{3}{4} + \frac{3}{4} + \frac{3}{4} = \frac{9}{4} = 2\frac{1}{4}$$

Mr. Turner spoke for $2\frac{1}{4}$ hours.

Sometimes mental math may help solve a problem. Multiply $6 \times \frac{1}{3}$.

Think:

How many thirds are there in 1?

$\frac{1}{3}$ $\frac{1}{3}$ $\frac{1}{3}$

6 thirds will be equal to 2.

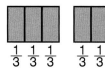

$\frac{1}{3}$ $\frac{1}{3}$ $\frac{1}{3}$ $\frac{1}{3}$ $\frac{1}{3}$ $\frac{1}{3}$

Multiply $8 \times \frac{3}{4}$. Rename the whole number as a fraction. $\frac{8}{1} \times \frac{3}{4}$ Multiply the numerators. Multiply the denominators. $\frac{8}{1} \times \frac{3}{4} = \frac{24}{4}$ Write the answer in simplest form. $\frac{24}{4} = 6$ $8 \times \frac{3}{4} = 6$	Multiplying fractions is simplified by using **cross-cancellation**. $8 \times \frac{3}{4} = \frac{8}{1} \times \frac{3}{4}$ Find a common factor of the numerator of one fraction and the denominator of the other fraction. $\frac{8}{1} \times \frac{3}{4}$ Divide with the factor, cross out, write the quotients. Multiply with the renamed fractions. $\frac{\overset{2}{\cancel{8}}}{1} \times \frac{3}{\underset{1}{\cancel{4}}} = \frac{6}{1} = 6$ $8 \times \frac{3}{4} = 6$

 **Check Understanding**

Solve.

a. Use a model.

$4 \times \frac{2}{3}$

b. Use cross-cancellation.

$8 \times \frac{1}{6}$

c. Use mental math.

$3 \times \frac{1}{4}$

Practice

Write a number sentence represented by the model.

Draw a model representing the number sentence.

4. $2 \times \frac{1}{8}$

5. 3 of $\frac{1}{5}$

6. $4 \times \frac{2}{7}$

Use the cross-cancellation method to solve.

7. $4 \times \frac{3}{20}$ 8. $3 \times \frac{2}{12}$ 9. $3 \times \frac{4}{9}$ 10. $6 \times \frac{1}{8}$

11. $5 \times \frac{5}{35}$ 12. $10 \times \frac{1}{6}$ 13. $4 \times \frac{7}{16}$ 14. $7 \times \frac{1}{21}$

Use mental math.

15. 2 of $\frac{1}{3}$ 16. $5 \times \frac{1}{5}$ 17. $4 \times \frac{1}{6}$ 18. $8 \times \frac{1}{16}$

 Apply

19. Rewrite the list of ingredients for making five batches of cookies.

Cookie Preserve

$\frac{1}{2}$ cup flour $\frac{1}{4}$ teaspoon salt

$\frac{1}{2}$ cup butter $\frac{1}{3}$ cup sugar

2 eggs   1 teaspoon vanilla

$\frac{2}{3}$ cup strawberries $\frac{3}{4}$ cup nuts

 Review

1. $\frac{1}{3} + \frac{2}{3}$ 2. $\frac{2}{7} + \frac{1}{7}$ 3. $\frac{1}{9} + \frac{4}{9}$ 4. $\frac{5}{8} + \frac{7}{8}$

5. $\frac{2}{5} - \frac{1}{5}$ 6. $\frac{8}{9} - \frac{2}{9}$ 7. $\frac{10}{13} - \frac{4}{13}$ 8. $\frac{2}{7} - \frac{1}{7}$

The fear of the LORD is the beginning of wisdom;
A good understanding have all those who do His
commandments. Psalm 111:10a

 Construct Meaning

Most large animals have large brains. However, animals with large brains are not necessarily more intelligent than animals or people with smaller brains. Use the table to compare the weight in grams and pounds of the human brain with the brains of animals.

Brain Weight

Elephant	6,000 gm	12 lb
Human	1,400 gm	? lb
Monkey	97 gm	0.194 lb
Dog	72 gm	0.144 lb
Cat	30 gm	0.06 lb
Rabbit	10 gm	0.02 lb
Owl	2.2 gm	0.0044 lb

If Mr. Tibbar is 5'10" and weighs 180 lbs, his brain is about $\frac{1}{60}$ of his weight. How many pounds does his brain weigh?

$\frac{1}{60} \times 180$ Rename the whole number as a fraction.

$\frac{1}{60} \times \frac{180}{1} = \frac{180}{60}$ Divide.

$\frac{180}{60} = 3$ **Mr. Tibbar's brain weighs about 3 pounds.**

Use the cross-cancelling method.

$\frac{1}{60} \times 180$ Rename the whole number as a fraction.

$\frac{1}{60} \times \frac{180}{1}$ Find a common factor of the numerator of one fraction and the denominator of the other fraction.

$\frac{1}{60_1} \times \frac{180^3}{1}$ 60 is a common factor.
Divide the numerator and denominator by 60.
Cross-cancel and write the quotient.

$\frac{1}{1} \times \frac{3}{1} = \frac{3}{1} = 3$ Multiply using the renamed fractions.

Find $\frac{3}{5} \times 10$ using a model.
- First, think in terms of fifths.
- Next, think how 10 can equally fit into the fifth model.
- Last, think 3 out of 5 equal groups.

       $\frac{3}{5}$ of 10 = 6

Estimate products using fractions. $\frac{2}{5} \times 321$
- Substitute the closest compatible number for the whole number.
    320 is the closest number evenly divisible by 5.
    $320 \div 5 = 64$. Substitute 320 in the place of 321. ⟶ $\frac{2}{5} \times 320$

- Substitute a **unit fraction**, which is a fraction with a numerator of 1. Use $\frac{1}{5}$ in place of the non-unit fraction $\frac{2}{5}$. ⟶ $\frac{1}{5} \times 320 = 64$

- Multiply the estimate of 64 by 2 to adjust the unit fraction of ⟶ $64 \times 2 = 128$
$\frac{1}{5}$ to $\frac{2}{5}$.
    $\frac{2}{5} \times 321$ is about 128.

180

Multiply Fractions and Whole Numbers

a. Multiply $\frac{1}{4} \times 9$.

b. Use cross-cancelling to solve $\frac{3}{10} \times 25$.

c. Estimate $\frac{3}{4} \times 215$

d. Draw a model to show $\frac{3}{4}$ of 12.

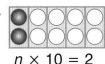 Practice

Use cross-cancelling to solve.

1. $\frac{1}{2} \times 6$

2. $\frac{3}{4} \times 12$

3. $\frac{1}{3} \times 15$

4. $\frac{2}{8} \times 8$

5. $\frac{3}{7} \times 14$

6. $\frac{7}{10} \times 15$

7. $\frac{2}{3} \times 9$

8. $\frac{5}{12} \times 16$

9. $\frac{4}{5} \times 15$

10. $\frac{4}{9} \times 12$

11. $\frac{2}{9} \times 15$

12. $\frac{3}{4} \times 8$

Identify *n* using the shaded part of each model.

13.

$n \times 10 = 2$

14.

$n \times 9 = 6$

15.

$n \times 12 = 4$

Estimate.

16. $\frac{1}{2}$ of 501

17. $\frac{1}{4} \times 79$

18. $\frac{1}{6}$ of 63

19. $\frac{1}{5}$ of 491

20. $\frac{2}{3} \times 304$

21. $\frac{3}{5} \times 547$

22. $\frac{5}{6} \times 311$

23. $\frac{3}{8}$ of 162

 Apply

24. Approximately $\frac{7}{10}$ of a person's body is made of water. If Brannon weighs 120 pounds, how many pounds of his body weight are water?

25. $\frac{9}{10}$ of a general group of people surveyed were recorded as being right-handed. 380 people participated in the survey.

   a. How many right-handed people were in the group?

   b. How many left-handed people were in the group?

26. Out of 640 left-handed people, $\frac{7}{8}$ of them were right-brain dominant. How many right-brain dominant people were found in the group?

27. Mrs. Stintson received a shipment of 200 elementary math books. $\frac{1}{2}$ were fifth grade books, $\frac{1}{4}$ were for grades 1–3, and $\frac{1}{4}$ were fourth grade books. How many math books were fourth grade books?

Lesson 85

Construct Meaning

Do not hold your breath for too long! Your brain requires oxygen in order to function. Without oxygen, the brain can survive only 3 to 5 minutes. When your body is at rest, the brain uses $\frac{1}{5}$ of the total amount of oxygen that is inhaled.

The physical education class is $\frac{3}{4}$ hour long. The students spent $\frac{2}{5}$ of the class running around the track. What fraction of an hour was spent running?

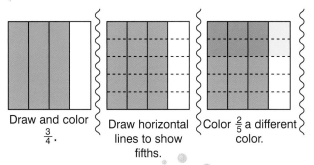

Draw and color $\frac{3}{4}$.

Draw horizontal lines to show fifths.

Color $\frac{2}{5}$ a different color.

Figure the fractional amount resulting in the overlapping color (green).

$$\frac{2}{5} \text{ of } \frac{3}{4} = \frac{6}{20} = \frac{3}{10}$$

The students spent $\frac{3}{10}$ of an hour running.

Cross-cancelling

Solve $\frac{2}{5} \times \frac{3}{4}$.
Find a common factor of the numerator of one fraction and the denominator of the other fraction.

$$\frac{2}{5} \times \frac{3}{4}$$

2 is a common factor. Divide both the numerator and the denominator by 2.

$$\frac{^{1}\cancel{2}}{5} \times \frac{3}{\cancel{4}_{2}}$$

Multiply the renamed fractions.

$$\frac{1}{5} \times \frac{3}{2} = \frac{3}{10}$$

Solve $\frac{2}{5} \times \frac{1}{6} \times \frac{3}{7}$.
Find the common factor of 2 and 6, **2**.
Divide both the numerator and the denominator by 2.

$$\frac{^{1}\cancel{2}}{5} \times \frac{1}{\cancel{6}_{3}} \times \frac{3}{7}$$

When you multiply a proper fraction by a proper fraction, the product will be less than 1.

Notice that there is another common factor, 3.
Divide both the numerator and the denominator by 3.

$$\frac{1}{5} \times \frac{1}{\cancel{3}_{1}} \times \frac{\cancel{3}^{1}}{7}$$

Multiply the renamed fractions.

$$\frac{1}{5} \times \frac{1}{1} \times \frac{1}{7} = \frac{1}{35}$$

Check Understanding

Write the multiplication equation.

a.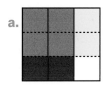

b.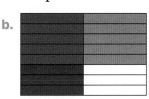

Solve.

c. $\frac{1}{3} \times \frac{4}{9}$ d. $\frac{3}{4} \times \frac{5}{6} \times \frac{1}{4}$

Write a number sentence for each model.

1.   2.   3.   4.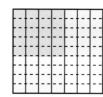

5.   6.    7. 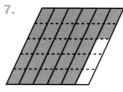   8.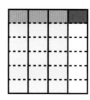

Draw a model to show the multiplication.

9. $\frac{1}{2} \times \frac{2}{7}$　　10. $\frac{5}{9} \times \frac{1}{4}$　　11. $\frac{2}{3} \times \frac{3}{5}$　　12. $\frac{3}{4} \times \frac{1}{4}$　　13. $\frac{1}{6} \times \frac{2}{5}$

Multiply by using cross-cancellation.

14. $\frac{1}{6} \times \frac{6}{7}$　　15. $\frac{2}{3} \times \frac{3}{5}$　　16. $\frac{5}{6} \times \frac{12}{15}$　　17. $\frac{3}{8} \times \frac{4}{9}$　　18. $\frac{3}{4} \times \frac{1}{3}$

19. $\frac{5}{6} \times \frac{3}{4}$　　20. $\frac{2}{3} \times \frac{3}{5} \times \frac{1}{6}$　　21. $\frac{2}{5} \times \frac{1}{4} \times \frac{5}{6}$　　22. $\frac{5}{9} \times \frac{6}{7} \times \frac{3}{10}$

23. If the organs in our bodies use $\frac{30}{35}$ of the available oxygen in our bloodstream and the brain uses $\frac{7}{30}$ of that amount, what fraction of the total oxygen does the brain use?

24. Melody played $\frac{2}{3}$ of the last half of the field hockey game. What fraction of the game did she play?

25. Three-fourths of the pie was left over, and Howard ate $\frac{1}{6}$ of the remaining amount. What fraction of the whole pie did he eat?

1. $\frac{1}{2} + \frac{3}{4}$　　2. $\frac{3}{6} + \frac{1}{9}$　　3. $\frac{6}{11} + \frac{1}{33}$　　4. $\frac{3}{7} + \frac{1}{4}$　　5. $\frac{3}{5} + \frac{2}{15}$

Construct Meaning

Intelligence is the ability to manipulate materials, anticipate, predict, learn, reason, and understand. Our intelligence is an aspect that makes us in God's image. However, being intelligent is very different from being wise. Wisdom is knowledge of what is true coupled with just judgment and insight.

> If any of you lacks wisdom, let him ask of God, who gives to all liberally and without reproach, and it will be given to him. James 1:5

A clinic specializing in I.Q. testing purchased three advertising spots on television. Each spot was $1\frac{1}{4}$ minutes long. How many minutes of advertising did the clinic purchase?

$3 \times 1\frac{1}{4}$

$1\frac{1}{4} + 1\frac{1}{4} + 1\frac{1}{4} = 3\frac{3}{4}$

Find $3 \times 1\frac{1}{4}$. Rename the whole number and mixed number as an improper fraction.

$\frac{3}{1} \times \frac{5}{4} = \frac{15}{4} = 3\frac{3}{4}$ Multiply.
Simplify.

The clinic purchased $3\frac{3}{4}$ minutes of advertising.

Find $\frac{3}{4} \times 1\frac{5}{9}$. Rename the mixed number as an improper fraction.

$\frac{\overset{1}{\cancel{3}}}{\underset{2}{\cancel{4}}} \times \frac{\overset{7}{\cancel{14}}}{\underset{3}{\cancel{9}}}$ Cross-cancel any common factors in each fraction.

$\frac{1}{2} \times \frac{7}{3} = \frac{7}{6} = 1\frac{1}{6}$ Multiply.
Simplify.

Find $2\frac{4}{5} \times 3\frac{1}{3}$. Rename the mixed numbers as improper fractions.

$\frac{14}{\underset{1}{\cancel{5}}} \times \frac{\overset{2}{\cancel{10}}}{3}$ Cross-cancel any common factors in each fraction.

$\frac{14}{1} \times \frac{2}{3} = \frac{28}{3} = 9\frac{1}{3}$ Multiply.
Simplify.

Estimating with Mixed Numbers

- Round each mixed number to the nearest whole number.

  $3\frac{2}{5} \times 1\frac{2}{3}$ Round, then multiply.

  $3 \times 2 = 6$

- Solve. $3\frac{2}{5} \times 1\frac{2}{3} = \frac{17}{5} \times \frac{\overset{1}{\cancel{5}}}{3} = \frac{17}{1} \times \frac{1}{3} = \frac{17}{3} = 5\frac{2}{3}$

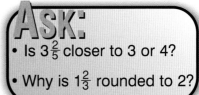

ASK:
- Is $3\frac{2}{5}$ closer to 3 or 4?
- Why is $1\frac{2}{3}$ rounded to 2?

Check Understanding

a. $4 \times 2\frac{3}{4}$

b. $\frac{2}{3} \times 1\frac{1}{4}$

c. $1\frac{3}{4} \times 2\frac{4}{5}$

d. $2\frac{2}{3} \times 3$

Multiply Fractions and Mixed Numbers

Estimate.

e. $2\frac{1}{4} \times 1\frac{3}{4}$

f. $6\frac{2}{9} \times 3\frac{2}{5}$

g. $1\frac{1}{5} \times 1\frac{1}{8}$

h. $7\frac{8}{9} \times 6\frac{1}{10}$

 **Practice**

Multiply. Write each product in simplest form.

1. $2\frac{1}{3} \times 6$

2. $2\frac{1}{7} \times \frac{2}{9}$

3. $3\frac{3}{5} \times 1\frac{2}{3}$

4. $3\frac{1}{4} \times 1\frac{3}{5}$

5. $\frac{5}{11} \times 7\frac{1}{3}$

6. $2\frac{1}{4} \times 8$

7. $4\frac{1}{6} \times \frac{3}{5}$

8. $9 \times 1\frac{2}{3}$

Estimate by rounding to the nearest whole number.

9. $2\frac{1}{4} \times 2\frac{2}{3}$

10. $3\frac{5}{6} \times \frac{2}{3}$

11. $4\frac{3}{8} \times 2\frac{4}{7}$

12. $5\frac{1}{7} \times 2\frac{5}{8}$

13. $3\frac{1}{2} \times 1\frac{3}{4}$

14. $8\frac{1}{3} \times 3\frac{2}{3}$

15. $4\frac{3}{8} \times 5\frac{2}{9}$

16. $10\frac{1}{5} \times 8\frac{8}{9}$

 Apply

17. Mina's father measured her height and marked it on the closet door. She discovered that she was $4\frac{3}{8}$ feet tall and that the door was $1\frac{3}{5}$ times her height. What is the height of the door?

18. Higher Connections Landscaping has planted daffodils that grow $2\frac{1}{2}$ feet high along a fence. The fence is $2\frac{1}{4}$ times as high as the daffodils. What is the height of the fence?

19. Mr. Aki owned $26\frac{1}{2}$ acres of land. Two years ago he purchased another $56\frac{3}{4}$ acres of land. Mr. Aki is selling $\frac{1}{3}$ of his total acres to his nephew. How many acres will Mr. Aki have after the sale?

20. Cody's car holds $24\frac{1}{2}$ gallons of gasoline. On his trip to Nebraska he started with $17\frac{5}{8}$ gallons. When he arrived, he had $\frac{1}{3}$ of that amount remaining in his tank. How many gallons did Cody use?

 **Review**

1. $\frac{1}{2} - \frac{1}{4}$

2. $\frac{2}{3} - \frac{1}{6}$

3. $\frac{5}{6} - \frac{3}{5}$

4. $\frac{3}{4} - \frac{3}{8}$

5. $\frac{2}{3} - \frac{4}{9}$

185

For the LORD is the great God, and the great King above all gods. In His hand are the deep places of the earth; The heights of the hills are His also. The sea is His, for He made it. Psalm 95:3–5a

God's wisdom in creating the earth is very evident. Seashells, for example, are simple but complex objects. The growth patterns on a seashell can be found to follow mathematical patterns—even patterns involving fractions.

Arco and Else were examining a seashell to find a pattern. They decided to divide the shell into fourths and look more closely at each section.

 Models can demonstrate dividing a whole number by a fraction. How many fourths will fit into or cover 1 whole?

$$1 \div \frac{1}{4} = \frac{1}{4}\frac{1}{4}\frac{1}{4}\frac{1}{4}$$ Four fourths will fit into 1 whole.

 How many $\frac{1}{3}$ parts will fit into 2 circles?
$2 \div \frac{1}{3} = 6$

 How many $\frac{1}{4}$ cups will fill 3 cups?
$3 \div \frac{1}{4} = 12$

 Models can help you divide a fraction by a fraction. A pie was divided into eighths. How many eighths are in $\frac{6}{8}$ of a pie?

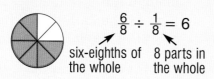 $\frac{6}{8} \div \frac{1}{8} = 6$

six-eighths of   8 parts in
the whole   the whole

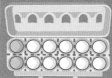

The egg carton has 12 sections.
How many eggs are in $\frac{2}{12}$ of the carton?
$\frac{2}{12} \div \frac{1}{12} = 2$
There are 2 eggs in $\frac{2}{12}$ of the carton.

 Models can help you divide a mixed number by a fraction.

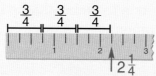
$$\frac{3}{4} \quad \frac{3}{4} \quad \frac{3}{4}$$

How many $\frac{3}{4}$ inches fit into $2\frac{1}{4}$ inches as seen on the ruler? $2\frac{1}{4} \div \frac{3}{4} = 3$

$2\frac{1}{4}$

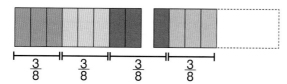
$$\frac{3}{8} \quad \frac{3}{8} \quad \frac{3}{8} \quad \frac{3}{8}$$

How many $\frac{3}{8}$ parts will fit into $1\frac{1}{2}$?

$1\frac{1}{2} \div \frac{3}{8} = n$ $n = 4$

 **Check Understanding**

Complete the number sentence for each model.

a.   b. 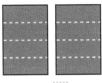 c. 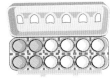 d.

$1 \div \boxed{} = 12$ $2 \div \boxed{} = 8$ $\frac{4}{12} \div \frac{1}{12} = \boxed{}$ $1\frac{4}{6} \div \frac{1}{6} = \boxed{}$

 **Practice**

Write the number sentence that matches the model.

$3 \div \frac{1}{3} = 9$

$\frac{2}{3} \div \frac{1}{12} = 8$

$1\frac{2}{3} \div \frac{1}{3} = 5$

$\frac{1}{2} \div \frac{1}{8} = 4$

1.   2. 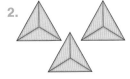   3.

4.

Use the model to find the quotient.

5.   6.   7.   8.

$1\frac{1}{3} \div \frac{1}{6}$ $\frac{5}{8} \div \frac{1}{8}$ $2 \div \frac{1}{3}$ $\frac{4}{5} \div \frac{1}{5}$

Draw a model for each number sentence.

9. $\frac{1}{2} \div \frac{1}{4} = 2$ 10. $2\frac{1}{2} \div \frac{1}{2} = 5$ 11. $\frac{5}{6} \div \frac{1}{6} = 5$ 12. $3 \div \frac{3}{8} = 8$

Complete the number sentence for each model.

13. 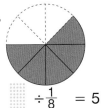   14. 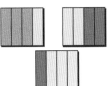   15. 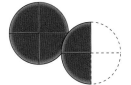   16.

$\boxed{} \div \frac{1}{8} = 5$ $3 \div \frac{3}{4} = \boxed{}$ $1\frac{1}{2} \div \boxed{} = 6$ $1 \div \boxed{} = \boxed{}$

 Review

1. $\frac{3}{7} + \frac{1}{4}$ 2. $\frac{2}{3} + \frac{1}{6}$ 3. $\frac{4}{9} + \frac{1}{2}$ 4. $\frac{4}{5} + \frac{2}{10}$

5. $\frac{1}{3} + \frac{1}{9}$ 6. $\frac{3}{14} + \frac{2}{7}$ 7. $\frac{3}{10} + \frac{2}{20}$ 8. $\frac{2}{9} + \frac{1}{3}$

Lesson 88

Construct Meaning

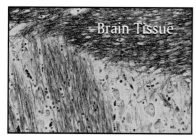

Brain Tissue

Ben Carson grew up in the inner-city of Detroit. Through hard work, motivation from his mother, and help from the Lord, he became a neurosurgeon. Dr. Carson refined a surgery technique to stop severe seizures by removing a fraction of the brain. This operation, a hemispherectomy, has helped many children lead healthy, normal lives.

To divide a whole number by a fraction, think: How many of this fraction are in this whole number?

How many $\frac{2}{3}$ are in 4 yards? $4 \div \frac{2}{3} = n$

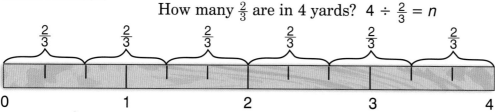

There are six $\frac{2}{3}$ in 4 yards.

Solve $4 \div \frac{2}{3}$.

The shortcut for dividing fractions is called "invert and multiply." Multiply the dividend (4) by the reciprocal of the divisor. A **reciprocal** is a fraction whose numerator and denominator have been reversed. The product of two reciprocals is 1.

$$4 \div \frac{2}{3} =$$
$$4 \times \frac{3}{2} =$$
$$\frac{12}{2} = 6$$

$$\frac{2}{3} \times \frac{3}{2} = \frac{6}{6} = 1$$

reciprocals

WHY DOES THE SHORTCUT WORK?

- Think about $1 \div \frac{1}{3}$. How many thirds fit into 1?

- Think about $1 \div \frac{2}{3}$. How many two-thirds fit into 1?

  In the model above, cover the portion to the right of the 1 mark.
  1 two-thirds part and $\frac{1}{2}$ of a two-thirds part equal 1.

  $1\frac{1}{2}$ two-thirds parts fit into 1.

- How many two-thirds parts would be in 4?
  4 times as many parts as in 1.
  So $4 \div \frac{2}{3}$ would be $4 \times 1\frac{1}{2}$, or $4 \times \frac{3}{2}$.

  $$4 \div \frac{2}{3} = 4 \times \frac{3}{2}$$

  $\frac{2}{3}$ and $\frac{3}{2}$ are reciprocals.

Check your answer.
Multiply the quotient by the divisor of the original problem.

dividend $\underbrace{4}$ $\div$ $\underbrace{\frac{2}{3}}_{\text{divisor}}$ $=$ $\underbrace{6}_{\text{quotient}}$ $6 \times \frac{2}{3} = \frac{{}^2\cancel{6}}{1} \times \frac{2}{3}_1 = \frac{2}{1} \times \frac{2}{1} = \underbrace{4}$ The product should match the dividend.

$$4 = 4$$

Divide Whole Numbers by Fractions

Check Understanding

Solve.

a. $2 \div \frac{1}{3}$ b. $6 \div \frac{1}{4}$ c. $3 \div \frac{1}{2}$ d. $8 \div \frac{2}{3}$ e. $4 \div \frac{1}{6}$

Practice

Find the quotient.

1. $2 \div \frac{2}{5} = n$

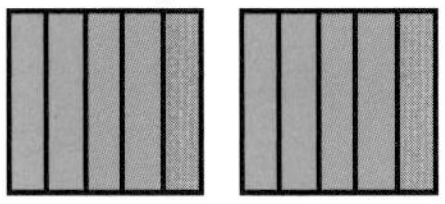

2. $2 \div \frac{2}{3} = n$

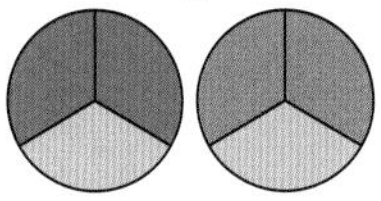

3. $3 \div \frac{1}{6} = n$

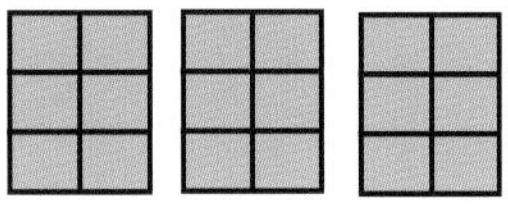

4. $1 \div \frac{1}{5} = n$

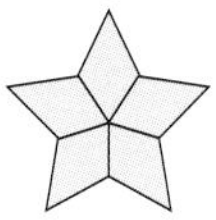

Write a division equation for each model.

5. 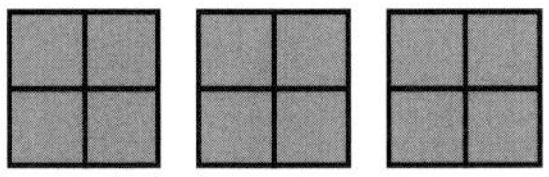

6. 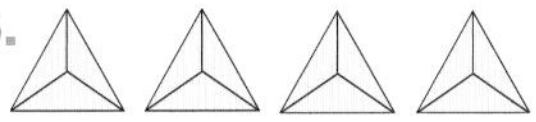

7. 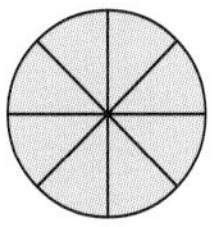

8. 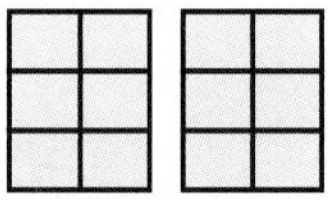

Find the quotient. Check your answer by multiplying.

9. $4 \div \frac{1}{2}$ 10. $3 \div \frac{1}{4}$ 11. $6 \div \frac{3}{5}$ 12. $9 \div \frac{3}{7}$ 13. $6 \div \frac{3}{4}$

14. $2 \div \frac{1}{6}$ 15. $4 \div \frac{2}{5}$ 16. $3 \div \frac{1}{8}$ 17. $8 \div \frac{4}{9}$ 18. $2 \div \frac{1}{11}$

Apply

19. If it takes four doctors 18 hours to perform a complicated neurosurgery and each doctor takes a turn every $\frac{3}{4}$ of an hour, how many turns will each doctor have during the surgery?

20. For each thirty-minute period of an hour-long medical program, a television station allows six minutes of commercials. How many $\frac{1}{3}$-minute commercials can be broadcast during a half-hour amount of time?

21. Charity knits one pair of baby booties every $\frac{3}{4}$ of an hour for the pediatric ward at the hospital. How many booties can she knit in six hours?

22. A parcel of land measuring 101 acres has been sold to a developer who plans to reserve one acre for a new neurosurgery clinic. The land will be broken into $\frac{5}{8}$-acre lots. How many lots will result?

23. During high fire danger season in the Deshuttes National Forest, every $\frac{3}{4}$ of an acre has one fire road built to contain any potential forest fires. If the southern part of the forest is 390 acres, how many fire roads have been built in that area?

Construct Meaning

Every human brain has different types of neurons (nerve cells) numbering from 10 to 100 billion. Neurons are very small cells that range in size from 4 to 100 microns wide (one micron is one-thousandth of a millimeter). It is the job of a neuron to transmit "messages" such as nerve impulses or sensory stimuli. Seeing, smelling, and tasting pizza are all "messages" transmitted by neurons.

Neuron

The Browns ate $\frac{3}{4}$ of a pizza at a family outing. If each serving is $\frac{1}{8}$ of a pizza, how many servings were eaten?

Use a model.

The drawing shows $\frac{3}{4}$ of the pizza. Count the number of eighths that are in $\frac{3}{4}$.

Six servings were eaten.

Divide.

$\frac{3}{4} \div \frac{1}{8}$

Remember the shortcut: Multiply the dividend by the reciprocal of the divisor.

$\frac{3}{4} \times \frac{8}{1}$ Reciprocal of $\frac{1}{8}$ is $\frac{8}{1}$ because $\frac{1}{8} \times \frac{8}{1} = \frac{8}{8} = 1$

$\frac{3}{4_1} \times \frac{8^2}{1}$ Cross-cancel.

$\frac{3}{1} \times \frac{2}{1} = \frac{6}{1} = 6$ Multiply.

Check your answer by multiplying.
Multiply the quotient by the divisor of the original problem.

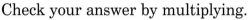

$\left(\frac{3}{4}\right) \div \frac{1}{8} = 6$

dividend   divisor   quotient

$6 \times \frac{1}{8} = \frac{6^3}{1} \times \frac{1}{8_4} = \frac{3}{1} \times \frac{1}{4} = \left(\frac{3}{4}\right)$

The product should match the dividend.

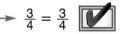 $\frac{3}{4} = \frac{3}{4}$ ✓

Check Understanding

Find the quotient.

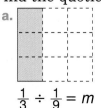

a.

$\frac{1}{3} \div \frac{1}{9} = m$

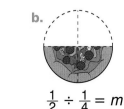

b.

$\frac{1}{2} \div \frac{1}{4} = m$

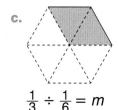

c.

$\frac{1}{3} \div \frac{1}{6} = m$

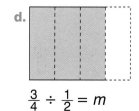

d.

$\frac{3}{4} \div \frac{1}{2} = m$

Divide.

e. $\frac{3}{4} \div \frac{1}{4}$ f. $\frac{1}{2} \div \frac{1}{4}$ g. $\frac{5}{6} \div \frac{1}{6}$ h. $\frac{2}{3} \div \frac{1}{3}$ i. $\frac{5}{8} \div \frac{3}{8}$

Find the quotient.

1.

$\frac{7}{8} \div \frac{1}{8} = x$

2.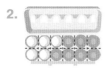

$\frac{5}{12} \div \frac{1}{12} = x$

3.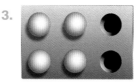

$\frac{2}{3} \div \frac{1}{6} = x$

4.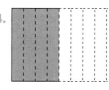

$\frac{1}{2} \div \frac{1}{8} = x$

Write the reciprocal.

5. $\frac{1}{2}$ 6. $\frac{4}{5}$ 7. $\frac{5}{8}$ 8. $\frac{1}{5}$ 9. 6   10. $\frac{7}{8}$

Find the quotient. Check by multiplying.

11. $\frac{7}{9} \div \frac{1}{9}$ 12. $\frac{9}{14} \div \frac{3}{14}$ 13. $\frac{2}{3} \div \frac{4}{9}$ 14. $\frac{6}{7} \div \frac{3}{14}$

15. $\frac{3}{5} \div \frac{1}{2}$ 16. $\frac{5}{9} \div \frac{5}{18}$ 17. $\frac{7}{9} \div \frac{1}{6}$ 18. $\frac{4}{5} \div \frac{2}{7}$

19. $\frac{2}{3} \div \frac{11}{12}$ 20. $\frac{3}{5} \div \frac{6}{7}$ 21. $\frac{3}{8} \div \frac{9}{16}$ 22. $\frac{3}{7} \div \frac{2}{3}$

23. Ellison has $\frac{5}{8}$ of the book remaining to read. He plans on reading $\frac{1}{4}$ of the book every night until it is finished. How many nights will Ellison have to read in order to finish the book?

24. The carpenter is making a shim for a file cabinet and has a piece of $\frac{1}{4}$-inch thick wood that is $\frac{6}{7}$ of a foot long. How many $\frac{1}{5}$-foot pieces can he cut from his piece of wood?

25. There are half a dozen eggs left in the egg carton and the recipe calls for $\frac{1}{6}$ of those. How many eggs will Beth need if she triples the recipe?

26. The sixth grade teacher has $\frac{5}{8}$ of an hour to complete the standardized testing sessions with her students. If each session takes $\frac{1}{5}$ of an hour, how many sessions will she complete?

Review

1. $\frac{2}{5} - \frac{1}{4}$ 2. $\frac{3}{5} - \frac{1}{3}$ 3. $\frac{5}{8} - \frac{3}{5}$ 4. $\frac{7}{8} - \frac{3}{4}$ 5. $\frac{5}{6} - \frac{7}{10}$

6. $\frac{9}{10} - \frac{3}{4}$ 7. $\frac{1}{5} - \frac{1}{8}$ 8. $\frac{3}{8} - \frac{1}{4}$ 9. $\frac{1}{2} - \frac{2}{5}$ 10. $\frac{3}{10} - \frac{1}{5}$

Lesson 90

Construct Meaning

Frontal Lobe

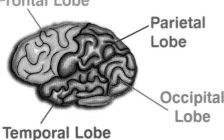

Parietal Lobe

Occipital Lobe

Temporal Lobe

The human brain is divided into four lobes. The lobes are separated by the various grooves and bumps on the surface of the brain. Each lobe performs a different function. The lobes are called the frontal lobe, occipital lobe, parietal lobe, and temporal lobe.

The parietal lobe may be divided into four equal sections. If the total surface area is $28\frac{1}{3}$ square inches, what is the surface area of each section?

$28\frac{1}{3} \div 4$

$\frac{85}{3} \div \frac{4}{1}$ Rename the mixed number as an improper fraction.

Rename the whole number as a fraction.

Use the shortcut:

$\frac{85}{3} \times \frac{1}{4}$ Multiply by the reciprocal.

$\frac{85}{12} = 7\frac{1}{12}$ Rename the improper fraction as a mixed number.

Each section is $7\frac{1}{12}$ square inches.

Solve $2\frac{2}{3} \div \frac{2}{3}$.

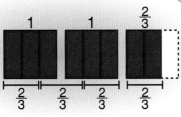

$1 \qquad 1 \qquad \frac{2}{3}$

$\frac{2}{3} \quad \frac{2}{3} \quad \frac{2}{3} \quad \frac{2}{3}$

Rename the mixed number as an improper fraction. $\frac{8}{3} \div \frac{2}{3}$

Multiply by the reciprocal. Cross-cancel. $\overset{4}{\underset{1}{\cancel{\frac{8}{3}}}} \times \overset{1}{\underset{1}{\cancel{\frac{3}{2}}}}$

Rename the improper fraction. $\frac{4}{1} \times \frac{1}{1} = \frac{4}{1} = 4$

Solve $2\frac{2}{9} \div 2\frac{2}{3}$. ═══════════

Rename the mixed numbers. $\frac{20}{9} \div \frac{8}{3}$

Multiply by the reciprocal. $\frac{20}{9} \times \frac{3}{8}$

Cross-cancel. Multiply. $\overset{5}{\underset{3}{\cancel{\frac{20}{9}}}} \times \overset{1}{\underset{2}{\cancel{\frac{3}{8}}}} = \frac{5}{3} \times \frac{1}{2} = \frac{5}{6}$

Estimating Quotients

Round each mixed number to the nearest whole number to estimate the quotient.

$6\frac{1}{9} \div 2\frac{3}{4}$ Round, then divide.

$6 \div 3 = 2$

$5\frac{2}{3} \div 1\frac{1}{5}$ Round, then divide.

$6 \div 1 = 6$

Check Understanding

Solve.

a. $\frac{6}{7} \div 1\frac{5}{7}$
b. $3\frac{1}{8} \div \frac{5}{6}$
c. $6\frac{2}{5} \div \frac{8}{15}$
d. $2\frac{1}{9} \div 2\frac{2}{9}$

192

Estimate.

e. $1\frac{3}{4} \div 1\frac{1}{6}$ f. $8\frac{2}{9} \div 4\frac{1}{4}$ g. $9\frac{1}{3} \div 3\frac{1}{4}$ h. $1\frac{7}{8} \div 1\frac{2}{9}$

 **Practice**

Write each mixed number as an improper fraction. Then write its reciprocal.

1. $4\frac{1}{2}$ 2. $1\frac{5}{8}$ 3. $7\frac{1}{7}$ 4. $3\frac{4}{9}$ 5. $8\frac{2}{3}$ 6. $6\frac{1}{9}$

Estimate the quotient.

7. $4\frac{1}{3} \div 2\frac{1}{5}$ 8. $9\frac{3}{5} \div 2\frac{2}{9}$ 9. $5\frac{6}{7} \div 3\frac{1}{8}$ 10. $15\frac{3}{8} \div 5\frac{3}{8}$

11. $13\frac{1}{4} \div 1\frac{2}{9}$ 12. $23\frac{3}{5} \div 5\frac{7}{8}$ 13. $8\frac{2}{31} \div 4\frac{3}{43}$ 14. $17\frac{18}{25} \div 2\frac{3}{4}$

Find the quotient.

15. $4\frac{1}{2} \div 12$ 16. $7\frac{4}{5} \div \frac{3}{5}$ 17. $4\frac{3}{8} \div 3\frac{1}{2}$ 18. $5 \div 1\frac{1}{7}$

19. $8\frac{1}{3} \div \frac{5}{9}$ 20. $\frac{5}{7} \div 1\frac{2}{3}$ 21. $\frac{2}{5} \div 3\frac{3}{5}$ 22. $5\frac{1}{4} \div 8\frac{1}{6}$

 Apply

23. Baby Jessica's weight at one year was about $2\frac{1}{2}$ times her weight at birth. At one-year of age she weighed $22\frac{1}{2}$ pounds. What was her weight at birth?

24. During a 30-minute television program there are about $5\frac{1}{3}$ minutes of advertising. If each commercial is an average of $\frac{2}{3}$ minutes long, how many commercials can be shown?

25. Elizabeth filled the bird feeder from a $10\frac{1}{2}$-pound bag. Every day she fed the birds with $\frac{1}{5}$-pound. How many days was she able to feed the birds from the $10\frac{1}{2}$-pound bag?

26. Lisel is covering the bathroom shelves in her house. She has $11\frac{1}{4}$ feet of shelving paper. How many shelves can she cover if each shelf is $1\frac{1}{2}$ feet long?

Review

1. $1\frac{1}{2} + 2\frac{1}{4}$ 2. $3\frac{2}{9} + 1\frac{1}{9}$ 3. $8\frac{1}{4} + 2\frac{1}{8}$ 4. $6\frac{7}{8} + 4\frac{1}{8}$

5. $7\frac{5}{9} + 3\frac{4}{9}$ 6. $2\frac{1}{5} + 3\frac{3}{4}$ 7. $2\frac{7}{8} + 2\frac{1}{8}$ 8. $3\frac{9}{10} + 4\frac{1}{5}$

Lesson 91

Construct Meaning

Mr. Boccelli's class has 4 boxes of materials for a science activity. There are 3 glass cylinders and 6 plastic cylinders in each box. If there are 20 students in the class, but 2 are absent, what is the maximum number of cylinders that may be given to each student?

$$\frac{4 \times (3 + 6)}{20 - 2}$$

ORDER OF OPERATIONS

★ Simplify the numerator.
1. Do the operations in parentheses first.
2. Multiply and divide from left to right.
3. Add and subtract from left to right
★ Simplify the denominator using the above steps.
★ Divide the numerator by the denominator.

• Do the operations in the numerator.

$$\frac{4 \times (3 + 6)}{20 - 2} = \frac{4 \times 9}{20 - 2} = \frac{36}{20 - 2}$$

• Do the operations in the denominator.

$$\frac{36}{20 - 2} = \frac{36}{18}$$

• Divide.

$$\frac{36}{18} = 36 \div 18 = 2$$

Each student may receive 2 cylinders.

The health food store has 4 pounds of almonds to divide evenly into jars. If each jar holds $\frac{2}{3}$ of a pound, how many will be filled by 4 pounds of almonds?

A **complex fraction** has a fraction in the numerator and/or the denominator.

complex fraction $\frac{4}{\frac{2}{3}}$ is $4 \div \frac{2}{3}$.

Multiply by the reciprocal. $\frac{4}{1} \times \frac{3}{2}$

Cross-cancel. $\frac{\overset{2}{4}}{1} \times \frac{3}{\underset{1}{2}}$

Multiply the renamed fractions. $\frac{2}{1} \times \frac{3}{1} = 6$

Simplify $\frac{2}{3}{12}$.

$\frac{\frac{2}{3}}{12}$ is $\frac{2}{3} \div 12$.

Multiply by the reciprocal. $\frac{2}{3} \times \frac{1}{12}$

Cross-cancel. $\frac{\overset{1}{2}}{3} \times \frac{1}{\underset{6}{12}}$

Multiply the renamed fractions. $\frac{1}{3} \times \frac{1}{6} = \frac{1}{18}$

Simplify $\frac{\frac{3}{8}}{\frac{5}{6}}$.

$\frac{\frac{3}{8}}{\frac{5}{6}}$ is $\frac{3}{8} \div \frac{5}{6}$.

Multiply by the reciprocal. $\frac{3}{8} \div \frac{5}{6} = \frac{3}{8} \times \frac{6}{5}$

Cross-cancel. $\frac{3}{\underset{4}{8}} \times \frac{\overset{3}{6}}{5}$

Multiply the renamed fractions. $\frac{3}{4} \times \frac{3}{5} = \frac{9}{20}$

194

Order of Operations with Fractions

 **Check Understanding**

Solve using the order of operations.

a. $\dfrac{1 + 3 \times 5}{4 \times 2}$

b. $\dfrac{6 + 40 \div 2}{16 - 14}$

c. $\dfrac{14 - 6}{2 \times (8 - 4)}$

Simplify.

d. $\dfrac{\frac{1}{2}}{3}$

e. $\dfrac{6}{\frac{3}{4}}$

f. $\dfrac{\frac{2}{5}}{\frac{1}{4}}$

 Practice

Solve.

1. $\dfrac{2 + 5 \times 6}{12 \div 3}$

2. $\dfrac{12 + 4 \times 2}{16 - 12 \div 1}$

3. $\dfrac{(6 + 4) \times 2}{18 \div (2 + 4)}$

4. $\dfrac{8 - 4 + 2 \times 7}{9 - 4 \times 2}$

5. $\dfrac{24 \div (2 + 6)}{(25 - 22) \div 4}$

6. $\dfrac{(2 + 8) \times 2 + 1}{(1 + 5) \div 2}$

7. $\dfrac{14 - 2}{16 \times 2 - 12}$

8. $\dfrac{10 - 6}{2 \times (4 + 3)}$

Simplify.

9. $\dfrac{8}{\frac{2}{3}}$

10. $\dfrac{\frac{4}{5}}{\frac{1}{5}}$

11. $\dfrac{\frac{5}{5}}{\frac{5}{8}}$

12. $\dfrac{\frac{3}{8}}{3}$

13. $\dfrac{6}{\frac{3}{4}}$

14. $\dfrac{\frac{4}{9}}{\frac{5}{6}}$

15. $\dfrac{\frac{1}{2}}{\frac{1}{3}}$

16. $\dfrac{\frac{3}{7}}{\frac{3}{4}}$

 **Apply**

17. The cookie recipe calls for $\frac{3}{4}$ cup of sugar for one batch of cookies. If Amber has a total of 9 cups of sugar, how many batches of cookies can she make? Write a complex fraction and simplify.

18. The watercolor class received six boxes of paintbrushes. There are 4 thin and 6 wide paintbrushes in each box. If there are 34 students in the class but 4 brought their own brushes, how many brushes will be given to each student? Solve using the order of operations. $\dfrac{6 \times (4 + 6)}{34 - 4}$

Challenge

19. $\dfrac{(6 + 4) \times 2}{(\frac{1}{3} + \frac{1}{3}) \times \frac{1}{2}}$

20. $\dfrac{(4 + 3) \times 2}{(\frac{1}{2} + \frac{1}{2}) \times 2}$

 Review

1. $1\frac{1}{2} + 2\frac{2}{3}$

2. $3\frac{4}{5} + 6\frac{1}{5}$

3. $6\frac{3}{8} - 5\frac{1}{8}$

4. $1\frac{6}{7} - \frac{5}{7}$

5. $\frac{4}{5} + 2\frac{1}{3}$

6. $3\frac{2}{5} - \frac{1}{4}$

7. $1\frac{8}{9} - \frac{1}{9}$

8. $4\frac{1}{9} + 2\frac{1}{3}$

© Copyright 2002

195

Practice

Each portion of the brain has particular functions. The prefrontal cortex is part of the frontal lobe and is responsible for problem solving, emotions, and complex thought. In this lesson, we will be exercising our prefrontal cortex.

1. On Megan's trip she kept track of her gas mileage. Her car averages $24\frac{1}{2}$ miles per gallon and the gas tank holds $10\frac{1}{4}$ gallons. How many miles can Megan travel on one tank of gasoline?

2. A resolution can be passed in the United States Senate by a $\frac{2}{3}$ majority vote. If there are 100 senators, use mental math to determine the number of votes which constitute a $\frac{2}{3}$ majority.

3. Inez wants to plant $\frac{5}{8}$ of her 56-foot-long garden with flowers. If she wants a larkspur plant every $\frac{1}{4}$ foot, how many larkspurs will she have in the garden?

4. Mr. George has decided to divide his land evenly among his four children. If he has $684\frac{3}{4}$ acres, how many acres will he give to each of his children?

5. Mr. Gundo donated several pounds of canned vegetables to the food bank. If $\frac{1}{6}$ of the vegetables were green beans, $\frac{1}{3}$ of the vegetables were tomatoes, and the remainder of the vegetables were sweet corn, what fraction of the vegetables were sweet corn?

6. Mrs. Meissner has $5\frac{1}{4}$ yards of material to make dresses for her two daughters. If each dress uses $3\frac{1}{4}$ yards of material, how much more material does she need to purchase?

7. The Ranchers Feed Store has a total of $26\frac{1}{4}$ bushels of feed to be loaded into containers. If each container can hold $3\frac{1}{4}$ bushels of feed, how many containers can they fill?

8. The Clarks plan to do volunteer work 6 hours a week. On Saturdays they work for $2\frac{1}{4}$ hours. They divide the rest of the time evenly over the weekdays. How much volunteer work do they do each weekday?

9. Jeff and Jayson went fishing with their grandfather. Jeff caught a fish weighing $10\frac{5}{8}$ pounds, and Jayson caught a fish weighing $12\frac{1}{16}$ pounds. How much more did Jayson's fish weigh than Jeff's?

10. Florence's monthly income is $1,485. She spends $\frac{1}{3}$ of her income on housing, $\frac{1}{5}$ goes into savings, and $\frac{2}{5}$ is spent on food. How much is left after housing, food, and savings?

Estimate using compatible numbers.

11. If $\frac{3}{5}$ of the students at West Wellingford Middle School exercise regularly and there are 392 students, how many students exercise regularly?

12. Approximately $\frac{1}{10}$ of a movie video's time is designated for previews. Sarah watched a video for 132 minutes. How many minutes of previews did Sarah watch?

13. The department store is advertising $\frac{1}{3}$ off all marked items in the store. The regular price for a pair of dress shoes is $88. If Floyd bought a pair of dress shoes, approximately how much money did he save?

Estimate by rounding to the nearest whole number.

14. It takes $1\frac{7}{8}$ yards of ribbon to make a bow for decorating a gift package. How many bows can be made from $15\frac{1}{3}$ yards of ribbon?

15. Miss Sanders, a secretary, can type $8\frac{1}{3}$ pages every hour. If she typed for $5\frac{7}{12}$ hours, approximately how many pages did she type?

16. The hike from Clear Springs to Copperhill Falls is $14\frac{3}{8}$ miles. A water pump is placed every $2\frac{3}{4}$ miles along the trail. How many water pumps are between Clear Springs and Copperhill Falls?

 **Construct Meaning**

Maris and Arthur purchased 230 licorice candies to share with their classmates. They decided to give away half of the licorice each week. How many weeks will it take for Maris and Arthur to give away all of their candy?

WEEK	1	2	3	4	5	6
Number of Candies	115	57.5	28.75			
Fraction Amount	$\frac{1}{2}$	$\frac{1}{4}$	$\frac{1}{8}$	$\frac{1}{16}$		

Copy and complete the chart to the sixth week.

After six weeks will all of the licorice be gone?

Will all of the licorice ever be given away? Explain your answer.

The **betweenness property** means that for any two numbers, there is another number between them.

To find the number halfway between $\frac{1}{2}$ and $\frac{1}{4}$, find the average of the numbers.

$\frac{1}{2} + \frac{1}{4}$ Add the numbers and divide by 2.

$\frac{2}{4} + \frac{1}{4} = \frac{3}{4}$

$\frac{3}{4} \div 2 = \frac{3}{4} \times \frac{1}{2} = \frac{3}{8}$

To find the number halfway between $\frac{1}{50}$ and $\frac{1}{100}$, find the average of the numbers.

$\frac{1}{50} + \frac{1}{100}$ Add the numbers.

$\frac{2}{100} + \frac{1}{100} = \frac{3}{100}$

$\frac{3}{100} \div 2$ Divide the sum by 2.

$\frac{3}{100} \times \frac{1}{2} = \frac{3}{200}$ $\frac{3}{200}$ is halfway between $\frac{1}{50}$ and $\frac{1}{100}$.

 **Check Understanding**

Find the number halfway between each pair.

a. $\frac{1}{3}$ $\frac{2}{3}$
b. $\frac{1}{2}$ $\frac{5}{8}$
c. $\frac{1}{10}$ $\frac{1}{100}$
d. $\frac{2}{5}$ $\frac{3}{5}$
e. $\frac{1}{9}$ $\frac{2}{9}$

Chapter Seven Study Guide

Solve.

1. $25 \times \frac{3}{5}$ *Lesson 83*

2. $85 \times \frac{1}{3}$ *Lesson 83*

3. $8 \times \frac{3}{4}$ *Lesson 83*

4. $\frac{2}{3} \times 5$ *Lesson 84*

5. $\frac{1}{4} \times \frac{2}{5}$ *Lesson 85*

6. $\frac{2}{3} \times 1\frac{1}{2}$ *Lesson 86*

Estimate by rounding to the nearest whole number.   *Lesson 86*

7. $2\frac{2}{3} \times 4\frac{1}{4}$

8. $3\frac{8}{9} \times 6\frac{1}{3}$

Use the model to find the quotient.   *Lesson 87*

9.

$1\frac{1}{2} \div \frac{1}{8} = x$

10.

$\frac{1}{2} \div \frac{1}{12} = x$

11.

$\frac{3}{5} \div \frac{1}{5} = x$

Estimate by using compatible numbers.   *Lesson 88*

12. $9 \div \frac{2}{5}$

13. $153 \div \frac{2}{3}$

Solve.

14. $8 \div \frac{1}{4}$ *Lesson 88*

15. $\frac{2}{5} \div \frac{1}{4}$ *Lesson 89*

16. $2\frac{3}{4} \div \frac{3}{4}$ *Lesson 90*

Estimate by rounding to the nearest whole number.   *Lesson 90*

17. $8\frac{1}{5} \div 2\frac{1}{9}$

18. $17\frac{3}{4} \div 2\frac{8}{9}$

Solve.

19. $\dfrac{4 + 12 - 12}{(8 + 4) \div 2 + 1}$ *Lesson 91*

20. Hillary spends $\frac{3}{7}$ of her $350 paycheck on rent and puts $\frac{1}{5}$ into savings. The rest she keeps as cash. What part of her check did she keep as cash?   *Lesson 92*

Lesson 94

Fraction Fiesta

Write a number sentence represented by each model.

1.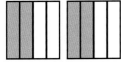

2.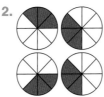

3.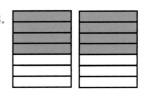

Complete the number sentence represented by each model.

4.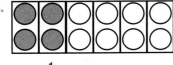

$\frac{1}{3} \times 12 = $ ▦

5.

▦ $\times 12 = 3$

6.

$\frac{2}{5} \times$ ▦ $= 10$

Solve.

7. $6 \times \frac{1}{4}$

8. $9 \times \frac{2}{3}$

9. $4 \times \frac{3}{4}$

10. $8 \times \frac{7}{8}$

11. $3 \times \frac{8}{9}$

12. $\frac{5}{12} \times 16$

13. $\frac{1}{2} \times 18$

14. $\frac{5}{6} \times 12$

15. $\frac{3}{5} \times 15$

16. $\frac{3}{4} \times 12$

17. One-fifth of 300 people and three-fifths of 275 people were surveyed and recorded as preferring pie over cake. How many people preferred pie over cake?

Complete the number sentence represented by each model.

18.

$\frac{3}{4} \times$ ▦ $=$ ▦

19.

$\frac{2}{3} \times$ ▦ $=$ ▦

20.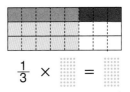

$\frac{1}{3} \times$ ▦ $=$ ▦

Solve.

21. $\frac{3}{4} \times \frac{1}{8}$

22. $\frac{5}{9} \times \frac{3}{5}$

23. $\frac{1}{4} \times \frac{2}{5} \times \frac{1}{3}$

24. $2\frac{2}{7} \times 5\frac{5}{6}$

25. $3\frac{4}{5} \times \frac{1}{2}$

26. $\frac{4}{5} \times 2\frac{2}{9}$

27. Two-fifths of the pizza were left over. Wendy ate one-sixth of that remaining amount. What fraction of the pizza did she eat?

Be diligent to present yourself approved to God, a worker who does not need to be ashamed, rightly dividing the word of truth. II Timothy 2:15

Find the quotient.

28.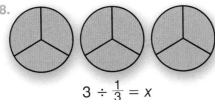

$3 \div \frac{1}{3} = x$

29.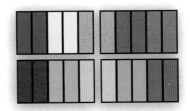

$4 \div \frac{2}{5} = x$

Solve.

30. $4 \div \frac{1}{4}$

31. $12 \div \frac{2}{3}$

32. $9 \div \frac{3}{4}$

33. $8 \div \frac{2}{9}$

34. $9 \div \frac{6}{7}$

35. $3\frac{4}{5} \div \frac{1}{5}$

36. $3\frac{1}{4} \div 2\frac{1}{6}$

37. $2\frac{3}{5} \div 1\frac{1}{2}$

38. $4\frac{1}{2} \div 3\frac{3}{8}$

39. Chandra is covering the rental house cupboards with shelving paper. She has $12\frac{1}{4}$ feet of paper. How many cupboards can she cover if each cupboard is $2\frac{1}{2}$ feet long?

40. If $6\frac{3}{4}$ pounds of almonds, $3\frac{1}{2}$ pounds of cashews, and $1\frac{5}{8}$ pounds of peanuts are divided equally to make 5 bags of mixed nuts, how much will each bag weigh?

Solve using the order of operations.

41. $\dfrac{(3 + 1) - 2}{6 \div 3 \times 2}$

42. $\dfrac{8 + 9 - 1}{8 \div 2 - 2}$

43. $\frac{1}{8} + \frac{1}{6} \times \frac{1}{2} \times 3$

Simplify each complex fraction.

44. $\dfrac{12}{\frac{2}{3}}$

45. $\dfrac{\frac{1}{2}}{\frac{1}{4}}$

46. $\dfrac{\frac{3}{4}}{\frac{3}{8}}$

47. Mr. Sprague is taking the train 3,500 miles. He will travel $\frac{1}{5}$ of the distance the first day and $\frac{1}{7}$ of the distance the second day. How many miles will he have left to travel after two days?

48. The Neurosurgery Clinic benefit dinner sold adult tickets for \$7.85. $\frac{4}{5}$ of the 300 people attending were adults. How much money was raised from the adult tickets?

49. Mrs. Fincham made three batches of $4\frac{1}{2}$ quarts each of blackberry jam. Later, she made $3\frac{1}{4}$ quarts of raspberry jam, $2\frac{1}{3}$ quarts of peach jam, and $1\frac{1}{2}$ quarts of strawberry jam. How many quarts of jam did Mrs. Fincham make?

Estimate using compatible numbers.

50. If $\frac{1}{5}$ of 201 boys and $\frac{2}{5}$ of 252 girls at Grace Academy exercise regularly, approximately what number of the students exercise regularly?

Chapter Theme

The theme of chapter 8 is Sacrifice and Service. In His Word, God tells us that we are His workmanship, created to walk in His light and to do good works. Christians are to study His Word, but not with the sole purpose of merely being receptacles of knowledge. Our learning is to lead us to love others and to serve them. We are to live with the constant awareness that He is at work around us, and that His desire is for us to join Him. In this chapter, you will read of well-known individuals who served God and sacrificed for Him. However, our personal acts of service may not bring fame. Yet every act, great or small, is precious to God when we serve out of sincere love.

8

Chapter

Integers

Lessons 95-104

I beseech you therefore, brethren, by the mercies of God, that you present your bodies a living sacrifice, holy, acceptable to God, which is your reasonable service.

Romans 12:1

The scale on a thermometer shows positive and negative integers.

54 and -2 are integers.

Andrew Lang was an NBA powerhouse for the Atlanta Hawks. In 1996 he was traded to the Minnesota Timberwolves. At the age of 13, he gave his life to Jesus Christ. One of his favorite Scripture passages is Proverbs 3:1–2. "My son, do not forget my law, but let your heart keep my commands; for length of days and long life and peace they will add to you." Transitioning from moderate weather (54°F) to cold winters (–2°F) was a negative for him. When he moved to Milwaukee to play for the Bucks, Andrew found the fellowship of the Christian players a positive.

Positive and negative integers are shown on the number line.

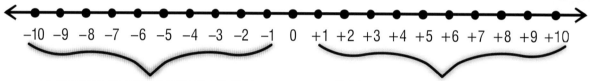

Negative integers are whole numbers to the left of 0, such as –2. They must have a negative sign in front of the number.

Positive integers are whole numbers to the right of 0, such as 54. They can be written with or without a positive sign in front of the number.

Zero is neither positive nor negative.

Integers include all of the positive whole numbers (1, 2, 3 . . .), all of the negative whole numbers (–1, –2, –3 . . .), and zero.

An integer and its **opposite** are the same distance away from zero with one being positive and one being negative. For example, 4 and –4 are opposites that are an equal distance from zero but are on opposite sides of zero.

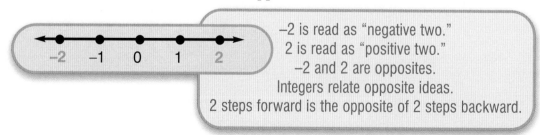

–2 is read as "negative two."
2 is read as "positive two."
–2 and 2 are opposites.
Integers relate opposite ideas.
2 steps forward is the opposite of 2 steps backward.

Provide the missing integer represented by the letter on the number line.

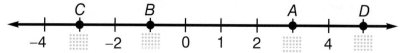

 Check Understanding

Write a positive or negative integer to describe the situation.

  a. Earned $16   b. Loss of nine yards   c. Salary increase of $300
  d. Temperature in Celsius of 22 degrees below 0   e. Debt of $25

 Practice

Write a positive or negative integer to describe the situation.

  1. $20 gift certificate   2. Bonus of $75   3. 15 meters below the surface
  4. Profit of three dollars 5. Six-point penalty   6. Three steps back on a game board
  7. Which two pairs of points represent opposite integers?

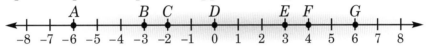

Write the opposite.

  8. 4   9. 11   10. –25   11. –7   12. 1

Write the opposite idea and the opposite integer.

  13. Gained six pounds; 6   14. 13 steps to the left; –13
  15. 10 minutes before takeoff; –10   16. Up five floors in an elevator; 5
  17. 47 feet above sea level; 47   18. 9° below zero; –9°

 Apply

19. Joe paid $4.00 each for five tickets to the
    basketball game. He had to cancel his plans, and sold
    the tickets to a friend, charging him $1.50 less per
    ticket. Find the total amount Joe's friend paid.

20. The Nates family bought a new sofa priced at
    $625.99. They paid tax that amounted to $37.56. The
    delivery charge was $25. Mrs. Nates had a $100-off coupon that she used. How
    much did the Nates family pay for the sofa?

 Review

Solve. Write the answer in simplest form.

1. $\frac{9}{11}$ 2. $\frac{5}{6}$ 3. 7 4. $8\frac{1}{2}$ 5. $1\frac{4}{7}$

   $+ \frac{6}{11}$ $- \frac{3}{4}$ $- 2\frac{4}{9}$ $- 3\frac{2}{3}$ $+ 6\frac{9}{14}$

Lesson 96

Construct Meaning

James Hudson Taylor's parents prayed for a son who would serve God in China. Their prayer was answered. He started the China Inland Mission which grew to 205 missionary stations, 849 missionaries, and 125,000 Chinese Christians working at the mission when he died in 1905.

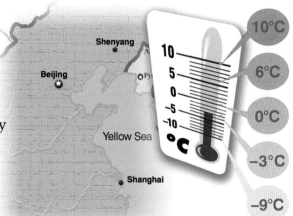

The average temperature for the month of December in Beijing, China, is –3°C, in Shenyang –9°C, and 6°C in Shanghai. Look at the thermometer to decide which city has the lowest average temperature for December.

⦿ Use a number line to compare two integers.
Do the integers on the number line become greater or less as they progress from left to right? The integer to the <u>right</u> always has <u>greater</u> value than the integer to the left.

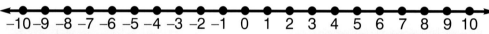

Compare 8 and 4.
8 is to the right of 4.
8 is greater than 4.
8 > 4 or 4 < 8.

Think
When there are two positive integers, the one farther from zero is greater.

Compare 1 and –7.
1 is to the right of –7.
1 > –7 or –7 < 1.

Think
A positive integer is always greater than a negative integer.

Compare 0 and –2.
0 is to the right of –2.
0 is greater than –2.
0 > –2 or –2 < 0.

Think
Zero is always greater than a negative integer.

Compare –6 and –9.
–6 is to the right of –9.
–6 is closer to 0 than –9.
–6 > –9 or –9 < –6.

Think
When there are two negative integers, the one closer to zero is greater.

⦿ Use a number line to order two or more integers.
Notice the placement of 1, –5, –2, and 3 on the number line.

The least to the greatest order is –5, –2, 1, and 3.
The greatest to the least order is 3, 1, –2, and –5.

Write > or <.

a. −5 ▦ (−2)   b. 7 ▦ (−6)   c. 0 ▦ (−9)   d. 1 ▦ 3   e. −8 ▦ 8

f. Write in order from least to greatest.
5   0   −9

g. Write in order from greatest to least.
−2   11   4   −7

Write > or <.

1. 9 ▦ 2   2. −3 ▦ 6   3. −5 ▦ 0   4. −8 ▦ (−12)
5. −5 ▦ 9   6. 4 ▦ (−3) 7. −7 ▦ (−4) 8. 1 ▦ (−8)
9. 6 ▦ 9   10. −2 ▦ (−4)

Write in order from least to greatest.

11. −1   −7   5   12. 27   −26   0   14
13. 1   −9   3   −3   9

Write in order from greatest to least.

14. −4   −1   −6   15. 2   −3   7   −5
16. 14   −15   3   26   −37

THE GREAT WALL, CHINA

Fill in the blanks with the words *greater* or *less*.

17. As you move from left to right on a number line, the integer farther to the right always has ▦ value than the integer to the left.

18. A negative integer is always ▦ than a positive integer.

19. Given two negative integers, the one farther away from 0 is ▦ than the one closer to 0.

20. Zero is always ▦ than a negative integer.

21. Write the integers that are represented by points *H*, *B*, and *G* in order from greatest to least.

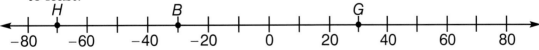

Write >, < or =.

1. 0.74 ▦ 0.82   2. 0.3 ▦ 0.35   3. 0.1 ▦ 0.100   4. 0.75 ▦ 0.745
5. 1.175 ▦ 1.18   6. $\frac{2}{3}$ ▦ $\frac{1}{2}$ 7. $\frac{2}{15}$ ▦ $\frac{4}{9}$ 8. $\frac{3}{6}$ ▦ $\frac{5}{10}$
9. $\frac{7}{8}$ ▦ $\frac{6}{7}$ 10. $\frac{3}{4}$ ▦ $\frac{5}{6}$

207

Construct Meaning

Payne Stewart (1957-1999) had career accomplishments in golf that included 18 professional titles, three major titles, and membership on five Ryder Cup teams. He spoke often of his faith in God and, after winning the Bay Hill Invitational, he gave the winner's check to a hospital in memory of his father who had a great impact on his early career.

Golfers at the 18th hole. St Andrews, Scotland

Ken's score on the first hole of the golf course was a bogie, which is one above par (+1). His score on the second hole was a birdie, which is one below par (–1). Was his final score par, above par, or below par after two holes?

Use counters to model the addition of integers.

A yellow counter represents 1.

A red counter represents –1.

When a yellow counter (1) is paired with a red counter (–1), the result is zero.

A 1 and a –1 cancel out each other. The result is a zero pair.

Use counters.

Ken was golfing par after the second hole.

Solve 2 + 3.
Place two yellow counters on the mat to represent 2.
Place three additional yellow counters to represent 3.
There are five yellow counters altogether.
Each yellow counter represents 1. The sum of 2 + 3 = 5.

Solve –4 + (–2).
Place four red counters on the mat to represent –4.
Place two additional red counters to represent –2.
There are six red counters altogether.
Each red counter represents –1. The sum of –4 + (–2) = –6.

Solve –3 + 4.
Place three red counters on the mat to represent –3.
Place four yellow counters to represent 4.
Pair up a red counter with a yellow counter to form a zero pair.
Take each zero pair off the mat because each zero pair has a value of zero.
One yellow counter remains, representing 1.

$$-3 + 4 = 1$$

Introduction to Addition of Integers

Use a pencil and paper to model the addition of integers.

⊕ Represents 1 with a positive counter.

⊖ Represents –1 with a negative counter.

Solve –7 + 2.

⊖⊖ ⊖ ⊖ ⊖ ⊖ ⊖
⊕⊕

Two zero pairs are formed and their value is zero.
Five negative counters remain.

$$-7 + 2 = -5$$

Draw positive or negative counters to represent the integers.

a. 3   b. –5   c. –3   d. 4   e. 2

Write a number sentence represented by the counters.

f. ⊖⊖⊖⊖⊖⊖⊖⊖
  ⊕⊕⊕⊕⊕

g. ⊕⊕⊕⊕⊕
  ⊖⊖⊖

Use positive and negative counters to find the sum.

h. –1 + (–3)   i. 2 + 4   j. –1 + 3   k. 3 + (–6)   l. –6 + (–2)

Draw positive or negative counters to find the sum.

1. –8 + 4   2. –6 + (–1)   3. 3 + (–5)   4. 2 + 7   5. –9 + 5

Write a number sentence represented by the counters.

6. ⊖⊖
  ⊕⊕⊕

7. ⊕⊕⊕⊕⊕⊕
  ⊖⊖⊖

8. ⊖⊖⊖⊖⊖
  ⊕⊕⊕⊕⊕

9. ⊖
  ⊕⊕⊕⊕

Write *positive* or *negative* to complete the sentence.

10. The sum of two positive integers is a _____ integer.

11. The sum of two negative integers is a _____ integer.

12. Ralph's golf score was par by the end of the seventh hole. He made an eagle (–2) on the eighth hole and a double bogie (2) on the ninth hole. Was his final score par, below par, or above par?

 Construct Meaning

Mel Trotter grew up with a godly mother and an alcoholic father. After years of walking in his father's footsteps, he took a train to Chicago where he visited the Pacific Garden Mission and trusted Christ as his Savior. His experience as a popular speaker and rescue worker led him to establish sixty-seven rescue missions across America.

A train's final destination is where its journey terminates. The answer on a number line is where the curved arrow terminates.

Steps to adding integers on a number line

1	*2*	*3*	*4*
Begin at the first addend.	To add a positive integer, move to the right.	To add a negative integer, move to the left.	The sum is where the arrow terminates.

Solve $2 + 6$. Add the positive integers on the number line.

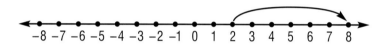

Begin at 2.
From 2, move six units to the right.
The curved arrow terminates on 8.
The sum of $2 + 6 = 8$.

Solve $-1 + (-4)$. Add the negative integers. Use the negative sign in the sum.

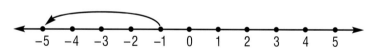

Begin at −1.
From −1, move four units to the left.
The arrow terminates on −5.
The sum of $-1 + (-4) = -5$.

Solve $-3 + 5$. Use the number line to add a positive and a negative integer.

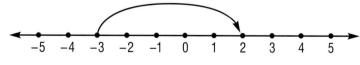

Begin at −3.
From −3, move five units to the right.
The arrow terminates on 2.
The sum of $-3 + 5 = 2$.

 Check Understanding

Draw a number line to find the sum.

a. $-6 + 3$ b. $-2 + (-3)$ c. $4 + 5$ d. $3 + (-5)$ e. $-1 + 1$

Add the integers.

f. $9 + (-4)$ g. $-4 + (-6)$ h. $-6 + 6$ i. $2 + 9$ j. $-3 + 7$

Find the sum. Draw a number line or use counters if needed.

1. −5 + (−1)   2. 4 + (−4)   3. 2 + 6   4. −8 + (−4)   5. 3 + 7

6. −2 + 5   7. 10 + (−3)   8. 5 + 7   9. −1 + (−4)   10. 6 + (−3)

Before drawing a number line to solve 3 + (−7) + 2, review the process by filling in the blanks. Use the bank.

BANK
7 arrow
−2 right
4 left
3 negative
2 sum

11. Begin at ▦.

12. Move ▦ units to the ▦.

13. Move ▦ units to the ▦.

14. The arrow terminates on ▦.

15. The ▦ of 3 + (−7) + 2 = −2.

Write the letter of the rule that applies to each problem for 16–20.

Rule A When integers with the same sign are added, add the integers, then use the same sign in the sum.

Rule B When integers with different signs are added, subtract the shorter distance from the longer distance and use the sign of the integer farther from zero.

16. −3 + 2 = −1   17. 3 + 3 = 6   18. 4 + (−7) = −3   19. −5 + (−1) = −6

Write the equation that matches each event in the scenario.

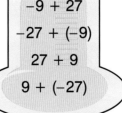
−9 + (−5) = −14
10 + (−14) = −4
12 + 12 = 24

20. For Tony's twelfth birthday, he received twelve one-dollar bills from a cousin and a twelve-dollar check from an uncle. He totaled both money gifts.

21. He bought a CD for $9 and a book for $5. He spent most of his birthday money.

22. He wanted to buy a hat that cost $14. He realized he was a few dollars short.

Write the expression that matches each temperature change.

−9 + 27
−27 + (−9)
27 + 9
9 + (−27)

23. The temperature was 27°F and rose 9 degrees.

24. The temperature was −9°F and rose 27 degrees.

25. The temperature was −27°F and dropped 9 degrees.

1. $\frac{1}{5} \times \frac{5}{7}$ 2. $\frac{2}{5} \times \frac{1}{4} \times \frac{5}{6}$ 3. $\frac{2}{3} \div \frac{1}{6}$ 4. $\frac{1}{4} \div \frac{1}{8}$ 5. $\frac{4}{5} \div \frac{1}{10}$

 Construct Meaning

Gabe planned to purchase *Daktar II* by Dr. Viggo Olsen, a surgeon and missionary to Bangladesh. Gabe went to a used bookstore and wrote a $9 check for the book. When he got home, he realized he only had $7 in his checking account. What is the difference between the amount of money he had in his account and the amount of the check he wrote?

To find the difference, subtract.
To subtract an integer, add the opposite.

$$7 \quad - \quad 9$$
$$7 \quad + \quad (-9)$$

Do not change the first integer.   The minus sign becomes a plus sign.   The second integer becomes an opposite.

Solve 7 – 9. Subtracting 9 is the same as adding –9.
$$7 - 9 = 7 + (-9) = -2$$

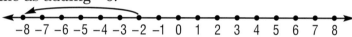

Solve –2 – 6. Subtracting 6 is the same as adding –6.
$$-2 - 6 = -2 + (-6) = -8$$

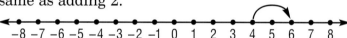

Solve 4 – (–2). Subtracting –2 is the same as adding 2.
$$4 - (-2) = 4 + 2 = 6$$

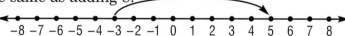

Solve –3 – (–8). Subtracting –8 is the same as adding 8.
$$-3 - (-8) = -3 + 8 = 5$$

Solve. Can you find a pattern in each list of answers?

4 – 3	2 – 2	6 – 3
4 – 2	2 – 1	6 – 2
4 – 1	2 – 0	6 – 1
4 – 0	2 – (–1)	6 – 0
4 – (–1)	2 – (–2)	6 – (–1)
4 – (–2)	2 – (–3)	6 – (–2)
4 – (–3)	2 – (–4)	6 – (–3)

 Check Understanding

Rewrite the subtraction problem as an addition problem. The first integer does not change. The operational minus (subtraction) sign becomes a plus (addition) sign. The second integer becomes an opposite. Do not solve.

a. 23 – (–14)   b. –74 – (–677)   c. –6,300 – 8,217   d. –3 – 4   e. 17 – 18

Subtraction of Integers

Complete the blanks.

 f. Consider 3 – 4. Subtracting 4 is the same as adding ▦ .

 g. Consider 7 – (–1). Subtracting (–1) is the same as ▦ ▦ .

 h. Consider –1 – (–6). Subtracting (–6) is the same as ▦ ▦ .

Subtract.

 i. 9 – 2

 j. 0 – 3

 k. –1 – 5

 l. Complete the pattern.

 4 – 3 = ▦
 4 – 2 = ▦
 4 – 1 = ▦
 4 – 0 = ▦
 4 – (–1) = ▦

Rewrite each subtraction problem as an addition problem. Solve.

 1. 9 – 2   2. 0 – 3   3. –1 – 5   4. 4 – (–8)   5. –5 – 4

 6. –3 – (–3)   7. –2 – 1   8. 6 – (–4)   9. 3 – 5   10. –9 – (–7)

Solve. Can you find the pattern in each list of answers?

11.	12.	13.
3 – 2	1 – 3	–2 – 1
3 – 1	1 – 2	–2 – 0
3 – 0	1 – 1	–2 – (–1)
3 – (–1)	1 – 0	–2 – (–2)
3 – (–2)	1 – (–1)	–2 – (–3)

14. Bangladesh is to the southeast of Nepal. The people in Bangladesh live less than one meter above sea level. Nearby Mt. Everest in Nepal is 8,848 meters above sea level. The Mariana Trench in the Pacific Ocean is 11,000 meters below sea level. What is the difference in meters between the summit of Mt. Everest and the bottom of the Mariana Trench?

15. Janie landed on number 18 on a game board. She took a card that told her to go ahead five spaces. Her next card told her to go back seven spaces. Where is she on the game board?

1. $\frac{6}{7} - \frac{2}{7}$ 2. $\frac{1}{2} - \frac{3}{8}$ 3. $\frac{3}{4} - \frac{1}{6}$ 4. $6\frac{2}{3} - 1\frac{1}{6}$ 5. $8\frac{3}{5} - 4\frac{2}{3}$

Construct Meaning

At a scuba diving class, Ray practiced descending in the water at 10 feet per minute. At this rate, how many feet below the surface will Ray be after three minutes?

The scuba diver descends at the rate of –10 feet per minute. In three minutes, he descends –10 + (–10) + (–10), a total of –30 feet. Repeated addition is made easy using multiplication.

$3 \times (-10) = -30$ *Multiply first. Then place the sign.*

Which sign do you use when multiplying two integers?

When the signs are the <u>same</u>, both positive or both negative, the product will be <u>positive</u>.

SAME SIGNS = POSITIVE PRODUCT
$$3 \times 3 = 9$$
$$-4 \times (-2) = 8$$

When the signs are <u>different</u>, one positive and one negative, the product will be <u>negative</u>.

DIFFERENT SIGNS = NEGATIVE PRODUCT
$$-5 \times 6 = -30$$
$$7 \times (-2) = -14$$

Multiplication of integers can be written in different ways.

Read: three times negative five
Write: $3 \times (-5)$ $3(-5)$ $(3)(-5)$ $3 \cdot (-5)$

Commutative Property of Multiplication

$-6 \times 3 = -18$ The order of the factors does
$3 \times (-6) = -18$ not change the product.

Associative Property of Multiplication

$(2 \cdot (-6)) \cdot (-4) = 48$ The grouping of the
$2 \cdot (-6 \cdot (-4)) = 48$ factors does not change the product.

Find a pattern.

$-1(3) = -3$ $(-1)(-5) = 5$ $1 \cdot (-4) = -4$
$-1(2) = -2$ $(-1)(-4) = 4$ $1 \cdot (-3) = -3$
$-1(1) = -1$ $(-1)(-3) = 3$ $1 \cdot (-2) = $ ▨
$-1(0) = 0$ $(-1)(-2) = $ ▨ $1 \cdot (-1) = -1$
$-1(-1) = $ ▨ $(-1)(-1) = 1$ $1 \cdot 0 = 0$

Check Understanding

Write a multiplication sentence for the addition sentence. Solve.

a. $-5 + (-5) + (-5) + (-5)$ b. $-20 + (-20)$ c. $-8 + (-8) + (-8) + (-8) + (-8)$

Write whether the product is *positive* or *negative*. Do not solve.

d. 21×13 e. $-9(4)$ f. $(-1)(-1)$ g. $(7 \cdot 3) \cdot (-5)$ h. $((-2) \times (-7)) \times (-1)$

i. Write the phrase, negative nine times nine, in three different ways.

j. Write two problems with each one illustrating a property of multiplication and identify the property shown.

Multiply.

k. −4 × 3   l. 2 · (−5)   m. (8)(−1)   n. (7)0   o. (−9)6

 **Practice**

Write a multiplication sentence for the addition sentence. Solve.

1. −6 + (−6)   2. −13 + (−13) + (−13) + (−13)   3. −100 + (−100) + (−100) + (−100) + (−100)

Multiply.

4. 5 × 6   5. −2 · 7   6. (−5)(−8)   7. 2 · (−3)   8. (−1)(−6)

9. 9(−3)   10. (−4)(−3)   11. 8(6)   12. 0 × (5)   13. −7 × (−4)

14. 4 · (−8)   15. (−9)(5)   16. −6 · (−2)   17. (10)7   18. −1 · 63

Solve to complete the pattern. Describe the pattern.

19. −2 × (−1)   20. 5 × (−2)
    −2 × 0   5 × (−1)
    −2 × 1   5 × 0
    −2 × 2   5 × 1

 Apply

21. Mr. Knowles put a lamppost in his front yard. The tool to dig the posthole went two feet below the ground level on the first attempt and one more foot on the second. Express the depth of the hole as a negative integer.

22. Due to a winter storm, the temperature dropped 20 degrees overnight to a low of −8°F. What was the temperature before it dropped?

23. Mrs. Eikenberry decorated her patio with seven flower pots each of which cost $5. Due to a windstorm she lost all of them. Write an equation to show the total monetary loss she suffered.

 Review

1. 0.4 × 0.2   2. 7 × 0.19   3. 30 × 0.05   4. $\frac{2}{5} \times \frac{3}{4}$ 5. $6\frac{1}{8} \times 1\frac{5}{7}$

 **Construct Meaning**

Eric Liddell was an athlete in the 1924 Olympics in Paris, France. The 100-meter race was his competition. It was scheduled for Sunday, but he did not believe in competing on the Lord's Day. He changed to the 400-meter race and set a new world record at 47.6 seconds. He had honored the Lord, and the Lord honored him.

How many times did Liddell run 100 meters in the 400-meter race?

The relationship between multiplication and division can be used to find quotients of integers.

$4 \times 100 = 400$

QUOTIENT ÷ DIVIDEND = DIVISOR
$400 \div 100 = 4$
$400 \div 4 = 100$

He ran 100 meters four times.

Read the related division problems for $-2 \times (-3) = 6$.
$6 \div (-3) = -2$
$6 \div (-2) = -3$

Read the related division problems for $-3 \times 4 = -12$.
$-12 \div 4 = -3$
$-12 \div (-3) = 4$

Which sign do you use when dividing integers?

When the signs are the <u>same</u>, both positive or both negative, the quotient will be <u>positive</u>.

SAME SIGNS = POSITIVE QUOTIENT
$42 \div 6 = 7$
$-18 \div (-2) = 9$

When the signs are <u>different</u>, one positive and one negative, the quotient will be <u>negative</u>.

DIFFERENT SIGNS = NEGATIVE QUOTIENT
$-28 \div 7 = -4$
$15 \div (-3) = -5$

Use a calculator to find the quotient.

$56 \div (-8)$
$238 \div 14$
$-180 \div 12$
$-84 \div (-4)$

 **Check Understanding**

Write the related division problems.

a. $6 \times (-2) = -12$ b. $9 \times 3 = 27$ c. $-30 \times (-5) = 150$

Write whether the quotient is *positive* or *negative*. Do not solve.

d. $-14 \div (-7)$ e. $25 \div (-5)$ f. $-8 \div 8$

Solve.

g. −880 ÷ 10   h. 63 ÷ (−7)   i. −75 ÷ (−25)

 **Practice**

Write the related division problems.

1. 6 × 4 = 24   2. −4 × (−5) = 20   3. −3 × 6 = −18   4. 9 × (−8) = −72   5. 7 × 12 = 84

Write whether the quotient is *positive* or *negative*. Do not solve.

6. 6 ÷ (−1)   7. −16 ÷ 4   8. −8 ÷ (−2)   9. 18 ÷ 9   10. −36 ÷ 4

Solve.

11. −24 ÷ (−6) 12. 0 ÷ (−2)   13. 49 ÷ (−7)   14. −35 ÷ 5   15. −48 ÷ (−8)

16. −27 ÷ 3   17. −32 ÷ (−4)   18. 60 ÷ 12   19. −28 ÷ (−14)   20. 105 ÷ 5

 Apply

21. If x represents a positive number and y represents a negative number, will their product be positive or negative? Will their quotient be positive or negative?

22. For problems a–d use the chart to the right to find the difference in high temperatures of the cities. Notice the temperatures are measured on a Celsius thermometer, which measures a warm day as 29°C.

	Saturday High	Sunday High
Baltimore, MD	10°C	15°C
Toronto, Canada	−2°C	−6°C
Chicago, IL	−5°C	3°C
Billings, MT	8°C	−7°C
Boulder, CO	11°C	4°C

   a. Saturday's high in Boulder and Chicago.

   b. Saturday's high in Billings and Toronto.

   c. Sunday's high in Toronto and Billings.

   d. Sunday's high in Baltimore and Boulder.

   e. Which day had the warmest recorded temperature?

   f. Which day had the coolest recorded temperature?

 Review

Rename as a mixed number.

1. $\frac{9}{5}$ 2. $\frac{15}{4}$ 3. $\frac{43}{6}$

Rename as an improper fraction.

4. $1\frac{2}{5}$ 5. $9\frac{1}{3}$ 6. $8\frac{1}{7}$

But now the LORD says: ..."for those who honor Me I will honor." I Samuel 2:30b

Lesson 102

Construct Meaning

To solve problems with positive and negative numbers, follow the color-coded steps of the Problem-Solving Guide.

PROBLEM-SOLVING GUIDE

Understand the question.
Analyze the data.
Plan the strategy.
Solve the problem.
Evaluate the result.

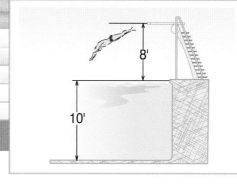

The diving board is eight feet above the surface of the water. The swimming pool is 10 feet deep. Taylor dove straight down from the diving board and touched the bottom of the pool. What is the difference between the height of the diving board and the bottom of the pool?

To find the difference, subtract. $8 - (-10) =$
To subtract an integer, add its opposite. $8 + 10 = 18$

18 feet is a logical answer.

Write the correct equation using positive and negative integers. Solve.

1. In their first football game, the Cougars had three penalties resulting in a total loss of 45 yards. Each penalty resulted in the same number of yards lost. How many yards did each penalty cost?

2. A dolphin ascended from seven feet below the surface of the water to 15 feet above the surface of the water in a vertical leap. How many feet did the dolphin ascend?

3. Chad owes Preston $9. Chad borrows $12 from Doug. How much money does Chad owe?

Solve.

4. At noon, the temperature at Snow Valley Elementary School was 23°F. The temperature dropped 36 degrees by eleven o'clock that night. What was the temperature at eleven o'clock?

5. Mr. Sanders scored two eagles and a bogie for the first three holes he golfed. What was his score after the first three holes?

Golfer's Facts	
Eagle	−2
Birdie	−1
Par	0
Bogie	1
Double Bogie	2

6. Pedro opened a savings account with $600. Since then he has made a withdrawal of $93 and a deposit of $75. What is Pedro's current balance?

7. The Branson High Mustangs had the football six yards away from the end zone, that is, six yards away from scoring a touchdown. The next play resulted in a gain of three yards. The play after that resulted in a loss of five yards. How far are the Mustangs now from scoring a touchdown?

8. Located near the Hudson River in New York State is Bear Mountain, a resort area that is 398 meters or 1,305 feet above sea level. The lowest temperatures for a period of five days were 4°F, −3°F, −7°F, −1°F, and 2°F. What is the average low temperature for the five-day period?

A battery, used to start an engine-car, truck, boat, tractor-has both a positive and a negative terminal.

9. Mr. Schneider placed a stationary marker at the end of his dock to measure the level of Crane Lake. He adjusted it so that zero was at normal water level. On July 31 the lake was three inches below normal. After a three-day rainstorm, Mr. Schneider read his marker as one inch above normal. Write an equation and find the number of inches the level of the lake increased in that three-day period.

Review

Complete the chart.

Polyhedron	Drawing	Number of Faces	Number of Vertices	Number of Edges
Triangular Prism		1.	2.	3.
Square Pyramid		4.	5.	6.

Construct Meaning

David purchased quadrant maps to locate canoe routes in a national park in Canada. Each map showed one of four regions of the park.

In mathematics, a **quadrant** is one of four regions on a coordinate grid.

A coordinate grid is formed by two intersecting lines called the coordinate axes. The horizontal line is called the *x*-axis. The vertical line is called the *y*-axis. The intersection of the horizontal and vertical lines is the origin. The *x*-axis and *y*-axis intersect to form four quadrants, which are numbered as shown.

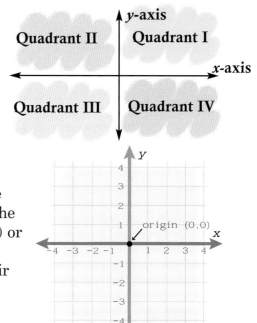

An ordered pair gives the location of a point on a coordinate plane. To plot a point, always start at the origin. The first number of the ordered pair, called the **x-coordinate**, tells how far to move to the right (+) or left (−). The second number, the **y-coordinate**, tells how far to move up (+) or down (−). The ordered pair (0,0) indicates the origin.

The instructions explain how to plot points $A(2,1)$ and $B(3,-4)$.

$A(2,1)$ Start at the origin.
            The *x*-coordinate is 2. Move two places to the right.
            The *y*-coordinate is 1. Move up one place.
            Plot the point and label it *A*.

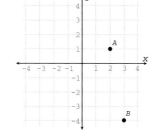

$B(3,-4)$ Start at the origin.
            The *x*-coordinate is 3. Move three places to the right.
            The *y*-coordinate is −4. Move four places down.
            Plot the point and label it *B*.

Check Understanding

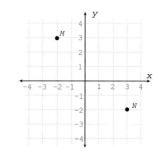

a. Write the coordinates for *M* and *N* as ordered pairs.
b. Points with a negative *x*-coordinate are ▨▨▨ of the origin.
c. Points with a negative *y*-coordinate are ▨▨▨ the origin.
d. Identify the quadrant for the ordered pair (−1,−3).

220

Chapter Eight Study Guide

1. ▦▦▦ include all of the positive ▦▦▦ numbers and all of the negative ▦▦▦ numbers and ▦▦▦ . *Lesson 95*

Write the opposite idea and the opposite integer. *Lesson 95*

2. 10 minutes after blastoff

3. 7 feet below the surface

Write > or < to compare. *Lesson 96*

4. 7 ▦ 3   5. −3 ▦ 0   6. 2 ▦ (−6)   7. −6 ▦ (−8)

Write in order from greatest to least. *Lesson 96*

8. 1   −17   5   −5   17

Write a number sentence represented by the counters. *Lesson 97*

9.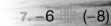

Add the integers. *Lesson 98*

10. 3 + 7   11. −1 + (−3)   12. −4 + 8

Subtract the integers. *Lesson 99*

13. −5 − 7   14. 8 − (−4)   15. −6 − (−9)

Multiply the integers. *Lesson 100*

16. 4 × 9   17. −7 × (−3)   18. −8 × 6

Divide the integers. *Lesson 101*

19. 16 ÷ (−2)   20. 84 ÷ 12   21. −56 ÷ 8

22. The low morning temperature was −8°F. By noon the temperature had risen 14 degrees. At night, the temperature dropped 7 degrees. What was the final temperature? *Lesson 102*

Plot and label the following points on a coordinate plane. *Lesson 103*

23. *A*(−3,−1)   24. *B*(2,4)

25. *C*(5,−4)

For we are His workmanship, created in Christ Jesus for good works, which God prepared beforehand that we should walk in them. Ephesians 2:10

Lesson 104

Positive and Negative Effects

Write the idea that is being defined.

1. Numbers to the right of zero on a number line
2. Neither positive nor negative
3. Positive and negative whole numbers and zero
4. The greater of two positive integers
5. The sum of two negative integers
6. Four times negative six
7. Formed by the *x*-axis and *y*-axis
8. The horizontal line on a coordinate grid
9. The location of a point on a coordinate grid
10. The starting place on a coordinate grid

IDEAS

negative integer
origin
the integer farther
 from zero
4 · (−6)
integers
coordinate grid
zero
x-axis
positive integers
ordered pair

Write the letters of the pair of integers representing opposites.

11.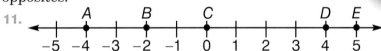

Write > or <.

12. −6 ⬚ 2

13. 0 ⬚ (−3)

14. 5 ⬚ (−5)

15. −13 ⬚ 12

Write in order from least to greatest.

16. 5 −8 0 −2

17. −3 4 −5 −4 3

Add or subtract.

18. −1 + 8

19. −5 + (−10)

20. 2 − 8

21. 9 − (−2)

22. −1 − (−5)

23. 4 + (−4)

24. −3 − 7

25. −6 + 5

Multiply or divide.

26. 7 ÷ (−7)

27. −5 × (−6)

28. 3 × (−9)

29. −6 ÷ (−3)

30. 0 × (−8)

31. −36 ÷ 6

32. 40 ÷ (−5)

33. −7 × 8

222

Chapter 8 • *Mathematics* Grade 6

Solve.

34. Some adventurous students assisted workers at a paleontological dig that was located 35 feet above sea level. Another group of scientists were working at a site 23 feet below sea level. What is the difference in elevation between the two sites?

35. At 8:00 P.M. the temperature outside was 5°F. By 10:00 P.M. the temperature had dropped 7 degrees. By midnight the temperature had dropped an additional 9 degrees. How many degrees did the temperature drop from 8:00 P.M. to 12:00 midnight?

36. At Friday night's football game, the running back carried the ball three times in the game. The first carry resulted in a 2-yard loss. The second carry resulted in a 3-yard gain. The third carry resulted in a 5-yard loss. What was the running back's total yards for the game?

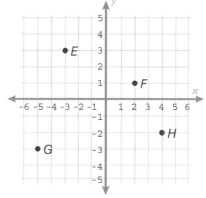

Use the coordinate grid.

37. Write the coordinates as an ordered pair for *E*.

38. Write the coordinates as an ordered pair for *F*.

39. Write the coordinates as an ordered pair for *G*.

40. Which quadrant contains *H*?

Your teacher will give you a copy of the four-quadrant grid found on Blackline Master M6-103B to plot and label the points.

41. *L*(–4,4)   42. *M*(2,3)   43. *N*(1,1)   44. *O*(6,–5)   45. *P*(–3,–4)

46. *Q*(–7,2)   47. *R*(4,7)   48. *S*(2,–3)   49. *T*(–6,–1)   50. *U*(–2,2)

Therefore by Him let us continually offer the sacrifice of praise to God, that is, the fruit of our lips, giving thanks to His name. Hebrews 13:15

Chapter Theme

As we mature in our Christian walk, we learn that we serve a God who is faithful to us. His design of mankind in His image means that we have the ability to reciprocate and be faithful to Him. The chapter 9 theme of Faith is a joyful reminder to us. We are motivated to be faithful to God because we can know and experience the depth of His love for us. Scripture gives us powerful examples of the people of God who chose to live by faith. Read the entire chapter of Hebrews 11 and reflect on those who chose to do exactly as God commanded. You will also have the opportunity to learn about some faithful people who have lived in modern times as you study this chapter of your math book. You will enjoy reading about David Simpich, who combines his love of God with his creative talents to design the exquisite marionettes that he uses to tell stories that delight both young and old.

9
Chapter
Perimeter, Area, and Volume

Now faith is the substance of things hoped for, the evidence of things not seen.

Hebrews 11:1

Lesson 105

Construct Meaning

Rosa and William plan to outline the front of their puppet stage with gold braid. How many inches of braid should they purchase? They need to know the **perimeter**, the distance around a figure, of the opening.

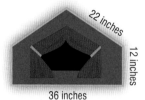

22 inches

12 inches

36 inches

Perimeter = sum of the lengths of the sides

P = 36 in. + 12 in. + 22 in. + 22 in. + 12 in.
P = 104 inches

Will a 3-yard package of braid be enough?

The perimeter of a rectangle is the sum of the lengths of all four sides. Since the opposite sides of a rectangle are congruent, the sum of twice the length of the base of the rectangle and twice the height is the perimeter.

Perimeter = 2 × base + 2 × height

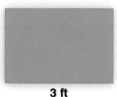

2 ft

3 ft

$P = 2b + 2h$

$P = (2 \cdot 3 \text{ ft}) + (2 \cdot 2 \text{ ft})$
$P = 6 \text{ ft} + 4 \text{ ft}$
$P = 10 \text{ ft}$

William said he finds the perimeter of a rectangle by adding the base and height, then multiplying by two. $P = 2(b + h)$

What mathematical property confirms that William's equation is the same as $P = 2b + 2h$?

Finding the perimeter of a square having a side length of s is easy.

Perimeter = 4 × side

$P = 4s$

s

s s

s

What would be the formula for the perimeter of a regular hexagon having a side length of s?

Check Understanding

Find the perimeter of each figure.
  a. A regular octagon with the measure of one side equal to 18 mm.
  b. A triangle with sides measuring 3 feet, 4 feet, and 5 feet.
  c. The base of a rectangle is 16 inches. The height is equal to one-half of the base.

Find the missing measurement.
  d. The perimeter of an equilateral triangle is 33.6 cm. What is the length of a side?
  e. The base of a rectangle is $4\frac{1}{2}$ inches and the perimeter is 14 inches. What is the height of the rectangle?

226

Find the perimeter of each figure.

1. 1 in., 1 in. (square)

2. 15 mm, 13 mm, 21 mm

3. 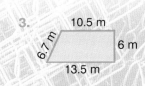 10.5 m, 6 m, 6.7 m, 13.5 m

4. 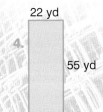 22 yd, 55 yd

Find the value of *x*.

5. 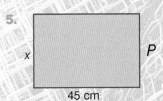 *x*, 45 cm $P = 151$ cm

6.   6 in., $4\frac{1}{2}$ in., *x* $P = 14\frac{1}{2}$ in.

7. Blackwater Christian Academy is planning to fence an outdoor basketball court with a rectangular enclosure that measures 75 feet by 120 feet. How many feet of fencing will be needed? If the fencing is purchased in rolls of 50 feet at a rate of $55 per roll, how much will the fencing cost?

8. Johanna and Max bicycled the entire Perimeter Road that forms the border of the Sprucewood Athletic Complex. The square athletic complex is a piece of property 2 miles on each side. How far did they travel?

9. Marci purchased three 15-foot rolls of wallpaper border for a room that measures 10 feet by 13 feet. She plans to place the border 4 feet from the floor. The doorway into the room is 3 feet wide. Does she have enough border to do the job? Explain.

10. Akins is building a rectangular pen for his dog, Mosley, using one 36-foot roll of fencing for three sides and the 26-foot side of his house as the fourth side. What is the width of the pen?

1. $\frac{2}{9} \div \frac{2}{3}$

2. $8 \div \frac{1}{2}$

3. $\frac{4}{5} \div \frac{2}{3}$

4. $\frac{3}{7} \div 5$

5. $2\frac{1}{2} \div \frac{1}{4}$

6. $26 \div 6\frac{1}{2}$

7. $2\frac{1}{2} \div 1\frac{1}{4}$

8. $3\frac{1}{2} \div 9\frac{1}{3}$

Construct Meaning

David Simpich is a professional puppeteer who designs and makes his own puppets and writes the script for each performance. In his unique form of storytelling, David is on the stage with his puppets, bringing them to "life." He is excited when his presentations result in dialogue and questions about the truths he is communicating. David's designs require the calculation of perimeter, proportion, and area.

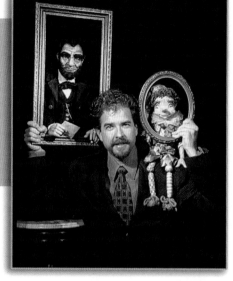

The **area** of a figure is the number of square units that cover the surface. What is the area outlined by a frame 3 inches by 5 inches?

We can count the squares or, for a rectangle, we can multiply the number of units of the base by the number of units of the height.

Area = base × height
$A = bh$
$A = 3$ in. × 5 in.
$A = 15$ square inches

What is the area of a square with side length s? Since the base and height are both equal to s, the area is the square of the side length. How is this related to "square" numbers?

$$A = s^2$$

Determining the area of a parallelogram that is not a rectangle is difficult if you are trying to count the unit squares. The same formula can be used, but recognize that the height of the parallelogram is not the length of the side. The **height** is determined by a line perpendicular to the two **bases**, one set of parallel sides.

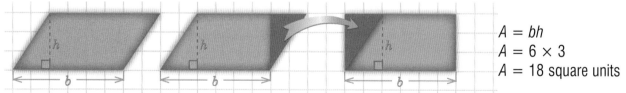

$A = bh$
$A = 6 × 3$
$A = 18$ square units

Imagine cutting off the right triangular portion of the parallelogram and moving it to the left side to fill in the triangular space. The base and height are now sides of a rectangle. Count the squares to check your calculated area.

Check Understanding

Find the area of each shaded figure.

a.

2 ft
8 ft

b.

27 cm
38 cm
27 cm

c.
9 in.
3 in. 9 in.
3 in.

Find the missing measurement.
  d. A rectangle with an area of 42 square inches has a base of 6 inches and a height of ▨ inches.

  e. A parallelogram with a height of 16 cm and an area of 64 square cm has a base of ▨ cm.

David with puppets from his Christmas presentation

1. What is the area of a rectangular stage that measures 12 feet by 8 feet?

2. What is the base length of a 190 square meter parallelogram that has a height of 19 meters?

3. How many one-foot square tiles should Ray buy for a room that measures 10 feet by 12 feet and a closet that measures 3 feet by 6 feet?

4. The game of checkers is played on a board 8 squares by 8 squares, alternating black and red. If each square is $1\frac{1}{2}$ inches on a side, what is the perimeter of the board? What is the area of the board? What is the area of the black surface only?

5. Glynn and Sue are ordering Christmas tree seedlings to plant on their farm. The instructions said to allow 36 square feet of space for each tree. What is the maximum number of trees they should plant on a one-acre plot of ground that measures 726 feet by 60 feet?

6. Glynn has 100 meters of fencing to enclose an area for a rectangular herb garden. What dimensions should he make the garden to have maximum area for planting?

1. $5\overline{)870}$
2. $8\overline{)4,808}$
3. $39\overline{)1,248}$
4. $1,000\overline{)48,000}$

5. $100\overline{)57,000}$
6. $9\overline{)65.79}$
7. $0.72\overline{)0.0432}$
8. $9.6\overline{)115.2}$

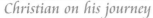

David Simpich says that math is very important in puppetry. He is careful to proportion each head so the cast of characters can work together in the show. The body of the puppet must be constructed so that the weight is properly centered. The wooden controls and strings must be measured, cut, and connected with precision to provide a device best suited for lifting, twisting, and tipping of the puppet as it speaks. Even the stage must be carefully balanced so the heavy lights do not pull the structure over. One of Mr. Simpich's productions is based on the story of Christian in John Bunyan's *The Pilgrim's Progress.*

Christian on his journey

Richard is cutting out large cardboard triangles to use as a background for his class puppet show. He cut one triangle from a rectangular piece of cardboard that measured 8 feet by 4 feet. What is the area of his triangle?

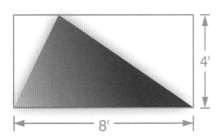

Richard recognized that the two remaining triangles could be put together to form a triangle congruent to the one he cut out.

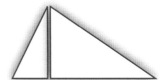

The area of the rectangle is equal to the base multiplied by the height. The area of Richard's triangle would be exactly half that area, since the two congruent triangles formed the rectangle. The **height** is the perpendicular distance from the **base** to the opposite vertex.

Area of a triangle = $\frac{1}{2}$ × base × height

$$A = \frac{1}{2} bh$$
$$A = \frac{1}{2} \cdot 8 \text{ ft} \cdot 4 \text{ ft}$$
$$A = 16 \text{ square feet}$$

Check Understanding

Find the area of each triangle.

a.
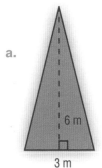
6 m

3 m

b.
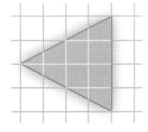

c.
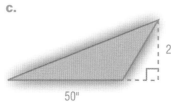
23"
50"

d.
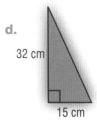
32 cm
15 cm

Find the area of each shaded figure.

1.

1.6 cm

1.2 cm

2.

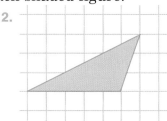

3.

8"

8"

4.

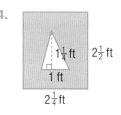

$1\frac{1}{4}$ ft $2\frac{1}{2}$ ft

1 ft

$2\frac{1}{4}$ ft

5. The area of a triangle is 40 square inches and its height is 8 inches. What is the measure of its base?

6. The area of a right triangle is 65 square centimeters. If one of the sides forming the right angle measures 10 centimeters, how long is the other side which forms the right angle?

7. What is the height and base of a triangle having an area of 18 square yards if the height and base are the same length? Could this be an equilateral triangle? Explain.

Apply

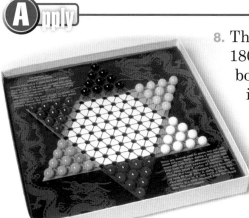

8. The game of Chinese checkers was invented around 1800. The blue equilateral triangle on Karol's game board has a base of 3 inches and a height of 2.6 inches. What is the area of the blue triangle? What is the area of the star playing surface? Think of the white hexagon as triangles.

9. What is the perimeter of the blue triangle? What is the perimeter of the star?

Review

1. 1.79×600

2. 16.2×8.1

3. 100×24.93

4. $\frac{3}{4} \times \frac{8}{9}$

5. $1\frac{1}{2} \times \frac{5}{6}$

6. $2\frac{3}{4} \times 5\frac{3}{5}$

Christian fighting Apollyon in The Pilgrim's Progress

Lesson 108

Construct Meaning

On his journey in *The Pilgrim's Progress*, Christian meets others along the way who give him counsel. Some give him good advice and encouragement. Others try to distract him from following God's path. Notice what Mr. Simpich communicates by the faces of these characters.

Faithful, Goodwill, and Hopeful

Mr. Simpich measured the circumference of a marionette's head in order to make its hat the proper size. What was he measuring? The **circumference** is the distance around a circle.

Start at one point and go completely around the circle. That distance is the circumference.

The ratio of the circumference of a circle to its diameter is always *pi*, or π.

$$\frac{\text{circumference}}{\text{diameter}} = \pi$$

Multiplying both sides of the equation by the diameter yields this formula.

> Circumference = π × diameter
>
> C = π*d*

The value of π is a nonrepeating decimal that rounds to 3.14. If the diameter of a circle is 5 cm, what is the circumference?

C = π*d*
C ≈ 3.14 × 5 cm
C ≈ 15.70 cm

The circumference of the marionette's head is 25 inches. What is the diameter rounded to the nearest inch?

C = π*d*

25 inches ≈ 3.14*d*

$\frac{25 \text{ inches}}{3.14} ≈ d$

7.96 inches ≈ *d*   The head diameter is 8 inches.

Ignorance, Mr. Worldly Wiseman, and Pliable

Check Understanding

a. Why is $C = 2\pi r$ true?
b. Use mental math. If $d = 100$ yards, what is C?
c. What is the radius of a circle if the circumference is 47.1 cm?
d. If the diameter of circle A is twice that of circle B, how do their circumferences compare?

Practice

Find the missing measurement. Round to the nearest tenth.

1.
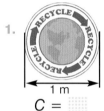
1 m
$C =$

2.

5 in.
$C =$

3.

$C = 57$mm
$d =$

4.

$r = 6$ cm
$C =$

Apply

5. Arlene baked a 9-inch diameter cake. She plans to use three rows of edible chocolate beads around the cake for decoration. How many 4-foot strands of beads should she purchase?

6. Zaki has a hat which measures 7 inches in diameter and another that has a circumference of 23 inches. Which is larger?

7. About how many times will the wheel of a bicycle go around in one mile if the diameter of the wheel is 26 inches? (Hint: 1 mile = 63,360 in.)

8. The diameter of the toy pictured at the left is 3 in. and there are 40 coils. If it could be totally unwound and stretched out, how long would it be? Round to the nearest inch.

Challenge

9. Lisa and Ricardo started on a two-mile circular nature hike. After hiking 0.5 mile they took a short-cut trail that went straight across and rejoined the circular path. How far had they walked by the time they returned to their starting point? Round to the nearest tenth of a mile.

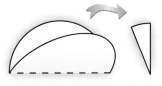

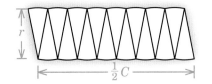

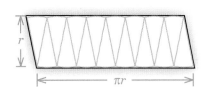

Start with a circle with a radius of 4 inches. Fold it in half, and then repeat, folding in half three more times. Unfold and cut the circle on the folds into 16 equal segments.

Arrange the segments as shown to approximate a parallelogram.

Notice that the height of the figure is equal to the radius, r, of the circle. The base of the figure is approximately equal to half of the circumference, C, of the circle.

Remember that $C = 2\pi r$. Half of the circumference is equal to πr. Use the formula for the area of a parallelogram to write a formula for the area of a circle.

Think:
The base is made of 8 of the 16 segments, or half of the circle.

$$A = bh$$
$$A = \pi r \times r$$
$$\boxed{A = \pi r^2}$$
Area = *pi* times the radius squared

Use the formula to find the area of a circle with a radius of 4 inches.

$A = \pi r^2$
$A = \pi (4 \text{ in.})^2$
$A \approx 3.14 \ (4 \text{ in.}) \ (4 \text{ in.})$
$A \approx 50.24$ sq in.

The area of a circle must be in square units!

 Check Understanding

a. Measure the height and length of the figure you constructed with the 16 segments and calculate the approximate area. Megan measured her figure as 4 inches by $12\frac{3}{4}$ inches.
$A \approx bh$
$A \approx 12\frac{3}{4}$ in. $\times$ 4 in.
$A \approx \frac{51}{4}$ in. $\times \frac{4}{1}$ in.
$A \approx 51$ in.   What is your calculated area?

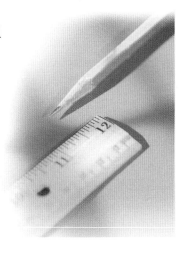

b. Was Megan's answer close to the value calculated using the formula for area of a circle?

c. What could account for slight variations?

 **Practice**

Find the missing dimensions. Use a calculator. Round to the nearest hundredth.

1. $r = 12$ in.
   $A \approx$ ▦

2. $d = 6$ cm
   $A \approx$ ▦

3. $A = 2$ sq m
   $r \approx$ ▦

4. $C = 31.4$ in.
   $r \approx$ ▦
   $A \approx$ ▦

5. $A = 3.14$ sq km
   $r \approx$ ▦
   $d \approx$ ▦

 Apply

Mary has some old textbooks that belonged to her great-grandparents. Some of the exercises written for students over one hundred years ago are not much different from those in modern textbooks. Solve these "old" problems. You may use a calculator, something Mary's great-grandparents did not have! Drawing a picture may help. Round your answer to the nearest whole number.

6. *Ex.* 53 Find the area of a circular pool with a radius of 6 feet.

7. *Ex.* 54 How much land is in a circular garden that requires 88 yards of fencing to enclose it?

8. *Ex.* 55 Find the side of a square which is equivalent in area to a circle whose diameter is 35 feet.

9. *Ex.* 56 The radius of a circle is 7.5 inches. Find the radius of a circle that has three times the area.

Rectangle	$S = b \times h$
Square	$S = b^2$
Parallelogram	$S = b \times h$
Triangle	$S = \frac{1}{2}b \times h$
Circle	$S = \pi R^2$

10. Look at the table of formulas shown above taken from one of the old geometry books. What does S represent? Why do you think they used an S? What other differences do you notice?

Imitate those who through faith and patience inherit the promises. Hebrews 6:12b

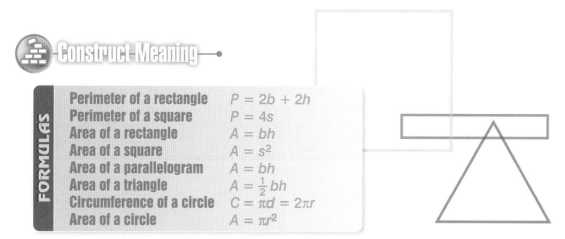

Construct Meaning

FORMULAS

Perimeter of a rectangle	$P = 2b + 2h$
Perimeter of a square	$P = 4s$
Area of a rectangle	$A = bh$
Area of a square	$A = s^2$
Area of a parallelogram	$A = bh$
Area of a triangle	$A = \frac{1}{2}bh$
Circumference of a circle	$C = \pi d = 2\pi r$
Area of a circle	$A = \pi r^2$

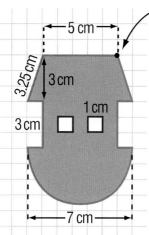

Gwen designed a border pattern for her younger brother's bedroom. Find the perimeter of the houseboat figure in the border pattern. The perimeter is the distance around the outside of the figure. Some measurements are included in the drawing. Others can be determined by adding or subtracting the given measurements. Gwen calculated the circumference of the semicircle first.

$$C = \pi d$$
$$\tfrac{1}{2}C = \tfrac{1}{2}(\pi d)$$
$$\tfrac{1}{2}C \approx \tfrac{1}{2}(3.14)(7 \text{ cm})$$
$$\tfrac{1}{2}C \approx 10.99 \text{ cm}$$

Then she added the distances in centimeters starting at the dot and moving clockwise around the figure.

$P \approx 3.25 \text{ cm} + 1 \text{ cm} + 3 \text{ cm} + 1 \text{ cm} + 10.99 \text{ cm} + 1 \text{ cm} + 3 \text{ cm} + 1 \text{ cm} + 3.25 \text{ cm} + 5 \text{ cm}$
$P \approx 32.49 \text{ cm}$

Find the area covered by the houseboat figure. Gwen divided the figure into pieces for which she could determine the area. Then she added or subtracted to find the shaded area.

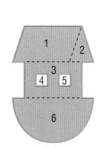

Area of figure $= A_1 + A_2 + A_3 - A_4 - A_5 + A_6$
$A_1 = bh = 5 \text{ cm} \times 3 \text{ cm} = 15 \text{ sq cm}$
$A_2 = \tfrac{1}{2}bh = \tfrac{1}{2} \times 2 \text{ cm} \times 3 \text{ cm} = 3 \text{ sq cm}$
$A_3 = bh = 5 \text{ cm} \times 3 \text{ cm} = 15 \text{ sq cm}$
$A_4 = s^2 = 1 \text{ cm} \times 1 \text{ cm} = 1 \text{ sq cm}$
$A_5 = s^2 = 1 \text{ cm} \times 1 \text{ cm} = 1 \text{ sq cm}$
$A_6 = \tfrac{1}{2}(\pi r^2) \approx \tfrac{1}{2} \times 3.14 \times 3.5 \text{ cm} \times 3.5 \text{ cm} \approx 19.23 \text{ sq cm}$

Determine the area of the figure by placing these values in the formula, adding or subtracting as necessary.

$A \approx 15 \text{ sq cm} + 3 \text{ sq cm} + 15 \text{ sq cm} - 1 \text{ sq cm} - 1 \text{ sq cm} + 19.23 \text{ sq cm}$
$A \approx 50.23 \text{ sq cm}$

Perimeter and Area of Irregular Figures

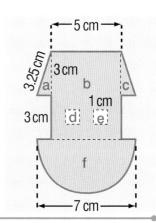

a. Gary divided the figure a different way. Will he arrive at the same answer? Explain.

b. Find the area of the figure using Gary's method.

c. If the room to be decorated with this border pattern measures 10 feet by 13 feet, how many feet of border will need to be painted?

Find the area of the shaded portion of each figure.

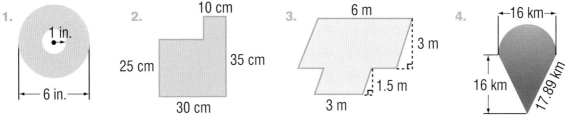

1.

2. 10 cm / 25 cm / 35 cm / 30 cm

3. 6 m / 3 m / 1.5 m / 3 m

4. 16 km / 16 km / 17.89 km

5. What is the perimeter of the figure in problem 2? problem 4?

Apply

6. Use a calculator and the distances on the map to estimate the area of each of the four states shown. The blue dotted lines have been drawn to help you divide Arizona into smaller areas.

7. There is only one place in the United States where four states meet at a common point. Where is that point and why do you think it is called Four Corners?

8. Compare your estimates in problem 6 to the actual areas given in the chart below. Explain why they vary.

Arizona	114,006 sq mi
Colorado	104,100 sq mi
New Mexico	121,598 sq mi
Utah	89,904 sq mi

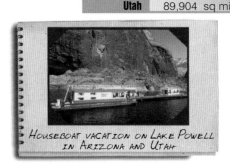

HOUSEBOAT VACATION ON LAKE POWELL IN ARIZONA AND UTAH

9. What is the perimeter of Utah? If you average 10 miles per day, about how long would it take you to walk the border of Utah?

A toy manufacturer will package cube puzzles of eight cubes each in decorative boxes. The cubes will be arranged in one of the ways shown below. If the company wants to select the arrangement of cubes with less surface area, which will be chosen?

Surface area is the sum of the areas of all the faces of a three-dimensional figure.

CUBE ARRANGEMENT #1   CUBE ARRANGEMENT #2

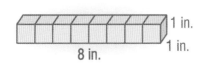

1 in.
1 in.
8 in.

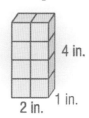

4 in.
2 in.   1 in.

Use a net of each cube arrangement to find each surface area. A **net** is a flat pattern that can be folded into a three-dimensional figure.

CUBE ARRANGEMENT #1   CUBE ARRANGEMENT #2

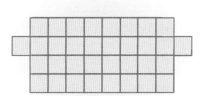

Surface Area = 34 square inches

Surface Area = 28 square inches

CALCULATING SURFACE AREA

What is the surface area of the rectangular prism shown? Find the area of each face. Then find the sum of all of the areas.

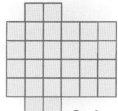

Area of top rectangle = 3 ft × 1 ft = 3 sq ft
Which other face has the same area?

Area of end rectangle = 2 ft × 1 ft = 2 sq ft
Which other face has the same area?

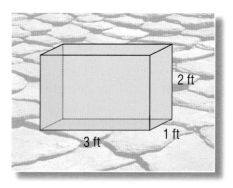

2 ft
3 ft   1 ft

Area of front rectangle = 3 ft × 2 ft = 6 sq ft
Which other face has the same area?

Surface Area = (2 × 3 sq ft) + (2 × 2 sq ft) + (2 × 6 sq ft)
Surface Area =   6 sq ft   + 4 sq ft   + 12 sq ft   = 22 sq ft

Surface Area of Prisms and Pyramids

A square pyramid has 5 faces, 1 square and 4 triangular. The net shows the dimensions of each face. Find the surface area of the square pyramid.

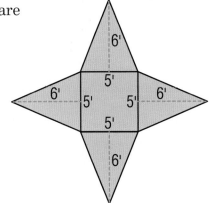

Area of square base = 5 ft × 5 ft = 25 sq ft
Area of one triangle = $\frac{1}{2}$ × (5 ft × 6 ft) = 15 sq ft
Surface Area = 25 sq ft + (4 × 15 sq ft)
Surface Area = 25 sq ft + 60 sq ft = 85 sq ft

 Check Understanding

a. What area formula is used to find the addends for determining the surface area of a triangular pyramid?

b. How can you find the surface area of a cube?

Practice

Write the number of faces of each three-dimensional figure.

1.
2.
3.
4.

Find the surface area of each figure.

5.  3 m, 3 m, 3 m

6. 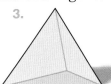 4 yd, 3 yd, 6 yd

7. 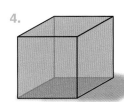 2 in., 4 in., 4 in.

8. h = 7 cm, 8 cm, 8 cm

Apply

9. Tyrone has a piece of wrapping paper that measures 48" by 24". Will he be able to wrap a box that measures 2' by 1' by 1' ? If not, how much additional paper will he need?

10. A photographer selected a box that measured 3' by 2' by 1', removed the 3' by 2' top, and placed the pups inside. What is the outside surface area of the box without the lid?

Lesson 112

🧱 Construct Meaning

A candy company will package colorful mints in clear plastic cylinders. The package designer must determine the surface area of the cylindrical container.

Picture the net of the cylinder. What shape does the curved side become? Which shapes are congruent?

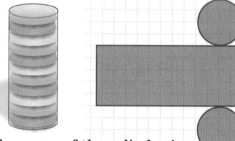

Consider each face of the mint container.

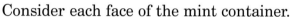
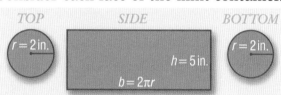

TOP   SIDE   BOTTOM

$r = 2$ in. $h = 5$ in. $b = 2\pi r$ $r = 2$ in.

The surface area of the cylinder is the sum of the areas of the 3 faces.

Surface Area of a cylinder = (2 × Area of circular base) + Area of rectangular side

---

Formulas You Need
Area of a circle = πr^2
Area of a rectangle = bh
Circumference of a circle = $2\pi r$

The base of the rectangle exactly matches the circumference of the circle. Why?

Since Circumference = $2\pi r$, we know that $b = 2\pi r$.

Remember: $\pi \approx 3.14$

Find the surface area of the container.

Area of a circular base	Area of the rectangular side
$A = \pi r^2$	$A = bh$ Think: $b = 2\pi r$
$A \approx 3.14 \times (2$ in. $\times 2$ in.$)$	$A \approx (2\pi r) \times 5$ in.
$A \approx 3.14 \times 4$ sq in.	$A \approx (2 \times 3.14 \times 2) \times 5$ in.
$A \approx 12.56$ sq in.	$A \approx (12.56) \times 5$ in.
	$A \approx 62.8$ sq in.

Surface Area = (2 × Area of circular base) + Area of rectangular side
      ≈ (2 × 12.56 sq in.)   + 62.8 sq in.
      ≈ 25.12 sq in.   + 62.8 sq in.
Surface Area ≈ 87.92 sq in.

✓ Check Understanding

CYLINDERS OF CHEESE

Write *true* or *false*.

a. The surface area of a cylinder is equal to
(2 × area of circular base) + (circumference of circular base × height).

b. Two cans of different heights may have circular bases that are congruent.

240

Use a calculator to find the circumference of each cylinder.

1.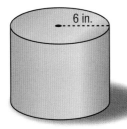
6 in.

2.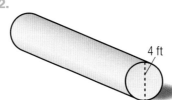
4 ft

3.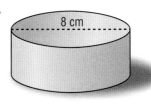
8 cm

Use a calculator to find the surface area of each cylinder.

4.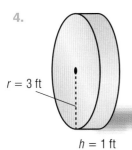
r = 3 ft
h = 1 ft

5.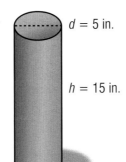
d = 5 in.
h = 15 in.

6.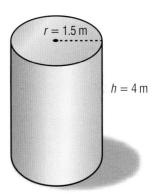
r = 1.5 m
h = 4 m

Apply

7. Describe how you would make a cylinder from construction paper. What measurements must match each other?

8. A cylinder jar was made to display colorful pasta. It cost $0.04 per square inch to manufacture the jars. What is the cost of producing a cylinder if it has a radius of 2 inches and a height of 6 inches? Round the surface area to the nearest tenth to calculate the cost.

9. How would you calculate the outside surface area of a cylinder that is open on one end?

10. Mrs. Clark has a piece of fabric to cover six juice cans to use as pencil holders for her kindergarten class. The bottom of the can will not be covered. The fabric measures 15" by 15". Does she have enough fabric if each can is five inches tall and has a circumference of nine inches? Explain.

The Washington Monument in Washington, D.C., was built as a memorial to our first president George Washington. It is one of our most unique and oldest national landmarks. Construction began on July 4, 1848 with the laying of the cornerstone containing a time capsule with information about George Washington, his family, the United States, the Smithsonian Institute, the capital city, some American coins, newspapers, and a Bible. The monument was not completed until 1884.

Memorial stones from various states, organizations, and foreign countries were installed in the interior walls. One marble stone is four feet long, two feet high, and one foot wide. What is the volume of that stone?

Volume is the number of cubic units that fill a three-dimensional space.

The volume of a prism can be determined by finding the area of the base and multiplying it by the height.

Volume = Area of Base × height of figure

$V = bh \times$ height of figure
$V = 4 \text{ ft} \times 1 \text{ ft} \times 2 \text{ ft}$
$V = 8$ cubic feet

$h = 2$ ft
$w = 1$ ft
$l = 4$ ft

For a rectangular prism the volume is calculated as the product of length, width, and height.
$V = lwh$

For a cube of side length s, the formula becomes
$V = s^3$.

Why are the units for volume called cubic units? The unit of measurement is multiplied by itself three times, or cubed.

$V = 1 \text{ cm} \times 1 \text{ cm} \times 1 \text{ cm}$
$V = 1 \text{ cm}^3$ or 1 cu cm

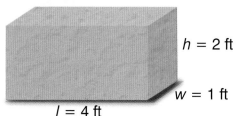

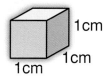

1cm
1cm
1cm

One cubic centimeter is equal to one milliliter. How many cubic centimeters would be equal to one thousand milliliters (one liter)?

Volume of Rectangular Prisms

a. Find the volume of a box that measures 2 in. by 15 in. by 8 in.

b. What is the volume of a cube that measures 3 cm on each side?

c. Find w if $V = 96$ cu cm, $l = 3$ cm, and $h = 4$ cm. Use $V = lwh$.

d. The volume of a container is 64 cubic yards. If the base measures 4 yd by 8 yd, what is the height?

e. If the height of a rectangular prism is doubled and the other measurements stay the same, what happens to volume?

Find the volume of each figure.

1. 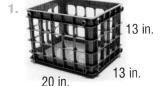 13 in. 13 in. 20 in.

2.  11 cm 20 cm 35 cm

3.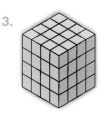

4. 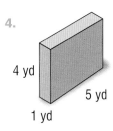 4 yd 5 yd 1 yd

Find the missing measurement for each figure.

5. $V = 32$ cu in. $h = $ ▦

6. $V = 1,000$ cu cm $w = $ ▦

7. $V = 12$ cu ft $l = $ ▦

8. $V = 70$ cu in. $w = $ ▦

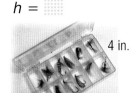 4 in. 8 in.

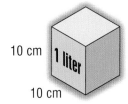 10 cm 1 liter 10 cm

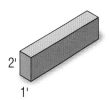 2' 1'

 5" $3\frac{1}{2}$"

9. If the length, width, and height of a rectangular prism are all doubled, what happens to the volume?

10. Sarah bought 16 gift boxes measuring 6 in. by 6 in. by 3 in. She plans to mail them all in one shipping box. Which box should she use? Think about how they will fit in the box. Explain your reasoning.

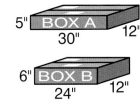 5" BOX A 30" 12" 6" BOX B 24" 12"

Solve the following problems Mary found in an old textbook.

11. *Exercise 195*   Find the cost of a 40-foot long piece of timber having a square end $1\frac{1}{2}$' on a side. The timber sells for $0.30 per cubic foot.

12. *Exercise 196*   Find the cost of a piece of marble that measures 2 feet by 4 feet and is 1 foot thick. Marble sells for $2.50 per cubic foot.

Mustard seeds

"If you have faith as a mustard seed, you will say to this mountain, 'Move from here to there,' and it will move; and nothing will be impossible for you." Matthew 17:20b

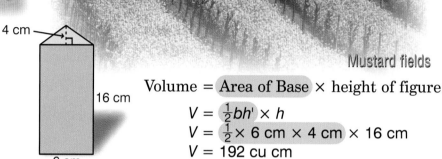

Mustard fields

The volume of a triangular prism can be determined by finding the area of the triangular base and multiplying it by the height.

4 cm

16 cm

6 cm

Volume = Area of Base × height of figure

$V = \frac{1}{2}bh' \times h$

$V = \frac{1}{2} \times 6\text{ cm} \times 4\text{ cm} \times 16\text{ cm}$

$V = 192$ cu cm

In the same way, the volume of a cylinder can be determined, except now the base is a circle. Be sure to find the radius of the circle.

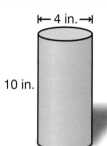

4 in.

10 in.

Volume = Area of Base × height of figure

$V = \pi r^2 \times h$

$V \approx 3.14 \times 2\text{ in.} \times 2\text{ in.} \times 10\text{ in.}$

$V \approx 125.6$ cu in.

For any cylinder:
$V = \pi r^2 h$

Calculate the volume of a 25-foot hose that has a diameter of $\frac{1}{2}$ inch.

$V = \pi r^2 \times h$

$V \approx 3.14 \times \frac{1}{4}\text{in.} \times \frac{1}{4}\text{in.} \times 300\text{ in.}$

$V \approx 58.875$ cu in.

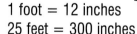

Think:
  1 foot = 12 inches
  25 feet = 300 inches

 Check Understanding

a. Name some everyday items that have a volume of about 1 cubic centimeter, one cubic inch, and one cubic foot.

b. How can you calculate the volume of material used to make each shape?

Find the volume of each figure.

1.
4 in.
11 in.
10 in.

2.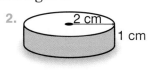
2 cm
1 cm

3.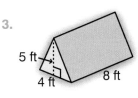
5 ft
4 ft
8 ft

4.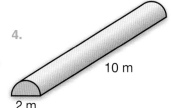
10 m
2 m

Find the missing measurement. You may use a calculator.

5. $V = 45$ cu ft

$h = $ ▦

3 ft   3 ft

6. $V \approx 314$ cu in.

$h = $ ▦ in.

10 in.

7. $V = 12$ cu cm

$l = $ ▦

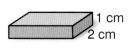
1 cm
2 cm

8. $V \approx 392.5$ cu m

$r = $ ▦

$d = $ ▦

10 m

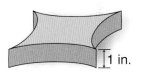

9. A 200-foot poinsettia greenhouse is built in a half-cylinder shape. The roof is 40 feet high at the tallest point. Calculate the volume of the greenhouse.

10. Butch built a triangular compost enclosure as shown below by using three sections of material left from another project. The height of the enclosure is 3 feet. Calculate the volume.

6 ft
8.5 ft
6 ft

11. Find the volume of this toy if the area of the base is 6 square inches.

1 in.

12. One of the greenhouses at Nour's Nurseries covers an area of 50 feet by 24 feet. The side walls are 8 feet tall and the floor-to-peak distance is 16 feet. Calculate the volume of the greenhouse.

16 ft
24 ft
50 ft
8 ft

(Hint: Think of the greenhouse as a rectangular prism that measures 50 feet by 24 feet by 8 feet and a triangular prism that is 50 feet long.)

 **Construct Meaning**

Formulas for Distance Around

Perimeter of a rectangle	$P = 2b + 2h$
Perimeter of a square	$P = 4s$
Circumference of a circle	$C = \pi d = 2\pi r$

Formulas may be used when you are given the value of one or more of the variables in the equation.

Steps for using formulas:
- Choose the correct formula.
- Write the numbers you know in the equation.
- If you are missing a factor or an addend, use an inverse operation.
- Solve.

Area Formulas

Area of a rectangle	$A = bh$
Area of a square	$A = s^2$
Area of a parallelogram	$A = bh$
Area of a triangle	$A = \frac{1}{2}bh$
Area of a circle	$A = \pi r^2$

$P = 40$ ft

What is the length of each side of the square?
Use $P = 4s$ and write the numbers you know in the formula.

$40 \text{ ft} = 4s$
$\frac{40}{4} \text{ ft} = \frac{4s}{4}$
$10 \text{ ft} = s$

Use the inverse operation and divide both sides of the equation by 4.

$C = 9.42$ cm

What is the diameter of the circle?
Use $C = \pi d$ and write the numbers you know.

$9.42 \text{ cm} \approx 3.14 \times d$
$\frac{9.42}{3.14} \text{ cm} \approx \frac{3.14 \times d}{3.14}$
$3 \text{ cm} \approx d$

Use the inverse operation.

 **Practice**

1. A group of middle school students and parents renovated their church preschool. Their first project was to fence a play area of 72 square feet. Determine the missing dimensions on the table by using the correct formula and inverse operations.

2. Write the dimensions of the base and height that will require the least amount of fencing to surround the play area.

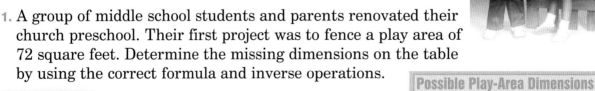

Possible Play-Area Dimensions

Area	Base	Height
72 sq ft	9 ft	▦ ft
72 sq ft	12 ft	▦ ft
72 sq ft	▦ ft	4 ft

3. A circular track for riding toys will be drawn on the concrete near the play area. The circumference of the track will be 47.1 feet. What will be the diameter of the riding track?

4. A toy chest shaped like a cube will be used for storage. If the surface area of the cube is 5,400 sq cm, what is the area of one face? What is the length of an edge of the cube?

5. The area of the classroom bulletin board is 30 square feet. A piece of butcher paper that is 6.25 feet long completely covers the bulletin board. What is the width of the paper?

6. The circumference of each table in the preschool is 7.85 feet. What is the diameter of each table?

Formulas for Volume	
Volume of a rectangular prism	$V = l \times w \times h$
Volume of a triangular prism	$V = \frac{1}{2} bh' \times h$
Volume of a cube	$V = s^3$
Volume of a cylinder	$V = \pi r^2 \times h$

7. The sandbox is a rectangular prism with a volume of 22.5 cubic feet. The length of one side is 5 feet, and the height is 1.5 feet. How wide is the sandbox?

8. What is the perimeter of the sandbox?

9. A tent shaped like a triangular prism has been set up for the children. The volume of the tent is 72 cubic feet and the area of the triangular base is 9 square feet. What is the height?

10. Some of the preschool toys are packaged in a cylindrical container. The area of the base of the container is 62.8 square centimeters. The volume of the cylinder is 2,512 cubic centimeters. What is the height of the toy container?

✓ Check Understanding

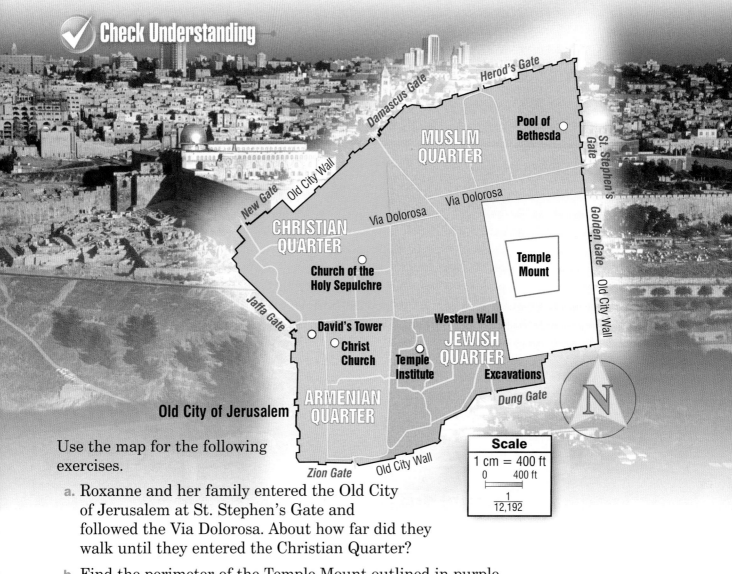

Old City of Jerusalem

Scale
1 cm = 400 ft
0   400 ft
$\frac{1}{12,192}$

Use the map for the following exercises.

a. Roxanne and her family entered the Old City of Jerusalem at St. Stephen's Gate and followed the Via Dolorosa. About how far did they walk until they entered the Christian Quarter?

b. Find the perimeter of the Temple Mount outlined in purple on the map. Estimate the area.

c. If you enter at the Damascus Gate, about how far do you walk before you enter the Jewish Quarter?

d. Is it closer to go from the Pool of Bethesda to the Church of the Holy Sepulchre, or from Christ Church to the Temple Institute?

e. Roxanne and Karen took the perimeter walking tour which goes along the top of the Old City Wall. Would it be reasonable to estimate that they walked 0.5 mile, 3 miles, or 10 miles? (There are 5,280 feet in one mile.)

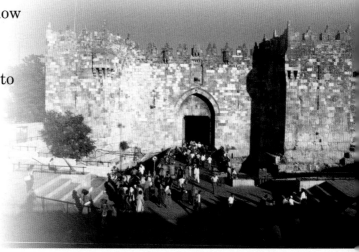

Chapter Nine Study Guide

1. What is the perimeter of a regular hexagon with the measure of one side equal to 7 cm? *Lesson 105*

2. Find the area of the parallelogram shown. *Lesson 106*

3. What is the area of the triangle shown? *Lesson 107*

4. Find the circumference of a 10-foot diameter circle. *Lesson 108*

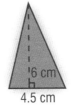

5. What is the area of a 4-inch radius bird feeder? *Lesson 109*

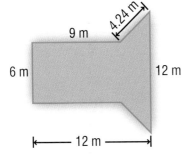

6. Find the perimeter of the symmetrical figure shown. Find the area. *Lesson 110*

7. Find the surface area of a box that measures 2 inches by 5 inches by 7 inches. *Lesson 111*

8. What is the surface area of a cylindrical rod with a diameter of 20 cm and a height of 40 cm? *Lesson 112*

9. Find the volume of a bird feeder that measures 3 inches by 3 inches by 14 inches. *Lesson 113*

10. What is the volume of a cylindrical hummingbird feeder with a diameter of 8 cm and a height of 25 cm? If one cubic centimeter equals one milliliter, does the feeder hold more or less than one liter? *Lesson 114*

11. Write the formula for finding the area of a triangle. If the base of a triangle is 6 cm and the area is 12 sq cm, what is the height? *Lesson 115*

12. Rhea measured the distance on her map between Sandpoint Lake and Loon Lake as $3\frac{1}{2}$ inches. How far will Rhea and David have to hike between the two lakes? *Lesson 116*

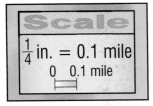

Scale

$\frac{1}{4}$ in. = 0.1 mile

0   0.1 mile

Lesson 117

Beneath the Surface

Write the letter of the correct word for each definition.

1. The distance around a circle
2. The number of square units that cover a surface
3. The distance around a polygon
4. A flat pattern that can be folded into a three-dimensional figure
5. The number of cubic units that fill a three-dimensional space

   a. area
   b. perimeter
   c. circumference
   d. volume
   e. net

Find the missing measurements.

6. $P =$
7. $A =$

1.6 m
4 m

$P = 22$ feet
8. $h =$
9. $A =$

h
3'

10. $P =$
11. $A =$

$\frac{3''}{4}$
$\frac{3''}{4}$

12. $P =$
13. $A =$

24 in.
45 in.
20 in.

$P = 14\frac{1}{2}'$
14. $x =$
15. $A =$

$3\frac{1}{2}'$
3'
x
6'

16. $P =$
17. $A =$

12.5 cm
7.5 cm
10 cm

18. $d =$
19. $C \approx$
20. $A \approx$

15 cm

$A \approx 314$ sq in.
21. $r =$
22. $d =$
23. $C \approx$

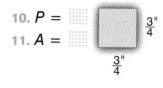

24. $r =$
25. $A \approx$

4 ft

Write *true* or *false*.

26. Cubic units are used to express volume.
27. A cylinder has only one base.
28. Square units are used to express area.
29. A triangular prism has 6 surfaces.
30. The surface area of a 1 cm cube is 6 sq cm.
31. $C = 5d$
32. The perimeter can be expressed in square units.
33. $r = 2d$
34. The area of a triangle is the product of the base and the height.

35. Find the perimeter of this swimming pool.

36. Find the area.

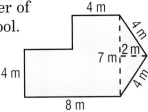

Find the surface area. Round to the nearest whole number.

37.

38.

39.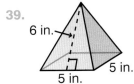

40.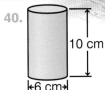

41. What is the volume of a rectangular prism that measures 1 ft by 2 ft by 3 ft?

42. What is the volume of a 2-inch radius jar that is 12 inches high?

43. Can a cylinder have the same volume as a cube? Explain.

44. Frieda has a cubic box that measures 12 inches on each side filled with packaging peanuts. She wants to transfer them to a box that measures 20 in. by 8 in. by 4 in. Will they all fit? Explain.

45. How tall is a 628 cubic centimeter cylinder that has a diameter of 10 cm?

46. What is the volume of a triangular prism building block with the measurements shown?

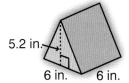

47. Use the map to find the approximate perimeter of Point State Park on Pittsburgh's Golden Triangle, formed by the intersection of three rivers.

    a. 0.3 mile   **b.** 1 mile   **c.** 7 miles

48. If Ken is at Third Avenue and Wood Street, about how far will he drive to get to the stadium?

    a. 0.5 mile   **b.** 1 mile   **c.** 5 miles

49. Do Third Avenue and Wood Street represent perpendicular or parallel lines?

50. About how wide is the Allegheny River at Point State Park?

Chapter Theme

God has given us both physical sight and spiritual sight. The gift of vision allows us to see color, the beauty of creation, and the faces of those whom we love. Our eyesight enables us to participate in sports, enjoy hobbies, and read great books. In chapter 10, you will learn some interesting facts about vision.

Moreover, God's Word tells us that the eye is the lamp of the body. Scripture often connects the idea of sight with the ability to see and understand the power and wisdom of God. Paul speaks of "the eyes of your understanding being enlightened." It is not the Lord's desire for His children to walk in darkness, as do those who have been given eyes but do not see. Our Father desires that our spiritual eyes are wide open to see everything He is doing around us.

10 Chapter

Ratio, Proportion, and Percent

Lessons 118-131

The lamp of the body is the eye. Therefore, when your eye is good, your whole body also is full of light.

Luke 11:34a

Lesson 118

Construct Meaning

Iris
Cornea
Pupil
Lens
Vitreous
Retina

Normal vision is noted as 20/20 vision. This means that at a 20-foot distance a person can read the small line on an eye chart. A person with 20/30 vision has slightly impaired vision. They would have to come <u>up to</u> 20 feet to see what normal vision could see at 30 feet.

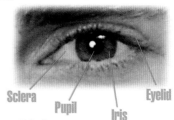

Sclera
Pupil
Iris
Eyelid

20/20 is one way to write a ratio. It can also be written as 20:20 or 20 to 20.

A **ratio** compares two quantities. In this group of individual eyes, the ratio of blue eyes to brown eyes is 2 to 6. This ratio compares one part to another part, blue to brown.

The ratio for brown to blue would be 6 to 2, 6:2, or $\frac{6}{2}$.

You can also write a ratio to compare one part to the whole.

$$\frac{\text{blue eyes}}{\text{eyes}} \qquad \frac{2}{8} \qquad \text{and} \qquad \frac{\text{brown eyes}}{\text{eyes}} \qquad \frac{6}{8}$$

> The order in which you write the ratio is important. 8:2 is different from 2:8.

- A bald eagle can fly up to 40 miles per hour. At this rate, how long would it take a bald eagle to fly 120 miles? **Equal ratios** show the same comparison.

$$\frac{40 \text{ miles}}{1 \text{ hour}} \quad \text{Finding an equal ratio is like finding an equivalent fraction.} \quad \frac{40 \text{ miles}}{1 \text{ hour}} \overset{\times 3}{\underset{\times 3}{=}} \frac{120 \text{ miles}}{n \text{ hours}} \quad n = 3$$

think

The bald eagle can fly 120 miles in 3 hours.

- A **ratio table** shows a series of equal ratios.

miles	40	80	120	160
hours	1	2	3	4

- Comparing cross products also shows equal ratios. To find the **cross products** of two ratios, multiply each numerator by the denominator of the other ratio.

Are $\frac{4}{8}$ and $\frac{6}{12}$ equal ratios?

$$\frac{4}{8} \qquad \frac{6}{12}$$

$4 \times 12 = 48 \qquad 8 \times 6 = 48$

$48 = 48$

$\frac{4}{8}$ and $\frac{6}{12}$ are equal ratios.

Are $\frac{3}{4}$ and $\frac{9}{15}$ equal ratios?

$$\frac{3}{4} \qquad \frac{9}{15}$$

$3 \times 15 = 45 \qquad 4 \times 9 = 36$

$45 \neq 36$

$\frac{3}{4}$ and $\frac{9}{15}$ are not equal ratios.

254

 Check Understanding

a. Write a ratio of eyeglasses to sunglasses.
b. Write a ratio comparing one part to the whole.

Use cross products to determine if the ratios are equal. Write *yes* or *no*.

c. $\frac{2}{3}$ $\frac{7}{12}$ d. $\frac{5}{14}$ $\frac{8}{10}$

Find the missing number.

e. $\frac{3}{16} = \frac{9}{}$ f. $\frac{3}{4} = \frac{}{8}$

 Practice

Write the appropriate ratio representing the relationship.

Optometrist Office	
Age Group	Number of patients
1–10 yr	8
11–20 yr	15
21–30 yr	32
31–40 yr	35
41–50 yr	53

1. Number of patients in the 1–10 age group to the number of patients in the 31–40 age group
2. Number of patients 20 and under to the number of patients 41–50
3. Number of patients 31–40 to the total number of patients

Copy and complete the chart.

4. 6 to 7 $\frac{6}{7}$ | $\frac{12}{}$ | $\frac{}{21}$ | $\frac{30}{}$ | $\frac{60}{}$

5. 4 to 9 $\frac{4}{9}$ | $\frac{8}{}$ | $\frac{}{27}$ | $\frac{16}{}$ | $\frac{}{45}$

6. 3 to 7 $\frac{3}{7}$ | $\frac{9}{}$ | $\frac{12}{}$ | $\frac{}{42}$ | $\frac{60}{}$

Write two equivalent ratios.

7. 2:7   8. $\frac{4}{5}$ 9. 5 to 9   10. $\frac{8}{18}$ 11. $\frac{6}{14}$

Find the missing number.

12. $\frac{7}{8} = \frac{14}{n}$ 13. $\frac{3}{9} = \frac{5}{n}$ 14. $\frac{4}{11} = \frac{12}{n}$ 15. $\frac{3}{8} = \frac{9}{n}$ 16. $\frac{3}{4} = \frac{15}{n}$

Use cross products to determine if the ratios are equal. Write *yes* or *no*.

17. $\frac{7}{12}$ $\frac{5}{9}$ 18. $\frac{3}{9}$ $\frac{2}{6}$ 19. $\frac{1}{2}$ $\frac{2}{5}$ 20. $\frac{4}{9}$ $\frac{2}{3}$

 Apply

21. An infant has a ratio of 1 to 4 skull length to body length. If a baby is 40 inches long, what is the length of her head?

22. The *Hometown Daily News* reported that 5 out of 9 people took advantage of the free eye examination service. If the population of the town is 3,600, how many people used the service?

23. The *Hometown Daily News* also reported that the Warriors baseball team's ratio of wins to losses was 9 to 7. Did the Warriors have more wins or losses? What fraction of their games did they win?

 **Construct Meaning**

Rod and cone cells

Our eyes have specialized cells called photoreceptors. The two types of photoreceptors are rod cells and cone cells. Rod cells enable us to see in dim light, and cone cells enable us to see color. The rod cells outnumber the cone cells 20 to 1.

20 to 1 is a ratio comparing two like quantities.

A **rate** is a ratio comparing two amounts having different units. A **unit rate** is a rate having 1 as the denominator.

• Jana plans to read 16 books in 8 months. How many books will she need to read each month?

$$\frac{16 \text{ books}}{8 \text{ months}}$$ Compare the number of books to the number of months.

Express the rate in number of books per month.

Divide the numerator and denominator by 8 to obtain a denominator of 1.

Think ÷ 8
$$\frac{16}{8} \xrightarrow{} \frac{\text{books}}{\text{months}} \xleftarrow{} \frac{2}{1}$$
Think ÷ 8

You can also set up the problem as an equation.

Let *n* equal the number of books completed in one month.

$$\frac{16}{8} = \frac{n}{1}$$

Use cross products.

$$\frac{16}{8} \bowtie \frac{n}{1} \rightarrow 8 \times n = 16 \times 1$$

Use the inverse operation; divide both sides of the equation by 8 to isolate *n*.

$$\frac{8n}{8} = \frac{16}{8} \rightarrow n = \frac{16}{8}$$

$$n = 2 \text{ books}$$

The unit rate is 2 books per month.

The unit rate can be written as: **2 books/month.** per↗

• Shannon owns a studio. She plans to have 5 new customers every 3 months. If all goes according to her plan, how many new customers will she have in one year?

Let *n* equal the number of ▓▓▓.

$$\frac{5 \text{ customers}}{3 \text{ months}} = \frac{n}{12 \text{ months}}$$

Why do we put 12 months in the denominator instead of 1 year?

Use cross products.

$$\frac{5}{3} \bowtie \frac{n}{12} \rightarrow 3 \times n = 5 \times \text{▓}$$

Do the inverse operation.

$$\frac{3n}{3} = \frac{60}{3} \quad n = \text{▓} \quad \text{The unit rate is ▓ per ▓.}$$

 **Check Understanding**

Express each ratio as a unit rate.

a. $26 for 2 shirts   b. 16 breaths in 4 minutes   c. $3.20 for 2 liters of juice

d. 345 miles in 3 hours   e. 5 yards of fabric for $16.50   f. 120 pages in 3 hours

 **Practice**

Write *ratio* or *rate* for each example.

1. 84 meters/minute   2. 14 pounds to 2 pounds   3. The speed limit in a school zone

4. $24 per box   5. 8 laps in one minute   6. 440 rod cells to 22 cone cells

Express each example as a unit rate.

7. 48 miles/2 gallons   8. 3 gallons of milk for $7.50

9. 2 pounds of cheese for $7.50   10. 12 packs of gum for $11.88

11. 104 miles in 2 hours   12. 90 math problems in 12 minutes

 Apply

13. If there are 42,000 rod cells in 3 square mm, how many rod cells are in 1 square mm?

14. The optometrist can do 20 routine eye exams in 100 minutes. How many eye exams can she do in 1 hour?

15. The display case at the optical shop holds 36 pairs of glasses in every three sections. How many glasses are in one section?

16. Miss Trudeau can type 256 words in 4 minutes. How many words can she type in one minute?

Use the table to answer the following questions.

Student	Pages every 2 hours
Jared	26
Oly	20
Gloria	22
Ping	32
Laurie	21

17. How many pages did Gloria read in one hour?

18. How many pages could Oly read in a 24-hour day?

19. What is the difference between Jared's hourly reading rate and Laurie's hourly reading rate?

 **Challenge**

Write the letter of the answer that is the better buy.

20. **a.** 2 pounds of hamburger for $6.25
     b. 3 pounds of hamburger for $7.50

21. **a.** 6 gallons of gasoline for $8.50
     b. 10 gallons of gasoline for $12.75

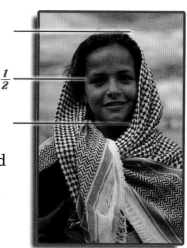

$\frac{1}{2}$

Construct Meaning

For it is the God who commanded light to shine out of darkness, who has shone in our hearts to give the light of the knowledge of the glory of God in the face of Jesus Christ. 2 Cor. 4:6

The distance between the features of a person's face are said to be proportional to one another. For example, the correct placement of the eyes on the head is half the distance from the top of the head to the bottom of the chin.

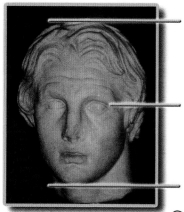

$\frac{1}{2}$

If a 12-inch sculpture of a head is being made and the eyes are placed at 6 inches, is the sculpture proportional?

An equation which shows that two ratios are equal is called a **proportion**.

Two ratios form a proportion if their cross products are equal. To find cross products of two ratios, multiply each numerator by the denominator of the other ratio.

Think:
$$\frac{1}{2} \times \frac{6}{6} = \frac{6}{12}$$
or
$$\frac{6}{12} \div \frac{6}{6} = \frac{1}{2}$$
$$\frac{1}{2} = \frac{6}{12}$$

$\frac{1}{2} = \frac{6}{12}$

$1 \times 12 = 2 \times 6$ Because the cross products are equal,
$12 = 12$ the faces are proportional.

Computer monitor displays have a contrast ratio shown as maximum to minimum darkness. One display has a contrast ratio of 225 to 15, and the other display has a maximum of 120. What must the minimum value of the second display be in order to have proportional displays?

To find the answer, write a proportion showing two equal ratios. Use cross products to solve for n.

$$\frac{225}{15} \xleftarrow{\text{maximum}} \xrightarrow{} \frac{120}{n}$$ $$\frac{225}{15} = \frac{120}{n}$$

Set up the equation with cross products. $225 \times n = 15 \times 120$
$$225n = 1{,}800$$

Use the inverse operation to isolate n. $$\frac{225n}{225} = \frac{1{,}800}{225}$$
$$n = \frac{1{,}800}{225}$$
$$n = 8$$

The minimum darkness is 8. Therefore, the contrast ratio is 120 to 8.

 **Check Understanding**

Solve for the unknown.

a. $\dfrac{6}{9} = \dfrac{10}{n}$ b. $\dfrac{8}{12} = \dfrac{r}{21}$ c. $\dfrac{1}{8} = \dfrac{x}{64}$ d. $\dfrac{t}{6} = \dfrac{6}{9}$ e. $\dfrac{25}{70} = \dfrac{5}{a}$

 **Practice**

Write the cross products. Write = or ≠.

1. $\dfrac{5}{7}$ ⬚ $\dfrac{8}{11}$ 2. $\dfrac{2}{5}$ ⬚ $\dfrac{10}{25}$ 3. $\dfrac{6}{8}$ ⬚ $\dfrac{9}{12}$ 4. $\dfrac{9}{25}$ ⬚ $\dfrac{3}{5}$

5. $\dfrac{6}{8}$ ⬚ $\dfrac{3}{4}$ 6. $\dfrac{150}{8}$ ⬚ $\dfrac{200}{12}$ 7. $\dfrac{36}{43}$ ⬚ $\dfrac{18}{20}$ 8. $\dfrac{64}{128}$ ⬚ $\dfrac{192}{384}$

Solve for the unknown.

9. $\dfrac{1}{4} = \dfrac{n}{20}$ 10. $\dfrac{t}{6} = \dfrac{3}{18}$ 11. $\dfrac{3}{8} = \dfrac{w}{12}$ 12. $\dfrac{6}{8} = \dfrac{3}{b}$

13. $\dfrac{y}{15} = \dfrac{4}{5}$ 14. $\dfrac{3}{4} = \dfrac{12}{r}$ 15. $\dfrac{x}{18} = \dfrac{5}{6}$ 16. $\dfrac{12}{f} = \dfrac{8}{14}$

17. $\dfrac{6}{15} = \dfrac{n}{20}$ 18. $\dfrac{5}{8} = \dfrac{t}{12}$ 19. $\dfrac{2}{6} = \dfrac{3}{d}$ 20. $\dfrac{4}{a} = \dfrac{8}{9}$

 Apply

Write a proportion and solve.

21. The placement of the nose on the face is $\dfrac{2}{3}$ the distance from the top of the head to the bottom of the chin. If an artist draws a nose 7 inches from the top of a 10-inch head, is the drawing proportional?

22. The proportion of the height of the head to the height of the body is 1 to 8. If a lady is 72 inches tall, what is the height of her head?

23. The customer service department at Bond's Optical helps an average of 20 customers in a four-hour period. What is the average number of customers they help in 16 hours?

24. The circumference of the thumb, wrist, neck, and waist of a person are all equally proportional to one another. If the ratio of thumb to wrist is 8 cm to 16 cm, what would be the wrist to neck ratio?

Construct Meaning

> He who dwells in the secret place of the Most High shall abide under the shadow of the Almighty. I will say of the LORD, "He is my refuge and my fortress; My God, in Him I will trust." Psalm 91:1–2

A natural consequence of light is a shadow. A shadow can be long or short, depending on the position of the sun in the sky. Mr. Jung, who is 6 feet tall, has a shadow measuring 4 feet in length. A nearby palm tree casts a shadow 30 feet long. What is the height of the palm tree?

30 ft

4 ft

A proportion can be used to determine the height of the tree. Let h represent the height of the palm tree.

$$\text{height} \longrightarrow \frac{6 \text{ feet}}{4 \text{ feet}} = \frac{h}{30 \text{ feet}} \longleftarrow \text{shadow length}$$

Use cross products to solve for h.

$$6 \times 30 = 4 \times h$$
$$180 = 4h$$
$$\frac{180}{4} = \frac{4h}{4}$$
$$45 = h$$

The palm tree is 45 feet high.

 **Check Understanding**

Write a proportion and solve.

a. Mrs. Aguilar is 5 feet tall and her shadow measures 8 feet. The shadow of a peach tree in her garden measures 32 feet. What is the height of the peach tree? Let h represent the height of the tree.

$$\frac{}{} = \frac{}{32 \text{ feet}} \qquad h = $$

b. A high school English class orders 45 books for 15 students. How many books would the English department need to order for 135 students?

Write a proportion and solve.

1. A kangaroo in Australia can be 2 meters in height. If the kangaroo casts a shadow of 3 meters and an eucalyptus tree casts a shadow of 24 meters, what is the height of the eucalyptus tree?

2. Homer's car can travel 260 miles on 10 gallons of gasoline. How many gallons of gasoline will the car need to travel 320 miles? Round your answer to the nearest tenth.

3. Mr. VanBuren uses a paint color called Cinderella to paint the inside of new houses. The color is made by mixing 1 pint of ruby red into 5 gallons of antique white. How much ruby red is needed to mix with 12 gallons of antique white?

4. Tweeties Bird Shop has 20 birds in every 6 cages. If the shop has 21 cages, how many birds are in the shop?

5. Early one morning Bryce traveled to Cape Canaveral, Florida, to see the launch of a rocket. Bryce is six feet tall and his shadow measures 16 feet. If the rocket's shadow is 488 feet long, what is the height of the rocket?

6. Maria is making uniforms for school children. Two boys' uniforms can be made from 5 yards of fabric. How many yards are needed to make 30 uniforms?

7. It was determined through a phone survey that 6 out of 10 Americans between the ages of 35 and 55 wear eyeglasses. If 420 people in the age group were surveyed, how many of them wear glasses?

8. An Emperor penguin is one of the largest types of penguins, reaching 4 feet in height. If a full-grown Emperor penguin casts a shadow of 6 feet and a nearby glacier's shadow measures 330 feet, how tall is the glacier?

Write in order from least to greatest.

1. 0   2   −1   8   2. 9   −3   −6   3. 6   −24   1   −1

Solve.

4. −8 + 7   5. 2 + (−4)   6. −3 + (−4)

Lesson 122

Construct Meaning

The eye is somewhat like a camera. It has similar parts and requires light in order to function at its best. Light from an object enters the eye through the cornea and is concentrated and focused by the lens. The curvature of the cornea carries out 80% of the focusing that the eye does. The lens completes the task. Together the lens and the cornea accomplish 100%, or all, of the focusing of the eye.

What percent of the focusing does the lens do?

100 − 80 = 20   20 out of 100 = 20%   The lens does 20% of the focusing.

Percent means per one hundred.
A **percent** (%) is a ratio that compares a number to one hundred.

Problem	Ratio	Fraction	Decimal	Percent
show 20 out of 100	20:100	$\frac{20}{100}$	0.20	20%
show 76 out of 100	76:100	$\frac{76}{100}$	0.76	76%
show $4 out of $100	4:100	$\frac{4}{100}$	0.04	4%

Sixteen out of 50 cameras inspected had faulty auto-focus units. What percentage of the cameras inspected had faulty units?

If a ratio has a denominator of 100, it can easily be expressed as a percent.

Write the ratio as a fraction. ⟶ $\frac{16}{50}$

Write a proportion with 100 as one of the denominators. ⟶ $\frac{16}{50} = \frac{a}{100}$

Solve the proportion using cross products. ⟶ $\frac{16}{50} = \frac{a}{100}$

$16 \times 100 = 50 \times a$

$\frac{1,600}{50} = \frac{50a}{50}$

$32 = a$

Rewrite the fraction as a percent. ⟶ $\frac{32}{100} = 32\%$

You can also solve this proportion by using multiplication.

$\overset{\times 2}{\frac{16}{50}} = \underset{\times 2}{\frac{a}{100}}$ $a = 32$

32% of the cameras had faulty auto-focus units.

Check Understanding

Write each ratio as a percent.

a. $\frac{6}{100}$ b. 72:100   c. 45.5 to 100

Solve for n.

d. $\frac{8}{50} = \frac{n}{100}$ e. $\frac{12}{25} = \frac{n}{100}$ f. $\frac{9}{15} = \frac{n}{100}$

 **Practice**

Write each ratio as a percent.

1. 8 to 100
2. 12:100
3. $\frac{16}{100}$
4. 45 to 100

Write as a fraction with a denominator of 100.

5. 11%
6. 44%
7. 9%
8. 85%

Solve.

9. $\frac{9}{25} = \frac{n}{100}$
10. $\frac{14}{32} = \frac{n}{100}$
11. $\frac{4}{20} = \frac{n}{100}$
12. $\frac{24}{60} = \frac{n}{100}$

13. $\frac{6}{8} = \frac{n}{100}$
14. $\frac{9}{16} = \frac{n}{100}$
15. $\frac{14}{50} = \frac{n}{100}$
16. $\frac{7}{8} = \frac{n}{100}$

 Apply

17. Write each ratio as a percent.

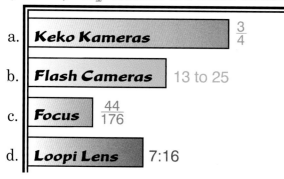

Ratio of Faulty Cameras to Perfect Cameras

a. **Keko Kameras** — $\frac{3}{4}$

b. **Flash Cameras** — 13 to 25

c. **Focus** — $\frac{44}{176}$

d. **Loopi Lens** — 7:16

18. Forty-five out of 100 types of cameras give away a carrying case with each camera purchase. What percentage of camera types do not give away a carrying case with each purchase?

19. If 11% of Eugene Bible College's student population have normal vision, what percent of the student population does not have normal vision?

20. Out of 96 photographs, Kerry and Jenny have taken 54. What percent of the photographs remain to be taken?

21. Dr. Zawel, an optometrist, evaluated 6 out of 24 patients in four hours. What percent of his patients did he evaluate in four hours?

22. On her business trip, Mrs. Sanders spent $100 on food and gasoline. If Mrs. Sanders spent $57 on food, what percent did she spend on gasoline?

 Construct Meaning

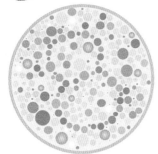

Both males and females can inherit a type of color blindness called red-green color blindness. An individual with this type of color blindness has trouble distinguishing between certain shades of red, brown, olive, and gold. Approximately 8 out of 100 males and 1 out of 100 females have red-green color blindness.

8 out of 100 or $\frac{8}{100}$ males have red-green color blindness. What percent of males have red-green color blindness?

Divide the numerator by the denominator to express $\frac{8}{100}$ as a decimal.

$$100\overline{)8.00} \quad \begin{array}{r} 0.08 \\ \underline{8\ 00} \\ 0 \end{array}$$

Write 0.08 as a percent.

Multiply. $0.08 \times 100 = 8$
Write the %. $0.08 = 8\%$.

OR

$0.08 = \frac{8}{100} = 8\%$

Multiply by 100 and write the %

Decimal $1.00 = 100\%$ Percent

Divide by 100 and remove the %

Convert a percent to a decimal.

Write 0.4% as a decimal.

$$\frac{0.4}{100} \quad 100\overline{)0.400} \quad \begin{array}{r} 0.004 \\ \underline{-400} \\ 0 \end{array}$$

$0.4\% = 0.004$

Convert a percent greater than 100% to a decimal.

Write 112% as a decimal.

$$\frac{112}{100} \quad 100\overline{)112.00} \quad \begin{array}{r} 1.12 \\ \underline{100} \\ 120 \\ \underline{100} \\ 200 \\ \underline{200} \\ 0 \end{array}$$

$112\% = 1.12$

Convert a decimal to a percent.

Write 0.013 as a percent.
Multiply. $0.013 \times 100 = 1.3$
Write the %. $0.013 = 1.3\%$

Convert a decimal greater than 1 to a percent.

Write 3.5 as a percent.

Multiply $3.5 \times 100 = 350$
Write the %. $3.5 = 350\%$

 Check Understanding

a. What is done to convert a decimal to a percent?

b. What is done to convert a percent to a decimal?

Write each decimal as a percent.

c. 0.36   d. 0.005   e. 2.13

Write each percent as a decimal.

f. 6%   g. 42%   h. 0.6%

Write if each decimal is *greater than* or *less than* 100%.

1. 0.05   2. 0.167   3. 2.13   4. 0.99   5. 1.80

Write each decimal as a percent.

6. 0.09   7. 0.5   8. 0.17   9. 0.35

10. 1.25   11. 0.003   12. 0.88   13. 2.5

Write each percent as a decimal.

14. 1%   15. 0.4%   16. 76%   17. 25%

18. 175%   19. 33%   20. 240%   21. 18%

Write >, < or =.

22. 0.4 ⬚ 4%   23. 15% ⬚ 1.5   24. 70% ⬚ 0.7   25. 0.09 ⬚ 90%

Use the table to answer the following questions.

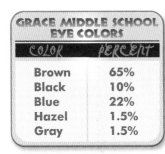

GRACE MIDDLE SCHOOL EYE COLORS	
COLOR	PERCENT
Brown	65%
Black	10%
Blue	22%
Hazel	1.5%
Gray	1.5%

26. What percent of the middle school population does <u>not</u> have brown eyes?

27. Which eye color makes up more than $\frac{1}{2}$ of the middle school population's eye color?

28. Which eye color is 0.1 of the middle school population?

29. Write the percent of students with gray eyes as a fraction with a denominator of 100.

30. What is the difference between the percent of blue eyes and the percent of hazel eyes?

Find the area.

1.

4 ft
6 ft

2.

26 cm
32 cm

3.
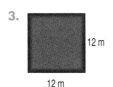
12 m
12 m

4.

5.2 mm
1.2 mm

Construct Meaning

Nearsightedness and farsightedness are terms that are used to describe conditions where the eye is unable to focus on objects at varying distances. For a nearsighted person, their distance vision, without glasses, will always be blurry.

3 out of 8 members of Sean's family wear glasses to correct nearsightedness. What percent of his family wears glasses?

Divide the numerator by the denominator → *Multiply by 100 and write the %*

Fraction   Decimal   **Percent**

Write as a fraction and simplify ← *Divide by 100 and remove the %*

To change a Fraction to a Percent:

Find the decimal equivalent of the fraction.

$\frac{3}{8}$ is $3 \div 8$

$$\begin{array}{r} 0.375 \\ 8)\overline{3.00} \\ \underline{24} \\ 60 \\ \underline{56} \\ 40 \\ \underline{40} \\ 0 \end{array}$$

Then write as a percent.

Multiply. $0.375 \times 100 = 37.5$
Write the %. $0.375 = 37.5\%$

 Or Use a proportion.

Write a proportion with 100 as one of the denominators.

$$\frac{3}{8} = \frac{n}{100}$$

Solve the proportion by using cross products.

$$3 \times 100 = 8n$$
$$300 = 8n$$
$$\frac{300}{8} = \frac{8n}{8}$$
$$37.5 = n$$

$$\frac{n}{100} = \frac{37.5}{100} = 37.5\% \text{ or } 37\frac{1}{2}\%$$

37.5% of the family wear glasses.

To change a Percent to a Fraction:

Write the percent as the numerator of a fraction having 100 as the denominator. Simplify.

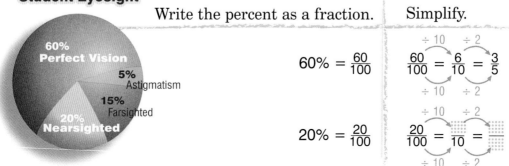

Carson Middle School Student Eyesight

60% Perfect Vision
5% Astigmatism
15% Farsighted
20% Nearsighted

Write the percent as a fraction.   Simplify.

$$60\% = \frac{60}{100}$$

$\div 10 \quad \div 2$
$$\frac{60}{100} = \frac{6}{10} = \frac{3}{5}$$
$\div 10 \quad \div 2$

$$20\% = \frac{20}{100}$$

$\div 10 \quad \div 2$
$$\frac{20}{100} = \frac{2}{10} =$$
$\div 10 \quad \div 2$

 **Check-Understanding**

Write the fraction as a percent using division.

a. $\frac{1}{4}$ b. $\frac{7}{8}$ c. $\frac{1}{3}$

Use a proportion to write the fraction as a percent.

d. $\frac{5}{8}$ e. $\frac{2}{5}$ f. $\frac{2}{9}$

 **Practice**

Write each fraction as a percent using division.

1. $\frac{3}{25}$ 2. $\frac{3}{5}$ 3. $\frac{4}{5}$ 4. $\frac{9}{16}$

 **USING A CALCULATOR**

5. $\frac{16}{32}$ 6. $\frac{8}{25}$ 7. $\frac{50}{25}$ 8. $\frac{13}{25}$ 9. $\frac{19}{90}$

Use a proportion to write the fraction as a percent.

10. $\frac{9}{36}$ 11. $\frac{8}{15}$ 12. $\frac{7}{20}$ 13. $\frac{6}{8}$ 14. $\frac{5}{16}$

Use mental math to find the percent.

15. $\frac{1}{2}$ 16. $\frac{7}{10}$ 17. $\frac{3}{4}$ 18. $\frac{1}{10}$ 19. $\frac{1}{4}$

 Apply

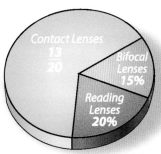

Lenses-R-Us Yearly Production

20. What fraction of bifocal lenses were made by Lenses-R-Us?

21. What percent of lenses produced were contact lenses?

22. What fraction of lenses produced were bifocal and reading lenses?

23. Jules took 9 pictures of his roll of 36 pictures last weekend. What percent of his pictures remain to be taken?

24. $\frac{2}{3}$ of the patients at Magnified Lenscrafters are nearsighted. What percent of the patients are nearsighted? Round to the nearest percent.

 Construct Meaning

Your word is a lamp to my feet and a light to my path. Psalm 119:105

The visible light spectrum that humans can see is basically the colors of the rainbow. Each color of light has a wavelength range measured in nanometers (nm). The wavelengths from purple to red range from about 400 nm to 700 nm. The total range of the spectrum spans 300 nm. The color yellow is about 17% of the 300 nm range of the spectrum.

Find the range of the yellow wavelength, which is 17% of 300 nm.

There are three ways to determine the percent of a number.

1 Change the percent to a decimal.

$$17\% = \frac{17}{100} = 0.17$$

Multiply.
```
    3 0 0
  × 0.1 7
  -------
  2 1 0 0
  3 0 0
  -------
  5 1.0 0   Place the decimal.
```

> You can also think of it as an equation.
>
> 17% of 300 is equal to a
> percent   whole   part
>
> $$0.17 \times 300 = a$$
> $$51 = a$$

2 Change the percent to a fraction and simplify.

$$17\% = \frac{17}{100}$$

Multiply.

$$\frac{17}{100} \times \frac{300}{1} = \frac{5,100}{100} = 51 \text{ nm}$$

> The yellow wavelength ranges 51 nanometers.

3 Use a calculator.

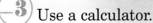   `51.` nanometers

---

Find 75% of 640.

Solve by using a decimal. $75\% = \frac{75}{100} = 0.75$ $0.75 \times 640 = 480$

Solve by using a fraction. $75\% = \frac{75}{100} = \frac{3}{4}$ $\frac{3}{4} \times \frac{640}{1} = \frac{1,920}{4} = 480$

Sometimes it is mentally easy to write the percent as a fraction, such as 75% is $\frac{3}{4}$ and 50% is $\frac{1}{2}$. At other times, it may be easier to change the percent to a decimal.

 **Check Understanding**

Find the percent of each number.

  a. 3% of 160   **b.** 40% of 860   **c.** 75% of 200   **d.** 20% of 80

 **Practice**

Find the percent of each number.

  1. 48% of 150   **2.** 6% of 30   **3.** 30% of 90   **4.** 10% of 120

  5. 8% of 150   **6.** 85% of 16   **7.** 80% of 15   **8.** 75% of 44

  9. 38% of 200   **10.** 95% of 30   **11.** 20% of 32   **12.** 36% of 75

 **USING A CALCULATOR**

Round to the nearest cent.

  13. 45% of $50.50   **14.** 25% of $128   **15.** 8% of $42.75   **16.** 85% of $601.25

 Apply

Solve. Round to the nearest cent if necessary.

17. The goal for the girls' soccer team fund-raiser is $1,250. They have raised 71% of the money. How much money have they collected?

18. The Ensada family received a phone bill for $65.75. If the bill is not paid on time, a late charge of 5% is added to the bill. How much is the late charge?

19. Many students participate in extra-curricular activities after school. In one sixth grade class of 30 students, 20% have band practice, 50% have intramural sports, and 10% are in chess club. How many students do not participate in extracurricular activities?

20. Jordy's youth group is raising funds for a missions trip to India. They need to raise a total of $5,500. In June they collected 25%, and in July they collected 45%. How much money remains to be collected?

21. Mohada's goal is to earn $250 by selling her crafts at the local market. During the first two weeks, she has collected 62% of the money. How much more money must Mohada earn in order to meet her goal?

 **Construct Meaning**

Dogs and cats have rod and cone cells in their eyes just as humans do. The rod cells in their eyes are numerous and enable dogs to see well at night. However, dogs do not see color very well because they only have two instead of three types of cone cells.

 If the central retina of the canine eye contains 51,250 rod and cone cells and 20% are cone cells, estimate the number of cone cells.

To estimate, round the number of rod and cone cells to the greatest place value.

51,250 is about 50,000.

20% can be thought of as two times 10%.
Remember that 10% can be written as $\frac{10}{100}$ or $\frac{1}{10}$.

10% of $50,000 = \frac{1}{10} \times \frac{50,000}{1}$
$= \frac{5,000}{1}$
$= 5,000$

To find 20%, multiply by 2. $2 \times 5,000 = 10,000$

> There are about 10,000 cone cells.

Sometimes you may need to round the percent to estimate.

Estimate 12% of 30.

Round to the nearest multiple of 10.

10% of 30 is $\frac{1}{10} \times \frac{30}{1}$

$\frac{30}{10} = 3$

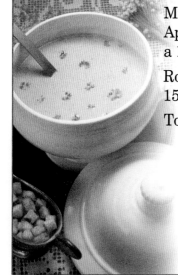

Miss Vaughn took a client out to dinner and her bill was $18.50. Approximately how much money should Miss Vaughn include for a 15% tip?

Round the dollars to the greatest place value. $18.50 = $20.00
15% can be thought of as 10% + 5%.

To find 15%

 Think: 10% of $20 = \frac{1}{10} \times $20 = 2

Think: 5% is half of 10%.
If 10% of $20 is $2, then 5% of $20 is $1.
$10\% + 5\% = 15\%$

$$\$2 + \$1 = \$3$$

 **Check Understanding**

Estimate each answer.

a. 20% of 200   b. 40% of $19.75   c. 15% of 2,143   d. 30% of 485

 **Practice**

Estimate each answer by rounding to the greatest place value.

1. 40% of 364,000   2. 60% of 4,210   3. 80% of 46   4. 20% of $15.65

5. 30% of 1,200   6. 10% of 82   7. 15% of 300   8. 25% of 180

Estimate each answer by rounding the percent to the nearest multiple of ten.

9. 12% of 600   10. 14% of 3,000   11. 62% of 80   12. 54% of 400

Use mental math to estimate each answer. Round numbers as needed.

13. 21% of 102   14. 10% of 48   15. 40% of 199   16. 29% of 200

 Apply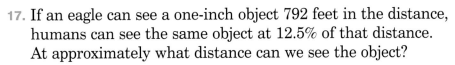

17. If an eagle can see a one-inch object 792 feet in the distance, humans can see the same object at 12.5% of that distance. At approximately what distance can we see the object?

18. The bones of a human are about 20% of our body weight. Estimate the weight of the bones of an 88-pound person.

Jazlyne's Monthly Budget

19% Food
30% Rent
10% Gas
26% Entertainment
15% Clothes

Total Budget $1,800

19. In Jazlyne's Monthly Budget, approximately how much does she spend on one-month's rent?

20. Estimate how much Jazlyne spends each month on gasoline for her car.

21. Approximately how much money does Jazlyne spend each month on entertainment and clothes?

22. If Jazlyne's family went out to dinner and spent $47.50 on the meal, how much money should they leave for a 15% tip?

 **Review**

Find the perimeter.

1.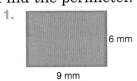
6 mm
9 mm

2.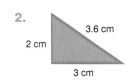
3.6 cm
2 cm
3 cm

3.
33 yd
70 yd

271

 **Construct Meaning**

Devon's basketball team made 70% of 200 shots. How many shots did the team make?
Recall how to find the percent of a number. Remember: percent × whole = part.

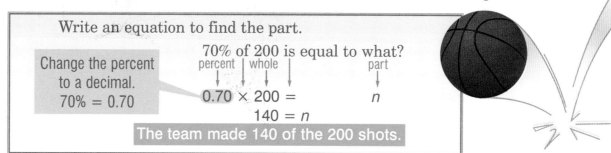

Write an equation to find the part.

Change the percent to a decimal.
70% = 0.70

70% of 200 is equal to what?
percent | whole | part

$0.70 \times 200 = n$

$140 = n$

The team made 140 of the 200 shots.

Devon is practicing shooting free throws. He made 17 out of 20 free throw attempts.
What percent of the throws did he make?

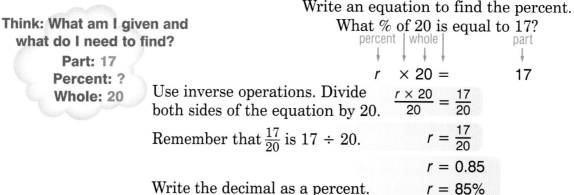

Think: What am I given and what do I need to find?
Part: 17
Percent: ?
Whole: 20

Write an equation to find the percent.
What % of 20 is equal to 17?
percent | whole | part

$r \times 20 = 17$

Use inverse operations. Divide both sides of the equation by 20.

$\frac{r \times 20}{20} = \frac{17}{20}$

Remember that $\frac{17}{20}$ is 17 ÷ 20.

$r = \frac{17}{20}$

$r = 0.85$

Write the decimal as a percent. $r = 85\%$

Devon made 85% of his free throws.

Helen answered 20 out of 25 questions on the literature quiz correctly.
What percent of the questions did she answer correctly?

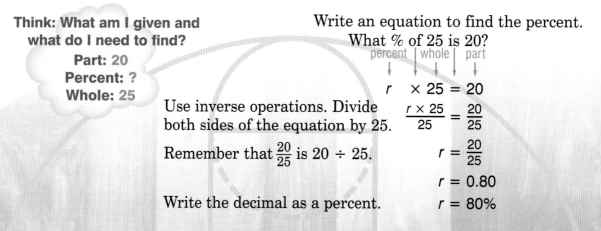

Think: What am I given and what do I need to find?
Part: 20
Percent: ?
Whole: 25

Write an equation to find the percent.
What % of 25 is 20?
percent | whole | part

$r \times 25 = 20$

Use inverse operations. Divide both sides of the equation by 25.

$\frac{r \times 25}{25} = \frac{20}{25}$

Remember that $\frac{20}{25}$ is 20 ÷ 25.

$r = \frac{20}{25}$

$r = 0.80$

Write the decimal as a percent. $r = 80\%$

Helen answered 80% of the questions correctly.

 **Check Understanding**

a. What percent of 40 is 16?

b. 9 is what percent of 36?

c. Kilan purchased four packages of four pairs of socks each. If five of the pairs are black, what percent of the socks are black?

 **Practice**

Solve for the unknown. Write the decimal answer as a percent.

1. $r \times 32 = 16$

2. $p \times 480 = 12$

3. $s \times 200 = 8$

4. $t \times 1,600 = 2$

5. $a \times 64 = 4$

6. $c \times 31,000 = 6,200$

Write an equation and solve.

7. What percent of 15 is 9?

8. 2 is what percent of 6?

9. 21 is what percent of 70?

10. What percent of 12 is 9?

11. What percent of 200 is 8?

12. 35 is what percent of 40?

 Apply

13. Russell purchased a bag containing 72 jelly beans. If 18 jelly beans were red, what percent of the jelly beans were red?

14. 15 out of the 24 students in Mr. Peterson's class use email to communicate with their friends. What percent of the class uses email?

15. Keysha ran for student council president. If she received 56 out of 80 votes, what percent of the votes did she receive?

16. Kelly is an underwater photographer. During one dive he took 24 pictures, and during another dive he took 42 pictures. If Kelly took a total of 102 pictures, what percent of the photographs did he take during the two dives? Round to the nearest percent.

 **Review**

1. $1 - (-1)$

2. $4 - (-6)$

3. $6 - (-2)$

4. $12 - (-1)$

5. $6 + (-3)$

6. $1 + (-1)$

7. $-1 + (-8)$

8. $3 + (-9)$

**Construct Meaning**

Polly put down a deposit of $3,000 on a new patio home. The deposit was 5% of the total cost of the home. What was the price of the home?

Think: What am I given and what do I need to find?
Part: $3,000
Percent: 5%
Whole: ?
Find the whole.

Write an equation to find the whole.

5% of *w* is $3,000.
percent | whole   part

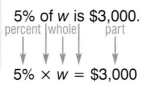

5% × *w* = $3,000

Change the percent to a decimal. 5% = 0.05
Use inverse operations. Divide both sides of the equation by 0.05.
Remember that $\frac{3,000}{0.05}$ is 3,000 ÷ 0.05.

0.05 × *w* = $3,000

$\frac{0.05 \times w}{0.05} = \frac{\$3,000}{0.05}$

$w = \frac{\$3,000}{0.05}$

w = $60,000

The price of the home was $60,000.

Recall: Find the Part

65% of 400 is what?
percent | whole | part

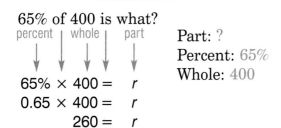

65% × 400 = *r*
0.65 × 400 = *r*
260 = *r*

Part: ?
Percent: 65%
Whole: 400

Recall: Find the Percent

What percent of 30 is 18?
percent | whole | part

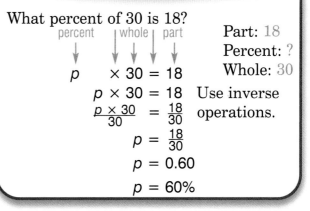

p × 30 = 18

p × 30 = 18
$\frac{p \times 30}{30} = \frac{18}{30}$

$p = \frac{18}{30}$

p = 0.60

p = 60%

Part: 18
Percent: ?
Whole: 30

Use inverse operations.

**Check Understanding**

a. Is there an equation that is used when either the part, percent, or whole is unknown? Explain.

Indicate what you need to find by writing *whole*, *part*, or *percent*. Solve the problem.

b. When Mrs. Stotmeir bought a car, she made a 25% down payment of $3,000. What was the purchase price of the car?

c. The park's naturalist estimated that 30% of the tide pools were damaged by the oil spill. If the park has 250 tide pools, how many were damaged?

Write an equation and solve.

1. Sixty percent of the Kennedy's 2,500-square-foot house is carpeted. How many square feet of carpet are there in the Kennedy house?

2. Cory purchased a kit to make a new go-cart. He made a 20% down payment of $20. What was the purchase price of the go-cart?

3. Seven hours or 14% of Roberto's work week is spent making service calls to customers. Determine the total hours in Roberto's work week.

4. At the Vandermeulen family reunion there were 40 people. If 18 of them were grandchildren, what percent of the people at the reunion were grandchildren?

5. In 1992, 4,000 people lived in Hoganville. In 1994, 52 people moved into town, and no one moved away. By what percent did the population of Hoganville grow? Round to the nearest percent.

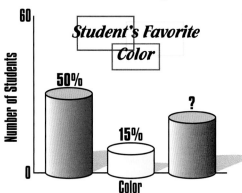

6. In a survey of 60 students, Joseph discovered that out of three colors, blue was the favorite.

    a. How many students chose blue as their favorite color?

    b. 21 out of 60 students chose red as their favorite color. What percent preferred red?

    c. How many of the students preferred the color yellow?

7. Freedom Fitness has used a circle graph to display their yearly budget.

    a. What percent of the budget is used on maintenance?

    b. How much money is used for purchasing new equipment?

8. If the Jackson's have driven 488 miles of their 1,220-mile trip, what percent of the trip have they completed?

9. Barry and Jana went out for dinner. Barry gave a 15% tip, which was $6.75. What was the total cost of dinner?

Lesson 129

 **Construct Meaning**

For Your lovingkindness is before my eyes,
And I have walked in Your truth. Psalm 26:3

Laser vision correction can be performed to correct certain
types of impaired vision. A laser is used to make tiny incisions
on the perimeter of the cornea in order to reshape the cornea,
thus correcting the vision.

The Peak View Center is offering a 12% discount on laser vision correction surgery. If
the cost per eye is regularly $1,150, how much will the surgery cost with the discount?

Write an equation to find the unknown part.

Change the percent
to a decimal.

12% of $1,150 is what?
12% × $1,150 = r
0.12 × $1,150 = r
$138 = r

Subtract to find
the discount price.

$1,150 − $138 = $1,012

The surgery will be $1,012 per eye.

Alternate Method

100% − % discount = % paid
100% − 12% = 88%

A 12% discount is 88% of the original price.

88% of $1,150 is what?
88% × $1,150 = r
0.88 × $1,150 = r
$1,012 = r

Mia purchased a sweater that was priced at $20. What was the total cost of the
sweater if the tax added was $8\frac{1}{2}$%?

Write an equation to find the part.

Change the percent
to a decimal.

$8\frac{1}{2}$% of 20 is what?
$8\frac{1}{2}$% × 20 = r
0.085 × 20 = r
$1.70 = r

Remember to think about
what is given and what
needs to be found.

Add the tax to the price to $20 + $1.70 = $21.70
find the cost of the sweater.   Mia paid $21.70 for the sweater.

 **Check Understanding**

Add the tax to find the total cost.

a. Book bag $24
   Sales tax 6%

b. Tennis shoes $55
   Sales tax 8%

Subtract to find the discounted price.

c. Sweatshirt $20
   Discount 15%

d. Jeans $32
   Discount 25%

e. Jacob purchased a jacket originally priced at $70.00 at a
   discount of 20%. How much did Jacob pay for the jacket?

276

 **ractice**

Find the amount of the sales tax.

1. Jacket $70
   Sales tax 6%

2. Watch $45
   Sales tax 3%

Find the amount of the discount.

3. Candles $16
   Discount 25%

4. Bed $400
   Discount 35%

Find the total cost.

5. Belt $12
   Sales tax 8%

6. Camera $200
   Sales tax $4\frac{1}{2}$%

Find the discounted price.

7. Amtrak $50
   Discount 20%

8. Chest $290
   Discount 10%

Use the advertised sales to determine the cost of each item.

Item	Original Price
9. 1 snare drum	$75.00
10. 3 azurites	$3.00 each
11. 1 model plane	$40.00
12. 2 vases	$65.00 each

 pply

13. Tito ordered a burrito, salsa, and soda from the menu of El Sombrero. What is the total cost of his bill?

14. If you have $4 to spend for lunch at El Sombrero's, what can you order? Write down the items you would purchase and calculate the total cost including tax.

15. Max's Home Furnishings is having a storewide sale. The regular price for a leather sofa is $1,500. With a discount of 30%, what is the cost of the sofa?

16. Troy lives in a state where the sales tax is 5%, and Wesley lives in a state where the sales tax is 7%. Both Troy and Wesley are looking at purchasing bicycles that are the same brand and model. The price of the bicycle for Troy is $115. The price of the bicycle for Wesley is $110. Who will pay more for the bicycle? How much more will he pay?

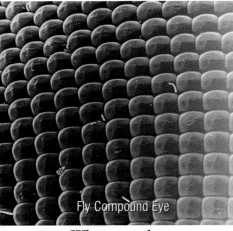

Construct Meaning

Compound eyes of a fly have 2 to 30,000 lenses that may project a type of "mosaic" picure. Insects usually have several eyes that may be simple or compound.

In terms of finances, simple or compound **interest** is money earned on a savings account or money paid for a loan.

Fly Compound Eye

• When you have money in an interest-earning bank account, the account earns interest for you. Simple interest is dependent on the principal, which is the original amount of money in the account, the interest rate, and the length of time.

$$\text{Interest} = p \quad \times \quad r \quad \times \quad t$$

principal   interest rate   time

Leaf Hopper Eye

Miss Sanchez deposited $5,000 in a savings account that has an annual interest rate of 8%.
What will be her account balance at the end of one year?

Find the interest earned.	$I = p \times r \times t$
Substitute the numbers.	$I = \$5,000 \times 8\% \times 1$
Write 8% as a decimal.	$I = \$5,000 \times 0.08 \times 1$
Add the interest to the principal to find the new balance.	$I = \$400$
	$\$5,000 + \$400 = \$5,400$

At the end of one year Miss Sanchez will have $5,400.

• When borrowing money from a bank, you have to pay interest on the loan.

Mr. Bellini borrowed $2,500 from First Bank at an annual interest rate of 7%. How much money will he have to pay at the end of the year?

Find the interest to be paid.	$I = p \times r \times t$
Substitute the numbers.	$I = \$2,500 \times 7\% \times 1$
Write 7% as a decimal.	$I = \$2,500 \times 0.07 \times 1$
Add the interest to the principal to	$I = \$175$
find the total amount to be paid back.	$\$175 + \$2,500 = \$2,675$

At the end of one year, Mr. Bellini will pay $2,675.

Check Understanding

a. Jeneane borrowed $1,450 from the bank at an annual interest rate of 9%. How much money will she have to pay at the end of the year?

b. Aselli has a savings account containing $5,000. If the account earns 4% interest every year, what will the balance of her account be in one year?

Chapter Ten Study Guide

Use cross products to determine if the ratios are equal. Write *yes* or *no*.

1. $\frac{4}{9}$ $\frac{2}{3}$ *Lesson 118*
2. $\frac{6}{7}$ $\frac{24}{28}$ *Lesson 118*

Express each example as a unit rate.

3. 48 miles/2 gallons
   Lesson 119
4. 12 pounds of apples/6 dollars
   Lesson 119

Solve.

5. $\frac{t}{6} = \frac{6}{9}$ *Lesson 120*
6. $\frac{8}{12} = \frac{r}{21}$ *Lesson 120*

7. If a migrating butterfly can fly 20 miles in 24 hours, how far can it fly in 4 days? *Lesson 121*

8. 24 out of 64 jelly beans were red. What percent of the jelly beans were red? *Lesson 122*

9. Write 62.5% as a decimal. *Lesson 123*

10. Write 0.35 as a percent. *Lesson 123*

11. Write $\frac{3}{8}$ as a percent. *Lesson 124*

12. Write 60% as a fraction. *Lesson 124*

13. Find 18% of 280. *Lesson 125*

14. Estimate 15% of 302. *Lesson 126*

15. What percent of $200 is $8? *Lesson 127*

16. Danika put down a deposit of $400 on a car. If the deposit was 13% of the total cost, what was the price of the car? Round to the nearest cent. *Lesson 128*

17. Teresa's new jeans were $32 plus 6% sales tax. How much did she pay for her new jeans? *Lesson 129*

18. A pad of drawing paper was on sale for 25% off. If the original price was $18, what was the sale price of the pad? *Lesson 129*

19. Katherine deposited $800 into a savings account that has a 7% annual interest rate. After one year, how much will Katherine have in her savings account? *Lesson 130*

Powerful Percents

1. Beaumont Motors sells new and used cars. There are 64 new cars and 49 used cars on the lot. Write the ratio of new cars to used cars in three forms.

Determine if the ratios are equal. Write *yes* or *no*.

2. $\frac{3}{9}$ $\frac{4}{12}$
3. $\frac{9}{12}$ $\frac{6}{8}$
4. $\frac{5}{6}$ $\frac{30}{45}$
5. $\frac{1}{4}$ $\frac{16}{40}$

Solve.

6. If the Howard School surveyed 72 students and found that 5 out of 9 students carried dictionaries, how many of the students carried dictionaries?

7. $\frac{5}{9} = \frac{35}{n}$
8. $\frac{w}{7} = \frac{24}{28}$
9. $\frac{2}{7} = \frac{a}{77}$
10. $\frac{18}{21} = \frac{6}{b}$

11. Mr. Hansen is 2 meters tall and has a shadow measuring 3 meters in length. If a nearby statue casts an 18-meter shadow, what is the height of the statue?

12. A stunt pilot may use 12 gallons of gasoline for every three hours of flying time. How many gallons of gasoline would be consumed in 10 hours of flight?

13. Two fudge chocolate chip cookies contain 130 calories. If Annette ate six cookies, how many calories did she consume?

14. For every 6 months of work, Mr. Griffin earns 7 vacation days. How many months does Mr. Griffin have to work before he earns 21 days of vacation?

Write the decimals as percents.

15. 0.79
16. 0.01
17. 1.5
18. 0.15
19. 0.065

Write the fractions as percents.

20. $\frac{3}{5}$
21. $\frac{3}{60}$
22. $\frac{5}{8}$
23. $\frac{1}{3}$
24. $\frac{7}{10}$

Write each percent as a decimal.

25. 19%   **26.** 80%   **27.** 104%   **28.** 5%   **29.** 0.3%

Write each percent as a fraction in simplest form.

30. 40%   **31.** $12\frac{1}{2}$%   **32.** 30%   **33.** 62.5%   **34.** 18%

Use the circle graph to answer each question.

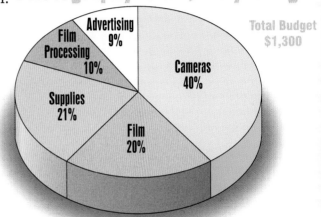

Photography Club Yearly Budget

Advertising 9%
Film Processing 10%
Supplies 21%
Cameras 40%
Film 20%
Total Budget $1,300

35. How much money will the club spend on cameras?

36. In the first two months of the year, the club used 72% of the $273 allocated for supplies. How much money did they spend?

37. How much more money will be used on film than on film processing?

Estimate.

38. 49% of 91   **39.** 32% of 79   **40.** 16% of 50   **41.** 10% of 25

Solve.

42. 198 is 99% of what?   **43.** $r = 14\%$ of 32   **44.** $16\% \times w = 3,200$

45. Sami deposited $900 into a savings account that has an annual interest rate of 4%. How much interest will he earn in a year?

46. The regular price of a computer is $1,200. There is a 30% discount on all computers at Computer Buy-It. What is the discounted price of the computer?

47. Mr. Harrington lives in a state where the sales tax is 5%. He bought a suit that cost $250. How much did Mr. Harrington pay for the suit?

48. The Old Lace Antique Shop sold a bracelet for 250% of their original purchase price. If the bracelet was sold for $150, at what price was the bracelet originally acquired?

49. Dr. Mitchell's salary of $3,100 a month will soon increase by 8.5%. By what amount will his salary increase?

50. Three boys from Nepal herd 300 yaks. Thapa is in charge of 40% of the herd. How many yaks does he herd?

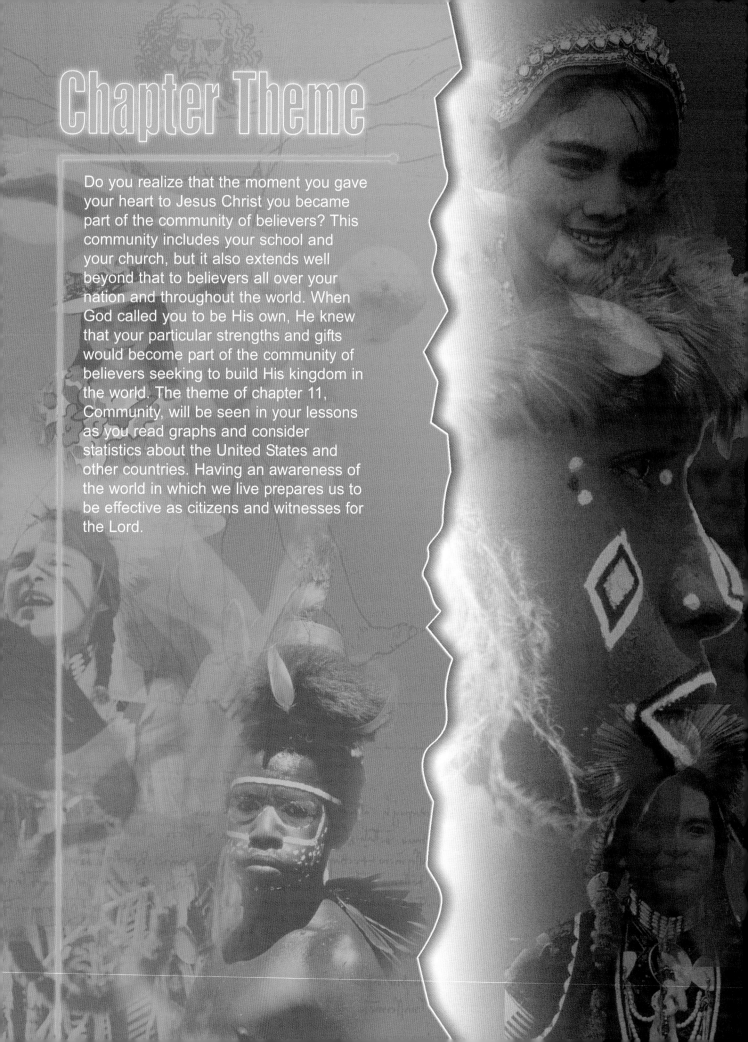

Chapter Theme

Do you realize that the moment you gave your heart to Jesus Christ you became part of the community of believers? This community includes your school and your church, but it also extends well beyond that to believers all over your nation and throughout the world. When God called you to be His own, He knew that your particular strengths and gifts would become part of the community of believers seeking to build His kingdom in the world. The theme of chapter 11, Community, will be seen in your lessons as you read graphs and consider statistics about the United States and other countries. Having an awareness of the world in which we live prepares us to be effective as citizens and witnesses for the Lord.

11

Chapter

Application of Statistics and Graphing

Lessons 132-141

And He has made from one blood every nation of men to dwell on all the face of the earth, and has determined their preappointed times and the boundaries of their dwellings, so that they should seek the Lord.

Acts 17:26-27a

Construct Meaning

Morena, who lives in Madrid, Spain, has been studying the demography of the community around her. **Demography** is the science of vital and social statistics of a population. She researched the Internet and the library, and used surveys to collect her data. She then organized the information in tables, graphs, and charts.

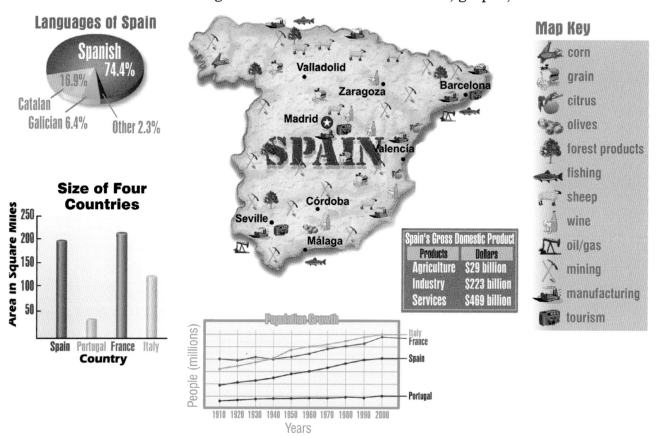

Surveys, questionnaires, experiments, and research enable us to collect information. Tables, charts, and graphs organize the information so that it can be easily analyzed.

A survey and a questionnaire must be given randomly to a group or sample of people to ensure that the data collected is representative of the entire population.

The type of table, chart, or graph that is constructed from the data depends on the <u>type</u> of data and the <u>form</u> of the data.

Check Understanding

a. Look at the chart displaying Spain's gross domestic product. What type of graph could be used to represent the data?

b. Is there another way you could organize the data represented on the map of Spain?

c. What type of graph would best show your changes in height since you entered school?

 **ractice**

Use the charts and graphs on the previous page to answer the following questions.

1. According to the Population Growth graph, which country had a decline in population from 1930 to 1940?

2. According to the bar graph, what is the approximate area of Spain?

3. Would the bar graph or a table be more useful in finding the exact square miles of the area of France?

4. What types of agriculture, industry, and services are located closest to Madrid?

5. Why is it important to make sure that a survey is given to a random sample of people?

6. Endida counted the colors of the Spanish dancers' dresses. Eight dancers wore red dresses, 12 wore blue dresses, 15 wore green dresses, and four wore yellow dresses. Organize the data in a table.
   a. What type of data is this?
   b. Why is a line graph not the best graph to use to represent this data?

7. A total of 3,214 cars have been sold by Garcia's Motor Company. The company's records show that 400 were sports cars, 861 were trucks, 823 were sedans, and 1,130 were SUVs. How can you transform this data so that it could best be represented by a circle graph?

8. Explain how to survey your class to determine what type of television program is preferred by sixth graders. What type of graph would best represent the data?

SPAIN'S POPULATION (millions)

Year	1910	1920	1930	1940	1950	1960	1970	1980	1990	2000
Number	19	21	23	25	28	30	34	37	38	40

9. Using the table above, describe how a line graph of Spain's population would change if the population recorded for 1950 was 14 million.

Lesson 133

Construct Meaning

Mean, median, and mode are called "measures of central tendency." They identify where the center of a set of data tends to lie.

- Investigate the length of egg noodles by measuring to the nearest tenth of a centimeter.
- Record the lengths on a data table.
- Make a histogram of the results.

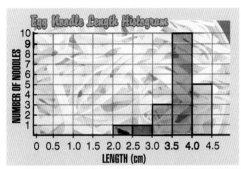

A **histogram** is a graph that uses bars to represent how many of a particular item are found in a given interval. This histogram shows that there are three noodles that have a length greater than 3.0 cm and less than or equal to 3.5 cm.

Length of Egg Noodles

1.	3.3 cm	11.	4.3 cm
2.	4.0 cm	12.	3.6 cm
3.	3.7 cm	13.	3.6 cm
4.	3.9 cm	14.	4.2 cm
5.	3.8 cm	15.	4.2 cm
6.	3.5 cm	16.	3.7 cm
7.	4.2 cm	17.	3.9 cm
8.	2.0 cm	18.	3.4 cm
9.	3.7 cm	19.	2.8 cm
10.	4.2 cm	20.	3.8 cm

Mean: the average of a set of numbers.

A histogram can be used to estimate the mean by locating the interval containing the greatest number of data (the tallest bar).

Since the interval 3.6 to 4.0 has the greatest number of data (10), the mean will be near this interval.

Is 3.8 a reasonable estimate of the mean?

Calculate the mean length of the noodles.

Find the sum of all the measurements and divide by 20.

73.8 cm ÷ 20 = 3.69 cm   Round to the nearest tenth.   **3.7 cm**

Median: the middle number in an ordered set of data.

Order the data set from least to greatest.

2.0, 2.8, 3.3, 3.4, 3.5, 3.6, 3.6, 3.7, 3.7, (3.7, 3.8) 3.8, 3.9, 3.9, 4.0, 4.2, 4.2, 4.2, 4.2, 4.3

Since there are two numbers in the middle of the data, the median is the average of the two numbers.   (3.7 + 3.8) ÷ 2 = 3.75 cm

Mode: the number or value that occurs the most often in a set of data.

On the data table, you can see that 4.2 occurs four times.

Sometimes no one number occurs more often, in which case there is no mode.

There may be more than one mode if more than one number occurs equally often.

Range: the difference between the greatest and least numbers in a set of numerical data.

4.3 – 2.0 = 2.3 cm

Conclusions about egg noodles.

The mean length is 3.7 cm.

The median number is 3.75.

The mode for egg noodle length is 4.2 cm.

The range for egg noodle length is 2.3 cm.

286

 **Check Understanding**

a. Why is it important to notice that an interval on the histogram actually reads 0 to 0.5 and 0.6 to 1 instead of 0 to 0.5 and 0.5 to 1?

b. How many egg noodles measure greater than 4 cm and less than or equal to 4.5 cm?

c. Explain how to estimate the mean by looking at a histogram.

 **Practice**

USING A CALCULATOR

Find the mean, median, mode, and range for each set of data.

1. 12 14 82 16 36 101
2. 420 500 62 500 68 322
3. 6 3 2 6 7 6 10 6
4. 84 90 8 16 50 16 8 70

 Apply

Use the table to answer the following questions.

Football Team Scores

	Game 1	Game 2	Game 3	Game 4	Game 5
Bulldogs	14	17	37	45	10
Saxons	23	21	7	39	28
Warriors	9	14	42	10	21

5. Rank each football team by their <u>mean</u> scores. If you could join any of the three teams, which team would you choose?

6. Rank each football team by their <u>median</u> scores. Which team would you choose according to this ranking?

7. If you were the owner of the Warriors and were reporting your scores to a football magazine, would it appear better for you to report your mean score or your median score?

House Prices in Sunnybrook

$75,000	$91,000	$89,000
$96,000	$95,000	$99,000
$82,000	$105,000	$96,000
$132,000	$78,000	$131,000
$77,000	$116,000	$112,000

8. Use the histogram above to estimate the mean price of a Sunnybrook house.

9. Use a calculator to calculate the mean. Round to the nearest dollar.

10. Find the median, mode, and range.

11. Write your conclusions about the house prices of Sunnybrook. Use the mean, median, mode, and range.

 **Construct Meaning**

Communities around the world have many needs. Shelter for the Homeless in Los Angeles, California, has been working to provide shelter and life skills for many people in need. One home involved in the program shelters and feeds a different number of people every night.

The table shows the number of people who came to the shelter each night during a three-week period.

Number of People at the Shelter/Night					
32	40	36	19	16	9
36	29	18	25	31	43
40	10	23	38	39	49
42	50	36			

 Organize the data as a stem and leaf plot.

- Find the numbers with the least value and with the greatest value in the table.

        9   50

    ones place   tens place

    Check for the least and greatest digits in the tens place to determine the digits that will become the stems.

- Use the digits from the tens place as the stems. List them vertically from least to greatest and draw a vertical line to their right.

```
      0|
      1|
      2|
      3|
      4|
Stems 5|
```

- The leaves will be the digits in the ones place. Fill in the leaves by writing the ones digit next to its stem.

```
      0|9
      1|9 6 8 0        Each time a number
      2|9 5 3          occurs, it is recorded
      3|2 6 6 1 8 9 6      on the plot.
      4|0 3 9 2 0
Stems 5|0      Leaves
```

- Arrange the leaves horizontally in order from least to greatest.

```
0|9
1|0 6 8 9        Describe the shape.
2|3 5 9          Is the plot symmetrical?
3|1 2 6 6 6 8 9
4|0 0 2 3 9
5|0
```

By looking at the numerically arranged stem and leaf plot, we can easily analyze the data.

What is the range of the number of people staying at the shelter?
    Range: The difference between the greatest value and the least value is 50 − 9 = 41.

What number of people visiting the shelter occurred the most often?
    Mode: The most common number is 36.   (It occurs three times.)

What number is in the middle of the ordered data set?
    Median: By counting we know there are 21 numbers. Therefore, the middle number would be the eleventh number, 36.

What is the mean?
    The original values can be constructed by combining the stem and leaf values. Use a calculator to add the data and divide the sum by 21. Rounding to the nearest whole number gives a mean of 31.

Check Understanding

a. Why is a stem and leaf plot helpful in organizing data?

b. How can the original values of a stem and leaf plot be reconstructed?

c. Explain how to find the median on a stem and leaf plot.

d. What does it mean when the median is larger than the mean?

The scores for the last math test of the year for a sixth grade class were recorded and arranged in a stem and leaf plot.

1. Find the mode, median, and mean of the data.

2. Explain how an extreme value, such as a score of 33, would affect the mean of the data.

3. Explain how well you think the students did on the test overall.

```
 3 | 3
 4 |
 5 |
 6 | 4
 7 | 1 3 5 8
 8 | 1 1 3 3 5 5 6 8
 9 | 3 5 7 7 9
10 | 0
```

Becca kept a daily log of her summer job earnings. In one month, she earned the following amounts: $9 $12 $25 $6 $9 $12 $15 $20 $14 $17 $13 $11 $17 $13 $12 $15 $18 $15 $20 $15.

4. Make a stem and leaf plot of the data.

5. Find the mode, median, and mean of the data.

6. Describe the shape of the plot.

7. If Becca worked approximately four hours a day, what was her mean hourly income?

Sonja just purchased an electronic game. The manufacturer made the claim: Up to 24 hours of continuous play! She tested the amount of time (in hours) that the manufacturer's batteries lasted, in the game, as follows:

12   9   12   8   5   13   24   6   12   14   4

8. Make a stem and leaf plot of the data.

9. Find the mode, median, and mean of the data.

10. According to Sonja's data, is the claim true? Is the manufacturer's claim a fair or a misleading statement?

Lesson 135

![Construct Meaning]

Each year facts and statistics are reported about the United States and the world, such as population growth, income, types of people groups, and new discoveries. The median income of residents in the United States is reported by region and ethnic background.

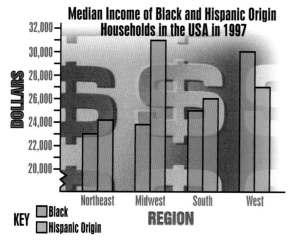

A **double bar graph** uses two sets of bars to represent and compare numbers for several items of the same units.

The graph here compares the median incomes of groups of people by region.

The <u>median</u> is the middle number in the set of ordered incomes. Would the graph change if the <u>mean</u> (average) income was displayed?

Why was a broken scale used on the bar graph?

A **triple bar graph** uses three sets of bars to represent and compare numbers for several items of the same units.

What is the title?

What is represented by the yellow bars?

State	1993	1995	1997
Texas	17.4%	17.4%	16.7%
Indiana	12.2%	9.6%	8.2%
Maine	15.4%	11.7%	10.7%

What information is presented on each axis?

Why may a graph with three bars be the best way to present this data?

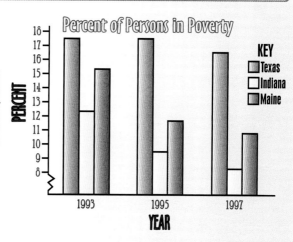

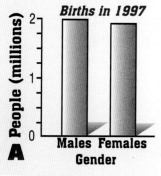

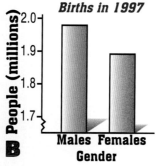

How are the two graphs different?

Which graph would give you the impression that there is a small difference between the number of males and females born?

Using the ratio of males born to females born, solve the following proportion. Round to the nearest whole number.

Explain what the broken line means on the vertical scale of Graph B.

$$\frac{1,985,000,000 \text{ males}}{1,895,000,000 \text{ females}} = \frac{x \text{ males}}{1,000 \text{ females}}$$

 **Check Understanding**

a. What is the benefit of a double or triple bar graph compared to a single bar graph?

b. Discuss the importance of the vertical scale.

c. What type of information can be displayed on a bar graph?

 **Practice**

Refer to the Median Income of Black and Hispanic Origin Households graph.

1. Why is it important to include a key on a bar graph?

2. In which region do those of Hispanic origin have the highest median income?

3. How could the scale of the vertical axis be changed to begin at zero?

Refer to the Percent of Persons in Poverty graph.

4. Which state's poverty percentage decreased by 4.7% between 1993 and 1997?

5. By looking at the graph, determine which state had the least amount of decrease between 1993 and 1997.

6. What is the general trend of the three states' poverty percentages from 1993 to 1997?

 Apply

Use the graph to answer the following questions.

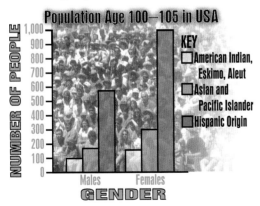

7. How does the population of Hispanic origin people compare to that of Asian and Pacific Islanders?

8. Make a general statement about the number of males and females, age 100–105.

9. Why do you think there are so many more Hispanic origin people than Asian or American Indian people in this age group in the United States?

10. Construct a double bar graph using the following data.

	Arkansas	Massachusetts	Colorado	New York
Number of counties	75	14	63	62
Number of state parks	50	129	44	152

Construct Meaning

The faces of communities grow and change over time. Changes may occur in population, economics, employment, and industry. Each type of change can be represented on a line graph.

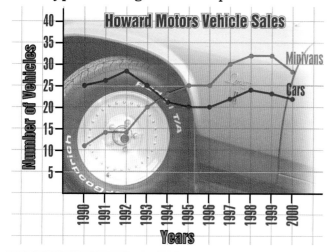

A **line graph** uses line segments to represent increases or decreases over a period of time.

By plotting several items on a line graph, a comparison over time can be made.

- What can be observed about the number of cars and minivans sold between 1992 and 1994?

- Which interval shows the greatest increase in minivan sales?

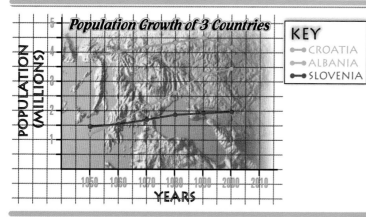

KEY
- CROATIA
- ALBANIA
- SLOVENIA

Compare the population growth by noticing the steepness and the direction of the slant in the line segments.

- Predict the population of all three countries in the year 2010.

- Did any country experience a loss in population? What might cause a loss in population?

Use the data table to construct a line graph.

- Draw the horizontal axis. Determine and label the interval of time.

- Draw the vertical axis. Determine what was measured and how. Determine the scale. (Note the largest and smallest measurement.)

- Choose one set of data to plot first, such as Zagreb, Croatia. Connect the points with line segments. Repeat for Tirana, Albania.

- Make a key.

- Label each axis and title the graph.

Mean Temperatures for the 17th of Each Month		
Month	Zagreb, Croatia	Tirana, Albania
Jan 17	31°F	46°F
Feb 17	43°F	52°F
Mar 17	48°F	43°F
Apr 17	43°F	50°F
May 17	68°F	71°F
June 17	64°F	72°F
July 17	79°F	70°F
Aug 17	74°F	92°F
Sept 17	50°F	78°F
Oct 17	55°F	53°F
Nov 17	33°F	67°F
Dec 17	45°F	60°F

 **Check Understanding**

a. Why is it important to title a graph and label each axis?

b. Can you predict the number of vehicles Howard Motors might sell in 2001?

c. Why is it advantageous to plot more than one set of data on one graph?

d. Is it important to plot time on the horizontal axis?

 **Practice**

Use the Howard Motors Vehicle Sales graph to answer the following questions.

1. Which vehicle type had an increase in sales by nine vehicles from 1992 to 1994?

2. What would happen to the slant of the lines if the intervals on the vertical scale changed from intervals of five to intervals of one?

Use the Population Growth graph to answer the following questions.

3. Which country has the slowest rate of population growth? Explain.

4. Which country has the greatest rate of population growth? Explain.

 Apply

Mrs. Felt's family has three children, Tiffany, Justin, and Evan. The graph displays the children's weights from birth until one year.

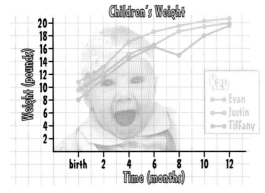

5. During which time interval did Evan gain the most weight?

6. Who had the greatest weight gain from birth to 12 months?

7. Do any of the lines show a loss in weight? Who lost weight?

8. What might be the cause of a baby's weight loss?

9. Make a line graph using the following data table.

Time	6:00 A.M.	7:00 A.M.	8:00 A.M.	9:00 A.M.	10:00 A.M.	11:00 A.M.	12:00 P.M.	1:00 P.M.	2:00 P.M.	3:00 P.M.	4:00 P.M.	5:00 P.M.	6:00 P.M.
Day 1	39°F	39°F	41°F	43°F	50°F	55°F	60°F	64°F	68°F	70°F	73°F	73°F	71°F
Day 2	45°F	45°F	48°F	50°F	55°F	61°F	68°F	75°F	77°F	79°F	80°F	79°F	78°F
Day 3	41°F	41°F	44°F	45°F	51°F	54°F	57°F	60°F	64°F	67°F	70°F	68°F	65°F

Lesson 137

Construct Meaning

Information can easily be misrepresented by figures and graphs, and may cause you to come to false conclusions. Carefully observe the following graphs.

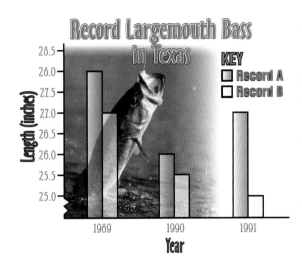

What is the graph showing?

In the year 1991, the bar for Record A is about how many times longer than the bar for Record B?

In 1991, what was the length of the Record B fish? What length was the Record A fish?

Does comparing the two bar lengths for 1991 relate well to comparing the actual lengths of the two fish? Explain.

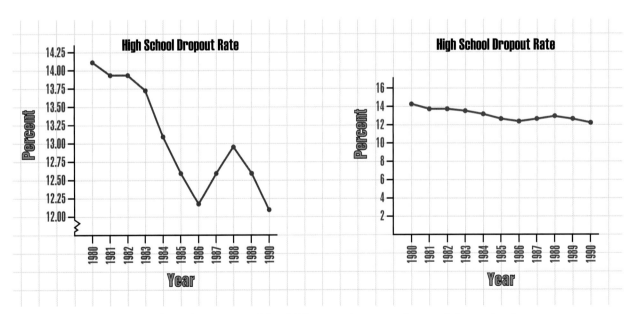

Why do the two graphs above provide different impressions although the same information is represented?

What impression does the graph on the left give you?

Use the graph on the left to determine the two-year period when the percent of dropouts decreased by the greatest number.

Why is it difficult to determine the answer to the question above using the graph on the right?

294

**Check Understanding**

The local newspaper published an illustration to show the number of houses sold in Speers County.

a. How is the illustration similar to a bar graph?

b. How is the size of the house picture related to the number of houses sold?

c. Explain how the house pictures may cause a reader to make incorrect conclusions.

Apply

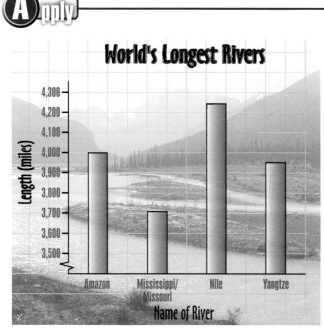

Use the bar graph to answer the following questions.

1. Which two rivers are about the same length?

2. The bar representing which river is more than twice as high as the bar representing the Mississippi/Missouri River?

3. Is the Nile River actually more than twice as long as the Mississippi/Missouri River? Explain.

4. Why is it easy to misinterpret this graph if you do not examine it carefully?

Use the line graph for the following problems.

5. What impression does the graph give you about U-Save's stock?

6. On which day did the stock gain the most points?

7. Explain why this graph may be misleading.

8. Draw a new graph that represents the information more accurately.

Approximate Land Area of the Earth

Approximate area of the continents:
57,130,000 square miles

Find the area of Asia.

USING A CALCULATOR

What is 30% of 57,130,000 square miles?

$n = 0.30 \times 57{,}130{,}000$ square miles

$n = 17{,}139{,}000$ square miles

The land area of Asia is 17,139,000 square miles.

What is the area of South America?

Construct Meaning

We do not often think of the whole world as being our community, but the world is the sum of all of our small communities.

A **circle graph** is a graph that compares parts of a whole, using different-sized sections of a circle.

The whole circle stands for the total area of the continents. Each section of the circle shows a percentage of the whole. The sum of the percents must be 100%.

If you know the total area of the continents, you can calculate the actual area of each continent.

Use the information in the table to construct a circle graph.

New Zealand Exports	Tons in Thousands	Percent	Degree
Logs	2,920	39%	140°
Other Forest Products	2,240	30%	108°
Dairy	700	9%	
Kiwi Fruit	470		
Other Exports	1,170		
TOTAL EXPORTS	7,500	100%	360°

• First, change the numbers to percents.

2,920 is what percent of 7,500?

$2{,}920 = n \times 7{,}500$

$\dfrac{2{,}920}{7{,}500} = \dfrac{n \times 7{,}500}{7{,}500}$

$0.389 = n$

$0.389 = 38.9\%$ Change the decimal to a percent.

Round 38.9% to 39%

• Next, find the portion of the circle represented by each export product in <u>number of degrees</u>. Remember that there are 360° in a circle.

What is 39% of 360°?

$39\% \times 360° = n$

$0.39 \times 360° = n$

$140° = n$ Round to the nearest degree.

CONSTRUCT YOUR CIRCLE GRAPH

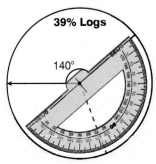

39% Logs

140°

→ Draw a 6-inch diameter circle with one radius pointing left.
→ Construct a central angle measuring 140°.
→ Using the second radius, align the protractor and construct the next central angle of 108°.
→ Proceed clockwise around the circle, constructing the remaining central angles.
→ Label each percent and title the graph.

Check Understanding

Use the Approximate Land Area of the Earth circle graph.

a. What is the fourth largest continent on the earth?

b. How many square miles is the land area of Africa?

Solve.

c. What is the central angle of a 42% section on a circle graph?

Practice

Use the circle graph to answer the following questions.

1. What two religions together make up more than $\frac{3}{4}$ of the total population of Africa?

2. How many people are Muslim?

3. What is the difference between the number of Christians and the number of people who practice ethnic religions in Africa?

Religions in Africa

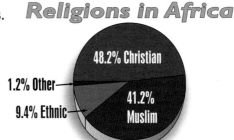

1.2% Other
9.4% Ethnic
48.2% Christian
41.2% Muslim

Total Population 748,130,000

Apply

Areas of Oceans

Arctic Ocean	4,732,000 square miles
Atlantic Ocean	41,000,000 square miles
Indian Ocean	28,500,000 square miles
Pacific Ocean	64,000,000 square miles

Use the table for the following problems.

4. What is the total area of all of the oceans?

5. What percent of the total is each ocean's area? Round to the nearest percent.

6. What will be the central angle of the section representing the Atlantic Ocean on a circle graph?

7. Construct a circle graph that compares ocean areas.

Use the circle graph below for the following problems.

World Imports

1% UK and Europe
12% Middle East and Africa
12% Americas
34% Australia and Pacific
31% New Zealand Coastal
10% Asia

Total Imports 2,678,000 tons

World Imports	Tons in Thousands	Percent	Central Angle
Asia	266	10%	36°
Australia and Pacific	902	34%	122.4°
Americas	311	12%	43.2°
UK and Europe	36	1%	3.6°
Middle East and Africa	328	12%	55°
New Zealand Coastal	835	31%	111.6°
TOTAL	**2,678**	**100%**	**360°**

8. A mistake was made when calculating a central angle. Find the mistake in the table, write the correct angle, and redraw the circle graph correctly.

9. What area imports the most products?

10. What three areas together have $\frac{1}{4}$ of the total imports?

Construct Meaning

Bar graphs and histograms have a similar appearance but represent different information.

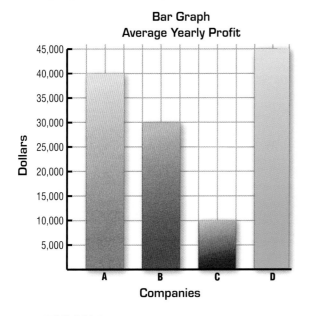

Bar Graph
Average Yearly Profit

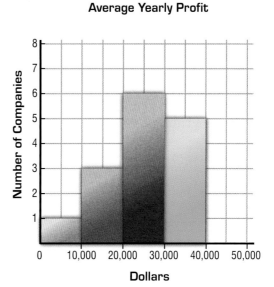

Histogram
Average Yearly Profit

BAR GRAPH

- Shows data for several different items
- Bar height equal to a specific quantity
- A bar graph cannot be made from a histogram.
- Question answered: What is the measurement for each item?

HISTOGRAM

- One variable divided into categories
- Bar height proportional to the number of items in the interval
- A histogram may be made from a bar graph.
- Question answered: How many items are in each interval?

Check Understanding

Determine the type of graph that would best represent the information. Write *bar graph* or *histogram*.

a. Comparing heights of trees in a city park
b. The number of cars sold in certain price ranges
c. The number of trees within various height ranges
d. Number of tickets sold each month
e. Number of ocean creatures living at various depth intervals

Choose the letter representing the type of graph that would best fit the information.

1. Bushels of plums harvested
2. Heartbeat during exercise
3. Number of shoes sold for certain brands
4. Percent of elementary children at various reading levels
5. Spending budget for a company
6. Hourly temperatures during one day

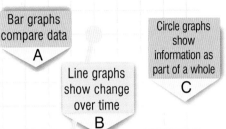

Bar graphs compare data
A

Line graphs show change over time
B

Circle graphs show information as part of a whole
C

7. Use the table to make a bar graph of the data.

The Megabyte Store

Sales Person	Ata	Gail	Blake	Glenda	Sara
Number of computers sold	20	25	16	18	35

The Gaffney, South Carolina, peach festival takes place every July. The list shows the number of bushels of peaches picked daily for 17 days.

> 35 40 62 70 81 73 68 65 54
> 90 42 45 36 48 51 44 8

8. Make a numerically ordered stem and leaf plot of the data.

9. Find the median, mode, mean, and range.

10. How does the number of bushels picked on the last day affect the mean?

All the ends of the world
Shall remember and turn to the LORD,
And all the families of the nations
Shall worship before You. Psalm 22:27

Construct Meaning

The map of Ivory Coast, West Africa, is a scale drawing of the country. A **scale drawing** represents an area or an object as it is, but is usually smaller or larger in size. The drawing is proportional to the actual area or object.

The key of the map shows you that 6 cm represents a distance of 300 miles. As a ratio, this is 6 cm:300 miles. The distance between Yamoussoukro and Abidjan is 2 cm on the map. What is the actual distance?

$$\frac{\text{map}}{\text{actual}} = \frac{6 \text{ cm}}{300 \text{ miles}} = \frac{2 \text{ cm}}{n}$$

Cross multiply. 6 cm × n = 300 miles × 2 cm

$$6 \times n = 600$$

$$\frac{6n}{6} = \frac{600}{6}$$

$$n = 100 \text{ miles}$$ The actual distance is **100 miles**.

Côte D'Ivoire

Yamoussoukro

Abidjan

Ivory Coast
6 cm = 300 miles

0   300

A **scientific illustration** is a type of scale drawing that is accurate in scale and physical detail. This scientific illustration is of a beetle called *Goliathus regius Klug* which is found on the Ivory Coast.

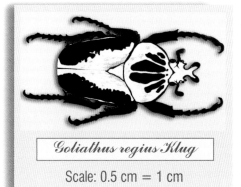
Goliathus regius Klug
Scale: 0.5 cm = 1 cm

The key states the scale is 0.5 cm to 1 cm. The scale drawing of the beetle is 5.5 cm long. Find its actual length using cross products.

$$\frac{0.5 \text{ cm}}{1 \text{ cm}} = \frac{5.5 \text{ cm}}{b}$$

0.5 cm × b = 5.5 cm × 1 cm

$$0.5 \times b = 5.5$$

$$\frac{0.5\,b}{0.5} = \frac{5.5}{0.5}$$

$$b = 11 \text{ cm}$$

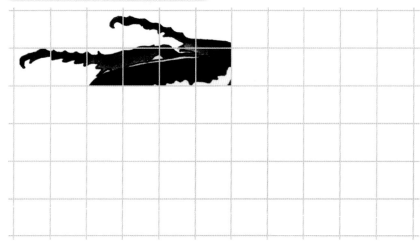

Use centimeter grid paper to make an actual-size scientific drawing of the beetle.

Chapter Eleven Study Guide

Write the letter of the matching item. *Lesson 132*

1. A graph that illustrates parts of a whole
2. A graph representing change over time
3. A graph showing comparisons

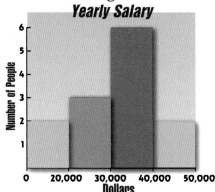

GRAPH TYPE
A. Bar graph
B. Circle graph
C. Line graph

Use the histogram for the following problems. *Lesson 133*

4. Estimate the mean salary.

5. How many people earn more than $20,000 but less than or equal to $30,000 per year?

6. Find the mean of the following salaries.
$18,500 $29,000 $17,000
$45,000 $36,500 $31,000

Use the stem and leaf plot for problems 7 through 10. *Lesson 134*

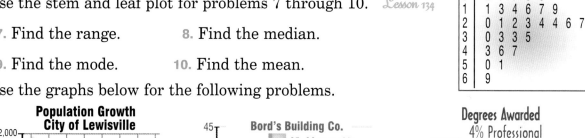

7. Find the range.   8. Find the median.

9. Find the mode.   10. Find the mean.

Use the graphs below for the following problems.

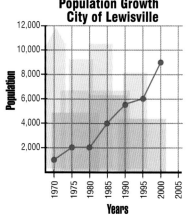
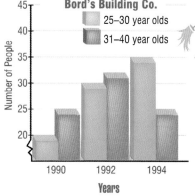
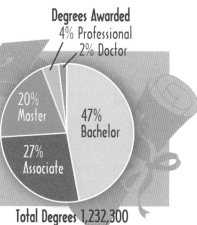

11. Explain the trend of numbers of 25 to 30-year-olds working at Bord's Building. *Lesson 135*

12. During which five-year period was the greatest population increase in Lewisville? *Lesson 136*

13. What impression do the bars on Bord's graph give you about the age of the employees in 1994? Is it a correct interpretation of the information? *Lesson 137*

14. Which two academic degrees make up just under ¾ of the total degrees offered? *Lesson 138*

15. State one difference between a bar graph and a histogram. *Lesson 139*

Global Graphs

1. Explain the importance of a random sample when conducting a survey.
2. List three ways of collecting data.

Use the graph for the following:
3. Approximately how many times larger is the bar for Rockhopper penguins than the bar for Fiordland penguins?
4. Approximately how many Snares Island penguin pairs are there?
5. Is the bar graph misleading?

PENGUIN BREEDING PAIRS

Dory researched the caffeine content of certain drinks. Eight ounces of brewed coffee has 135 mg, tea has 50 mg, cola has 34 mg, and hot chocolate has 5 mg of caffeine.
6. Explain the type of graph that would best represent this information.
7. Could a circle graph be used to represent this information? Explain.

Write the letter of the correct word for each definition.
8. The difference between the greatest and least number in a set of numerical data
9. The middle number in an ordered set of data
10. The number that occurs the most often
11. The average of a set of data

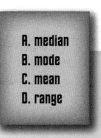

A. median
B. mode
C. mean
D. range

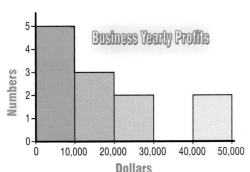

Business Yearly Profits

Business Yearly Profits

$2,000	$16,500	$46,300
$10,000	$13,125	$25,500
$7,000	$4,560	$21,100
$41,000	$9,000	$14,000

12. Use the histogram to estimate the mean.
13. What is the interval on the horizontal axis?
14. Find the median.
15. Use the Business Yearly Profits data to find the mean.

16. Make a stem and leaf plot of the hospital data.
17. Find the range.   18. Find the mode.
19. Find the median.   20. Find the mean.
21. How can you estimate the mean on a stem and leaf plot?
22. If the hospital administrator is seeking financial support, is it fair for him to say, "We have 101 patients who stay at General Hospital each night"?

Number of Patients at General Hospital

99	73	99	50	86
87	78	74	56	82
100	93	91	61	101

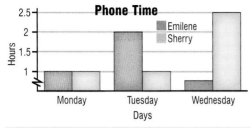

23. On what day did Sherry talk on the phone over three times as long as Emilene?
24. Explain the broken line on the vertical axis.
25. How is a double bar graph beneficial over a single bar graph?

Number of people speaking a language other than English at home

Spanish	17,339,000	Italian	1,309,000
German	1,547,000	Chinese	1,249,000
French	1,702,000	Tagalog	843,000

26. Make a bar graph from the table.
27. How is your bar graph more helpful than the table?

Write *bar*, *line*, *circle*, or *histogram* to indicate the most appropriate graph.
28. Percents of languages spoken in Denmark
29. Favorite pizza survey
30. Number of students 4 feet to $5\frac{1}{2}$ feet tall
31. Population growth of 2 towns
32. Temperatures of El Paso, Texas, for a month
33. Salaries of 20 people

Use the circle graph for problems 34 through 37.
34. Find the dollar amount of the shoe sales.
35. Find the sum in dollars of jewelry, cosmetics, and sportswear sales.
36. Which department had just over one-fourth of the total sales?
37. Which department sold $27,500 in merchandise?

Fashion Boutique

26% shoes
55% clothing
3% sportswear
6% cosmetics
10% jewelry

Total Sales: $50,000

38. Use the percentages below to make a circle graph.

U.S. Foreign-born Citizens in 1990

Latin America	42.5%	Asia	25.2%
Europe	22%	All other	10.3%

39. Which graph appears to show rapid growth of sales?
40. Which months show equal sales?
41. Which month had the greatest sales increase from the previous month?
42. How are the vertical scales different?
43. Explain how either graph could be thought of as misleading.

Write *true* or *false*.
44. A bar graph can be made from a histogram.
45. A histogram uses one variable.
46. The vertical scale of a line graph is not important.
47. Percents on a circle graph total 100%.
48. There can be more than one mode in a set of data.
49. The vertical scale of any graph must always start with zero.
50. A bar graph can be made using percents.

Chapter Theme

Our sovereign God, who is the same yesterday, today, and forever, is the author of everything, including mathematical probability. The chapter 12 theme of Overcoming Great Odds is a reminder that we serve a God who is certain to love us and care for us in all circumstances. In this chapter, you will learn the story of Renée Bondi, whose trust in God to care for her in all the trials of life has helped her overcome circumstances that might otherwise have defeated her. Jesus Christ offers you His strength and peace to walk through all of the difficulties of life. He does not say He will probably be there for you, but instead promises to never leave or forsake you. Trust Him.

12 Chapter

Introduction to Probability

Lessons 142-150

"These things I have spoken to you, that in Me you may have peace. In the world you will have tribulation; but be of good cheer, I have overcome the world."

John 16:33

 **Construct Meaning**

Many people fail when attempting to climb a mountain. There are many odds against a climber, such as weather, altitude, and personal limitations. But, despite the odds, some people are overcomers and reach the summit.

Probability is the likelihood that a given event will occur. Probability can be written as a ratio, fraction, or percent.

When an event is <u>certain</u>, the probability is 1 or 100%.
When an event is <u>not possible</u>, the probability is zero. The closer the probability is to zero, the less likely the event will occur.

Respond to the following statements as *certain*, *possible*, or *not possible*.
• It will snow in your town in the next few days.
• You will have a spelling test this year.
• Two regular number cubes can have a sum of thirteen.
• After you are married, you will have a child that is a girl.
• There will be a tomorrow.

Mathematical (theoretical) probability is a ratio of the number of favorable outcomes to the number of possible outcomes.

heads   tails

$$P = \frac{\text{Number of Favorable Outcomes}}{\text{Number of Possible Outcomes}}$$

If you toss a coin, what is the probability that it will be heads?

$$P(\text{heads}) = \frac{\text{Number of Favorable Outcomes (heads)}}{\text{Number of Possible Outcomes (heads, tails)}} = \frac{1}{2} \text{ or } 50\%$$

If you toss a pattern stick like the one shown here, what is the probability that it will land pattern side up?

$$P(\text{pattern}) = \frac{\text{Number of Favorable Outcomes (pattern)}}{\text{Number of Possible Outcomes (pattern, plain)}} = \frac{1}{2} \text{ or } 50\%$$

We can predict the number of favorable outcomes based on the mathematical probability and a known number of trials.

pattern   plain

For 20 trials, what would be the predicted number of times the pattern stick will land on its plain side?

$$\frac{1}{2} = \frac{n}{20}$$

mathematical probability   number of tosses or trials

Use a proportion.

$$\frac{1}{2} = \frac{n}{20}$$
$$2n = 20$$
$$n = 10$$

The predicted number of favorable outcomes is 10.

 **Check Understanding**

Determine how many outcomes are possible for each statement.

a. Rolling a regular number cube

b. Flipping a dime

c. Choosing a day in April at random

d. Randomly choosing a letter of the alphabet

 **Practice**

Write *certain*, *possible*, or *not possible*.

1. A baby boy was born today.

2. A regular number cube can roll a zero.

3. You will have your wisdom teeth pulled.

4. There will be clouds in the sky tomorrow.

Solve.

5. If $P(\text{an event}) = \frac{10}{10}$, what can you conclude about the event?

6. Give an example of an event with five outcomes.

7. If the mathematical probability was $\frac{1}{4}$ for spinning red on a spinner, what would be the predicted number of reds in 40 trials?

$$\frac{1}{4} = \frac{n}{40}$$

8. If the mathematical probability was $\frac{3}{8}$ for spinning blue on a spinner, what would you predict the outcome to be for spinning blue in 40 trials?

 Apply

9. Predict the $P(\text{pattern})$ for 30 trials of tossing a pattern stick.

10. Perform a probability experiment by tossing a pattern stick 30 times. Record your results in a tally table each time *pattern* or *plain* is tossed.

Pattern — Plain

a. How many times did you toss *pattern*?
b. How many times did you toss *plain*?
c. How does the number of times you tossed *pattern* compare to the predicted outcome from problem 9?

Suppose you roll a regular number cube.

11. List the possible outcomes on a regular number cube.

12. $P(\text{even number}) = $ ⬚

13. $P(7) = $ ⬚

14. $P(\text{a number less than 5}) = $ ⬚

 Construct Meaning

Perform an experiment using a spinner.

First, observe the spinner.
- How many colors does it have?
- How is the spinner divided?
- Predict the outcomes for each color.

Next, spin the pointer 20 times and record the color on a chart like the one below by placing an ✗ in the column representing the color.

red   blue   yellow

Answer the following:
- Did yellow or blue have more marks? How many more?
- Is the spinner equally likely to land on yellow, blue, or red?
- What fraction of the spinner is red? What is the mathematical probability of landing on red?

Experimental probability is a ratio of the number of times an event actually occurred to the number of trials.

Calculate your experimental probability for red, for blue, and for yellow.

If the spinner landed on red five times, then $P(\text{red}) = \dfrac{5}{20}$ ← number of times the pointer landed on red
← number of trials

How does the experimental probability differ from the mathematical probability?
Perform another experiment with a different spinner.

First, observe the spinner.
- How many colors does it have?
- How is the spinner divided?
- Predict the outcomes for each color.

Next, spin the pointer 20 times and record the color on a chart as was done previously.

Answer the following:
- What fraction of the spinner is blue? What is the mathematical probability of landing on blue?
- Is the spinner equally likely to land on each color?
- What was your experimental probability for blue? red? yellow?

Fair or Unfair?

UP-SIDE-DOWN ————————————————————————— ODD-COUPLE

Materials: paper cup, paper, and pencil to tally results
Rules of the Game:
1. Play in groups of three.
2. Each player chooses a position to be: up, side, or down.

UP   SIDE   DOWN

3. Take turns tossing the cup straight up into the air and allow it to drop to the ground.
4. Each person gets one point when the cup lands in their position.
5. Play 20 rounds.

Is this game fair or unfair? Explain.

Materials: 2 regular number cubes, paper, and pencil
Rules of the Game:
1. Play in pairs.
2. One player chooses to be the number 8 and the other chooses to be numbers 10 and 11.
3. Roll two number cubes.
4. Add the face-up numbers. Player 1 gets a point if the sum is 8 and Player 2 gets a point if the sum is 10 or 11.
5. Roll the number cubes until the sum of the two players' points is 40.
6. The player with the most points is the winner.

Is this game fair or unfair? Explain.

Check Understanding

a. Discuss what might happen to the experimental probability, compared to the mathematical probability, if 40 trials were performed rather than 20.

b. If the probability of getting yellow on a spinner is 80%, what is the probability of not getting yellow?

c. Can the probability of an event be less than 0? Explain.

Practice

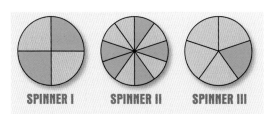

SPINNER I   SPINNER II   SPINNER III

1. Which spinner most likely produced the following set of data: green, yellow, yellow, yellow, yellow, yellow, yellow, yellow, green, green, yellow?

2. Which two spinners have equally likely outcomes?

A spinner is labeled with letters from A to E. Find each experimental probability based on the data set: A, A, B, C, A, E, E, D, A, B, B, B, A, C, E, A, A, B, E, A

3. $P(A)$ 4. $P(C)$ 5. $P(B)$ 6. $P(F)$ 7. Which letter in the data set had the lowest experimental probability?

Use the spinner to find each mathematical probability.

8. $P(\text{purple})$ 9. $P(\text{black})$ 10. $P(\text{orange})$ 11. $P(\text{not blue})$

12. Which colors have equally likely outcomes?

Solve.

13. If $P(\text{red}) = \frac{3}{8}$, $P(\text{pink}) = 0.45$, $P(\text{blue}) = 35\%$

    a. Are all the probabilities equally or unequally likely?

    b. Which outcome has the greatest probability of occurring?

Apply

Design a spinner like the one below and complete the following.

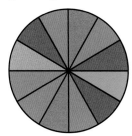

14. Predict the outcome for each color in an experiment of 24 trials.

15. Perform a probability experiment with 20 trials.

16. What is your experimental probability for each color?

17. Which colors have equally likely outcomes?

Construct Meaning

The greater the number of events involved in a probability problem, the more complicated the outcomes become. Two ways to organize the outcomes of probability problems are tree diagrams and sample spaces.

A **tree diagram** is a diagram that uses lines as branches representing all possible outcomes of a given situation. It shows not only the number of outcomes, but also what the outcomes are.

Kirsten is tossing a penny and a nickel at the same time. What are the possible outcomes for one toss? A tree diagram shows the possible outcomes.

There are two outcomes for both the penny and the nickel: heads or tails.

Follow the branches in the diagram to see each possible outcome. For example, if the toss of the penny is heads and the toss of the nickel is heads, the branch is drawn from TOSS to penny/heads to nickel/heads. This is one possible outcome (heads, heads). Copy the chart and list the possible outcomes.

Possible Outcomes	
Penny	**Nickel**
H	**H**
H	

The Fundamental Counting Principle can also help you find the possible outcomes when one choice is selected from each of two or more categories.

The **Fundamental Counting Principle** states that the total number of possible outcomes is the product of the number of items in each category.

Lunch	Toppings	
hamburger or sandwich	lettuce cheese tomato	

2 choices for lunch $\times$ 3 choices for toppings =

6 possible outcomes

Toss three coins

2 outcomes for penny $\times$ 2 outcomes for nickel $\times$ 2 outcomes for dime =

8 possible outcomes

Another way to organize possible outcomes is called a sample space.
A **sample space** is a table or list that shows all possible outcomes of a given situation.

What are the possible outcomes when spinning the two spinners at the same time? Make a sample space.

• Label a table with the possible outcomes from the colored spinner on the top horizontal axis.

• Label the vertical axis with the possible outcomes from the number spinner.

• Then bring the number from the first row over into the box and the letter from the first column down into the box. Continue until all the possible outcomes are shown.

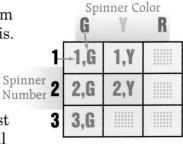

Spinner Color

	G	Y	R
1	1,G	1,Y	
2	2,G	2,Y	
3	3,G		

Spinner Number

 **Check Understanding**

a. If you flip a penny, a nickel, and a dime at the same time, what are the possible outcomes and how many are there? Show your answer using a tree diagram.

b. Hutchin's Café serves three flavors of ice cream (chocolate, vanilla, and strawberry) and two toppings (caramel and hot fudge). Construct a sample space showing all the possible servings with one flavor of ice cream and one topping.

c. What information does the Fundamental Counting Principle give you? a tree diagram?

 **Practice**

1. Does a sample space show the same information as a tree diagram?

2. If you were to flip a single coin one time, would a tree diagram be helpful? Explain.

3. How many possible outcomes are there when rolling a six-sided number cube and tossing a penny?

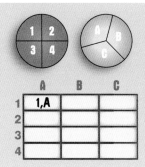

4. Copy and complete the sample space for all of the possible outcomes.

5. How many outcomes are there for spinning the spinners at the same time?

6. Could you have calculated the number of possible outcomes by using the Fundamental Counting Principle? Explain.

7. Copy and complete the tree diagram showing all the possible outcomes for choosing plaid shorts or plain shorts with a yellow, green, or flowered shirt.

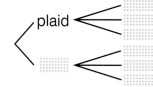

 Apply

8. Gloria is decorating her room. She can choose from cream, blue, or pink paint for the walls and tan, brown, or yellow carpet for the floor. What are all the possible outcomes?

9. The school cafeteria is offering sandwiches for lunch. Four types of meat are available: ham, turkey, roast beef, and tuna. Three toppings are available: lettuce, cheese, or pickles. Each student also has a choice of white or wheat bread. Make a tree diagram to show all of the possible sandwiches that can be made using one meat, one topping, and one type of bread.

10. In a board game called *Possibly So* the players each roll a six-sided number cube and toss a token that is red on one side and blue on the other. How many possible outcomes are there for one turn?

Lesson 145

 **Construct Meaning** — The Pan-American Wheelchair Games are held for paraplegic athletes. Often athletes are assigned lanes on the track according to their previous individual race times. Sometimes the athletes may be arranged in the lanes by randomly drawing names out of a hat.

Arrangements are important when considering probabilities.

Place a red, green, and blue color tile in a bag. Draw out one tile at a time and record the color and the order in which each was drawn. Use two draws as one trial. Replace the two drawn tiles back into the bag after each trial.

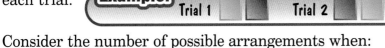

Example: Trial 1 ▢ ▢ Trial 2 ▢ ▢ Trial 3 ▢ ▢

Consider the number of possible arrangements when:

- The order in which the colors are drawn matters. (Blue/red is <u>not</u> the same as red/blue.)
- The order does not matter. (Blue/red is the same as red/blue.)

Let's explore by arranging color tiles.

Colors	Number of Tiles Chosen	Arrangements when Order Matters	Arrangements when Order Does Not Matter
Red Blue Green	⭐ 2	(9 tile pairs shown) Total ___6___	(3 tile pairs shown) Total ___3___

 **Check Understanding** —

a. Copy and complete the chart.

Colors	Number of Tiles Chosen	Arrangements when Order Matters	Arrangements when Order Does Not Matter
Red Blue Green	⭐ 3	(tiles shown) Total ┊┊┊	Total ┊┊┊

b. What patterns have you noticed?

c. Do you think there will always be more arrangements where order matters than where order does not matter?

1. Copy and complete the chart. Use color tiles or colored paper squares to model each arrangement. As you continue finding the designated arrangements, you may find it easier to list the colors in an abbreviated manner such as red, blue, green as r/b/g.

Colors	Number of Tiles Chosen	Arrangements when Order Matters	Arrangements when Order Does Not Matter
Red Blue Green Yellow	2	Total	Total
Red Blue Green Yellow	3	Total	Total
Red Blue Green Yellow	4	Total	Total
Red Blue Green Yellow Orange	2	Total	Total

2. Explain the method you used to arrive at the possible arrangements.

3. Estimate how many possible outcomes there are using all five colors and choosing five tiles when the arrangement order <u>does</u> matter and when it <u>does not</u> matter.

 **Construct Meaning**

Remember the arrangements you made with red, blue, green, and yellow color tiles? You determined that there were 24 ways to make an arrangement of four tiles when the order mattered. An arrangement when order matters is called a **permutation**.

You also made **combinations**, which are arrangements when the order does not matter.

Taylor has 3 quarters, 6 dimes, and 2 nickels. How many different ways can he make change for a dollar?   **3**

Does the order matter when making change?

Is this a permutation or a combination?

Quarters	Dimes	Nickels
3	2	1
2	5	0
2	4	2

The Fundamental Counting Principle can make it easier to determine the number of possible outcomes for a permutation. Let's explore.

If Ormand draws from a bag containing four color tiles, one each of red, green, blue, and yellow, how many possible permutations are there using all four colors?

- *Draw One*
  Draw one tile from the bag. How many possible colors could be drawn?

   ④

- *Draw Two*
  One tile has been removed. How many possibilities for the second draw?

   ③

- *Draw Three*
  Two tiles have been removed. How many possibilities for the third draw? ②

- *Draw Four*
  Three tiles have been removed. How many possibilities for the fourth draw? ①

Use the Fundamental Counting Principle. Think of each draw as a category.

    Draw One   *Draw Two*   *Draw Three*   *Draw Four*
④ possibilities × ③ possibilities × ② possibilities × ① possibility = 24 possible outcomes

This is also called a 4 factorial (4!) $4 \times 3 \times 2 \times 1 = 24$

A **factorial** is the product of all the whole numbers from 1 to n, starting with n. It is written as $n!$

The number of permutations of n objects or categories is represented by the expression: $n \times (n - 1) \times (n - 2) \times (n - 3) \ldots$

    If $n = 4$: $4 \times 3 \times 2 \times 1 = 4! = 24$

Note that the n factorial is appropriately used when an item is <u>removed</u> from the possibilities.

Check Understanding

a. How would the number of possible outcomes change if you were finding permutations by placing the tile back into the bag each time one was drawn?

b. Todd dropped his five-page report and scattered the pages. Find the number of possible orders of the pages when he gathers them back together.

Write *permutation* or *combination*.

c. The number of games played by the members of a chess club when they play each other

d. The number of different phone numbers made with only the digits 1, 3, and 5 when the digits may be repeated

Write *permutation* or *combination*.

1. The number of different lock "combinations" with numbers 0 to 12 if each "combination" has three numbers (Hint: Should this really be called a combination lock?)

2. The number of different two-topping sundaes that can be made using four toppings

3. The number of ways to choose three class representatives from Mrs. Smalley's class of 15 students

4. The number of ways to make social security numbers

Evaluate the expression.

5. 9!   **6.** 3!   **7.** 8!   **8.** 10!

Use factorials or the Fundamental Counting Principle to determine the number of possible outcomes.

9. Three softball pitches called as a ball or a strike

10. Casey, Lorna, Wells, and Aeysha finishing first, second, third, or fourth place in the 100-meter dash

11. The order of adding six ingredients to homemade chili

12. Choosing three desserts from four choices

13. The Penuela family is taking a family portrait. There are five members in the family seated in a row.

14. Selecting a captain and co-captain from among four girls

Lesson 147

 Construct Meaning

Blaise Pascal, a Frenchman who lived in the 1600s, was considered to be a mathematical prodigy. He invented the first calculating machine, the syringe, and the hydraulic press. Among his most famous writings is the *Pensées*, where he states what is called Pascal's Wager.

Pascal's Wager is man's way of reasoning about faith in God. One can be certain of God's existence. Is there any certainty about rolling number cubes or is it merely chance?

> ### Pascal's Wager
> "If God does not exist, one stands to lose nothing by believing in him anyway, while if he does exist, one stands to lose everything by not believing."

Roll two number cubes at the same time. For each roll, what sums are possible? Is each sum equally likely?

With a partner, take turns rolling two number cubes a total of 36 times. Before you begin, choose a sum that you think will occur most often.

Record your results on a **line plot** like the one shown.

```
                              x
                              x                 x
             x        x   x                     x
     _____
       1  2  3  4  5  6  7  8  9  10  11  12
```

Now which sum do you think will occur the most often? Explain.

Make a Number Cube Sum Chart

Copy and complete the chart to show mathematical probability.

Write the sum of the number cubes in each square.

Next, choose a different color for each sum and color the appropriate square on your chart with that color. For example, color all sums of 2 green, and all sums of 3 red.

	1	2	3	4	5	6
1	2	3	4	5		
2	3	4				
3	4					
4						
5						
6						

Calculate Mathematical Probability

How many different ways can you roll a sum of 9?

Which sum occured the most often?

Ask the following questions for each sum: How many times can a sum of ▦ occur?

How many possible outcomes are there for rolling two number cubes?

What is the mathematical probability for rolling a sum of 3?

$$P(\text{sum of 3}) = \frac{\text{Favorable Outcomes (2)}}{\text{Possible Outcomes (36)}} = \frac{2}{36} \text{ or } \frac{1}{18}$$

What is the mathematical probability for rolling a sum of 10? $P(\text{sum of 10}) = $ ▦

 **Check Understanding**

Use your Number Cube Sum Chart to answer.

a. Describe a pattern you see.   b. *P*(sum of 8)   c. *P*(sum of 7)

 **Practice**

Use your Number Cube Sum Chart for problems 1 through 4.

1. *P*(doubles)   2. *P*(not 7)   3. *P*(12)   4. *P*(odd)

5. What is the experimental probability for rolling a sum of 7 shown on your line plot?

6. How does your experimental probability of rolling a 7 compare to the mathematical probability of rolling a 7?

Globe Trader Cards, Inc. has released its latest packs of hockey trading cards, each containing one of eight rookie cards. Assume that the company produces an equal number of each rookie card and, when you buy a pack, your chance of getting any of the eight rookies is the same.

7. How many packs do you think you would have to purchase to get all eight rookie cards?

8. a. Is it possible to get all eight rookie cards with only eight purchases?

   b. Would you expect that to happen? Why or why not?

9. Simulate the rookie card scenario by using an octahedral die. Toss the octahedron until all the numbers have been rolled at least once. Record each number as it occurs, including numbers that are rolled more than one time. This simulates the number of packs that would need to be purchased in order to get all eight rookie cards.

   a. Run three trials and record your results on a tally table.

   b. According to your tally table, estimate the least number of purchases that you would have to make in order to get all eight cards at least once.

   c. According to your three trials, what is the mean number of purchases needed to get all eight rookie cards?

   d. Give an example of another way to simulate this scenario other than with an octahedral die.

Rookie Card	Trial 1	Trial 2	Trial 3
#1			
#2			
#3			
#4			
#5			
#6			
#7			
#8			
TOTAL			

Lesson 148

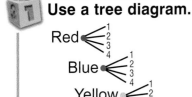 **Construct Meaning**

In 1988, Renée Bondi suffered an accident that left her a quadriplegic. She has overcome this hardship by allowing the Lord to work in her circumstance showing her purpose and hope. Currently, Mrs. Bondi is a speaker and a singer who encourages others through difficult times. Her faith in God's sovereignty has allowed her to overcome great odds.

A game required Danell to spin a red on a spinner and roll a 3 on a four-sided polyhedral die in order to move a space on the game board. What is the probability that this event will occur? This type of probability problem is called a compound event. A **compound event** is a combination of two or more single events.

THREE WAYS TO DETERMINE THE PROBABILITY OF A COMPOUND EVENT

 Use a tree diagram.

Red $\begin{array}{c}1\\2\\3\\4\end{array}$
Blue $\begin{array}{c}1\\2\\3\\4\end{array}$
Yellow $\begin{array}{c}1\\2\\3\\4\end{array}$

List
R,1   B,1   Y,1
R,2   B,2   Y,2
R,3   B,3   Y,3
R,4   B,4   Y,4

Possible outcomes for (red, 3) : one
Total possible outcomes: twelve

Therefore, $P(\text{red}, 3) = \frac{1}{12}$

Use the Fundamental Counting Principle.
The spinner has three possible outcomes.
The die has four possible outcomes.
Red, 3 has only one favorable outcome.

$3 \times 4 = 12$ possible outcomes

$P(\text{red}, 3) = \dfrac{\text{Favorable outcomes (1)}}{\text{Possible outcomes (12)}} = \frac{1}{12}$

 Multiply the probabilities of the individual favorable outcomes.
What is the probability of rolling a 3? $\frac{1}{4}$
What is the probability of landing on red on the spinner? $\frac{1}{3}$

$P(\text{red}, 3) = \frac{1}{4} \times \frac{1}{3} = \frac{1}{12}$

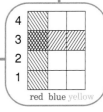

red blue yellow

What is the probability of rolling a 6 on a number cube twice in a row?

Find the individual probability of rolling a 6.
Possible outcomes: 1   2   3   4   5   ⑥
There is $\frac{1}{6}$ chance of rolling a 6 the first time and a $\frac{1}{6}$ chance of rolling a 6 the second time.

$P(6, 6) = \frac{1}{6} \times \frac{1}{6} = \frac{1}{36}$

There is a 1 in 36 chance of rolling 6 twice in a row.

a. The probability of rolling a 3 on a number cube twice in a row, $P(3, 3) =$ ▦ .

b. The probability of tossing tails, heads, tails on a penny, nickel, and dime, $P(T, H, T) =$ ▦ .

c. In your own words, explain how to find the probability of a compound event.

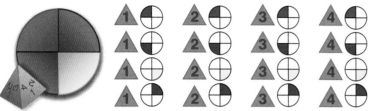

1. How many possible outcomes are there for rolling the die and spinning the spinner?
2. $P(2, \text{red})$
3. $P(4, \text{blue})$

Five number cards are placed into a hat: 1, 2, 5, 8, and 9. Each time a card is drawn, it is placed back into the hat.

4. $P(2)$
5. $P(\text{odd number, even number})$
6. $P(8, \text{odd number})$
7. $P(\text{even number, odd number, even number})$

Two pattern sticks are thrown into the air.

8. How many possible outcomes are there for each stick?
9. How many ways can two sticks land?
10. What is the probability that the first stick will land pattern side up and the second stick will land plain side up?

11. What is the mathematical probability for each color on the spinner and each number on a six-sided number cube?
12. Using the mathematical probability, predict the number of times you would roll a 4 in 36 trials.
13. Predict how many times you would spin a green in 40 trials.
14. Calculate the mathematical probability for rolling a 4 and spinning a green at the same time.

Construct a spinner matching the one shown for problems 11–14. Perform an experiment using the spinner and a number cube. Do 48 trials and record your results in a table.

15. What is your experimental probability for 4, green?
16. How does this compare to the mathematical probability of 4, green, that you calculated in problem 14?

TABLE	
cube	spinner
2	red
6	blue

Construct Meaning

The sixth grade at Wilson Middle School has several probability booths at the school fair.

At the Egyptian Triangle Dart Booth, a dart is randomly thrown at a target. If the dart hits the target, what is the probability that it will land in the yellow triangle?

$$P(\text{triangle}) = \frac{\text{area of the triangle}}{\text{area of the rectangle}} = \frac{\frac{1}{2}bh}{bh} = \frac{\frac{1}{2}(6 \times 9)}{6 \times 9} = 0.5 \text{ or } 50\%$$

There is a 50% chance the dart will land on the triangle.

At the Coin Toss Booth, a coin is randomly tossed onto a flat target with a square hole. Assuming that the coin lands on the target, what is the probability that it will land in the hole?

$$P(\text{hole}) = \frac{\text{area of the hole}}{\text{area of the rectangle}} = \frac{2 \times 2}{9 \times 6} = \frac{4}{54} \approx 0.074 \approx 7.4\%$$

There is about a 7.4% chance the coin will land in the hole.

At the Sticky Vortex Booth, a sticky ball is randomly thrown at a sticky target. If the ball hits the target and sticks, what is the probability that it will land in the gray part of the target?

$$P(\text{gray}) = \frac{\text{half the area of the circle}}{\text{area of the square}} = \frac{\frac{1}{2}(\pi r^2)}{s^2} \approx \frac{19.23}{49} \approx 0.3925 \approx 39\%$$

There is about a 39% chance the ball will hit the gray part of the target.

At the Bag-O-Beans Toss, a bean bag is thrown through one of three holes in a target board. If the bag hits the target, what is the probability that it will go through one of the holes?

$$P(\text{holes}) = \frac{\text{total area of three holes}}{\text{area of the triangle}} \approx \frac{3 \times 78.5}{\frac{1}{2}(48 \times 48)} \approx \frac{235.5}{1{,}152} \approx 0.2 \approx 20\%$$

There is about a 20% chance the bean bag will go through one of the holes.

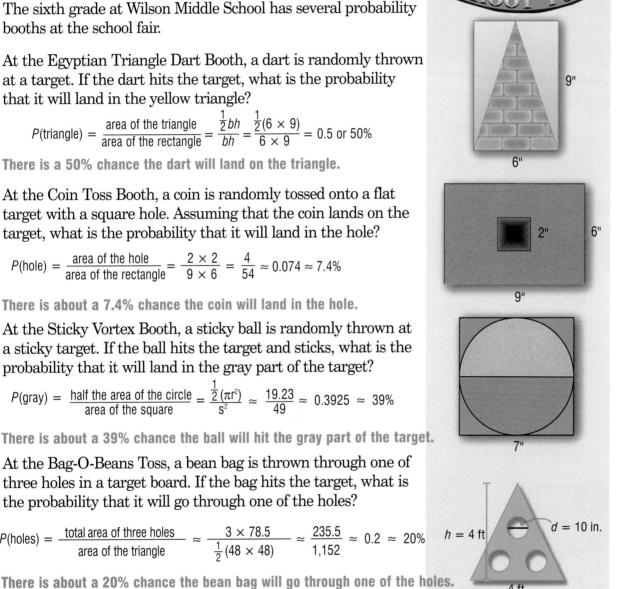

Apply

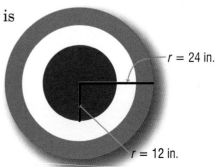

At the Archery Booth, an arrow is randomly shot toward a target. What is the probability that an arrow hitting the circle target will hit the red part of the target? (Hint: Change inches to feet.)

$$P(\text{red}) = \frac{\quad}{\quad} = \quad = \quad \%$$

Chapter Twelve Study Guide

1. If a coin is tossed 40 times, what would you expect the probability to be for heads? *Lesson 142*

2.  a. Which colors are equally likely events? *Lesson 143*
   b. P(orange)

3. The Hot Pan Pizza Shop take-out menu offers thick or thin crust, mozzarella or cheddar cheese, and pepperoni, sausage, or chicken toppings. Show the possible combinations using a tree diagram. *Lesson 144*

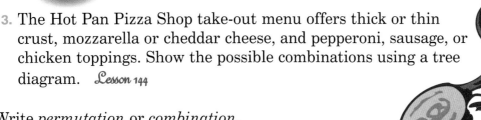

Write *permutation* or *combination*.

4. Awarding gold, silver, and bronze medals *Lesson 145*

5. Selecting people to be on the city planning committee *Lesson 146*

Solve.

6. If a regular number cube is rolled, find: *Lesson 147*
   a. $P(1)$ b. P(even)   c. $P(7)$

7. If two regular number cubes are rolled, find: *Lesson 147*
   a. P(sum of 10)   b. P(sum of 6)   c. P(sum of 1)

8. If a penny and a number cube are tossed at the same time, what is the probability that the penny will be heads and the number cube will be 6? *Lesson 148*

9. If a nickel is tossed and a spinner is spun at the same time, what is the probability that the spinner will land on red and the nickel will be tails? *Lesson 148*

10.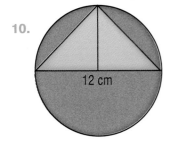
    12 cm

    If a randomly thrown dart hits the target, what is the probability that the dart will hit the triangle? *Lesson 149*

Perfecting Probabilities

1. If a dime is tossed 50 times, what would you predict for the number of times that heads would be an outcome?

2.  This spinner is spun 40 times. What would you predict for the number of times that purple would be an outcome?

3. Draw two different spinners where the colors have equally likely outcomes.

4. The result of spinning one of the spinners below was: blue, blue, green, blue, green, blue, blue, blue, green, green. Write the letter of the spinner that most likely produced the results.

 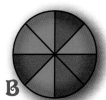  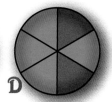

A   B   C   D

Write the letter of the term that matches the definition.

5. The middle number in a set of data
6. An arrangement where the order matters
7. An arrangement where the order does not matter
8. A ratio of the number of favorable outcomes to the number of possible outcomes
9. A combination of two or more single events
10. A ratio of the number of times an event actually occurred to the number of trials

a. mathematical probability
b. permutation
c. compound event
d. median
e. experimental probability
f. combination

11. Sparkling Teeth Toothbrushes come in four colors: yellow, purple, green, or red. The toothbrushes may also have soft or firm bristles. Construct a tree diagram showing all the possible Sparkling Teeth Toothbrushes. How many different toothbrushes are made by Sparkling Teeth?

12. Kayleen wants to have a picture matted and framed. Find the number of different combinations that can be made if there are nine choices of colors for the matte and six styles of frames.

A number cube is rolled twice. Identify the probability for each pair.

13. $P(4, 4)$ 14. $P(1, 6)$ 15. $P(\text{odd, even})$ 16. $P(\text{greater than 4, greater than 4})$

17. $P(0, 1)$ 18. $P(\text{even, even})$ 19. $P(7, 6)$ 20. $P(\text{even, 3})$

A coin is tossed and a spinner is spun at the same time.

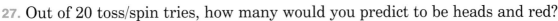

21. Make a sample space of all the possible outcomes.

22. *P*(heads, red) 23. *P*(tails, blue) 24. *P*(heads, orange)

25. *P*(tails, not blue) 26. What are the least likely outcomes?

27. Out of 20 toss/spin tries, how many would you predict to be heads and red?

A number cube was rolled, and the results of 20 trials were recorded on the tally table.

28. How many possible outcomes are there for rolling a number cube?

29. What is the mathematical probability for rolling a 6?

30. What is the experimental probability for rolling a 6?

31. What is the experimental probability for rolling a 2?

32. Why is the experimental probability for rolling a 2 different from its mathematical probability?

NUMBER CUBE TALLIES

1	2	3	4	5	6

There are three doors. Behind two of the doors is a goat and behind one of the doors is the grand prize.

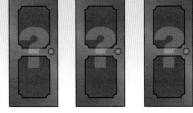

33. What is the probability that there is a grand prize behind the door you choose?

34. What is the probability that there is a goat behind the door you choose ?

35. Two 8-sided number dice are rolled. Copy and complete the chart of number sums.

36. How many possible outcomes are there for rolling the two 8-sided number dice?

37. How many times did a sum of 8 occur?

38. How many times did a sum of 16 occur?

39. Which sum occurs most frequently?

40. *P*(sum of 12) 41. *P*(sum of 16)

42. *P*(sum of 2) 43. *P*(sum of 14)

44. *P*(doubles) 45. *P*(not a sum of 10)

46. *P*(sum is odd) 47. *P*(sum of 3)

48. 3! 49. 6! 50. 4!

Chapter Theme

Mankind, created in the image of God, is called to excellence. David gave voice to this characteristic of God when he wrote, "O Lord, our Lord, how excellent is Your name in all the earth." As you consider the chapter 13 theme of Excellence, ask yourself how your actions might be different if you decided to live with excellence as a daily personal goal. The writer of the book of Proverbs says, "Listen, for I will speak excellent things." Search the Bible for the wisdom that will guide you in your quest for excellence. The apostle Paul tells us to "approve the things that are excellent." Take time to reflect on what the world might call excellent as opposed to the things that God calls excellent. Test against the word of God the things that you participate in and approve. An excellent God would not create His children in His image and call them to mediocrity. He has set you apart for excellence.

13

Chapter

Measurement

Lessons 151-160

LORD, make me to know my end,
and what is the measure of my days, . . .
Indeed, You have made my days as handbreadths.

Psalm 39:4a, 5a

Lesson 151

 **Construct Meaning**

Isaiah 12:5 says, "Sing to the LORD, For He has done excellent things; This is known in all the earth." As children of our heavenly Father, we need to follow this example of excellence in the details of our lives. Mr. Safford demonstrated his integrity as a Christian by keeping excellent records of the hours he worked. Use the portion of Mr. Safford's time card to find the number of hours and minutes he worked on February 10.

Employee: Jim Safford

Date	A.M. In	A.M. Out	A.M. Time Worked	P.M. In	P.M. Out	P.M. Time Worked	Total
2/10	7:52	12:07	4 hr 15 min	1:05	5:55	4 hr 50 min	

Mr. Safford rounded 7:52 A.M. to 8 A.M. and 12:07 P.M. to 12 noon. The difference between 8 A.M. and noon is four hours. Since he began working 8 minutes before 8 A.M. and continued for 7 minutes past noon, he added 15 minutes to the 4 hours to calculate his morning work time. The amount of time that passes in a designated time period is the **elapsed time**.

Did Mr. Safford calculate his afternoon hours correctly on his time card? Explain how you would calculate the time.

> 60 seconds (sec) = 1 minute (min)
> 60 minutes = 1 hour (hr)
> A.M. begins at 12:00 midnight.
> P.M. begins at 12:00 noon.

What is the total time worked by Mr. Safford on February 10?

```
  4 hr 15 min
+ 4 hr 50 min
-------------
  8 hr 65 min
```

Regroup 8 hr 65 minutes as
8 hr + 1 hr + 5 min   **9 hr 5 min**

How much longer did Mr. Safford work on February 10 than he worked on the previous day if his time for the previous day was 7 hours 50 minutes?

```
  9 hr  5 min        8 hr 65 min
- 7 hr 50 min      - 7 hr 50 min
              -----------------
                    1 hr 15 min
```

You cannot subtract 50 minutes from 5 minutes, so regroup 1 hour as 60 minutes and add it to the 5 minutes. Subtract.

OLD ROYAL OBSERVATORY

Greenwich, England

Check Understanding

Find the sum or difference.

a.
```
  5 hr 13 min
+ 2 hr 20 min
```

b.
```
  12 hr 10 min
-  6 hr 20 min
```

c.
```
  7 hr 15 min
+ 1 hr 45 min
```

Write the elapsed time.

d. Piano practice from 4:00 P.M. to 4:45 P.M.

e. Read a book from 11:50 A.M. to 12:30 P.M.

f. Left car in parking garage from 9:15 A.M. to 11:37 A.M.

Find the sum or difference.

1.   8 hr 13 min
  − 6 hr 20 min

2.   4 hr 30 min
  + 1 hr 45 min

3.   15 hr
  − 10 hr 35 min

4.   3 min 4 sec
  − 1 min 8 sec

5.   18 hr 18 min
  + 3 hr 3 min

6.   13 min 8 sec
  − 9 min 7 sec

7.   2 hr 24 min
  + 4 hr 32 min

8.   6 hr 37 min
  + 8 hr 49 min

Write the elapsed time.

9. 4:45 P.M. to 6:15 P.M.

10. 1:10 A.M. to 4:14 A.M.

11. 11:49 A.M. to 12:29 P.M.

12. 6:50 A.M. to 8:05 P.M.

13. 12:02 P.M. to 12:20 A.M.

14. 9:13 P.M. to 3:19 A.M.

15. Mr. Safford left for home at 6:10 P.M. He stopped to get gasoline which took 15 minutes. He arrived home at 6:50 P.M. How much driving time was his trip home?

16. Dinner is served at 6:15 P.M. It took 48 minutes to prepare dinner. What time did the family begin preparing dinner?

17. The space shuttle landed on Friday at 9:30 A.M. It had been in space for 9 days, 3 hr, and 17 min. At what time did it blast off?

18. Compute the amount of time that Flight 164 was in the air.
It departed Tampa at 6:30 A.M. and arrived in
Atlanta at 7:57 A.M.
It departed Atlanta at 9:04 A.M. and arrived in
Washington, D.C., at 11:02 A.M.
It departed Washington, D.C., at 11:58 A.M. and arrived in New York City at 1:32 P.M.

19. The Boston Marathon is the oldest marathon in the United States. In 1972, women were officially acknowledged in the running of the 76th Boston Marathon. New Yorker Nina Kuscisik was the first official female winner with a time of 3:08:58, which is 3 hours, 8 minutes, and 58 seconds. In 2001, Catherine Nderba of Kenya won the women's race, completing the course of 26 miles and 385 yards in 2:23:53. What is the difference in the winning times?

Write as a ratio, fraction, decimal, and percent.

1. 43 out of 100

2. 25 cents out of 100

3. 80 out of 100

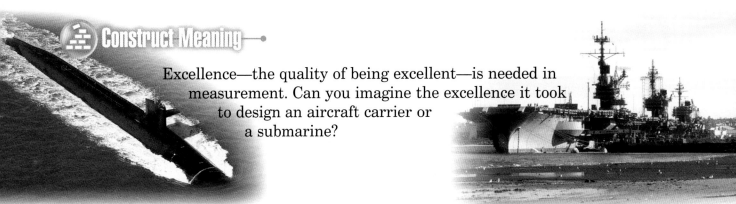

Construct Meaning

Excellence—the quality of being excellent—is needed in measurement. Can you imagine the excellence it took to design an aircraft carrier or a submarine?

Tom's goal is to build a doghouse that has a height of 45 inches. What will be the height in feet and inches?

Steps to convert from one unit to another:
1. Decide whether to multiply or divide.
2. Use the equivalent units of length to compute.

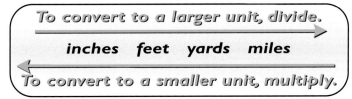

To convert to a larger unit, divide.

inches   feet   yards   miles

To convert to a smaller unit, multiply.

Customary Units of Length
12 inches (in.) = 1 foot (ft)
3 feet = 1 yard (yd)
36 inches = 1 yard
5,280 feet = 1 mile (mi)
1,760 yards = 1 mile

Converting inches into feet is converting to a larger unit. Divide 45 inches by 12 inches.

```
      3 feet 9 inches
12) 45
    36
     9
```

The height of Tom's doghouse will be 3 feet 9 inches.

Tom bought 5 yards 2 feet of trim for the roof of the doghouse. How many feet did he buy? Convert to a smaller unit by multiplying.

```
  5   number of yards of trim
× 3   number of feet in 1 yard
 15   number of feet in 5 yards
```

15 feet + 2 feet = 17 feet
Tom bought **17 feet** of trim.

Tom was given a piece of carpet that was 5 feet 2 inches long and another piece 4 feet 11 inches in length.

Find the total length of the carpet.

```
   5 ft  2 in.
+ 4 ft 11 in.
   9 ft 13 in.   Regroup 13 in. as 1 ft 1 in.
 10 ft 1 in. total
```

Find the difference in length of the pieces.

```
   5 ft  2 in. = 4 ft 14 in.   Regroup 1 ft as 12 in.
 - 4 ft 11 in. = 4 ft 11 in.
                      3 in. difference
```

Check Understanding

a. 2 mi = ⬚ yd   b. 72 in. = ⬚ yd   c. 54 ft = ⬚ yd   d. 5,283 ft = ⬚ mi ⬚ yd

e. 44 in. = ⬚ yd ⬚ in.   f. 11 ft = ⬚ yd ⬚ ft   g. 3 yd 2 ft = ⬚ in.   h. 5 yd = ⬚ in.

Write the letter of the most reasonable estimate of length.

1. A pencil
   a. 6 in.
   b. 6 ft
   c. 6 yd

2. The distance between Mexico City and Paris
   a. 5,716 ft
   b. 5,716 yd
   c. 5,716 mi

3. A skateboard
   a. 3 in.
   b. 3 ft
   c. 3 yd

4. A long goal in football
   a. 48 in.
   b. 48 ft
   c. 48 yd

Complete.

5. 60 in. = ___ ft

6. 6 yd = ___ ft

7. 34 ft = ___ yd ___ ft

8. 108 in. = ___ yd

9. 3 mi = ___ ft

10. 7 yd 1 ft = ___ ft

11. 77 in. = ___ ft ___ in.

12. 3 ft 6 in. = ___ in.

13. 1,767 yd = ___ mi ___ yd

Solve.

14. 8 yd 2 ft
    + 5 yd 1 ft

15. 10 ft 9 in.
    − 5 ft 11 in.

16. 9 ft 6 in.
    + 1 ft 5 in.

17. 5 yd 4 ft
    − 3 yd 5 ft

18. 20 ft 5 in.
    − 6 ft 7 in.

19. 17 yd 21 in.
    + 3 yd 25 in.

20. 8 yd 2 ft 4 in.
    + 3 yd 4 ft 5 in.

21. 7 yd 2 ft 4 in.
    − 4 yd 3 ft 6 in.

22. Brad jumped six feet in the high jump. Garrett jumped 60 inches. Who made the highest jump?

23. Sally used 23 feet of ribbon for her craft. Bonnie used 8 yards. Who used more ribbbon?

24.
$\frac{1}{4}$ ft = ___ in.
$\frac{1}{3}$ ft = ___ in.
$\frac{1}{2}$ ft = ___ in.
$\frac{3}{4}$ ft = ___ in.

Use your ruler to complete the table. Then complete the statements. Marsha's cell phone is 4 inches long, or ___ foot long. Todd climbed to the top of a pole that is 4 yards 9 inches tall, or 12 ___ feet.

Review

1. Order the factors of 35 from least to greatest.

2. Order the factors of 24 from least to greatest.

3. List the first five multiples of 12.

4. List the first five multiples of 36.

Lesson 153

Construct Meaning

Dr. Viggo Olsen wanted his medical career to be characterized by excellence. It took about 15 years of studying at a university, a medical college, in laboratories, and in hospitals to become a certified surgeon. He explains that prescriptions for children and infants must be calculated accurately so they get the proper dosage.

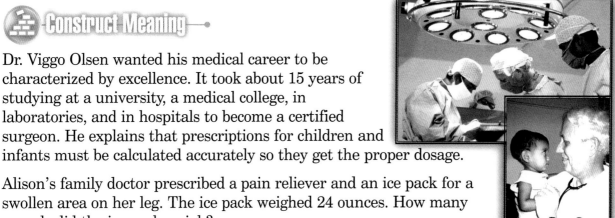

Alison's family doctor prescribed a pain reliever and an ice pack for a swollen area on her leg. The ice pack weighed 24 ounces. How many pounds did the ice pack weigh?

Customary Units of Weight
16 ounces (oz) = 1 pound (lb)
2,000 pounds = 1 ton (T)

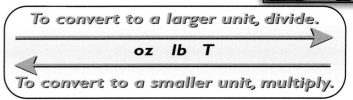

To convert to a larger unit, divide.

oz   lb   T

To convert to a smaller unit, multiply.

24 oz = ⬚ lb ⬚ oz   To convert to a larger unit, divide.

$$16\overline{)24}$$ 1 pound 8 ounces
$$\underline{16}$$
$$8$$

The ice pack weighed 1 pound 8 ounces.

Fractions of a Pound
$\frac{1}{8}$ lb = 2 oz
$\frac{1}{4}$ lb = 4 oz
$\frac{1}{2}$ lb = 8 oz
$\frac{3}{4}$ lb = 12 oz

You can think of 1 pound 8 ounces as $1\frac{8}{16}$ pounds, or $1\frac{1}{2}$ pounds.

How many pounds are in 2 tons? To convert to a smaller unit, multiply.

2 T = ⬚ lb   2 T × 2,000 lb = 4,000 lb
                    in a T

How can you convert fractions of a pound to ounces?

$2\frac{1}{4}$ lb = ⬚ oz $2\frac{1}{4}$ lb × 16 oz = $\frac{9}{4} × \frac{16^4}{1}$ = 36 oz
                        in a lb

or

(2 lb × 16 oz) + ($\frac{1}{4}$ lb × 16 oz) = 32 oz + 4 oz = 36 oz
    in a lb   in a lb

To add and subtract ounces, pounds, and tons, you may need to regroup.

```
                    5    20   16 oz = 1 lb                      3    2,059   2,000 lbs = 1 T
  3 lb  8 oz        6 lb  4 oz              8 T 139 lb          4 T    59 lb
+ 2 lb  9 oz      – 3 lb  7 oz            + 2 T 764 lb        – 1 T    74 lb
  5 lb 17 oz =      2 lb 13 oz             10 T 903 lb          2 T 1,985 lb
  6 lb  1 oz   16 oz = 1 lb
```

 **Check Understanding**

Complete.

a. 5 lb = ⸱⸱⸱ oz   b. $3\frac{1}{2}$ T = ⸱⸱⸱ lb

c. 128 oz = ⸱⸱⸱ lb   d. 65 oz = ⸱⸱⸱ lb ⸱⸱⸱ oz

Solve.

e.　38 lb　6 oz
　+ 23 lb 12 oz

f.　7 T　98 lb
　− 2 T 187 lb

 **Practice**

Write *oz*, *lb*, or *T* to indicate the most appropriate unit of measurement.

1. Adult human
2. Letter
3. Helicopter
4. Killer whale
5. Chocolate bar
6. A ball of yarn
7. A quarter
8. Dumbbells for weight lifting

Complete.

9. 2 lb = ⸱⸱⸱ oz
10. 9,000 lb = ⸱⸱⸱ T
11. 6 T = ⸱⸱⸱ lb
12. 48 oz = ⸱⸱⸱ lb

13. 90 oz = ⸱⸱⸱ lb ⸱⸱⸱ oz
14. $2\frac{3}{4}$ lb = ⸱⸱⸱ oz
15. $1\frac{1}{2}$ T = ⸱⸱⸱ lb
16. 96 oz = ⸱⸱⸱ lb

17. 7 lb 7 oz = ⸱⸱⸱ oz
18. 56 oz = ⸱⸱⸱ lb ⸱⸱⸱ oz
19. $3\frac{1}{8}$ lb = ⸱⸱⸱ oz
20. 500 lb = ⸱⸱⸱ T

Solve.

21.　17 lb 14 oz
　+ 12 lb 12 oz

22.　12 T　397 lb
　+ 20 T 1,700 lb

23.　24 T　600 lb
　− 13 T 1,400 lb

24.　9 lb 4 oz
　− 8 lb 5 oz

 Apply

25. Mrs. Hurley divided $7\frac{1}{2}$ pounds of pretzels evenly among her 20 students. How many ounces did each student receive?

26. Before Cara was diagnosed with the flu, she weighed 98 lb 4 oz. She became dehydrated and went to the doctor. In his office she weighed 96 lb 14 oz. How many pounds had she lost?

27. Mrs. Brown bought bananas for 49¢ per pound. If she bought 96 oz of bananas, how much did she pay for them?

28. A truck driver pulls in at a weigh station. If his truck weighs 13,500 pounds, is he over the 7-ton limit? Explain.

 Review

Name the following polygons.

1.
2.
3.
4.
5.

 **Construct Meaning**

It is recommended that people drink at least eight cups of fluids a day to maintain good health. Micah drank one pint of milk, one cup of juice, and one quart of water. Does he need to take in more fluids before the end of the day?

Use the table to answer the question.

Customary Units of Capacity
3 teaspoons(tsp) = 1 tablespoon (tbsp)
2 tablespoons = 1 fluid ounce (fl oz)
8 fluid ounces = 1 cup (c)
2 cups = 1 pint (pt)
2 pints = 1 quart (qt)
4 quarts = 1 gallon (gal)

1 quart of water = 2 pints = 4 cups
1 pint of milk = 2 cups
1 cup of juice = 1 cup
_____
7 cups

Micah needs to drink one more cup of liquid before the end of the day.

Micah had a gallon container, the largest customary unit of capacity, and wondered how many teaspoons, the smallest customary unit of capacity, it would take to fill it. To convert a greater unit to a smaller unit, multiply.

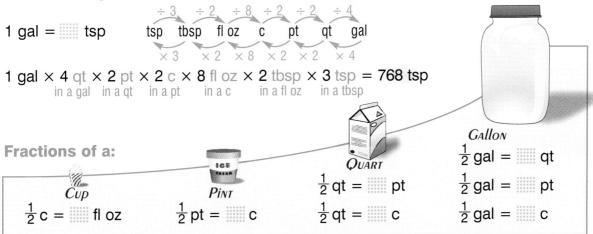

1 gal = ⬚ tsp

$\div 3 \quad \div 2 \quad \div 8 \quad \div 2 \quad \div 2 \quad \div 4$

tsp tbsp fl oz c pt qt gal

$\times 3 \quad \times 2 \quad \times 8 \quad \times 2 \quad \times 2 \quad \times 4$

1 gal × 4 qt × 2 pt × 2 c × 8 fl oz × 2 tbsp × 3 tsp = 768 tsp
in a gal in a qt in a pt in a c in a fl oz in a tbsp

Fractions of a:

Cup
$\frac{1}{2}$ c = ⬚ fl oz

Pint
$\frac{1}{2}$ pt = ⬚ c

Quart
$\frac{1}{2}$ qt = ⬚ pt
$\frac{1}{2}$ qt = ⬚ c

Gallon
$\frac{1}{2}$ gal = ⬚ qt
$\frac{1}{2}$ gal = ⬚ pt
$\frac{1}{2}$ gal = ⬚ c

You may need to regroup to add or subtract customary units of capacity.

```
   4 gal  2 qt
 + 2 gal  2 qt
 ─────────────
   6 gal  4 qt   4 qt = 1 gal
   ⬚ gal
```

```
       14    3
      15 qt  1 pt   2 pt = 1 qt
 −     9 qt  2 pt
 ─────────────────
       ⬚ qt  ⬚ pt
```

```
        8    20
        9 gal  4 c   16 c = 1 gal
 −      4 gal  15 c
 ─────────────────────
        ⬚ gal  ⬚ c
```

 **Check Understanding**

Complete.

a. 8 pt = ⬚ qt
b. 3 gal 2 qt = ⬚ qt
c. $\frac{1}{4}$ c = ⬚ fl oz

Solve.

d.
```
   8 tbsp  2 tsp
 − 5 tbsp  3 tsp
```

e.
```
   5 gal  3 qt  7 fl oz
 + 1 gal  2 qt  9 fl oz
```

 **ractice**

Write *divide* or *multiply* to indicate which operation would be used for each conversion.

1. Cups to pints
2. Gallons to quarts
3. Teaspoons to tablespoons
4. Fluid ounces to cups
5. Pints to cups
6. Gallons to cups

Write the equivalent measures that must be considered and solve.

7. 28 c = ▦ pt
8. 11 gal = ▦ qt
9. 20 qt = ▦ c

Solve.

10. 2 gal = ▦ qt
11. 18 tsp = ▦ tbsp
12. 5 c = ▦ fl oz
13. 3 fl oz = ▦ tbsp
14. 10 pt = ▦ qt
15. 28 qt = ▦ gal
16. 6 qt = ▦ c
17. 4 tbsp = ▦ fl oz
18. 8 c = ▦ gal
19. 5 pt = ▦ fl oz

Write the letter of the most reasonable measurement.

20. A full tank of gasoline
21. A full can of soda
22. Amount of salt in a casserole
23. A carton of ice cream

a. 12 fl oz   b. 2 qt
c. 1 tsp   d. 16 gal

Write *tsp*, *c*, *qt*, or *gal* to indicate the appropriate unit of measurement.

24. eyedropper
25. thermos
26. washing machine
27. bottle of sauce

Solve.

28. 8 gal 3 qt
   + 5 gal 2 qt

29. 13 c 6 fl oz
   − 10 c 7 fl oz

30. 24 qt 4 c
   − 18 qt 6 c

31. 10 qt 1 pt
   + 26 qt 1 pt

 pply

32. The Coupon Station grocery store sells apple juice for $1.98 per gallon, $0.55 per quart, and $0.26 per pint. Which size is the better buy?

33. Elsie is making three apple pies for a fund-raiser at school. Each pie needs five cups of sliced apples. She has sliced three quarts of apples. Has she sliced enough apples to make three pies? Explain your answer.

34. One cup of apple juice contains 117 calories, and one cup of grapefruit juice contains 96 calories. How many more calories are in a quart of apple juice than in a quart of grapefruit juice?

 **Construct Meaning**

Meteorologists use a variety of tools to provide excellent weather forecasts locally, nationally, and internationally. A thermometer measures temperature. **Fahrenheit** (°F) is the customary scale for measuring temperature commonly used in the United States. **Celsius** (°C), the metric scale for measuring temperature, is used in most parts of the world.

A weather forecast may include the high and low temperatures. The high temperature for Concord, New Hampshire, is forecasted at 80°F and the low is forecasted at 66°F. What is the difference between the high and low for Concord?

$$80°F - 66°F = \underline{}$$

 **Check Understanding**

Write the most reasonable temperature.

a. A cool day at the beach
   29°F   65°F   96°F
b. A cold glass of milk
   0°F   25°F   40°F
c. A warm, sunny day
   83°C   11°C   28°C
d. A cup of hot tea
   85°C   30°C   162°C

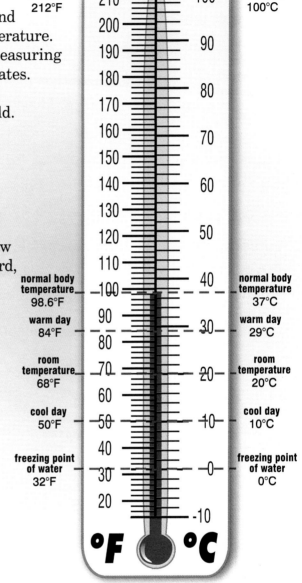

Write the most reasonable activity to do at the given temperature.

e. 78°F   in-line skating or snow skiing   f. 103°F   running or swimming

Write the most reasonable article of clothing to wear at the given temperature.

g. 5°C   sweater or sleeveless shirt   h. 40°C   jacket or swimsuit

Find the difference between the high and low temperatures.

i. San Antonio, TX   j. Tel Aviv, Israel
   high: 102°F   high: 26°C
   low: 78°F   low: −9°C

Write the letter of the most reasonable temperature.

1. A snowman   **a.** 50°F   **b.** 32°F   **c.** 75°F
2. A mild fever   **a.** 100°F   **b.** 38.6°F   **c.** 115°F
3. A hot bowl of soup   **a.** 180°F   **b.** 72°F   **c.** 105°F
4. Oven for baking cookies   **a.** 85°F   **b.** 110°F   **c.** 375°F
5. Ice cubes   **a.** 0°C   **b.** 32°C   **c.** 5°C
6. A cold glass of orange juice   **a.** 23°C   **b.** 5°C   **c.** 0°C

Write the letter of the most reasonable activity for the given temperature.

7. 45°F   **a.** jogging   **b.** ice skating on a pond
8. 30°F   **a.** waterskiing   **b.** snowboarding

Find the difference between the high and low temperatures.

9. Flagstaff, AZ   10. Madrid, Spain
   high: 81°F   high: 12°C
   low: 40°F   low: −1°C

Water can exist in a steam, liquid, or ice form. Write *steam*, *liquid*, or *ice* to indicate the form of water at the given temperature.

11. 43°F   12. 279°F   13. 164°F   14. 19°F

15. On a December morning, it is 5°C in London, England, and 41°F in New York City. After a temperature rise of 15 degrees on the Celsius scale in London and 15 degrees on the Fahrenheit scale in New York City, which city has the warmest temperature? Explain.

16. On July 4, the high temperature in Johannesburg, South Africa, was 22°C. On July 5, the high temperature was 18°C. The three-day average high temperature for July 4 through July 6 was 18°C. What was the high temperature on July 6?

17. When a meterologist says, "It feels colder than the thermometer reads," he may be referring to the wind chill factor. On a snowy night in Denver, Colorado, the actual temperature was 14°F. The wind chill factor made it feel 16 degrees colder. What was the temperature with the wind chill factor taken into account?

 **Construct Meaning**

While traveling in Europe, Brad's family saw a sign that read 3 kilometers. The family went to a soccer game where the ball was kicked 40 meters. The depth of the hot tub at the hotel was 9 decimeters. They purchased a package of postcards with a pen. Each postcard was 15 centimeters long, and the pen tip was one millimeter in thickness. Brad knew he had a lot to learn about the metric system of measuring length.

Metric Units of Length
10 millimeters (mm) = 1 centimeter (cm)
10 centimeters = 1 decimeter (dm)
1,000 millimeters = 1 meter (m)
100 centimeters = 1 meter
10 decimeters = 1 meter
1,000 meters = 1 kilometer (km)

1 cm

1 dm

Examples of metric units of length	
millimeter	the thickness of a metal staple
centimeter	the width of your little finger
decimeter	the width of a small box of tissues
meter	the height of a kitchen counter
kilometer	the distance a person walks in 15 minutes

The basic unit of metric length is a meter. Since the metric system is based on 10, it is easy to convert from one unit to another.

To convert to a larger unit, divide.

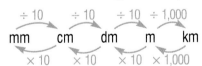

$\div 10 \quad \div 10 \quad \div 10 \quad \div 1,000$

mm   cm   dm   m   km

$\times 10 \quad \times 10 \quad \times 10 \quad \times 1,000$

To convert to a smaller unit, multiply.

Convert to a larger unit, divide by 10.

50 mm = ▦ cm

50 mm ÷ 10 mm = 5 cm
in a cm

4 dm = ▦ mm

4 dm × 10 cm × 10 mm = 400 mm
in a dm   in a cm

Convert to a smaller unit, multiply.

0.28 km = ⬚ m   0.28 × 1,000 m = 280 m
                                        in a km
                                                    Convert to a smaller unit, multiply.

110 mm = ⬚ m   110 ÷ 1,000 mm = 0.11 m
                              in a m
                                              Convert to a larger unit, divide.

 Check Understanding

Select *mm*, *cm*, *dm*, *m*, or *km* as the most appropriate unit of measurement.

a. The height of an adult   b. The length of a pencil
c. The length of a chalkboard eraser   d. The eye of a caterpillar
e. The distance between Detroit and Seattle

Decide if you are converting to a smaller or a larger unit to determine if you multiply or divide. Solve.

f. 12 cm = ⬚ mm   g. 6 dm = ⬚ cm   h. 8.7 cm = ⬚ m

 **Practice**

Write *mm*, *cm*, *dm*, *m*, or *km* as the appropriate unit of measurement.

1. The length of a swimming pool   2. The length of an ant
3. The diameter of a golf ball   4. The distance from Texas to Florida
5. The head of a straight pin   6. The length of a basketball court
7. A candy bar

Write the letter of the most reasonable measurement.

8. The width of a classroom   9. The thickness of a paperback book
   a. 7 cm   b. 7 m   c. 7 km   a. 19 mm b. 19 dm c. 19 km
10. The length of a calculator   11. The length of a river
   a. 12 mm b. 12 cm c. 12 m   a. 48 cm b. 48 m c. 48 km

Compute.

12. 8 cm = ⬚ mm   13. 2,000 m = ⬚ km   14. 65 dm = ⬚ cm
15. 9 dm = ⬚ m   16. 7 m = ⬚ cm   17. 664 mm = ⬚ m
18. 3 cm = ⬚ m   19. 0.48 km = ⬚ m   20. 5,000,000 mm = ⬚ km

 Apply

21. Dave and Derek are running in a 5-kilometer race. Dave has finished 3 kilometers and Derek has finished 2 kilometers. How many more <u>meters</u> has Dave run than Derek?

© Copyright 2002   **337**

Dr. Olsen witnesses to patients.

The Olsen family arrives in East Pakistan.

The Memorial Christian Hospital, founded by Dr. Olsen and others

Construct Meaning

Dr. Olsen's lifestyle of excellence is seen with his family, his patients, and his career. His advice to sixth graders is to work hard and study well to develop thinking skills.

Medicine may be given to a patient with a medicine dropper that contains about one milliliter of liquid. The basic unit of capacity in the metric system is the liter, which holds a little more than a quart.

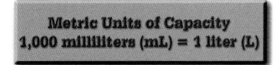

Metric Units of Capacity
1,000 milliliters (mL) = 1 liter (L)

1 milliliter

1 liter

How many liters are equivalent to 4,000 milliliters?

$4,000 \text{ mL} = \boxed{} \text{ L}$

You are converting to a larger unit, so divide.
$4,000 \div 1,000 = 4$
There are 4 liters in 4,000 milliliters.

Dividing by 1,000 is equivalent to moving the decimal point three places to the left.

$97 \text{ mL} = \boxed{} \text{ L} \qquad 97 \div 1,000 = 0.097 \qquad 97 \text{ mL} = 0.097 \text{ L}$

Multiplying by 1,000 is equivalent to moving the decimal point three places to the right.

$52 \text{ L} = \boxed{} \text{ mL} \qquad 52 \times 1,000 = 52,000 \qquad 52 \text{ L} = 52,000 \text{ mL}$

Check Understanding

Write *mL* or *L* as the more appropriate unit of measurement.

  a. A full tank of gasoline   b. The amount of vanilla in a recipe

Write the most reasonable measurement.

  c. The milk for a bowl of cereal   d. The hot pepper sauce in a recipe
    12 mL   120 mL   1.2 L   1 mL   100 mL   1 L

Compute.

  e. $8 \text{ L} = \boxed{} \text{ mL}$ f. $7.5 \text{ mL} = \boxed{} \text{ L}$ g. $0.49 \text{ L} = \boxed{} \text{ mL}$ h. $150 \text{ mL} = \boxed{} \text{ L}$

Choose the more appropriate unit of measurement. Write *mL* or *L*.

1. The amount of water in a hot tub
2. A sip of punch
3. A drop of contact lens solution
4. The amount of water in a fish tank

Write the letter of the most reasonable measurement.

5. Enough water to fill a bathtub
   a. 1 L
   b. 10 L
   c. 100 L

6. One dosage of nose spray
   a. 0.5 mL
   b. 50 mL
   c. 0.5 L

7. A serving of ice cream
   a. 2 mL
   b. 2 L
   c. 200 mL

8. A cyclist's full water bottle
   a. 1 mL
   b. 1 L
   c. 10 L

Compute.

9. 7 L = ▓ mL
10. 30 mL = ▓ L
11. 473 mL = ▓ L
12. 0.081 L = ▓ mL
13. 0.6 mL = ▓ L
14. 2.8 L = ▓ mL
15. 18 L = ▓ mL
16. 24 mL = ▓ L

17. Miss Canon is mixing paint for her class to paint pictures of animals in the wild. The directions say one cup of powdered paint will make 0.25 L. How many cups are needed to make 2 liters?

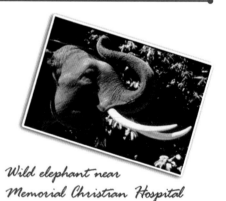

18. Elephants need a lot of drinking water, so they are restricted to habitats where there is an adequate water supply. If an elephant drank 3,000 mL in one gulp, how many liters would it have consumed?

Wild elephant near Memorial Christian Hospital

250 mL
200
150
100
50

19. Martha is making a chocolate pudding recipe. It calls for one liter of whole milk. If she uses the measuring cup on the left, how many times should she fill the cup to the 250 mL line?

20. Mrs. Watts poured a cup of coffee. Is a cup of coffee closer to 250 milliters or 250 liters?

Write the answer in simplest form.

1. $\frac{8}{9} \times \frac{1}{5}$
2. $\frac{3}{8} \times \frac{6}{11}$
3. $\frac{4}{5} + \frac{3}{4} + \frac{3}{10}$
4. $\frac{7}{8} - \frac{2}{5}$
5. $\frac{9}{12} \div \frac{3}{4}$

Lesson 158

Construct Meaning

Is it weight, mass, or does it matter? In science class Cameron learned that he would weigh a different amount on Mars. A weighing scale indicates the gravitational pull on a person toward Earth. **Mass** is the measure of how much matter is in an object. Cameron's weight would change from planet to planet, but his mass would remain the same.

The basic unit of mass in the metric system is a gram.

Metric Units of Mass
1,000 milligrams (mg) = 1 gram (g)
1,000 grams = 1 kilogram (kg)

 a grain of salt

1 milligram   **1 gram**   **1 kilogram**

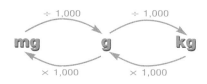

To convert to a larger unit, divide by 1,000 which means to move the decimal point three places to the left.

To convert to a smaller unit, multiply by 1,000 which means to move the decimal point three places to the right.

Cameron's mother read the Nutrition Facts on a package of blueberry muffins. In one muffin there are 40 milligrams of cholesterol and 24 grams of carbohydrates.

40 mg = ▢ g
24 g = ▢ mg

Was the gram count higher in cholesterol or carbohydrates?

Understand the relationship between volume, capacity, and mass.

Volume is the number of cubic units that fill a three-dimensional space.	Capacity is the volume expressed in terms of liquid measurement.	Mass is a measure of how much matter is in an object.
1 cubic centimeter	**1 milliliter**	**1 gram**

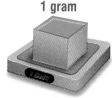

1 cubic centimeter of water has a capacity of 1 milliliter and a mass of 1 gram.

Check Understanding

Write *mg*, *g*, or, *kg* to select the most appropriate unit of measurement.
a. person   b. calculator   c. ladybug   d. plum   e. bicycle   f. stamp

Write the most reasonable measurement.
g. A box of cereal
   500 mg   500 g   500 kg

h. The amount of iron in a multivitamin
   27 mg   27 g   27 kg

340

Compute.

i. 3 g = ⬚ mg   j. 6,000 g = ⬚ kg   k. 450 mg = ⬚ kg

Write *mass*, *capacity*, or *volume*.

l. A cube that is 1 cm on each side has a ⬚ of 1 cubic centimeter.

m. A cubic centimeter has a ⬚ of 1 milliliter.

n. A cubic centimeter of water has a ⬚ of 1 gram.

 **Practice**

Write *mg*, *g*, or *kg* to select the most appropriate unit of measurement.

1. An ant   2. A big rock   3. A slice of cheese   4. A toothpick   5. A cracker

Write the most reasonable measurement.

6. A comb
   16 mg   16 g   16 kg

7. A dollar bill
   300 mg   300 g   300 kg

8. A newborn baby
   4 mg   4 g   4 kg

9. A bag of sugar
   2.27 mg   2.27 g   2.27 kg

Compute.

10. 57 g = ⬚ kg   11. 802 mg = ⬚ g   12. 1.92 kg = ⬚ g   13. 0.0059 kg = ⬚ mg

Complete.

14. A container holds 136 cubic centimeters of water. It has a capacity of ⬚ milliliters. The water has a mass of ⬚ grams.

 Apply

15. The Barnett family has two pet dogs. Their poodle has a mass of 5.75 kg and their terrier has a mass of 11,800 g. What is the total mass of both pets?

16. A can of corn has a mass of 497 grams. If the empty can has a mass of 65 grams, how many grams of corn are in the can?

17. A bag of tortilla chips has a mass of 382.7 grams. What is its mass in milligrams? in kilograms?

 **Review**

1. 6.4 + 413.77 + 0.089   2. 0.94 − 0.817   3. 1.7 × 0.38   4. 9.69 ÷ 1.7

Construct Meaning

"Excellence in Products and Services" is the motto for Mr. Watson's computer company. He explains to his clients that computers use a system of binary numbers.

Here is a procedure that models binary numbers. Take one foot of ribbon, double it, then double those, and double those.

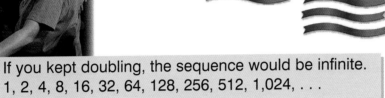

If you kept doubling, the sequence would be infinite.
1, 2, 4, 8, 16, 32, 64, 128, 256, 512, 1,024, . . .

In the binary system of numbers, there are only two digits: 0 and 1. Computers read electric signals that represent 1's and 0's. Each place value in the binary system represents a power of two.

The base ten system uses ten digits. Each place value is a power of ten.

10^3	10^2	10^1	10^0
1,000	100	10	1

The base two system uses two digits. Each place value is a power of two.

2^3	2^2	2^1	2^0
8	4	2	1

Think of a light bulb. If it is on, it represents 1 of that place value. If it is off, it represents a 0 for that place value.

Base ten number	Binary Place Value				Binary number
	8	4	2	1	
1					0001
2					0010
3					0011
4					0100
5					0101
6					0110
7					0111
8					1000
9					1001
10					1010

Check Understanding

Write the base ten number and the binary number shown.

a.

8	4	2	1

b.

16	8	4	2	1

c.

32	16	8	4	2	1

Write the base ten number for each binary number.

d. 10101   e. 11011   f. 110011   g. 1011

Do you know where computer scientists got the term *bit*, which means a single unit of information? (Hint: Look at the words *bi*nary digi*t*.)

Chapter Thirteen Study Guide

Find the sum or difference. *Lesson 151*

1. 3 hr 29 min
    + 5 hr 45 min

2. 17 min 14 sec
    − 9 min 36 sec

Write the elapsed time. *Lesson 151*

3. 7:08 A.M. to 12:19 P.M.

4. 5:37 P.M. to 7:26 P.M.

Solve. *Lesson 152*

5. 9 yd 2 ft
    + 6 yd 2 ft

6. 30 ft   9 in.
    − 18 ft 11 in.

7. 4 mi =   ft
8. 110 in. =   yd   in.
9. 63 ft =   yd

Solve. *Lesson 153*

10. 8T 1400 lb
     − 4T 1700 lb

11. 24 lb 13 oz
     − 17 lb 11 oz

12. 60 oz =   lb   oz
13. $2\frac{1}{2}$ T =   lb
14. 16 lb =   oz

Solve. *Lesson 154*

15. 24 qt 2 c
     − 19 qt 3 c

16. 5 gal 3 qt
     + 3 gal 2 qt

17. 3 qt =   c
18. $\frac{1}{2}$ gal =   pt
19. 9 tsp =   tbsp

Find the difference between the high and low temperatures. *Lesson 155*
20. Frankfurt, Germany   high: 37°C   low: −8°C

Write *multiply* and *divide* to complete the sentences.
21. When converting from a smaller unit of measure to a larger unit, you   .
    When converting from a larger unit to a smaller unit, you   .

Compute.
22. 9 cm =   mm
23. 723 m =   km *Lesson 156*
24. 4 L =   mL
25. 75 mL =   L *Lesson 157*
26. 6 g =   kg
27. 317 mg =   g *Lesson 158*

Write the base ten number for the binary number.
Draw a base two place value chart if needed.
28. 1100   *Lesson 159*
29. 0101
30. 10111

Praise Him for His mighty acts;
Praise Him according to His
excellent greatness! Psalm 150:2

Measured by Excellence

Select the letter of the equivalent unit of measurement.

1. 5,280 feet
2. 100 centimeters
3. 8 fluid ounces
4. 2,000 pounds
5. 1,000 grams

a. 1 cup
b. 1 kilogram
c. 1 ton
d. 1 meter
e. 1 mile

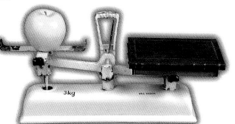

Find the sum or difference.

6.
```
   6 hr 25 min
+  3 hr 48 min
```

7.
```
  14 min 26 sec
−  8 min 39 sec
```

8.
```
  6 ft 4 in.
− 5 ft 9 in.
```

9.
```
  9 lb  2 oz
− 6 lb 10 oz
```

10.
```
  6 T   238 lb
+ 1 T 1,961 lb
```

11.
```
  9 T 248 lb
− 5 T 786 lb
```

12.
```
  5 gal 3 qt
+ 3 gal 2 qt
```

13.
```
  11 qt 1 pt
−  8 qt
```

14.
```
  4 gal 3 qt 1 pt
+ 1 gal 2 qt 1 pt
```

Write the elapsed time.

15. Pizza was ordered at 5:39 P.M. and delivered at 6:26 P.M.

Choose the most likely temperature required for each.

16. Friends tossing snowballs	27°F	80°F	29°C
17. Children wearing wool coats	62°F	8°C	78°F
18. People riding in a canoe	92°F	10°C	38°F
19. Oven temperature for baking cookies	40°C	212°F	350°F
20. Preschoolers running in the sprinklers	38°F	35°C	50°F

Choose the most appropriate unit of measurement.

21. The length of a large whale	inches	feet	miles
22. The mass of a gnat	milligrams	grams	kilograms
23. The weight of a pear	pounds	ounces	tons
24. The amount of milk in a large pitcher	milliliters	liters	tablespoons
25. The amount of water in a swimming pool	gallons	fluid ounces	milliliters
26. The distance between Washington, D.C., and San Francisco, California	centimeters	meters	kilometers

Write the letter of the most reasonable measurement.

27. The weight of a cat   **a.** 13 c   **b.** 13 lb   **c.** 13 T
28. Capacity of a glass of milk   **a.** 8 pt   **b.** 8 tsp   **c.** 8 fl oz
29. The length of a cell phone   **a.** 9.5 cm   **b.** 9.5 m   **c.** 9.5 ft
30. An amount of ink in a pen   **a.** 3 c   **b.** 3 L   **c.** 3 mL
31. The weight of a sports utility vehicle   **a.** 2 kg   **b.** 2 T   **c.** 2 lb

Compute.

32. 3 yd =   ft
33. 6 L =   mL
34. 5,295 ft =   mi   yd
35. 2,400 mL =   L
36. 4 lb =   oz
37. 168 in. =   ft
38. 100 oz =   lb   oz
39. 7 pt =   c
40. $2\frac{1}{2}$ T =   lb
41. 80 cm =   mm
42. 3 gal 8 qt =   gal
43. 18,000 mg =   g
44. 5,000 m =   km
45. $2\frac{1}{4}$ gal =   qt

Solve.

46. Patty invited her friends to watch two videos at a sleepover. One video was 127 minutes long and the other was 185 minutes long. It is now 7:45 P.M. and they have to be in bed by 1:00 A.M. Will Patty and her friends have enough time to view both videos?

47. Which is a better buy, 3 quarts of ice cream for $1.89 or 5 pints for $1.89?

48. Bruce is building a fenced-in area for his dog. He has fencing that is 20 ft 8 in. long. He needs fencing that is 18 ft 10 in. long. How much should be trimmed off to have the length he needs?

49. Before the race, Daryl hydrated by drinking one liter of water. How many milliliters is this?

50. Josh is 125 centimeters tall. Rob is 1.5 meters tall. Who is taller?

Chapter Theme

God said that He desires for mankind to have dominion over all that He created. Have you ever reflected on the meaning of dominion in this context? The chapter 14 theme of Stewards of Creation will give you an opportunity to consider what your responsibilities are as a Christian living among all that God created. Dominion of the earth and God's creatures does not imply selfishness or carelessness. The enjoyment and use of the earth's resources and animals are complex issues that require study. Psalm 111:2 says, "The works of the LORD are great, studied by all who have pleasure in them." Give praise to God daily for what He has given us. Pray that Christians will be part of the process of developing and preserving God's creation in ways that please Him.

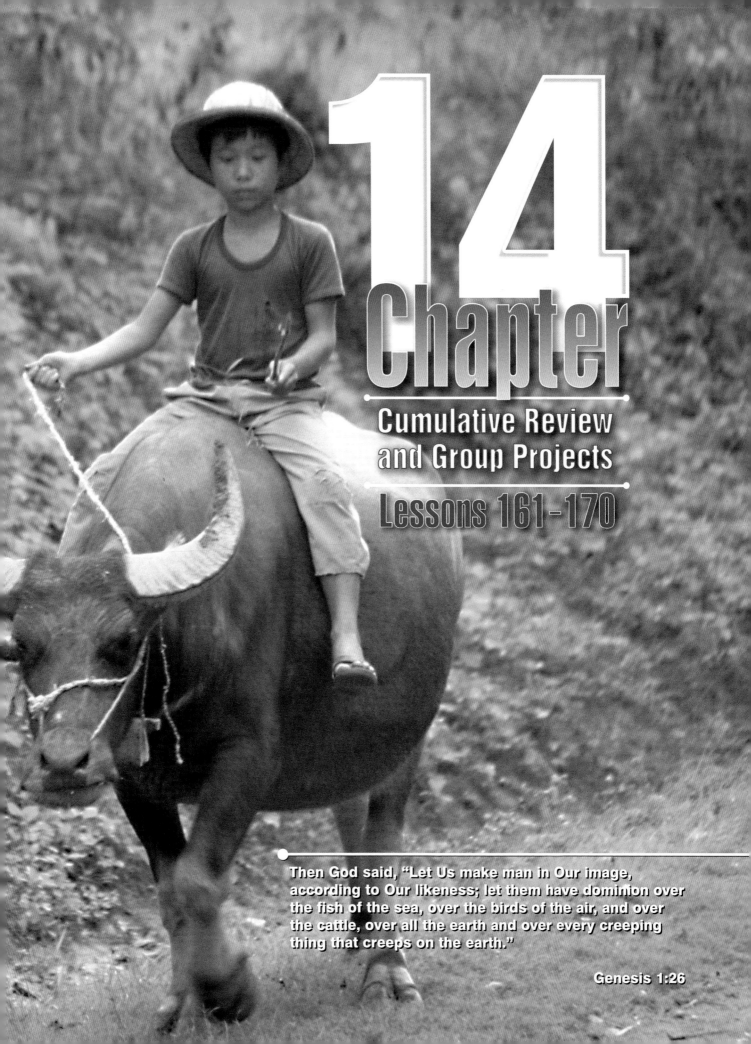

14

Chapter

Cumulative Review and Group Projects

Lessons 161-170

Then God said, "Let Us make man in Our image, according to Our likeness; let them have dominion over the fish of the sea, over the birds of the air, and over the cattle, over all the earth and over every creeping thing that creeps on the earth."

Genesis 1:26

Lesson 161

Write the letter of the addition property illustrated by each number sentence.

a. Associative (Grouping) Property
b. Zero Property
c. Commutative (Order) Property

1. $36 + 0 = 36$
2. $14 + 20 = 20 + 14$
3. $53.1 + (5.43 + 2.19) = (53.1 + 5.43) + 2.19$
4. $2 + 8 + 7 = 8 + 2 + 7$

Solve for n.

5. $n - 53 = 142$
6. $83 + n = 99$
7. $n + 14 = 23$
8. $n - 249 = 101$

Solve.

9. $14.036 - 9.8$
10. $0.6 - 0.003$
11. $442,319 + 9,222$
12. $942 - 618$
13. $303.89 + 14.031$
14. $4036.8 - 4014.28$
15. $8.1 + 2.36 + 4.03$
16. $30,421 - 21,801$

Write using exponents.

17. $3 \times 3 \times 3 \times 6 \times 6 \times 6$
18. $5 \times 5 \times 5 \times 5 \times 5$
19. 4 to the sixth power

Write in scientific notation.

20. 50,252

Find the greatest common factor.

21. 16 and 48
22. 21 and 63
23. 81 and 9
24. 12 and 54

Write the letter of the multiplication property illustrated by each number sentence.

25. $6 \times (4 \times 8) = (6 \times 4) \times 8$
26. $14 \times (2 + 5) = (14 \times 2) + (14 \times 5)$
27. $23 \times 1 = 23$

a. Distributive Property
b. Multiplication Identity Property of One
c. Associative Property of Multiplication

Solve.

28. To be a member of the Safari Club, Jonathan has to pay $85 a month for the first year and $70 a month each following year. If Jonathan has been a member for four years, how much money has he paid to the club?

29. Hillary's Safari wagons seat five people each. How many wagons will be needed to seat 114 people?

Tyger, Tyger, burning bright
In the forest of the night,
What immortal hand or eye
Could frame thy fearful symmetry?
excerpt from *The Tyger*
by William Blake

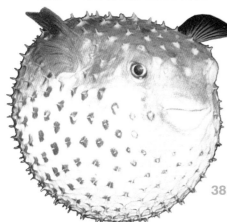

Find the average.

30. 72   83   99   100

31. 15   20   13   18   15

Divide.

32. 5,600 ÷ 80

33. 300 ÷ 75

34. 350,000 ÷ 7,000

35. $8\overline{)96}$

36. $30\overline{)2,760}$

37. $4\overline{)7.68}$

38. $9\overline{)45,108}$

39. $0.09\overline{)0.468}$

Solve.

40. The company Christmas dinner cost $3,412.50. If the average cost per meal was $18.75, how many employees attended the Christmas dinner?

41. Mary Ann has $815 in her savings account. She purchased new binoculars and will have payments of $30 a month for six months. How much money will remain in Mary Ann's account after she has paid for the binoculars?

42. $72\overline{)1,080}$

43. $0.32\overline{)38.4}$

44. $26\overline{)1.0738}$

45. $7.25\overline{)0.29}$

Use the correct order of operations to solve.

46. $15 + 8 \times 2 = y$

47. $20 - 6 \div 2 + 5 \times 4 = n$

48. $(7 \times 8) + 6 = a$

He clasps the crag
with crooked hands;
Close to the sun in
lonely lands,
Ring'd with the azure
world, he stands.

The wrinkled sea
beneath him crawls;
He watches from his
mountain walls,
And like a thunderbolt
he falls.

The Eagle
by Alfred,
Lord Tennyson

Solve.

49. If a six-pack of root beer costs $1.35, estimate the price per can using compatible numbers. How much would three cans cost?

50. Joyel attends a college where the yearly total cost is $13,800. She received a $1,800 scholarship, which is deducted from the total bill. What monthly amount will Joyel pay if the amount is spread over nine months?

Write the letter of the correct word for each definition.

1. An angle having a measure less than 90°
2. Lines in a plane that never intersect
3. The distance around a polygon
4. The relationship between map distance and actual distance
5. An angle having a measure of 90°
6. A part of a line between two endpoints
7. The circumference of a circle divided by the diameter
8. The number of square units that cover a surface
9. An angle that measures 180°
10. A two-dimensional flat surface that extends without end in all directions

a. perimeter
b. right angle
c. line segment
d. area
e. parallel
f. plane
g. acute angle
h. scale
i. π
j. straight angle

Write *true* or *false*.

11. An equilateral triangle has at least one obtuse angle.
12. A scalene triangle has no congruent sides.
13. A right triangle has one right angle.
14. Congruent line segments can be different lengths.
15. The sum of the measures of two supplementary angles is 180°.
16. A quadrilateral must have four right angles.
17. The bisector of an angle divides it into two congruent angles.
18. A trapezoid is a quadrilateral having only one pair of parallel sides.
19. A prism is a polyhedron with only one base.
20. All squares are rectangles.

Use the circle diagram for problems 21 through 25.

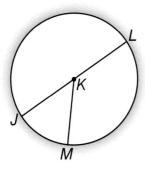

21. Name a diameter.
22. If $\overline{JL}$ is 2 cm, what is the radius of circle K?
23. What is the circumference of circle K?
24. What is the area of circle K?
25. If $\angle JKM$ measures 50°, what is the measure of $\angle MKL$?

Use the triangle diagram for problems 26 through 31.

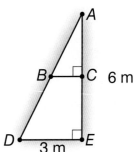

26. Name two similar triangles.
27. Which angle is congruent to $\angle ABC$?
28. If $\overline{AC} \cong \overline{CE}$, what is the length of $\overline{BC}$?
29. If the length of $\overline{AB}$ is 3.35, what is the perimeter of $\triangle ABC$?
30. What is the area of $\triangle ADE$?
31. If the measure of $\angle A$ is 25°, what is the measure of $\angle D$?

Find the missing measurements.

32. $P =$
33. $A =$

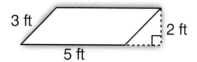

1½ in.
4 in.

34. $P =$
35. $A =$

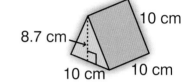

3 ft
2 ft
5 ft

36. What is the volume of a box that measures 2 feet by 3 feet by 6 feet?

37. What is the volume of a cylinder that has a diameter of 10 in. and a height of 5 in.?

38. What is the volume of a triangular prism with the measurements shown?

10 cm
8.7 cm
10 cm   10 cm

39. Find the surface area of the triangular prism in problem 38.

Draw a coordinate grid, labeling each axis. Plot and label the following points.

40. $A(5,4)$
41. $B(1,2)$
42. $C(3,0)$

43. If Kamey measures a distance of 8 inches on her map between two lighthouses, what is the actual distance between them?

SCALE
¼" = 1 mile

Find the sum or difference.

44. 6 hr 35 min
   + 3 hr 45 min

45. 5 pt
   − 2 pt 1 c

46. 8 lb 2 oz
   − 4 lb 8 oz

Complete.

47. 642 g = ___ kg
48. 8 ft = ___ in.
49. 32 qt = ___ gal

50. The oceanography boat left the dock at 7:30 A.M. and returned at 4:00 P.M. How much time elapsed between the boat's departure and return?

Write the fraction represented by the shaded portion of each model.

1.

2.

3.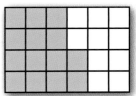

Find the missing number.

4. $\frac{1}{5} = \frac{}{30}$

5. $\frac{8}{9} = \frac{32}{}$

6. $\frac{2}{3} = \frac{}{24}$

7. $\frac{10}{25} = \frac{}{75}$

Simplify.

8. $\frac{12}{36}$

9. $\frac{24}{100}$

10. $\frac{14}{28}$

11. $\frac{3}{9}$

Write each decimal as a fraction in simplest form.

12. 0.375

13. 0.625

14. 0.7

15. $0.\overline{6}$

Solve for the unknown.

16. $y \times 5 = 300$

17. $\frac{n}{42} = 126$

18. Mr. Gerhardt is building a deck $10\frac{3}{4}$ feet long. He purchased boards that are six feet long. To make a length of $10\frac{3}{4}$ feet he will need to use one board and part of another. How long will the second board need to be?

Solve. Write the answer in simplest form.

19. $\frac{3}{8} + \frac{2}{8}$

20. $\frac{5}{6} - \frac{1}{2}$

21. $\frac{1}{2} + \frac{1}{6}$

22. $\frac{1}{4} + \frac{5}{12}$

23. $\quad 4\frac{2}{7}$
$\quad +6\frac{1}{2}$

24. $\quad 5\frac{1}{2}$
$\quad -1\frac{1}{8}$

25. $\quad 9\frac{4}{9}$
$\quad -5\frac{2}{9}$

26. $\quad 6\frac{5}{12}$
$\quad -3\frac{1}{6}$

Estimate by rounding to the nearest whole number.

27. $4\frac{3}{4} + 2\frac{1}{3} + 6\frac{1}{4}$

28. $30\frac{1}{3} - 14\frac{7}{8}$

29. $1\frac{8}{11} - 1\frac{1}{4}$

30. $5\frac{1}{2} + 6\frac{1}{2}$

31. Chana is making a blue outfit. The blouse pattern calls for $2\frac{1}{2}$ yards of fabric and the skirt pattern calls for $3\frac{2}{5}$ yards of fabric. Chana purchased $7\frac{1}{2}$ yards of fabric. How much fabric will be left over?

32. The top shelf in Terran's tool cabinet is 6 ft $4\frac{1}{8}$ in. high. The ceiling of the garage is $7\frac{1}{2}$ feet. Will a 1 ft $\frac{5}{8}$ in. square box fit on the top shelf?

33. A fruit basket contains apples, pears, and nectarines. If $\frac{2}{5}$ are apples and $\frac{1}{4}$ are pears, what fraction are nectarines?

Complete the number sentence represented by each model.

34.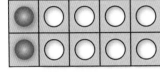

$$\frac{1}{5} \times 10 = \square$$

35.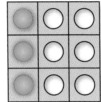

$$\square \times 9 = 3$$

36.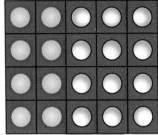

$$\frac{8}{20} \times \square = 8$$

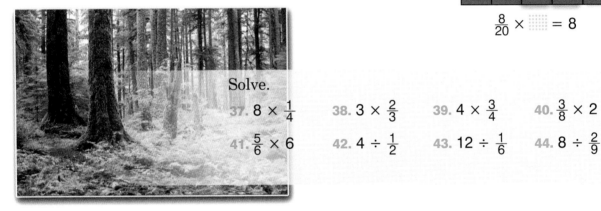

Solve.

37. $8 \times \frac{1}{4}$

38. $3 \times \frac{2}{3}$

39. $4 \times \frac{3}{4}$

40. $\frac{3}{8} \times 2$

41. $\frac{5}{6} \times 6$

42. $4 \div \frac{1}{2}$

43. $12 \div \frac{1}{6}$

44. $8 \div \frac{2}{9}$

Simplify each complex fraction.

45. $\dfrac{\frac{1}{3}}{\frac{1}{2}}$

46. $\dfrac{\frac{2}{5}}{8}$

47. $\dfrac{\frac{3}{4}}{\frac{2}{5}}$

48. $\dfrac{\frac{2}{3}}{4}$

49. Mr. Hous is driving 1,200 miles to his grandparents' house. The first day he plans to drive $\frac{3}{5}$ of the way. How many miles will he need to drive on the second day before arriving at his grandparents' house?

50. Ms. Swaney collected $21\frac{3}{4}$ pounds of bark from trees for a research project. If she divides it evenly between three sample containers, how many pounds will be in each container?

1. Which two points on the number line represent opposite integers?

Write > or <.

2. –5 ▦ 2   3. –3 ▦ 3   4. –12 ▦ (–11)   5. 0 ▦ (–1)

Solve.

6. –1 + 10   7. – 5 + (–12)   8. 4 – (–1)

9. –8 – 6   10. –12 + 3   11. 6 + (–6)

12. 3 – 9   13. 12 – (–11)

Use the coordinate grid.

14. Write the coordinates of *A* as an ordered pair.

15. Which quadrant contains point *B*?

Solve.

16. –2 × 6   17. 12 ÷ (–12)   18. –3 × (–8)   19. 2 × (–7)
20. –12 ÷ (–3)   21. –42 ÷ 6   22. 40 ÷ (–8)   23. –3 × (–3)

24. At 12:00 A.M. the temperature outside was –22°F. During the day the temperature rose a total of 9 degrees and then dropped a total of 12 degrees by 12:00 A.M. the next day. What was the temperature at that time?

25. An engineer started digging a well at an elevation of 13 feet above sea level. The completed well was 25 feet deep. What is the elevation of the bottom of the well?

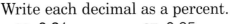

Write each decimal as a percent.
26. 0.31   27. 0.05
28. 1.75   29. 0.785

Write each fraction as a percent.
30. $\frac{4}{10}$ 31. $\frac{3}{5}$
32. $\frac{7}{8}$ 33. $\frac{3}{4}$

Write each percent as a decimal.
34. 21%   35. 110%
36. 70%   37. 9%

Solve.

38. Gregory puts 65% of his earnings into a savings account. Last month he earned $150 for doing yard work. How much money did he deposit in the savings account?

39. Jaymie's savings account earns an annual interest rate of 3%. Her savings account balance is $290. How much interest will she earn in a year?

40. During the after-Christmas sale at the department store, every item will be sold at a 40% discount. If the price of a dress shirt is $30.50, how much will it cost after the discount?

41. 4.8% of the monthly grocery bill of $250 was spent on milk. How much money was used to purchase milk?

Use mental math to estimate.
42. 49% of 81
43. 16% of 40
44. 9% of 20
45. 6% of 25
46. 95% of 102

Solve.
47. $\frac{4}{9} = \frac{20}{n}$
48. $\frac{8}{13} = \frac{n}{39}$
49. $\frac{3}{8} = \frac{45}{n}$
50. $\frac{2}{7} = \frac{n}{84}$

Write the letter of the correct word for each definition.

1. A graph that uses bars to represent how many of a particular item are found in a given interval
2. The average of a set of numbers
3. A graph that uses two sets of bars to represent and compare numbers for several items of the same unit
4. A graph that uses line segments to represent increases or decreases over a period of time
5. The difference between the greatest and least number in a set of numerical data
6. A graph that compares parts of a whole

a. mean
b. histogram
c. line graph
d. range
e. circle graph
f. double bar graph

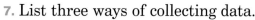

7. List three ways of collecting data.
8. Why is it important to take a random sample when giving a survey?

Use the circle graph to answer the following questions.

9. How much do the Clark's spend on groceries in a year?
10. Which two budget parts account for just under $\frac{1}{3}$ of the budget?
11. Which part has a budget of $778.50 a year?
12. Which two parts have the same budget amount?

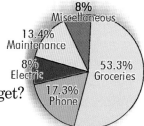

Clark's Yearly Household Budget

8% Miscellaneous
13.4% Maintenance
8% Electric
17.3% Phone
53.3% Groceries

Total: $4,500

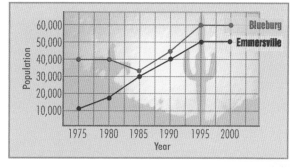

Blueburg
Emmersville

Population
60,000
50,000
40,000
30,000
20,000
10,000
1975 1980 1985 1990 1995 2000
Year

Use the line graph to answer the following questions.

13. What city has the greatest sustained rate of population growth?
14. What city has experienced a loss in population? during which years?
15. Predict each city's population for the year 2005.

Write *true* or *false*.

16. A bar graph always uses intervals of time.
17. The sum of the degrees on a circle graph is 360°.
18. A histogram can be made from a bar graph.
19. When there are two middle numbers in an ordered set of data, the median is the average of the two numbers.
20. More than one <u>type</u> of data can be represented on a bar graph.
21. The horizontal scale of a line graph is usually time.

Write *bar*, *line*, *circle*, or *histogram*.

22. Temperatures of Casablanca, Morocco, for one year
23. Favorite colors of the sixth grade
24. Number of houses priced between $100,000 and $125,000
25. Percentages of England's total exports

Write the letter of the correct word for each definition.

26. The likelihood that a given event will occur
27. An arrangement where order does not matter
28. The middle number in a set of data
29. A ratio of the number of times an event actually occurred to the number of trials
30. A combination of two or more single events
31. A table or list showing all possible outcomes

a. median
b. experimental probability
c. combination
d. probability
e. compound event
f. sample space

The tally table shows the results of 25 rolls of a number cube.

32. What is the mathematical probability for rolling a 4?
33. What is the mathematical probability for rolling a 1?
34. What is the experimental probability for rolling a 3?
35. What is the experimental probability for rolling a 4?

Number Cube Tallies

1	2	3	4	5	6
II	III	III	IIII I	IIII I	IIII

The number cube is rolled twice. Determine the probabilities.
36. $P(1, 4)$
37. $P(5, 5)$
38. $P(\text{even, odd})$
39. $P(\text{odd, 3})$
40. $P(\text{less than 3, 6})$
41. $P(\text{greater than 3, less than 3})$

42. Johnson's Deli offers sandwiches made of four types of bread, five types of meat, and six toppings. How many different sandwiches can be made using one type of bread, one meat, and one topping?

43. Maggie can wear a plaid or red skirt with a white, blue, or yellow shirt to school. Use a sample space to determine all the possible outfits.

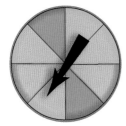

Use the spinner for the following problems.
44. $P(\text{green})$
45. $P(\text{blue})$
46. Which two colors are equally likely to occur?
47. If the spinner is spun 20 times, predict the outcome for orange.
48. Predict the outcome for landing on blue when the spinner is spun 40 times.

Solve.
49. How many possible arrangements can be made with two pattern sticks that are plain on one side and patterned on the other side?
50. If two pattern sticks are tossed, what is the probability that both will land plain side up?

Lesson 166

1. Connie and her friends Peter, Josh, and Annie have formed a band. One person plays the bass, one plays the guitar, one person is the singer, and another person plays the synthesizer. They are eating lunch while seated at a square table in the park.

   Use logic to determine what each person does in the band. Here are your clues:
   • Pete is seated across the table from the bass player.
   • The person on Connie's left is the singer.
   • Annie does not play the bass.
   • The girl on Josh's right is the guitar player.

   Discuss your thinking with a partner and list each person's part in the band.

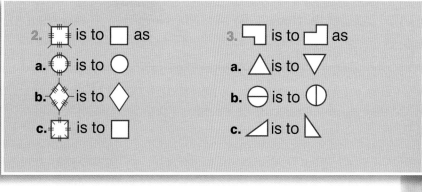

2. ▨ is to □ as
   a. ◯ is to ◯
   b. ◈ is to ◇
   c. ▨ is to □

3. ⌐ is to ¬ as
   a. △ is to ▽
   b. ⊖ is to ⦶
   c. ◿ is to ◺

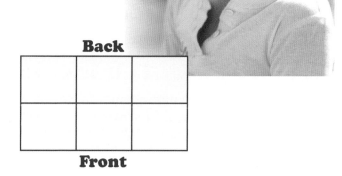

4. Use logic to determine how the six colors are placed on the grid. Draw an identical grid and color it correctly.

Clues

   • Blue is in front of yellow.
   • Red is in between yellow and purple.
   • Blue is adjacent to orange and to yellow.
   • Green has both the blue and the orange to its left.

Back

Front

GOING ACROSS LOGICALLY

Eight American scientists have traveled to Brazil to study the rich diversity of plants and animals in the rain forest. The expedition, which is guided by two young Brazilians, has come to an abrupt halt at the edge of a piranha-infested river. However, one of the Americans, each of whom is over six feet tall and weighs more than 200 pounds, has found an old raft drifting down the river. The members of the group have discovered that, unfortunately, the raft can only bear the weight of one hefty American or two slender guides. Can the raft be used to get everyone across the river? If so, how many crossings will it take to get everyone to the other side?

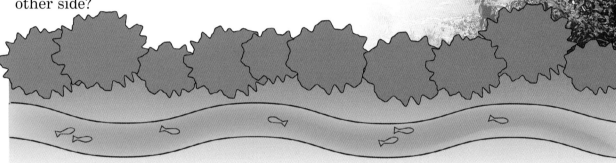

Use two colors of cubes or tiles with one color representing the 8 Americans and the other representing the 2 guides. Move them in the most logical manner across the river, keeping the weight restrictions in mind, to determine the number of crossings necessary.

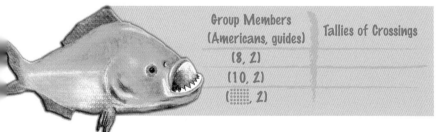

Group Members (Americans, guides)	Tallies of Crossings
(8, 2)	
(10, 2)	
(⠿, 2)	

Construct a tally table like this one. Make a mark in the row to show each time the raft crosses the river in either direction.

CROSSINGS QUESTION ONE: How many trips will it take to get the eight Americans and two guides to the other side?

CROSSINGS QUESTION TWO: Find the number of crossings necessary if the group has ten Americans and two guides.

CROSSINGS QUESTION THREE: Set up your own group with a specific number of Americans and two guides. Find the number of crossings needed.

CROSSINGS QUESTION FOUR: Identify the rule you observed that allowed you to know the number of crossings as soon as you knew the number of Americans in the group.

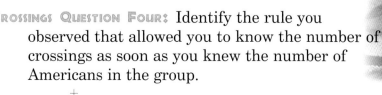

Construct Meaning

Skill and training are required for building structures that are able to withstand the pressures of use and natural forces. Knowledge of geometry is required to construct anything from a house to a bridge.

Work in groups of three. Use masking tape, craft sticks, newspaper, straws, or other construction materials to construct the following polygons.

triangle

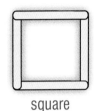

square

pentagon

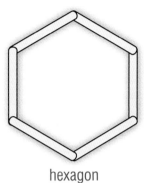

hexagon

Compare the following features of the shapes.
- The number of angles
- The size of the angles
- The number of sides
- The length of the sides

Place the hexagon perpendicular to a table and press down slightly on the top of the shape. Observe the measures of the angles as pressure is applied.

Do the measures of the angles change as you press down?

Can you apply much pressure before the shape collapses?

Repeat the exercise for each shape. Which shape appears to be the strongest? Explain.

The triangle is the strongest shape. When pressure is applied to the top, the weight is disbursed down the sides of the triangle. The third side holds the angles rigid. When an object is **rigid,** it is stiff or unyielding and maintains its shape.

For this reason, triangles are used in constructing a truss in a building or a bridge.

There are many styles of bridge construction such as beam and truss, suspension, or arch. The style of the bridge to be built depends on the span it must cross, the load it must carry, the clearance below the bridge, cost, and appearance.

1. You and the members of your group will build a bridge of your own design.

Materials
50 craft sticks
masking tape

Goal
To design and build a bridge that will span 12 inches and withstand the pressure of textbooks placed on its top

Rules
- The bridge must be at least three craft sticks long.
- There is a limit of 50 craft sticks per group.
- The bridge must be structurally sound and able to stand on its own.

2. Decide ahead of time how the testing of the bridges will be conducted. Will you gently add textbooks one at a time just until the bridge begins to show signs of breaking or until it collapses? Test your bridge.

Possible Designs

The 503-meter Sydney Harbour Bridge in Australia is the fourth longest steel arch bridge in the world.

Lesson 168

Fermi problems are named after Enrico Fermi, who was a Nobel Prize-winning physicist. Fermi asked his students unique and seemingly impossible questions that were designed to help them learn to think for themselves. A **Fermi problem** is a problem where the exact information needed to solve the problem is not given, but a reasonable answer can be obtained.

Strategies for Fermi Problems:
1. Break the problem into smaller parts.
2. Make estimates and assumptions.
3. Devise a method. Several methods can lead to one reasonable answer.

How many ping-pong balls will fill a medium-sized soft suitcase?

- Break the problem into smaller parts.
  What is the size of a ping-pong ball?
  What is the size of a medium-sized soft suitcase?
- Make an assumption about the size of the ping-pong ball.

$1\frac{1}{2}$-inch diameter (approximate)

Make an assumption about the size of the suitcase.

24 in. × 16 in. × 10 in.

- Devise your method by reasoning: We have round objects fitting into a square object. How can I simplify the problem and still make an accurate estimate?

Use a $1\frac{1}{2}$-inch cube instead of a ping-pong ball.

The original question becomes: How many $1\frac{1}{2}$-inch cubes will fit into a 24 in. by 16 in. by 10 in. suitcase? Round to the nearest whole number.

Number of cubes $= \dfrac{\text{volume of suitcase}}{\text{volume of cube}} = \dfrac{24 \text{ in.} \times 16 \text{ in.} \times 10 \text{ in.}}{1.5 \text{ in.} \times 1.5 \text{ in.} \times 1.5 \text{ in.}} = \dfrac{3{,}840 \text{ cu in.}}{3.375 \text{ cu in.}} = 1{,}138 \text{ cubes}$

What could you do to make your estimate more accurate?
Assume that because ping-pong balls are spheres, 1,138 may fill only 80% of the suitcase. How many ping-pong balls would fill the entire suitcase?

$$80\% \text{ of } x = \text{ping-pong balls}$$
$$0.80\, x = 1{,}138$$
$$\dfrac{0.80\, x}{0.80} = \dfrac{1{,}138}{0.80}$$

1,423 ping-pong balls would fill the suitcase.

$$x = 1{,}422.5$$

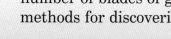

a. Work in groups of three to consider the following question. What is the total number of blades of grass in an average-sized front yard? Discuss various methods for discovering a reasonable answer.

Answer the following questions in your group. Write down every part of your strategy for solving each problem.

1. How many jelly beans will fit in a one-liter jar?

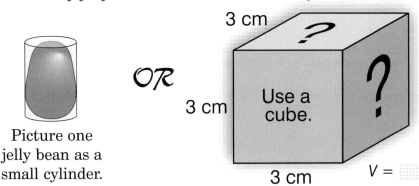

Picture one jelly bean as a small cylinder.

3 cm

OR

3 cm   Use a cube.   ?

3 cm   V =

1 liter is 1,000 cu cm

2. How many standard ballpoint pens would it take to draw a straight line around the equator of the earth?

Circumference at the equator: 24,901.55 miles

3. How many 8 $\frac{1}{2}$" by 11" sheets of paper will your math class use in one school year?

4. How many square inches of pizza is consumed by your sixth grade class in one school year?

The diameter of a medium pizza may be 14 inches.

5. How many six-sided number cubes will fit in your classroom?

Mr. Splurge was quite upset when he calculated the amount of money spent on last year's family vacation. This year the four members of the Splurge family will stay within a budget for their vacation by traveling to the nearby city of Conservationville, spending one night in a reasonably priced hotel, and spending only one day at one of the attractions close to Conservationville.

The Splurge family consists of Mr. and Mrs. Splurge and Charlie and Charlotte, the eleven-year-old twins. Your task is to plan and record on paper their family day by following these guidelines:

- The maximum budget is $275.

- Select a motel to spend one night.

- Choose meals from the menu for each person—breakfast and dinner or only dinner (depending on the motel you select).

- Select one attraction to visit, and purchase souvenirs and activities found at that attraction.

- Do not plan for lunch. The family has sack lunches prepared.

When the activity is complete, compare with others in the class. If your budget was reduced to $225, how would your selections change?

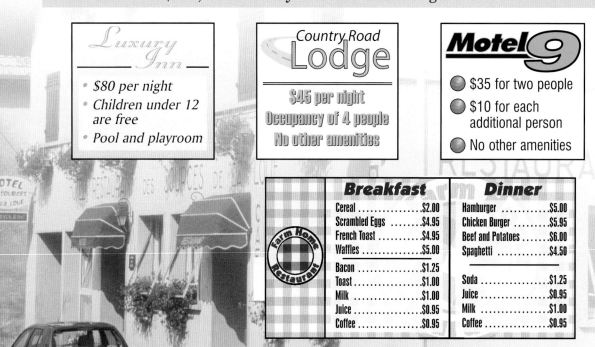

Luxury Inn
- *$80 per night*
- *Children under 12 are free*
- *Pool and playroom*

Country Road Lodge
$45 per night
Occupancy of 4 people
No other amenities

Motel 9
- $35 for two people
- $10 for each additional person
- No other amenities

Farm Home Restaurant

Breakfast		Dinner	
Cereal	$2.00	Hamburger	$5.00
Scrambled Eggs	$4.95	Chicken Burger	$5.95
French Toast	$4.95	Beef and Potatoes	$6.00
Waffles	$5.00	Spaghetti	$4.50
Bacon	$1.25		
Toast	$1.00	Soda	$1.25
Milk	$1.00	Juice	$0.95
Juice	$0.95	Milk	$1.00
Coffee	$0.95	Coffee	$0.95

ENTRANCE FEE
$35 PER PERSON

FAMILY PHOTO
WITH COSTUMES $13.00
WITHOUT COSTUMES $10.00

SOUVENIRS
BOARD GAME $30.00
MUG $5.00

SPECIAL EVENT
KNIGHTS OF WONDER
$5.00 PER PERSON

ENTRANCE FEE
$30 ADULTS
$20 CHILDREN UNDER 18

FAMILY PHOTO
WITH ANIMAL $15.00
WITHOUT ANIMAL $10.00

SOUVENIRS
STUFFED ANIMAL $8.00
WILD ANIMAL BOOK $12.00

SPECIAL EVENT
HUG THE KOALA
$3.00 PER PERSON

ENTRANCE FEE
$40 PER PERSON
CHILDREN UNDER 12
HALF PRICE

FAMILY PHOTO
$10.00

SOUVENIRS
COMPUTER GAME $45.00
T-SHIRT $15.00

SPECIAL EVENT
TECHNO ROLLER COASTER
$3.00 PER PERSON

Many games require thinking and strategizing in order to play, and often the player who has thought through his or her strategy will be the most successful.

Let's do some strategizing!

Quash Tactics

Materials
15 blue and 15 yellow color tiles
3 six-sided number cubes
2 to 5 players

How to Play:
1. Blue color tiles represent 1 and yellow color tiles represent –1. When you have a pair of one blue and one yellow, they quash each other and become zero. You may remove the pair from your playing area by placing them in the center pile at any time.

$$\blacksquare + \square = 0 \qquad \blacksquare\blacksquare + \square\square = 0$$
$$1 + -1 \qquad\qquad 2 + -2$$

2. Make a pile of 15 tiles of each color in the center of your group's playing area. Use 30 tiles of each color if playing in groups of four or five. Each individual is a team.

3. Take turns rolling three number cubes. The game ends after each person has seven turns.

4. On each turn, take the sum of any combination of cubes in any combination of color tiles.

For example: Roll  possible combinations:

3	6	9 and 5	5
5	6	11 and 3	3
3	5	8 and 6	6

- Decide on the best combination. In this case, it would be taking 8 blue and 6 yellow color tiles, or 8 yellow and 6 blue color tiles.
- Remove 6 blue and 6 yellow because 6 + (–6) = 0
- You are left with 2 blue.

8 blue   6 yellow   =   2 blue

5. After each player has seven turns, the player with zero tiles or the fewest tiles wins.

As a class, discuss the strategies you used while playing Quash. Play the variations.

Variations:
- Each player starts with five tiles of any one color.

- Odd-numbered sums can be taken only in blue tiles and even-numbered sums can be taken only in yellow tiles. (You may need additional tiles. This variation is more difficult.)

How does using either variation change your strategy?

The Last Straw

Materials:
10 straws
2 players

How to Play:
- Players alternate turns.
- Each player can draw only one or two straws on a turn.
- The player who takes the last straw is the winner.

Variation:
Each player starts with ten straws and adds either one straw or two straws to the pile on one turn. The player who puts the twelfth straw in the pile is the winner.

Devise a winning strategy for the game and one for the variation. Explain why it will always work. A **winning strategy** is a method for one player to win no matter what the other player does.

3-D Tic-Tac-Toe

Three-dimensional Tic-Tac-Toe can be very challenging. Three variations of the game are shown here. The goal is to get 3 (or 4, depending on the version) in a row, horizontally, vertically, or diagonally on one plane or across all three (or four) planes. Use the grids provided by your teacher to play with a partner.

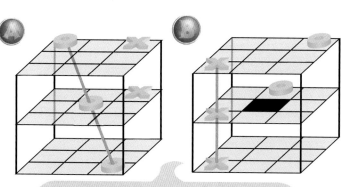

Version B has a block in the center space. This space cannot be used.

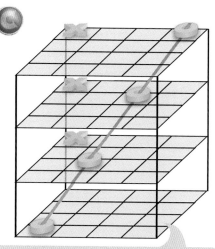

Version C has four planes. Be sure to visualize your moves carefully.

Table of Measures

Customary Units

Temperature
in Degrees Fahrenheit (°F)
32°F = freezing point of water
212°F = boiling point of water
98.6°F = normal body temperature

Length
12 inches (in.) = 1 foot (ft)
3 feet = 1 yard (yd)
36 inches = 1 yard
5,280 feet = 1 mile (mi)
1,760 yards = 1 mile

Weight
16 ounces (oz) = 1 pound (lb)
2,000 pounds = 1 ton (T)

Capacity
3 teaspoons (tsp) = 1 tablespoon (tbsp)
2 tablespoons = 1 fluid ounce (fl oz)
8 fluid ounces = 1 cup (c)
2 cups = 1 pint (pt)
2 pints = 1 quart (qt)
4 quarts = 1 gallon (gal)

Metric Units

Temperature
in Degrees Celsius (°C)
0°C = freezing point of water
100°C = boiling point of water
37°C = normal body temperature

Length
10 millimeters (mm) = 1 centimeter (cm)
10 centimeters = 1 decimeter (dm)
1,000 millimeters = 1 meter (m)
100 centimeters = 1 meter
10 decimeters = 1 meter
1,000 meters = 1 kilometer (km)

Mass
1,000 milligrams (mg) = 1 gram (g)
1,000 grams = 1 kilogram (kg)

Capacity
1,000 milliliters (mL) = 1 liter (L)

Units of Time

60 seconds (sec) = 1 minute (min)
60 minutes = 1 hour (hr)
24 hours = 1 day (d)
7 days = 1 week (wk)
about 4 weeks = 1 month (mo)
365 days = 1 year (yr)
52 weeks = 1 year
12 months = 1 year
366 days in a leap year
10 years = 1 decade
100 years = 1 century
1,000 years = 1 millennium

Formulas

Perimeter   polygon $P = $ sum of the lengths of the sides
            rectangle $P = 2b + 2h$
            square $P = 4s$

Circumference   circle $C = \pi d = 2\pi r$

Area   parallelogram $A = bh$
        rectangle $A = bh$
        square $A = s^2$
        triangle $A = \frac{1}{2} bh$
        circle $A = \pi r^2$

Volume   rectangular prism $V = l \times w \times h$
        cube $V = s^3$
        triangular prism $V = \frac{1}{2} bh' \times h$
        cylinder $V = \pi r^2 \times h$

Symbols

$+$	plus or positive	$\bullet A$	point A
$-$	minus or negative	$\overleftrightarrow{AB}$	line AB
$\times$	times	$\overline{AB}$	line segment AB
$\cdot$	times	$\overrightarrow{AB}$	ray AB
$\div$	divided by	$\angle B$	angle B
$<$	is less than	$\angle ABC$	angle ABC
$>$	is greater than	$\triangle ABC$	triangle ABC
$=$	is equal to	$\mathscr{P}$	plane $\mathscr{P}$
$\neq$	is not equal to	π	pi ($\pi \approx 3.14$)
$\approx$	is approximately equal to	(a,b)	ordered pair with x-coordinate a
$\circ$	degree		and y-coordinate b
$\%$	percent	$a{:}b$	ratio of a to b or $\frac{a}{b}$
$\parallel$	is parallel to	$P(E)$	the probability of event E
$\perp$	is perpendicular to	$n!$	n factorial
$\cong$	is congruent to	$\sqrt{x}$	the square root of x
$\llcorner$	right angle	x^n	x to the nth power

© Copyright 2002

Grade Six

abundant number A number having a proper factor sum greater than the number itself. (p. 152)

acute angle An angle that measures less than 90°. (p. 102)

acute triangle A triangle with three acute (less than 90°) angles. (p. 106)

addend A number added to one or more other numbers.

addition The mathematical operation that combines two or more addends to obtain a sum.

algebraic expression A mathematical phrase that uses numbers and symbols. Contains at least one variable and one operation symbol. (p. 56)

A.M. *Ante meridiem*. The time period beginning at midnight and continuing until noon. (p. 326)

angle An angle is formed by two rays with a common endpoint. (p. 102)

area The number of square units that cover a surface. (p. 228)

Associative (Grouping) Property of Addition Grouping addends differently does not change the sum. (p. 12) (6 + 2) + 5 = 6 + (2 + 5)

Associative (Grouping) Property of Multiplication The grouping of factors may change without changing the product. (p. 34) (3 × 2) × 6 = 3 × (2 × 6)

average The sum of the values in a set of data divided by the number of values. Also called the *mean*. (p. 92)

balance The amount of money in a savings account or the amount owed on a debt. (pp. 26, 278)

bar graph A graph that uses horizontal or vertical bars to represent and compare numerical data. (p. 290)

base (**1**) One side of a triangle. (p. 230) (**2**) One of the parallel sides on a quadrilateral. (p. 108) (**3**) One of the parallel and congruent faces on a prism or cylinder. (pp. 112, 118) (**4**) The face opposite the vertex of a pyramid or cone. (pp. 112, 118)

base number The number used as a repeated factor. (p. 48)

betweenness property For any two numbers, there is another number between them. (p. 198)

binary system A base two place value system. (p. 342)

bisect To divide in half, or into two congruent parts. (p. 104)

capacity The volume expressed in terms of liquid measurement. (p. 332)

Celsius The metric scale for measuring temperature. Expressed as °C. (p. 334)

center The point at the exact middle of a circle. (p. 116)

centimeter (cm) A metric unit of length. 100 centimeters equal 1 meter. (p. 336)

central angle An angle formed by two radii of a circle. (p. 116)

chord A line segment drawn between any two points on a circle. (p. 116)

circle A set of points in a plane that are all an equal distance from a fixed point, the center. (p. 116)

circle graph A round graph that compares parts of a whole using different-sized sections of a circle. (p. 296)

circumference The distance around a circle. (p. 232)

combination An arrangement when the order does <u>not</u> matter. (p. 314)

Commutative (Order) Property of Addition Changing the order of addends does not change the sum. (p. 12)
$$4 + 8 + 2 = 8 + 4 + 2$$

Commutative (Order) Property of Multiplication The order of factors may change without changing the product. (p. 34)
$$5 \times 6 \times 7 = 6 \times 5 \times 7$$

compass A tool used for constructing circles and arcs. (p. 104)

compatible numbers Numbers that can be paired together in order to make mental computing easier. (p. 12)

complementary angles Two angles with the sum of their measures equal to 90°. (p. 102)

complex fraction A fraction that has a fraction in the numerator and/or the denominator. (p. 194)

composite number A whole number that has more than two factors. (p. 40)

compound event A combination of two or more single events. (p. 318)

concave polygon For any two points inside the polygon, the line segment between them may be partially outside the polygon. (p. 110)

concentric circles Circles that lie in the same plane and have the same center. (p. 116)

cone A three-dimensional figure with a circular base and a curved surface that forms a single vertex opposite the base. (p. 118)

congruent angles Angles having the same measure. (p. 102)

congruent line segments Line segments having the same length. (p. 98)

congruent triangles Triangles having sides of equal lengths. (p. 106)

convex polygon For any two points inside the polygon, the line segment between them is completely within the polygon. (p. 110)

coordinate One of the numbers in an ordered pair. (p. 126)

coordinate plane A plane on which points are described as ordered pairs. A set of perpendicular lines framed by the *x*-axis and the *y*-axis used to graph these points is a coordinate grid. (p. 126)

cross-cancellation A method used to simplify multiplying fractions. (p. 178)

cross product For two ratios, the product of one numerator and the other denominator. (p. 254)

cube A prism with six congruent square faces. (p. 112)

cubed Raised to the third power. (p. 48)

cup (c) A customary unit of capacity equal to 8 fluid ounces. (p. 332)

customary system The measurement system used primarily in the United States.

cylinder A three-dimensional figure with two circular bases that are congruent and parallel. (p. 118)

D

data Individual facts or items of information.

decagon A polygon with ten sides. (p.110)

decimal system A base ten place value system that uses a decimal point.

decimeter (dm) A metric unit of length. 10 decimeters equal 1 meter. (p. 336)

deficient number A number having a proper factor sum less than the number itself. (p. 152)

degree (°) Standard unit of measurement for angles or temperature. (pp. 102, 334)

demography The science of vital and social statistics of a population. (p. 284)

denominator The number below the line in a fraction that tells the total number of equal parts in a whole. (p. 132)

diagonal A line segment, which is not a side, connecting two vertices of a polygon. (p. 110)

diameter The distance from one side of the circle to the other through the center. (p. 116)

difference The result of subtracting one number from another.

digit A symbol used for writing numbers: 0, 1, 2, 3, 4, 5, 6, 7, 8, and 9.

discount An amount or a percentage of the original price taken off of the original price.

Distributive Property The product remains the same whether the factor is multiplied by the sum of the addends or by each addend. (p. 34) $5 \times (3 + 2) = (5 \times 3) + (5 \times 2)$

dividend A number that is divided.

divisible A number is divisible by another number if it can be divided by that number with no remainder.

division The mathematical operation that separates a number into equal groups or an equal number of groups to give a quotient.

divisor The number that divides the dividend.

dodecagon A polygon with twelve sides. (p. 110)

edge The intersection of two faces of a polyhedron. (p. 112)

elapsed time The amount of time that passes in a designated time period. (p. 326)

endpoint The point at the end of a line segment or ray.

equally likely Given events with the same or equal chance of occurring. (p. 308)

equal ratios Ratios that show the same comparison. (p. 254)

equation A mathematical sentence that has an equal sign. (p. 18)

equilateral triangle A triangle with three congruent sides. (p. 106)

equivalent decimals Different decimals that have the same value.

equivalent fractions Fractions that name the same amount or number. (p. 132)

estimate An approximate answer for a calculation.

Euler's formula A formula that relates the number of edges, faces, and vertices of a polyhedron. (p. 113) $E = F + V - 2$

expanded notation A number expressed as the sum of the nonzero digits with appropriate place value for each. (p. 4) $2,000 + 100 + 6$

experimental probability A ratio of the number of times an event actually occurred to the number of trials. (p. 308)

exponent The number of times the base number is used as a factor. (p. 48)
6^3 — exponent

expression A mathematical phrase containing operation symbols and numbers and/or variables.

face A flat surface of a polyhedron. (p. 112)

factor A number multiplied by another number to find a product.

factorial The product of all the whole numbers from 1 to *n*, starting with *n*. Written as *n*!. (p. 314)

Fahrenheit The customary scale for measuring temperature. Expressed as °F. (p. 334)

Fermi problem A problem where the exact information needed to solve the problem is not given, but a reasonable answer can be obtained. (p. 362)

fluid ounce (fl oz) A customary unit of capacity equal to 2 tablespoons. (p. 332)

foot (ft) A customary unit of length equal to 12 inches. (p. 328)

fraction A number that describes part of a whole or part of a set. (p. 132)

frequency The number of times a certain item appears in a set of data.

Fundamental Counting Principle The total number of possible outcomes is the product of the number of items in each category. (p. 310)

gallon (gal) A customary unit of capacity equal to 4 quarts. (p. 332)

geometry The branch of mathematics that identifies and studies points, lines, plane figures, and three-dimensional shapes.

gram (g) The basic unit of mass in the metric system. (p. 340)

graph A drawing that shows and compares information in an organized way.

greatest common factor (GCF) The largest common factor of two or more numbers. (p. 42)

height (1) The perpendicular distance between two parallel bases. (p. 228) (2) The distance between a base and the opposite vertex. (p. 230)

hendecagon A polygon with eleven sides. (p. 110)

heptagon A polygon with seven sides. (p. 110)

hexagon A polygon with six sides. (p. 110)

histogram A graph that uses bars to represent how many of a particular item are found in a given interval. (p. 286)

improper fractions A fraction that has a numerator equal to or greater than the denominator. (p. 138)

inch (in.) A customary unit of length. (p. 328)

inequality A statement that two expressions are not equal. (p. 140)

integers All positive and negative whole numbers and zero. (p. 204)

interest Money earned on a savings account or money paid for a loan. (p. 278)

interest rate The percent used to calculate the money earned on a savings account or money paid for a loan. (p. 278)

intersecting lines Lines that meet at a point. The point at which they meet is the point of intersection. (p. 100)

interval The number of units between the lines on the scale of a graph.

inverse operation The opposite of a mathematical operation. Addition and subtraction are inverse operations. Multiplication and division are inverse operations.

isosceles triangle A triangle with at least two congruent sides. (p. 106)

kilogram (kg) A metric unit of mass equal to 1,000 grams. (p. 340)

kilometer (km) A metric unit of length equal to 1,000 meters. (p. 336)

Grade Six

least common denominator (LCD) The smallest common multiple of two or more denominators. (p. 134)

least common multiple (LCM) The smallest multiple that is common to two or more numbers. (p. 134)

line A straight path of points that extends without end in both directions, named by any two points. (p. 98)

line graph A graph that uses line segments to represent increases or decreases over a period of time. (p. 292)

line of symmetry A line that divides a figure into congruent halves that are mirror images of each other.

line plot A graph that uses an × to represent a quantity and show comparisons. (p. 316)

line segment A part of a line between two endpoints. (p. 98)

liter (L) The basic unit of capacity in the metric system. (p. 338)

mass The measure of how much matter is in an object. (p. 340)

mathematical (theoretical) probability A ratio of the number of favorable outcomes to the number of possible outcomes. (p. 306)

mean The sum of the values in a set of data divided by the number of values. Also called the *average*. (p. 286)

median The middle number in a set of data when the numbers are listed from least to greatest. (p. 286)

meter (m) The basic unit of length in the metric system. (p. 336)

metric system The international measurement system used by most nations of the world.

mile (mi) A customary unit of length equal to 5,280 feet or 1,760 yards. (p. 328)

milligram (mg) A metric unit of mass. 1,000 milligrams equal 1 gram. (p. 340)

milliliter (mL) A metric unit of capacity. 1,000 milliliters equal 1 liter. (p. 338)

millimeter (mm) A metric unit of length. 1,000 millimeters equal 1 meter. (p. 336)

minuend The number from which another number is subtracted to find the difference.

mixed number A number that has a whole number part and a fraction part. (p. 138)

mode The number or value that occurs the most often in a set of data. (p. 286)

multiple The product of a select number and another whole number. (p. 36)

multiplication The mathematical operation that combines groups of equal size a certain number of times to obtain a product.

Multiplication Identify Property of One If one factor is 1, the product will be the other factor. (p. 34) $1 \times 17 = 17$

negative integers All whole numbers less than zero. (p. 204)

net A flat pattern that can be folded into a three-dimensional figure. (p. 238)

nonagon A polygon with nine sides. (p. 110)

number line A line that shows numbers in order at appropriately spaced intervals.

numerator The number above the line in a fraction that tells the number of equal parts being considered. (p. 132)

numerical expression A mathematical phrase that uses numbers and at least one operation symbol to name a known quantity. (p. 56)

obtuse angle An angle that measures greater than 90° but less than 180°. (p. 102)

obtuse triangle A triangle with one obtuse (greater than 90°) angle. (p. 106)

octagon A polygon with eight sides. (p. 110)

opposite integers An integer and its opposite are the same distance away from zero, one positive and one negative. (p. 204)

ordered pair The location of any given point (*x,y*) on a coordinate plane. (p. 126)

order of operations The rules for determining in what order to perform mathematical operations:
1. Do operation(s) inside parentheses.
2. Multiply and divide from left to right.
3. Add and subtract from left to right. (p. 74)

origin The point (0,0) on a coordinate plane. (p. 126)

ounce (oz) A customary unit of weight. (p. 330)

outcome A possible result in a probability problem. (p. 306)

parallel lines Lines in a plane that never intersect. (p. 100)

parallelogram A quadrilateral having opposite sides parallel and congruent. (p. 108)

pentagon A polygon with five sides. (p. 110)

percent Means per one hundred. A ratio that compares a number to one hundred. (p. 262)

perfect number A number which is equal to the sum of its proper factors. (p. 152)

perimeter The distance around a figure. (p. 226)

period A group of three digits separated by commas from other periods. (p. 2)

permutation An arrangement when the order matters. (p. 314)

perpendicular lines Lines that meet to form right (90°) angles. (p. 100)

pi (π) The ratio of the circumference of a circle to its diameter. (p. 232)   π ≈ **3.14**

pictograph A graph that presents data by using symbols to represent numbers.

pint (pt) A customary unit of capacity equal to 2 cups. (p. 332)

place value A multiple of ten that tells how much a digit represents. (p. 2)

plane A two-dimensional flat surface that extends without end in all directions, named by a script letter. (p. 98)

plane figure A flat figure having two dimensions.

plane of symmetry A plane that divides a figure into two parts that are mirror images of each other. (p. 124)

P.M. *Post meridiem*. The time period beginning at noon and continuing until midnight. (p. 326)

point An exact location in space, identified by a capital letter. (p. 98)

polygon A closed plane figure formed by line segments. (p. 110)

polyhedron A three-dimensional figure made of flat surfaces that are polygons. (p. 112)

positive integers All whole numbers greater than zero. (p. 204)

pound (lb) A customary unit of weight equal to 16 ounces. (p. 330)

prime factorization Factoring a number into prime numbers. (p. 40)

prime number A whole number that has exactly two factors, 1 and the number itself. (p. 40)

principal The original amount of money invested in savings or the amount borrowed on a loan. (p. 278)

prism A polyhedron with two congruent and parallel bases. All other faces are parallelograms. (p. 112)

probability The likelihood that a given event will occur. (p. 306)

product The result of multiplying two or more factors.

proper factors All the factors of a number <u>except</u> the number itself. (p. 152)

proportion An equation which shows that two ratios are equal. (p. 258)

protractor An instrument used for constructing and measuring angles. (p. 102)

pyramid A polyhedron with one polygon base. All other faces are triangles that meet at a common vertex. (p. 112)

quadrant One of four regions on a coordinate plane. (p. 220)

quadrilateral A polygon with four sides. (p. 108)

quart (qt) A customary unit of capacity equal to 2 pints. (p. 332)

quotient The result of dividing one number by another.

radius The distance from the center to any point on the circle. (p. 116)

range The difference between the greatest number and the least number in a set of numerical data. (p. 286)

rate A ratio comparing two amounts having different units. (p. 256)

ratio A pair of numbers that compares two quantities. (p. 254)

ratio table A table that shows a series of equal ratios. (p. 254)

ray A part of a line that begins at one point and extends without end in one direction. (p. 98)

reciprocal A fraction whose numerator and denominator have been reversed. The product of two reciprocals is 1. (p. 188)

rectangle A parallelogram with opposite sides congruent and four right angles. (p. 108)

reflection A transformation that turns, or flips, a figure over on a line or plane of symmetry. (p. 124)

reflex angle An angle that measures greater than 180°. (p. 102)

regular polygon A polygon with congruent sides and congruent angles. (p. 110)

remainder The number that is left over after dividing. It is always less than the divisor.

repeating decimal A decimal number where one or more of the digits repeat continuously. (p. 148)

rhombus A parallelogram having all sides congruent. (p. 108)

right angle An angle that measures 90°. (p. 102)

right triangle A triangle with one right (90°) angle. (p. 106)

rigid Stiff or unyielding. (p. 360)

Roman numerals An ancient Roman system for writing numbers. (p. 28)

rotation A transformation that turns a figure around a fixed point. (p. 124)

rounding Adjusting a number to a given place value.

sales tax A tax imposed on the cost of goods or services computed as a percentage of the price.

sample space A table or list that shows all possible outcomes of a given situation. (p. 310)

scale (1) Numbers that define the intervals along the side or bottom of a graph. (2) The relationship of the map or model distance and the actual distance between two points. (p. 248)

scale drawing A proportional drawing that represents an area or an object as it is, usually smaller or larger in size. (p. 300)

scalene triangle A triangle with no congruent sides. (p. 106)

scientific illustration A drawing that is accurate in scale and physical detail. (p. 300)

scientific notation A number expressed as a decimal between one and ten multiplied by a power of 10. (p. 48) 6.36×10^{12}

side (1) One of the rays forming an angle. (p. 102) (2) One of the line segments forming a polygon. (p. 108)

similar triangles Triangles having angles of equal measures. (p. 106)

simplest form A fraction is in simplest form, or lowest terms, when the greatest common factor of the numerator and denominator is 1. (p. 136)

skew lines Lines that are not in the same plane and do not intersect. (p. 100)

sphere A three-dimensional figure where every point is the same distance from the center. (p. 118)

square A rectangle having all sides congruent. (p. 108)

squared Raised to the second power; multiplied by itself. (p. 48)

square root ($\sqrt{}$) A number which, when multiplied by itself, yields the given number. (p. 60)

standard notation A number expressed using the digits 0, 1, 2, 3, 4, 5, 6, 7, 8, and 9. (p. 2)
4,245

statistics The branch of mathematics that deals with collecting, organizing, and analyzing data.

stem and leaf plot A diagram that displays numerical data by breaking each value into a "stem" part and a "leaf" part. (p. 288)

straight angle An angle that measures 180°. (p. 102)

subtraction The mathematical operation that gives the difference between two numbers.

subtrahend The number subtracted from another number to find the difference.

sum The result of adding two or more addends.

supplementary angles Two angles with the sum of their measures equal to 180°. (p. 102)

surface area The sum of the areas of all the faces of a three-dimensional figure. (p. 238)

symmetry The ability of a figure to be divided into two congruent halves.

tablespoon (tbsp) A customary unit of capacity equal to 3 teaspoons. (p. 332)

teaspoon (tsp) A customary unit of capacity. (p. 332)

terminating decimal A decimal number that ends on the right. (p. 148)

tessellation A pattern of congruent shapes that covers a plane with no overlaps and no holes.

Grade Six

three-dimensional figure A geometric figure that takes up space.

ton (T) A customary unit of weight equal to 2,000 pounds. (p. 330)

transformation A change in the location or position of a figure by a translation, rotation, and/or reflection. (p. 124)

translation A transformation that slides a figure in a straight line, changing the location but not the orientation. (p. 124)

trapezoid A quadrilateral having only one pair of parallel sides. (p. 108)

tree diagram A diagram that uses lines as branches representing all possible outcomes of a given situation. (p. 310)

triangle A polygon with three sides. (p. 106)

triangular numbers Numbers of a sequence that can be shown by dots arranged in the shape of a triangle. (p. 10)

unequally likely Given events that do <u>not</u> have the same chance of occurring. (p. 309)

unit fraction A fraction with a numerator of 1. (p. 180)

unit rate A rate having 1 as the denominator. (p. 256)

variable A symbol used in algebra to stand for a number or a set of numbers. (p. 56)

vertex (**1**) The common endpoint of two rays. (p. 102) (**2**) The point at which two sides of a polygon meet. (p. 110) (**3**) The point at which edges of a polyhedron meet. (p. 112)

volume The number of cubic units that fill a three-dimensional space. (p. 242)

whole number Any of the numbers 0, 1, 2, 3, and so on. (p. 2)

winning strategy A method for one player to win no matter what the other players do. (p. 367)

word form A number expressed in words. (p. 2)
six hundred fifty-two

x-axis The horizontal axis on a coordinate grid. (p. 126)

x-coordinate The first number of an ordered pair. (p. 126)

yard (yd) A customary unit of length equal to 3 feet or 36 inches. (p. 328)

y-axis The vertical axis on a coordinate grid. (p. 126)

y-coordinate The second number of an ordered pair. (p. 126)

zero pair A number and its opposite. (p. 208)

Zero Property of Multiplication Multiplying any factor by 0 results in a product of zero. (p. 34)
$17 \times 0 = 17$

Zero Property of Addition The sum of a number and zero is that number. (p. 12)
$5 + 0 = 5$

378

estimation, 14, 16, 44, 46, 188
expanded notation, 4
and fractions, 70, 138, 140, 160,
    164, 166, 168, 178, 180, 184,
    192
integers, 204, 206, 208, 210, 212,
    214, 216
meaning of, 2
multiplying, 34, 36, 38, 40, 42, 44,
    46
naming, 2
number sense, 10
place value of, 2, 4, 6, 8, 14, 38
reading and writing, 2
rounding, 8, 14, 16, 44, 46, 78, 92
square root, 60
standard notation, 2, 4
subtracting, 14, 16, 18, 20
writing expressions, 56, 74
Word names for numbers
decimals, 144, 146
fractions, 144, 146, 160
integers, 204, 214
whole numbers, 2

Yard, 328

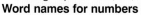

Zero pair, 208
Zero Property
in addition, 12
in division, 70, 76, 82, 84, 88, 86
in multiplication, 34
Zero(s)
in addition, 12, 14
in decimals, 24, 54
in division, 70, 76, 82, 84, 86, 88
in estimation, 46
in integers, 204, 206, 208, 210,
    212
in multiplication, 34, 46, 50, 54
in place value, 2, 4, 6
in powers of ten, 48
in quotients, 76, 82
in rounding, 8, 46, 88
in subtraction, 14